AF605848

TRAGEDY IN HEGEL'S EARLY THEOLOGICAL WRITINGS

Indiana Series in the Philosophy of Religion

Merold Westphal, editor

TRAGEDY IN HEGEL'S EARLY THEOLOGICAL WRITINGS

PETER WAKE

Indiana University Press
Bloomington and Indianapolis

This book is a publication of
Indiana University Press
Office of Scholarly Publishing
Herman B Wells Library 350
1320 East 10th Street
Bloomington, Indiana 47405 USA

iupress.indiana.edu

Telephone 800-842-6796
Fax 812-855-7931

∞ The paper used in this publication meets the minimum requirements of the American National Standard for Information Sciences—Permanence of Paper for Printed Library Materials, ANSI Z39.48–1992.

Manufactured in the United States of America

Cataloging information is available from the Library of Congress.

ISBN 978-0-253-01251-7 (cloth)
ISBN 978-0-253-01261-6 (ebook)

1 2 3 4 5 19 18 17 16 15 14

For Isabelle

CONTENTS

ACKNOWLEDGMENTS

This work was conceived while I was a student in the Philosophy Department at DePaul University. I wish to acknowledge, first and foremost, David Krell for the inspiration he provided during these years. His seminars on Hölderlin and Greek tragedy were decisive in shaping this book on Hegel. I also extend my deep thanks to Will McNeill for the close reading he gave to earlier versions of this text and for his continued support. Bill Martin, Michael Naas, and Angelica Nuzzo have each, in their own distinct ways, shaped the approach to philosophical texts reflected in this work. Kevin Carey, Sarah Dwyer, Laura Santos, and Mark Walter read sections of the book at various stages of its development, and I am grateful for their comments and our discussions. My thanks to Merold Westphal for his faith in the project and to Dee Mortensen at the University of Indiana Press for her advice and patience during its completion. My thanks also to Mary Lou Bertucci for her meticulous work in copyediting the manuscript.

I am particularly grateful to my students and colleagues at Saint Edward's University for their friendship and for the many conversations we have had about the ideas that animate this book. Evidence of these conversations can be found on virtually every page. I owe a special debt of gratitude to the members of the Philosophy Department at Saint Edward's. Thanks to William Zanardi, Mark Cherry, Jack Green Musselman, and Stephen Dilley for their encouragement and collegiality. My thanks as well to Richard Bautch, Lou Brusatti, Kerstin Somerholter, and the late Harald Becker, all of whom assisted in various ways in refining the work. I would also like to recognize George Martin for the St. Edward's Presidential Research Grants that made much of the writing and editing of this volume possible.

Above all, I give my most heartfelt thanks to Phil and Irene Wake for the innumerable ways in which they have lent their support during the long process of completing this project; and to Renée for her generous, indomitable spirit.

LIST OF ABBREVIATIONS

Citations that give both the German and the English sources will always list the German first. I have occasionally modified English translations and have indicated when I have done so.

G. W. F. Hegel

D — *The Difference between Fichte's and Schelling's System of Philosophy.* Translated by W. Cerf and H. S. Harris. Albany: SUNY Press, 1977. Referred to in the text as the *Differenzschrift.*

FK — *Faith and Knowledge.* Translated by W. Cerf and H. S. Harris. Albany: SUNY Press, 1977.

L — *Love.* In *Early Theological Writings.* Translated by T. M. Knox, 302–308. Philadelphia: University of Pennsylvania Press, 1971. Seventh paperback printing 1992.

LFA — *Hegel's Aesthetics: Lectures on Fine Art.* Translated by T. M. Knox. 2 vols. Oxford: Oxford University Press, 1998.

LJ — *The Life of Jesus.* In *Three Essays (1793–1795),* edited and translated by P. Fuss and J. Dobbins, 104–165. Notre Dame, IN: University of Notre Dame Press, 1984.

LPR — *Lectures on the Philosophy of Religion.* Edited by P. C. Hodgson. Translated by R. F. Brown et al. 3 vols. Berkeley: University of California Press, 1995.

LWH — *Lectures on the Philosophy of World History, Introduction: Reason in History.* Translated by H. B. Nisbet. 3 vols. Cambridge: University of Cambridge Press, 1992.

N — *Hegels theologische Jugendschriften.* Edited by Herman Nohl. Tübingen: Mohr, 1907.

NL — *Natural Law: The Scientific Ways of Treating Natural Law, Its Place in Moral Philosophy, and Its Relation to the Positive Sciences of Law.* Translated by T. M. Knox. Philadelphia: University of Pennsylvania Press, 1975.

OP — "The Oldest Program toward a System in German Idealism." In D. F. Krell, *The Owl of Minerva,* 17, 1 (1985): 8–13. This translation of "The

Oldest Program" is embedded within a longer article by David Farrell Krell.

P *The Positivity of the Christian Religion.* In *Early Theological Writings,* translated by T. M. Knox, 67–181. Philadelphia: University of Pennsylvania Press, 1971. Seventh paperback printing 1992.

PdG *Phänomenologie des Geistes.* Hamburg: Felix Meiner Verlag, 1988.

PH *The Philosophy of History.* Translated by J. Sibree. New York: Dover Publications, Inc., 1956.

PR *Elements of the Philosophy of Right.* Translated by A. Wood. Cambridge: Cambridge University Press, 1991.

PS *Phenomenology of Spirit.* Translated by A. V. Miller. Oxford: Oxford University Press, 1977.

SC *The Spirit of Christianity and Its Fate.* In *Early Theological Writings,* translated by T. M. Knox, 182–301. Philadelphia: University of Pennsylvania Press, 1971. Seventh paperback printing 1992.

TE *The Tübingen Essay.* In *Three Essays, 1793–1795,* translated by P. Fuss and J. Dobbins, 30–59. Notre Dame, IN: University of Notre Dame Press, 1984. This fragment is also known by its first words "Religion ist eine . . ."

W *Werke in zwanzig Bänden,* edited by E. Moldenhauer and K. M. Michel. Frankfurt am Main: Suhrkamp Verlag, 1969–1971. Reference to this edition of Hegel's work is cited by volume followed by page number.

Friedrich Hölderlin

FH *Sämtliche Werke und Briefe.* Edited by Michael Knaupp. 3 vols. Munich: Carl Hanser Verlag, 1992.

Immanuel Kant

Ak *Kants gesammelte Schriften.* Edited by the Royal Prussian Academy of Sciences and Its Successors. Berlin: Reimer; later Berlin and New York: Walter de Gruyter, 1902–1938, 1968.

TRAGEDY IN HEGEL'S EARLY THEOLOGICAL WRITINGS

INTRODUCTION

Monotheism of Reason and the Heart, Polytheism of the Imagination and Art

The following study addresses what I will call G. W. F. Hegel's early theologico-political writings. It focuses primarily on a series of unpublished, fragmentary works that Hegel produced while living in Bern (1793–1796) and Frankfurt (1797–1800). I will, however, make no attempt to engage these early writings as if the later system did not exist. Indeed, one of the aims of revisiting them is to read parts of Hegel's later systematic texts through the earlier ones with the hope of capturing a spirit of engagement and an openness to future events that is too often concealed behind the still-lingering image of Hegel's work as a triumphalist philosophy of historical progress, a totalitarian theory of the Absolute, and the last stand of the onto-theological tradition.[1] Hegel's early thought amounts to a thoroughgoing challenge to religious dogmatism and a rejection more specifically of the "positive" use of abstract, impersonal, metaphysical categories when conceiving of the divine. The force of Hegel's challenge ought to give us pause before this persistent image of his work.

More narrowly, this study of Hegel's early writings can be understood as an excavation of two intertwining dialectical movements related to the "Religion" section of the *Phenomenology of Spirit*. As such, it is, in part, an attempt to read Hegel "backward," from his future to his past. The first movement concerns the transition from Greek polytheism to Christian monotheism as presented in the "Religion" section of the *Phenomenology*. The second movement concerns the transition, found at the culmination of the section on "Spirit," from the moral view of the world to religious consciousness by way of the dialectic of conscience. That is, it concerns the need to move beyond the limits of Kantian moralism by way of the tragic recognition, born of the withdrawal of "beautiful souls," that to act is always to act violently.[2]

The "Religion" section of the *Phenomenology* recounts the progression of consciousness from "natural religion" through "religion in the form of art" to "revealed religion." The religion of art describes the development of ancient Greek religious consciousness in three moments—the abstract, living, and spiritual works of art—and, within the spiritual work, Hegel ascertains three specific shapes that correspond to epic, tragic, and comic poetry. I unearth the prehistory of this movement in Hegel's earlier writings through the moments of religion in the form of art, as they anticipate the revealed religion to come. That is, I investigate the prehistory of the logical priority that Hegel gives to Christian monotheism over ancient Greek polytheism and its tragic mythology. This, in turn, helps reveal the distinct character of Hegel's conception of modernity as a synthesis of the Greek and Christian traditions.[3] Of particular interest in this regard is the intensity of Hegel's early condemnation of Christianity and its historical unfolding. When he first compares the religion of the ancient Greek *polis* with Christianity, the latter is found lacking in its ability to help manifest the idea of autonomy, and, for the young Hegel, this lack gives rise to the perceived need for a new, modern mythology. When, however, we read Hegel "forward," that is to say, chronologically, from his early writings in Tübingen, Bern, and Frankfurt through to the composition of the *Phenomenology* in Jena and beyond, we see a shift from a valorization of Greek religion and culture to the eventual rehabilitation of Christianity. What appears at first glance to be left behind with this shift is the need for a distinctly modern religion informed by ancient Greek tragedy.

The call for such a new, modern mythology is made decisively in a fragment known as "The Oldest Program toward a System in German Idealism." The text is thought to have been produced by Hegel in January 1797, after moving from Bern to join his friend Friedrich Hölderlin in Frankfurt.[4] Although the fragment is clearly written in Hegel's hand, there has been controversy over whether it represents his own thought or whether he had simply copied a text that was originally produced by Hölderlin or F. W. J. Schelling.[5] The debate is of such interest because the fragment can be read as a kind of manifesto first proclaiming the project that has come to be known as German Idealism. That is, the author of "The Oldest Program" presents in a concise and inspired way the project, born of enthusiasm over the French Revolution, to fulfill the promise of autonomy articulated in Immanuel Kant's Critical philosophy. From the perspective of his descendants, however, Kant's philosophy was itself an unfulfilled promise. His escape from dogmatic metaphysics, his grounding of moral action on pure practical reason alone, and his strategy for moving from an age of enlightenment to an enlightened age were all achieved through the precise determination of proper limits. We can know only appearances and the conditions of their possibility; we are free only to submit to the moral law; we may argue as much as we want, but we must obey. The task that Kant's Critical philosophy posed, as his offspring saw it, was to reconcile what stands on the opposite sides of these borders.

"The Oldest Program" sets out this task in a way that anticipates the general structure of the transition from "Spirit" to "Religion" in the *Phenomenology*. Of particular importance to this study is the call at the end of the fragment for a *sensuous religion* grounded in Beauty, what the author of "The Oldest Program" describes as a "monotheism of reason and the heart, [a] polytheism of the imagination and art" (OP 12). This is a mythology that is consonant with reason and as necessary for philosophers as it is for nonphilosophers. Ideas are to be made aesthetic—"mythological"—so that they will have universal appeal, but, at the same time, they must conform to rationality so as not to shame the philosophers. Thus, the people will be made rational, and, like a "music-making Socrates," the philosophers will be made sensuous.[6] This is, at heart, a call to overthrow all superstitions about an afterworld and a transcendent God, as well as the institutions—a mechanistic state and hypocritical church—that profit from these beliefs. As such, it is the call for what can be described as a mythology of *immanence.*

The call to immanence found in "The Oldest Program" corresponds to the overarching ambition of Hegel's early writings to determine the proper form and content of what he refers to as a *Volksreligion*. In a series of texts written in Bern prior to the composition of "The Oldest Program," Hegel sets this type of sensuous, public religion in stark opposition to what he saw as the rigid hierarchy and orthodoxy that plagued contemporary Christianity. Although these Bern writings were originally published under the title *Hegels theologische Jugendschriften,* Hegel is as concerned with the political as he is with the theological or the religious.[7] The core position that he defends in these theologico-political writings is that a *Volksreligion* can potentially serve as a means of bridging the gap, opened by Kant's second *Critique,* between practical reason and sensibility; or, to put the problem in the political register, a *Volksreligion* was the means of overcoming the divide that existed between, on the one hand, the random power of a despotic state and, on the other, our autonomous ethical reason.[8] Hegel's consistent intention in his early texts, then, was to determine the kind of mythology that would best supplement a free political order, and his model for such a living religion was that of the ancient Greeks. He conceived of the Greek version of a *Volksreligion* as fulfilling the "supreme need of the human spirit" (W 1:406/SC 289).[9] This is the need, as he described it, "to unite subject with object, to unite feeling [*Empfindung*], and feeling's demand for objects, with the intellect [*Verstand*], to unite them in something beautiful, in a god, by means of the imagination" (ibid.). I will argue that Hegel comes to see this union of subject and object occurring through the distinctly *tragic* expression of beauty found in Greek *Volksreligion.* In light of this, Hegel's Bern and Frankfurt writings, and the historical analyses of Greece and Christianity that they contain, can be read, in effect, as his evolving response to the following series of questions that he implicitly posed to himself throughout this early period: *How was this beautiful, living form of Greek religion killed, and how can its spirit be revitalized? Why has Christianity failed to produce the kind of harmony evident in Periclean Athens?* Or (to use Gilles Deleuze's formulation of the question that he saw motivating Spinoza's *Theologico-Political Treatise*), "*Why does a religion that invokes love and joy inspire war, intolerance, hatred, malevolence, and remorse?"*[10] Finally, *Is it possible to establish a new, distinctly modern* Volksreligion *and do so within the parameters of Christianity?*

I will pose to Hegel the same questions that he implicitly posed to himself. But in stark contrast to the extremely ambitious nature of the project on which Hegel, along with Schelling and Hölderlin, embarked—the project heralding a new, modern religion, a project described in "The Oldest Program" as "the very last and the grandest of humanity's works" (OP 13)—my scope is modest. It is not only oriented by a physical relocation, namely, Hegel's move from Bern to Frankfurt, but, more importantly, a philosophical relocation or reorientation that is expressed so succinctly in "The Oldest Program." In the service of drawing out this reorientation, I will provide a detailed account of what could be called a pair of "false starts" that take place before and after the production of "The Oldest Program." The central focus of part 1 of the book (chapters 1 and 2) is Hegel's Bern text, *The Positivity of the Christian Religion,* which was composed between 1795 and 1796, thus prior to "The Oldest Program."[11] By way of the categories of Kant's practical philosophy, this text, as the first false start, confronts the insidious relation between the *polis* and "positivity," or what could also be called, with Kant in mind, "dogmatism."[12] Although Hegel is especially concerned with *religious* dogmatism, his analyses can be extended to other domains where a historically contingent trait is "essentialized"—posited as objectively true—based on the authority of an external and supposedly incontrovertible power. Hegel's conceptual and historical analyses of positivity raise the question of how to combine Kantian practical philosophy and its brand of Enlightenment morality and politics with the (Greek) imperative for a unified collective imagination that limits the very need for self-reflective moral reasoning. Part 2 (chapters 3, 4, and 5) consists primarily of a close reading of *The Spirit of Christianity and Its Fate,* written in Frankfurt between 1798 and 1800. In *The Spirit of Christianity,* Hegel traverses much of the same terrain that he covered in *The Positivity of the Christian Religion,* but he does so in a way that the full force of dialectic thinking becomes evident. When the unity of Periclean Athens as the historical proof of the possible concrete existence of the moral law is disrupted, a shift occurs in Hegel's thinking, and it can be expressed through a reorientation of three central themes that I concentrate on in my reading of the *Positivity:* (i) Greece, while still an ideal of *beauty,* is no longer understood primarily in terms of *moral* beauty, but an explicitly *tragic* form of it. Beauty of this kind does not belong solely to nature and life but to their demise as well. (ii) Kant's moral philosophy is relegated to the status of positivity. (iii) Jesus is no longer conflated with Kant but is now portrayed as a tragic hero. I will argue that tragedy in this context is the *poetic* articulation of the conflicts that arise with the penetration of the principle of subjective freedom into the substance of Greek ethical life. The centrality of Greek tragedy in *The Spirit of Christianity,* then, can be read as a sign of Hegel's recognition of the conflict between his earlier, Bern-era understanding of the free Greek *polis* and Kant's moral philosophy. What this last point entails is that the historical consequences of Jesus's doctrine can no longer be isolated from the fundamental idea that it articulates. This is to say, Jesus and the movement founded in his name are *fated.*

Despite the references I will make to Hegel's later works, they are not the measure against which the worth of the early, decidedly nonsystematic writings is determined. *The Positivity of the Christian Religion* and *The Spirit of Christianity and Its Fate* are described as "false starts" not because they are deemed to be false relative to a later, complete, and true system. I refer to them as false starts because Hegel clearly thought of them in this way—rightly or wrongly—and did not choose to complete and publish them. Hegel famously chided Schelling for his very public education, the error of Schelling's precocious string of early publications being that he did not present his philosophical work as a complete and unified front.[13] Hegel's editors and the resilience of the written word have managed, however, to circumvent the discretion that he attempted to maintain. This question, then, arises: why delve into these earlier texts? It is not with the intention of catching Hegel in any compromising positions. Nor is the aim simply to draw attention to consistencies and inconsistencies that exist between his early, unpublished texts and his later published ones. It is, instead, from a sense of fidelity to the spirit of Hegel's thought and its rigorous incorporation of what is incomplete within the concept of truth itself. This fidelity to Hegel's account of the nature of truth is, at the same time, a fidelity to the logic of fidelity itself—a logic at play in the heart of the later dialectic. Instead of understanding Hegel's dialectic as an oscillation between two opposed extremes, it should be conceived in terms of its self-producing and self-determining character. The negation of an original position or determination does not come about, in truth, through a confrontation with an "other" standing against it. Instead, the initial negation of a position takes place when it is adhered to with unwavering fidelity. When a position is shown this kind of devotion, it becomes radicalized to the point of self-contradiction. The initial negation of a position is an *infidelity* that comes through excessive *fidelity.* My approach to Hegel's early theologico-political writings will be characterized by the utmost fidelity to them.

Studies of Hegel's early texts by Wilhelm Dilthey, Georg Lukács, Adriaan Peperzak, Werner Hamacher, and Christoph Jamme, among others, are continual points of reference in my own close reading of them. It is, however, H. S. Harris's monumental two-volume work on this material, *Hegel's Development,* that continues to dominate the field in the English-speaking world, and my understanding of Hegel's early thought is indebted to Harris's genetic study. More specifically, I agree with Harris that Hegel's Bern and Frankfurt-era writings are unified by the question of the possibility and form of a modern *Volksreligion*. I also agree that these texts are marked by a mounting tension between Hegel's affiliation with Kant and the Hellenic ideal that is the reason for his concentration on *Volksreligionen*.[14]

Despite this indebtedness, I depart from Harris in a number of ways. The most obvious is my much more narrowly defined focus on Greek tragedy as a mythology of immanence. Harris, of course, addresses the theme of tragedy, but he does so within the context of his chronological reconstruction of the development of Hegel's early thought in general. References to Greek tragedies and the categories of the aesthetics of tragedy arise in a sporadic fashion throughout Harris's study because they arise sporadically in Hegel's own works from this period. In contrast to Harris's panoptic approach, tragedy is the often discreet thread that I follow through these labyrinthine early writings, for, as I have noted, the hybrid political, aesthetic, religious, and protophilosophical institution of tragedy constitutes the substance of the Greek *Volksreligion* as the historical realization of a living politico-religious formation. The use of *Schicksal,* fate, is only the most readily apparent indication of the importance of tragedy. I argue that tragedy is a particular theme through which the significance of these Bern and Frankfurt essays can be grasped as a whole and, thus, it is much more prominent thematically than the number of explicit references to Greek tragedies might imply.

Moving beyond the strict letter of Hegel's texts and placing tragedy at center stage are further warranted when we read them alongside contemporaneous works by Schelling and Hölderlin. With Dieter Henrich and David Farrell Krell, as well as Harris,[15] I take the contested authorship of "The Oldest Program" to be, above all, a reflection of the overlapping projects of Hegel and his friends, and I read their intense engagement with the tragic age of the Greeks as intimately related to the call for a new, modern mythology so central to this program.[16] Situating Hegel's early writings within this broader project clarifies the tragic spirit that shapes his own early writings. The move beyond the letter of Hegel's texts is also warranted by the significant role that tragedy plays in his subsequent work. I have mentioned the tragic fate of the "beautiful soul" in the "Conscience" chapter of the *Phenomenology of Spirit* and the importance of tragic theater in the chapter on "The Religion of Art," but we might also consider the account of the eternal tragedy of "absolute ethical life" found in the Jena "Nature Law" essay, the figure of Nemesis in the *Science of Logic,* the necessary sacrifice of the world historical individual as presented in the *Lecture on World History,* and, of course, the analysis of tragedy in the *Lectures on Aesthetics.* Reading these earlier writings from the perspective of the later system amounts in some instances to following the hermeneutic principle of moving from the clear into the obscure; when this is the case, it allows us to understand the early Hegel better, perhaps, than he understood himself.[17] Thus, I have attempted to balance the study of Hegel's early writings on their own terms with occasional retroactive analyses from the perspective of the later system. I have also extended this approach to subsequent reflections on tragedy and early Christianity by those who write in Hegel's wake, such as Friedrich Nietzsche, Sigmund Freud, Martin Heidegger, Theodor Adorno, Jacques Derrida, Jacob Taubes, and Alain Badiou.

I depart from Harris's study methodologically in adopting this circular approach. Harris ultimately reads the early writings in order to better understand the *Phenomenology of Spirit*. He claims that the young Hegel aspired to be a *Volkserzieher* on the model of Socrates or Jesus, that is, he aspired to be an enlightener first of his people and then of humanity as such.[18] A central aim of Harris's study is to explain why Hegel laid aside this earlier aspiration, grounded as it was in religious-aesthetic intuition, to become a philosopher committed to "the discursive mode of expression that typifies Hegel's later systematic work."[19] While Hegel had decided to become a professional philosopher by the time he wrote the *Systemfragment* of 1800, Harris claims that he, nevertheless, already had an intimation of this calling two years earlier:

> He stands on the brink of becoming a philosopher in the full sense, committed to understanding the world, rather than to changing it. But he does not yet know that this is his sun, he has not yet come out of the Cave into the world of Absolute Knowledge, the sunlight of the Absolute Idea. It is a steep and difficult slope that he has yet to climb. . . . The present book [*Toward the Sunlight, 1770–1801,* the first volume of *Hegel's Development*] is the story of his sojourn among the shadows and the picture-makers.[20]

Although Harris's goal is to comprehend how this sojourn prepared Hegel to become the author of the *Phenomenology of Spirit,* he still provides an immanent interpretation of the early development in the service of this goal. He aspired to "think with the young Hegel," which is to say that the meaning of particular passages and texts is not determined with reference to the way in which they either anticipate or fall short of the later, properly philosophical system.[21] Interpreting the early texts in light of the later system was, as Harris noted, methodologically barred to him in *Hegel's Development.* Looking back at the first volume of this study some twenty-five years after its publication, he recognized, however, that by making this methodological choice he was denying himself an important tool for interpreting obscure passages and for clarifying the significance of revisions that Hegel made to his work.[22] Indeed, Harris acknowledges that "it is perfectly good

Hegelian method to go round the circle of thought in either direction."[23] At the same time, he also warns of the danger that "one may make Hegel think rather more clearly than he actually did."[24]

My goal has not been to make Hegel appear more coherent than he may have been; nor have I read Hegel's early writings as a propaedeutic to the *Phenomenology*. As I have noted, my reading is oriented by "The Oldest Program," which is to say that I read these texts in terms of the project of German Idealism in its inception. Instead of asking how Hegel's Bern and Frankfurt writings can be subsumed within an account of the climb toward a future philosophical science, I ask, in effect, how they help to provide greater substance to the project of German Idealism as expressed in "The Oldest Program" fragment. My periodic references to the Hegel's later writings are made in the service of both clarifying these earlier texts and drawing attention to the way in which his early concentration on tragedy and the fate of living religions finds expression in his subsequent works. I attempt to formulate the very precise set of questions that Hegel raises in his early writings concerning tragedy and the fate of a religion of love in particular, but I do not presume to answer them in a way that outstrips Hegel's own thinking at the time. Instead, I go no further than the *aporia* that Hegel ultimately confronts when he attempts to interpret the figure of Jesus and the fate of Christianity through an idea of tragedy shorn of either Aristophanic or Dantean comic reconciliation. Hegel's later systematic work can be read as a response to this *aporia*, but, of course, it is not the only one.

While I have tried to avoid the danger of superimposing Hegel's later, more developed ideas onto the early texts, I may, however, be courting another kind of danger. Harris writes of *Hegel's Ladder*, his equally comprehensive commentary on the *Phenomenology of Spirit*, that it attempts to prove that the *Phenomenology* is, indeed, a science, and he sees the denial of science, its slow fragmentation, as leading to nothing less than "the great bonfire" of what he calls very generally "deconstruction."[25] He clarifies the identity of these arsonists in the very last footnote of the second and final volume of *Hegel's Ladder*.[26] They are the "spiritual children of Kierkegaard and Nietzsche," those who first separate the *Phenomenology of Spirit* from the *Science of Logic* and then proceed to tear it to pieces and set it ablaze. My own study reflects the view that the offspring of Kierkegaard and Nietzsche can be valuable readers of Hegel. I agree with John Russon, for example, when he writes that it is "by no means clear that there is a significant difference between the philosophical methods, goals, or results of Hegel's philosophy and the philosophies of such figures as Heidegger, Merleau-Ponty, and Derrida."[27] With their focus on the relation that exists between Greece and modernity, the concern with *life* and the limits of moral reason, the centrality of the aesthetic and the insufficiencies of traditional theoretical modes of expression, Hegel's early writings not only portend the

Phenomenology and the later system, but some of the most prominent movements in subsequent continental European philosophy, including deconstruction. Simon Critchley has said of "The Oldest Program" that the call found in this "strange and wonderfully naïve text"[28] to reconcile the dualisms of the Critical philosophy through art, thereby mixing the philosophical and the poetic in the service of an emancipatory religious and political project guided by the ideals of freedom and equality, "neatly crystallizes a number of themes in post-Kantian thought."[29] As Hegel's Bern and Frankfurt writings, in their evolution, are almost entirely consonant with "The Oldest Program," the following study serves in part to make the project it announces appear less strange and, perhaps, less naïve. Here is a sketch of the course that it follows.

In chapter 1, "Positivity and Historical Reversal," I present Hegel's understanding of positivity as the ossification of life into dead structures, and I draw specific attention to the way in which he comes to conceive of different historically situated "collective subjectivities" (Greek, Jewish, Christian, and modern) in relation to this guiding notion of positivity. I argue that Hegel is primarily concerned with the forms of positivity that have come to define modernity, and I develop his idea of a divided modern world with the help of his Jena-era *Differenzschrift* (1801) and *Faith and Knowledge* (1802) essays, as well as Hölderlin's *Hyperion*. Hegel's critical judgment concerning his contemporary world is oriented by his idea of the ancient Greek *polis* as the concrete, historical manifestation of Kantian autonomy, and this Greek manifestation of a free political and religious order is grounded, as I have indicated, in the *immanence* and *beauty* of its *Volksreligion*.

Hegel does not only judge his contemporary society in relation to the Athenian *polis* but also the birth of the first Christian communities. He finds in early Christianity a confrontation, in the name of free virtue, with the same kind of ossified culture and religion that he himself is facing. I argue that his account of the path that Christianity follows, from its inception as an attempt to fulfill the moral law to its fall back into positivity, stands as a warning to the present. The warning concerns the tension between the moral core of a religion and the need to appeal to positive elements, like miracles, as a means of communicating this moral essence in a historical context where the imagination has been shaped by positive tropes.

While chapter 1 describes the general trajectory of the history of Christianity as a return to the positivity that it had originally opposed, chapter 2, "On Expansion," documents in a more detailed manner examples of this reversal. In this way, it provides a richer account of the history of Christianity as the source of modern subjectivity. Hegel holds that the will to expansion is the most pronounced expression of the dominance of positivity in Christianity, and I argue that, for Hegel, the source of this outward drive is an experience of resentment born of both a terrorized imagination and the idea of a transcendent God with whom we share nothing in common. The *internalization* of the expansionist will ultimately leads to an asceticism that exists at the heart of the divided modern subject.

With the move from Bern to Frankfurt and the composition of *The Spirit of Christianity and Its Fate,* the conceptual foundation of the *Positivity*—which is grounded in the fixed (positive) oppositions between morality and positivity, life and death, truth and falsity—become unhinged, as the nature of each term is seen to exist only through intercourse with its opposite. The movement from one extreme to the other follows the path of self-negation through strict fidelity. The gesture that *Jesus* adheres to with such fidelity is that of *withdrawal* in the service of a love beyond the law, and, for Hegel, this is a gesture that is reflected in the experience of baptism. I argue that his description in *The Spirit of Christianity* of this experience as a form of withdrawal from the world provides a phenomenological account of the essence of Christianity and its history. Hegel reconstructs this history by way of a tragic understanding of the concepts of freedom, spirit, fate, and catharsis. That is to say, he develops a poetic history informed by the categories of tragic drama.

In chapter 3, "The Idea of Freedom as Independence," I analyze the portrait that Hegel provides of the world from which Christianity withdraws. This world is very much defined by the positivity that I analyze in earlier chapters, although it is now conceived according to an immanent logic of spirit and fate. That is, by using the tragic concept of *fate,* Hegel is, in effect, advancing the position that collective subjectivities can no longer be thought of as embodying immobile essences; rather, they are determined by the specific ideas that they adopt, and their histories are, in turn, presented as the unfolding of the contradictions inherent in these ideas. Hegel understands the *spirit* of Judaism through the idea of freedom conceived in terms of separation and independence. Its *fate* is the reversal of this spirit. That is, the fate of the spirit of independence is dependence, more specifically, the dependence on a foreign, transcendent God. He attempts to draw out the significance of this fate by comparing the different modes of tragedy and sacrifice that characterize Greeks and Jews. My thesis regarding Hegel's deeply reductive account of Judaism is that he elevates his Greek ideal to the status of an "original human essence" and, in doing so, posits the spirit of the Jews as the perversion of an original, harmonious community that never existed.

In chapters 4 ("Withdrawal and Exile") and 5 ("Dialectic of Love"), I reconstruct what I understand to be Hegel's conception of the essence of Christianity in light of his reflections on tragedy. "Immanent transcendence" is my expression for this essence, and I argue that he conceives of this in terms of a synthesis of (i) withdrawal, as a separation from separation, and (ii) the experience of love.

The gesture of withdrawal is expressed for Hegel most powerfully in the Sermon on the Mount, and I claim in chapter 4 that it is motivated at its core by a need that extends beyond the authority of codified moral and religious laws. Conceiving of the life and teaching of Jesus in terms of the need to fulfill the law, is, in turn, coupled with an explicit break with Kantianism. Indeed, I argue that, for Hegel, Kant's moral doctrine becomes another expression of positivity. The sacrifice of the strict universality of the Kantian moral law would be an infinite gain, for it would inaugurate an immanent relation to the world defined by love that Hegel sometimes calls "pure life."

Tragedy is so crucial to Hegel's analysis of Jesus and the movement to pure life that he embodies because it both expresses the inevitable transgressions *against* pure life and presents the catharsis of these violations. As love is the fulfillment, *qua* life, of the law, so fate is the fulfillment of transgressions against life. The spirit of Christianity, defined as it is for Hegel by the aspiration to overcome the domination of the law, attempts to negate this negation of life through the reconciliation of fate *as such*. The promise of Christian withdrawal is that, through the extreme gesture of *distancing* and *passivity*, a novel form of *engagement* and *activity* will arise. The baptismal rupture from the world and the withdrawal into the desert are to be followed by a return to the world in the form of a free subjectivity unfettered by the burden of fear (positivity) or reverence for the law (Kantianism).

In chapter 5, I consider Hegel's position that the proper aim of religion is to achieve a living identity of objectivity and subjectivity, and I do so in conjunction with his further claim that love can only achieve this living identity in a *fleeting* manner. The problem for Hegel, then, becomes how the love that Jesus embodied and conveyed to his friends and disciples can be made *objective*, how it can be "substantialized" as an institution. My thesis is that, for Hegel in Frankfurt, Christianity never progresses beyond a merely transient unity of (subjective) feeling and (objective) expression. He argues further that Christianity's failure to fulfill the proper aim of religion is determined by its spirit. The spirit of love as the "immanent transcendence" of fate fails in its aspiration to overcome all alien objectivity and instead provokes a colossal fate of its own. The Christian tradition and the modernity that issues from it reside within this fate.

Hegel's conclusion regarding the failure of Christianity to reconcile itself with the fate that its spirit engenders leaves him open to questioning what religious form (or in the terms of "The Oldest Program," what new, modern mythology) will allow for "universal freedom and equality of spirits" to prevail (OP 13). Can that which is founded on the gesture of withdrawal ground such a mythology? Can it ground that which is necessary to bring together subject and object in an immanent, substantial union? Can this attempt to withdraw from all fate *ever* work to fulfill the idea of life? I make the case throughout my reading of Hegel's early theologico-political writings that these questions are also a revealing way of framing Hegel's subsequent work, and I do so with reference to passages from the later system that address them. In the conclusion, "Comedy, Subjectivity, and the Negative," I allude specifically to the way in which the transition that dominates Hegel early writings, that is, the transition from Greek *Volksreligion* to Christianity on the way to modernity, is presented in the *Phenomenology*. In the 1807 text, the dialectical advance from the Greek "religion of art" to "revealed religion" depends on the collapse of Greek tragedy in laughter.

PART 1

Positivity and the Concrete Idea of Freedom

ONE

Positivity and Historical Reversal

> In thinking, I raise myself above all that is finite to the absolute and am *infinite consciousness,* while at the same time I am *finite self-consciousness,* indeed to the full extent of my empirical condition. Both sides, as well as their relation, exist for me [in] the essential unity of my infinite knowing and my finitude. These two sides seek each other and flee from each other. . . . I am not *one* of the parts caught up in the conflict but am both of the combatants and the conflict itself. I am the fire and water that touch each other, the contact and the union of what utterly flies apart.
>
> —Hegel, *Lectures on the Philosophy of Religion*

Positivität: Either Life or Death

It is apparent from his earliest writings that, for Hegel, religions live and die. In his pre-Jena writings, the model for religious *life* is consistently the *Volksreligion* of ancient Greece. The sign of *death* is what he calls "positivity" (*Positivität*), and this characterizes the religion of Hegel's own time. Most concretely, the "positive" elements of a religion are its statues, creeds, dogma, codified moral laws, and theologies,[1] but, for Hegel, "positivity" means, in essence, artificially fixing what is inherently fluid. More pointedly, it is a kind of fundamentalism, insofar as this term refers very narrowly to the naturalizing or essentializing of "contingent, historically conditioned traits."[2] "Positive" law, as opposed to "natural" law, is not self-given but is instead posited by a dominant, external authority. It gives rise, in turn, to a broadly legalistic caste of mind. When it is not simply an automatic adherence to the law, legalistic thinking reduces duties to a kind of calculus: "a dead letter is laid down as a foundation and on it a system is constructed prescribing how men are to act and feel" (W 1:181/P 137).[3] A positive liturgy, then, is one that presents rituals and texts as if they were fixed and indisputable facts.[4] The practices that Hegel associates with positive religion are an insult to life: "To mouth incomprehensible prayers, to read masses, to recite rosaries, to perform meaningless ceremonies, this is the activity of the dead. Man here attempts to become a sheer object [*Objekt*], to allow himself to be ruled entirely by something that is foreign."[5] In sum, "a positive religion is a contranatural or a supernatural one, containing concepts and information transcending understanding and reason and requiring feeling and actions which would not come naturally to men: the feeling are forcibly and mechanically stimulated, the actions are done to order or from obedience without any spontaneous interest" (W 1:217/P 167). The letter is, as Hegel writes, dead.

Among the most significant positive elements found in early Christianity was the emphasis placed on Jesus's own personality. In *The Positivity of the Christian Religion,*[6] written in 1795–1796 while employed as a Hofmeister at the von Steiger home in Bern, Hegel describes the effect of this emphasis pointedly: the authority of Jesus's words was not based in the substance of what he says but on the fact that he said them. For Hegel, this misunderstanding was encouraged by Jesus's adoption of the role of a messiah and, most importantly, by the fact that he performed miracles as a sign of his divine nature. Like a fetish, the positive aspects of a religion come to take the place of that which they were initially supposed to serve. The fetish that usurps the place of the divine is able to triumph only with the collapse of the *fluidity* between signifier (miracle) and signified (divinity), for meaning is established precisely through this fluidity. The opposition between signifier and signified may remain but in a fixed form, with no possibility of commerce between the two. The effect is that both terms lose their validity.[7] Thus, the miracles that are meant to signify the divine nature of Jesus *qua* universal morality—Jesus is divine because of a potentiality he shares with all human beings—become fetishized when Jesus is judged to be divine because of the miracles that he performs. We might still acknowledge the opposition between miraculous acts and the divine, but divinity is now located in Jesus alone. As such, a living relation with the divine is lost for those of us who cannot perform these miracles. We can only look up to or kneel before an alien being, and this, for the young Hegel, is nothing short of death. Thus, the way to God through the miraculous seems to make the possibility of reaching the destination impossible.

The *Positivity* is guided by the overarching question of how Christianity, as a religion that Hegel understands at this point to be grounded in Jesus's teaching of free virtue, falls prey to precisely the kind of tyranny that it was originally established to challenge. That is, how does a religion born of a struggle *against* positive faith become contaminated by, and ultimately overwhelmed by, positivity itself? The supposition of Hegel's detailed response in the *Positivity* essay is, again, that a vital religious community must protect itself from positive elements. Hans-Georg Gadamer writes of Hegel's later dialectic that it aims "to dissolve in spirit's being at home with itself everything 'positive,' everything estranged and alien."[8] For the Hegel of *The Positivity of the Christian Religion,* it would seem that everything positive simply works to contaminate, corrupt, and undermine life. The dialectical thinking that *dissolves* everything positive *in* spirit is absent. What we wish to track, however, in our reading of Hegel's early writings is the subtle emergence of the dialectical pattern of thought that conceives of living practices as arising from the *incorporation* of these positive elements.

Conviction and the Proper Name "Hegel"

Hegel's investigation into the origins of the fall of Christianity into positivity begins with an analysis of the essence of Christianity as a living religion. This analysis, in turn, begins with a rejection of the need for a confession of faith. In an attempt to uncover what Christianity is in itself, the convictions of the author, and his personality generally, are deemed irrelevant: "a dry sketch of that kind would have encouraged the opinion that the author regarded his individual conviction as something important and that his personality came under review along with the whole matter at issue" (W 1:105 / P 68). Although Hegel is driven to investigate the origins of Christianity by the particular historical situation that he confronts and although this is determinative for why he looks back to this particular place and point in history (first-century Judea), he eschews the particularity of his own name and personality. By the very fact that Hegel discounts the relevance of a first-person declaration of faith, his text begins, in effect, by raising the question of the relation between faith and knowledge. He proceeds by first determining the essence of religion as such before asking whether Christianity conforms to this essence, but his general assumption throughout is that this essence is supplied by rational reflection alone. If, however, disinterested theoretical reflection can determine the character of the proper object of faith, what is the need for faith? Is it simply a nonreflective means of instilling the beliefs that reason alone could establish freely? And is it, then, simply a crutch for those unable, or unwilling, to employ their rationality? If so, what is to stop religious faith from functioning in the service of paternalistic deception and pacification? As Dostoevsky's Grand Inquisitor confesses,

> The most painful secrets of their conscience, all, all they will bring to us, and we shall have an answer for all. And they will be glad to believe our answer, for it will save them from the great anxiety and terrible agony they endure at present in making a free decision for themselves. And all will be happy, all the millions of creatures except the hundred thousand who rule over them. For only we, we who guard the mystery, shall be unhappy.[9]

By way of contrast with the tidy solution that sees reflection as the arbiter of rationally acceptable articles of faith, we should consider "The Oldest Program toward a System in German Idealism" fragment, written in the very first weeks of 1797, and so after the composition of the *Positivity.* The text is written in the first person, but, given that its authorship is a matter of debate, it is perhaps a collective "I," an "I" that is "we"[10]:

> we so often hear that the great mass of men must have a *sensuous religion*. Not only the great mass of men, but the philosopher too, needs

> it. Monotheism of reason and of the heart, polytheism of the imagination and art, that is what we need!
>
> First, I shall speak here of an idea which, as far as I know, no human mind has ever entertained—we must have a new mythology; but this mythology must remain in service to the ideas, it must become a mythology of reason.
>
> Until we make the ideas aesthetic, i.e., mythological, they will have no interest for the *people;* and, conversely, until the mythology is rational, the philosophers will perforce be ashamed of it. Thus the enlightened and unenlightened must at long last clasp hands; mythology must become philosophical, and the people rational, while philosophy must become mythological, in order to make the philosophers sensuous. Then eternal union will prevail among us. No more the contemptuous glance, no more blind quaking of the people before their sages and priests. (OP 12–13)

In "The Oldest Program," we find neither a personal confession of faith nor a simple, Enlightenment defense of the capacity of theoretical reason to police religious doctrine, but instead a call for a future revolution in spirit characterized by a union beyond this disjunction, a union that would mark an end to positivity. As the poetic body of faith, the mythological must not be considered mere ornamentation but must instead play an essential role in achieving this union. To form the sensuous philosopher, the "polytheism of the imagination" is as crucial to the philosopher as is the "monotheism of reason" to the nonphilosopher. The author of the fragment writes, "The philosopher must possess as much aesthetic force as the poet," and poetry "will again become what she was in the beginning—*the instructress of humanity*" (OP 11). The position of the sensuous philosopher, and sensuous reason, is not to stand apart from the people as wise men or secularized priests and relieve the weight of the painful secrets of their conscience with promises of heaven. The vision of the author of "The Oldest Program" is defined by both freedom and equality, as well as a faith that is immanent to the extent that it is directed toward "neither God nor immortality *outside themselves*" (OP 10). Is Hegel in agreement, at least implicitly, with this thoroughgoing reciprocity of reason and mythology in *The Positivity of the Christian Religion?* I will argue that he is not, or at least not resolutely so. A sign of his unwillingness to accept this reciprocity is the vehemence of his challenge to positivity itself. With the exclusion of the positive elements of religious practices, the possibility of producing a mythology that will be of interest to anyone other than the nonsensuous philosopher is greatly diminished.

We will return to the broadly Kantian Enlightenment position on the relation between faith and reason that Hegel advances in the *Positivity* essay. We will do so, however, by way of a circuitous route that skips from Hegel's Bern writings (1795–1796) over "The Oldest Program" (1797) to a pair of essays, the *Differenzschrift* (1801) and *Faith and Knowledge* (1802), that were produced while Hegel was working with Schelling on the *Critical Journal* in Jena. We turn to these two essays in particular at this point because of the sharp criticisms they raise to this Kantian Enlightenment position. Thus, when we return, after a relatively brief stay in Jena, to Bern and the account of reason and faith that Hegel defends in the *Positivity,* we will do so fully cognizant of his own subsequent criticisms of it. Only then will we move forward again, in part 2 of the book, to an intermediary position between Bern and Jena. Geographically, this is Frankfurt. Conceptually, it is the point where Hegel adopts the position that, to borrow the words of "The Oldest Program," "the idea that unifies all, [is] the idea of *beauty.*" It is a point where, I will argue, Hegel concurs with the assertion that "the supreme act of reason, because it embraces all ideas, is an aesthetic act; and that only in *beauty* are *truth and goodness* of the same flesh" (OP 10–11). We will find, in other words, Frankfurt-era writings by Hegel that corroborate, and elaborate on, the protospeculative position sketched in "The Oldest Program." Further, we will see that Hegel builds on this position in *The Spirit of Christianity and Its Fate* when he argues that Greek tragedy is the model for the imaginative correlate of reason.

Faith and Knowledge in Modernity

Hegel's first acknowledged publication, "Differenz des Fichte'schen und Schelling'schen Systems der Philosophie" (Jena, 1801), also known as the *Differenzschrift,* challenges the Kantian conceptualization of the relation between faith and reason presented in the *Positivity* essay by advancing one of his earliest philosophical defenses of the speculative principle of the unification of opposites. Indeed, he claims that speculative philosophy is the fulfillment of philosophy as such. He goes on to describe "speculation" in a way that shows the centrality of the sensuous reason heralded in "The Oldest Program" fragment:

> The sole interest of [speculative] Reason is to suspend such rigid antitheses [reason and sensibility, intelligence and nature, absolute subjectivity and absolute objectivity]. But this does not mean that Reason is altogether opposed to opposition and limitation. For the necessary dichotomy is one factor in life. Life eternally forms itself by setting up oppositions, and totality at the highest pitch of living energy is only possible through its own re-establishment out of the deepest fission.

> What Reason opposes, rather, is just the absolute fixity which the intellect [*Verstand*] gives to the dichotomy [*Entzweiung*]. (W 2:21 / D 90–91)

Speculative thought aims to achieve unification, but a unification that contains within itself difference and opposition. To assume that any opposition or limit is unchanging or fixed is an offense to speculative reason. As we will see, if "life" is the name that Hegel gives to this unification in Jena, in his earlier Bern writings, it was given the historical and geographical location of ancient Greece. The conclusions that Hegel will draw from his investigations into the historical development of Christianity, along with its relation to Greece, are summarized concisely in a subsequent passage from the *Differenzschrift:*

> As a culture grows and spreads, and the development of those outward expressions of life into which dichotomy can entwine itself becomes more manifold, the power of dichotomy becomes greater, its regional sanctity is more firmly established and the strivings of life to give birth once more to its harmony become more meaningless, more alien to the culture as a whole. Such few attempts as there have been on behalf of the cultural whole against more recent culture, like the more significant beautiful embodiment of far away or long ago, have only been able to arouse the modicum of attention which remains possible when the more profound, serious connection of living art can no longer be understood. (W 2:23 / D 92)

What Hegel calls "positivity" in Bern takes the philosophical form of *Entzweiung,* while "life" is conceptualized as speculative reason. Dichotomy insinuates itself into a living culture by way of the most peripheral aspects of it, thereby disrupting the harmony of the whole. While speculative reason is "speculative" insofar as it incorporates dichotomies within itself, the power of dichotomy can overwhelm. Greece is the ideal of unification, or "life" ("the more significant beautiful embodiment of far away or long ago"), insofar as it manifests a cultural whole that achieves, through "art's all-embracing coherence," the highest aesthetic perfection.[11] The living union that Greece embodies ultimately flourishes through the proliferation of dichotomies, but to do so, it must avoid their rigid polarization.

We find the specific application of speculative reason to the opposition between faith and reason in a text titled *Faith and Knowledge* (1802), written a year after the *Differenzschrift.* In *Faith and Knowledge,* Hegel sets out his living, speculative relation of faith and reason by way of a contrast with the modern, nonspeculative idea of what he calls "practical faith." This is a position established by Kant but pushed to its logical conclusion by Fichte, and it purports to resolve the conflict between faith and reason, religion and philosophy, from the side of philosophy.

For Hegel, this apparent accomplishment of philosophy is a meager one: "the positive element with which Reason busied itself to do battle, is no longer religion, and victorious Reason is no longer Reason. The new born peace that hovers [*schweben*] triumphantly over the corpse of Reason and faith, uniting them as the child of both, has as little of Reason in it as it has of authentic faith" (W 2:288/FK 55). The effect is that, from the side of religion, God becomes something incomprehensible and unthinkable; or, in philosophical terms, "the supersensuous is incapable of being known by Reason; the highest Idea does not at the same time have reality" (W 2:289/FK 56). As a result, faith is empty, while knowledge is limited to what is finite and empirical. This mutual enervation leads to false sanctuary in an endlessly receding "beyond." The infinite resides where it can never, in principle, be reached. It thus becomes

> too vacuous for cognition so that this infinite void of knowledge could only be filled with the subjectivity of longing and divining [*Subjektivität des Sehnens und Ahnens*]. Thus what used to be regarded as the death of philosophy, that Reason should renounce its existence in the Absolute, excluding itself totally from it and relating itself to it only negatively, became now the zenith of philosophy. By coming to consciousness of its own nothingness, the Enlightenment turns this nothingness into a system. (Ibid.)

If, as Hegel claims, this Enlightenment system is a "vain tumult of activity without a firm core" (W 2:288/FK 56, translation altered), faith is enlisted to supplement this fragile edifice. This fragility is most apparent in Fichte's philosophy, because the divide that separates how things are from how they ought to be is most severe. For Fichte, the substance of this *ought* is what he calls the "moral world order," and it exists, and can only exist, through faith. As a result, it will always be outside the ego. Hegel, the emerging speculative philosopher, criticizes this position by arguing that the ego and the moral world order are dependent on each other for their identity. The loss of the one extreme cancels the other. The infinitely extended striving toward the reconciliation of the phenomenal realm of the finite and the noumenal realm of an infinite kingdom of ends represents faith in the form of an "empirical infinity" (W 2:346/FK 108). This is the infinity of an endless series, or what Hegel will later call the "bad infinite." This view condemns Fichte—and Kant—to a dualism that cannot simply be overcome by the appeal to a "beyond."

The reconciliation of religious faith and reason, as Hegel conceives it in 1802, is fundamentally at odds with Fichte's "practical faith" and its infinite progress toward the moral world order. The redemption of true religion is not projected into an infinite future as the regulative moral ideal of perpetual peace. It is not reconciliation infinitely deferred, thus never achieved. Instead, it provides a reconciliation that is genuinely possible and like Spinoza's infinity of the intellect, it would incorporate the finite into the infinite.[12] Only in this way is it possible to overcome the division (*Entzweiung*) defining Fichte's philosophy and modern culture as such. As Hegel had already written in the *Differenzschrift,* it is precisely the existence of *Entzweiung* that gives rise to the need for philosophy *as* speculation (see W 2:20/D 89).

Fichte is condemned to dualism because of his assumption of "difference as an in-itself" (W 2:424/FK 181). This is to say, for Fichte, the difference between the finite and infinite is absolute. Since freedom is defined by the striving toward the point of reconciliation, reaching this point would mean that the "whole worth of man would fall away because this freedom exists only by negating and it can only negate while what it negates exists" (ibid.). Freedom is defined as an infinite struggle against nature, or the natural element in the "self," a struggle without, we could say, catharsis. The dualism of Fichte's position and its existential consequences are most explicitly revealed at the point when, as Hegel writes, the "I" recognizes that it is a "manifestation, determined by the universe, of a force of nature that determines itself, . . . that it is nature which acts in him, that he is subject to the eternal laws of nature, to strict necessity." We must not hide "the sadness, the loathing [*Abscheu*], the horror [*Entsetzen*] . . . which seizes upon his inmost heart at such a conclusion" (W 2:417–418/FK 175–176).[13] Hegel rejects Fichte's reaction to nature in the most strenuous way. He condemns what he calls,

> the monstrous arrogance, the conceited frenzy of this self who is horrified, filled with loathing and sadness, at the thought that he is one with the universe, that eternal nature acts in him—to be filled with loathing, be horrified and sad over the resolve to subjugate oneself to the eternal laws of nature and to its hallowed and strict necessity, to be in despair because one is not free, free from the eternal laws of nature and its strict necessity, to believe that one makes oneself indescribably miserable by this obedience—all this presupposes an utterly vulgar view of nature and of the relation of the singular person to nature. (W 2:418/FK 176)

This view is, at heart, void of reason (*Vernunft*), mired as it is in the logic of reflection and mere understanding (*Verstand*).[14] As such, "the absolute identity of subject and object is entirely alien to it, and its principle is their absolute non-identity" (ibid.). The desperation of the Fichtean "I" follows precisely from the inability to reconcile itself with the necessity of nature, and this inability stems from the principle of nonidentity at the core of Fichte's thought. This failure is inevitable insofar as freedom is understood as freedom *from* necessity, not a union with it. As the association between Fichte and the Enlightenment makes clear, the philosophical shortcomings of the Fichtean system, and the *Entzweiung* at its core, mirror the cultural experience of Enlightenment modernity as an illness of the human spirit, as despair (*Verzweiflung*). Its symptom is the dominance of *Reflexionsphilosophie* and this concomitant absence of speculative unification.

Ultimately, Fichte's appeal to an endless progression lacks any proper sense of fulfillment or measure. Hölderlin gives voice to this condition in the second volume of *Hyperion*, published in October 1799. Hyperion writes to his friend Bellarmin,

> So I arrived among the Germans. I did not demand much and was prepared to find even less. I came there humbly, like homeless, blind Oedipus to the gates of Athens, where the sacred grove received him; and fair souls came to greet him—
>
> How different my experience!
>
> Barbarians from the remotest past, whom industry and science and even religion have made yet more barbarous, profoundly incapable of any divine emotion, spoiled to the core for the delights of the sacred Graces, offensive to every well-conditioned soul through the whole range of pretense to pettiness, hollow and tuneless, like the shards of a discarded pot—such, my Bellarmin! were my comforters.

This barbarism manifests itself in a dearth of festivals, and one wonders if this absence of festivals corresponds to a lack of a proper measure:

> I tell you: there is nothing sacred that is not desecrated, is not debased to a miserable expedient among this people; and what even among savages is usually preserved in sacred purity, these all-calculating barbarians pursue as one pursues any trade, and cannot do otherwise; for where a human being is once conditioned to look, there it serves its ends, seeks its profit, it dreams no more—God forbid!—it remains sedate; and when it makes holiday and when it loves and when it prays, and even when spring's lovely festival, when the season of reconciliation for the world dissolves all cares and conjures innocence into a guilty heart, when, intoxicated by the sun's warm rays, the slave in his joy forgets his chains, and the enemies of mankind, softened by the divinely living air, are as peaceable as children—when the caterpillar itself grows wings and the bees swarm, even then the German sticks to his petty tasks and scarcely deigns to notice the weather!

Finally, Hölderlin draws a stark contrast between this portrait of a sterile modernity and a harmonious ideal of unity forged by artistic beauty:

O Bellarmin, where a people loves Beauty, where it honors the Genius in its own artists, there a common spirit is astir like the breath of life, there the shy mind opens, self-conceit melts away, and all hearts are relevant and great and enthusiasm brings forth heroes. The home of all men is with such a people and gladly can the stranger linger there. But where divine Nature and her artists are so insulted, ah! there life's greatest joy is gone, and any other star is better than earth. There men grow ever more sterile, ever more empty, who yet were all born beautiful; servility increases and with it insolence, intoxication grows with troubles and, with luxury, hunger and dread of starvation; the blessing of each year becomes a curse, and all gods flee. (FH 1:754–57)[15]

Hölderlin's ideal of unity born of a love of artistic beauty is an articulation of the idea of the *hen kai pan,* the "One and All." He adopted the phrase from Jacobi, who had used it to describe, and condemn, Lessing's Spinozism,[16] and we find this same expression attached to an entry that Hölderlin made in Hegel's *Stammbuch* when they were students together, with Schelling, at the Tübingen Stift.[17] This idea is also at play in Hegel's own writing whenever there is a systematic unity in which the individuality of those who are united is maintained. For Hegel, the model for the *hen kai pan* is at once the organic unity of biological life and the ancient Athenian *polis.*[18] The idea of the *hen kai pan* provides a way of thinking about development and unification without falling prey to what we have described as the Fichtean infinite progression; thus, it is in light of this idea that Hegel criticizes Kant's "kingdom of ends" and Fichte's "moral world order." For Hegel, in 1802, religion is the mode of being in which "we consciously have experience of the Absolute."[19] "Authentic faith" (W 2:288/FK 55), then, is not spurred by the regulative ideal of perpetual peace but is animated by the thought of the *hen kai pan.* In religious intuition, the finite is reconciled with the infinite.

Kant in Athens

Although the difference in the character of the prose is stark, both Hölderlin's *Hyperion* and Hegel's early Jena essays condemn the fragmentation that they find in modernity. A confrontation with modernity is already present in Hegel's Bern-era writings, but instead of taking the form of a challenge to the Fichtean absolute subject, he frames it, as we have seen, in terms of positivity. What is also consistent is that this fragmentation is related to the dichotomy in modernity between faith and knowledge, religion and reason, necessity and freedom. Despite this continuity, however, when he wrote the *Positivity,* Hegel understood himself to be allied to the Kantian moral position, so to read the *Differenzschrift* and *Faith and Knowledge* essays is to see how Hegel would criticize his own position in Bern.

Hegel's most immediate intellectual opponents in the *Positivity* were not Kant and Fichte, but those like his former theology professor at the Stift, Gottlob Christian Storr (1746–1805), who attempted to appropriate Kant's thought to bolster orthodox Christianity. Storr's strategy was essentially to expand the postulates of pure practical reason to the point where they came to encompass all traditional dogmas.[20] More concretely, Storr argued that both miracles and the character of Jesus ought to be employed as proof of Jesus's divinity. Hegel judged this to be a misuse of Kant in the service of positive religion and a ruse to subordinate reason to supernatural revelation in the name of reason itself. As the author of "The Oldest Program" writes, "Finally come the ideas of a moral world, divinity, immortality—the overthrow of all belief in a hinterhaven, the prosecution by reason itself of that hypocritical priesthood that has recently begun to ape reason" (OP 10).[21] Hegel's aim in the *Positivity* will be, in part, to defend Kant against this kind of appropriation; he does so, moreover, by presenting Jesus as a moral teacher who would have shunned theological arguments premised on his miraculous acts.

Given this focus, it may be tempting to conclude that the *Positivity* specifically, and all of Hegel's pre-Jena writings more generally, are largely unconcerned with engaging philosophical issues. This conclusion would seem to imply further that it was only after moving to Jena that Hegel comes to prioritize philosophy and conceptual thought over religious representation and artistic intuition (even when what is being defended philosophically is religion's exclusive access to the Absolute [see W 2:290–291/FK 58]). It is certainly true that the texts written before Hegel's move to Jena forgo explicit philosophical analysis in favor of explicating the historical developments of religious and economic thought and practice.[22] If he is less involved with explicitly philosophical questions in the *Positivity*, however, it is not because he assigns a secondary role to philosophy but because he defers at the time so thoroughly to Kant.[23] Philosophical issues were of less pressing concern because they had been decided by the Critical philosophy. The emphasis of Hegel's *Positivity* attests less to the importance that he places in philosophy than to the specific role that he assumes for himself. His concern, as mentioned above, is with the means of bridging the divide that Kant introduces between practical reason and sensibility and of overcoming the division that existed between autonomous ethical reason and autocratic political rule. This leads to the investigation of the form and content of a mythology that would best supplement a free political order. But if his project was initially conceived as a supplement to Kant's philosophical achievements, Hegel will come to engage philosophical questions more directly when his own historical investigations serve to undermine the Kantian position.[24] This will take place in Hegel's *Spirit of Christianity and Its Fate,* for its historical investigations afford the distance from Kant's thought that, in turn, allows for the explicitly philosophical challenges he makes to Kant and Fichte in the early Jena essays.

Hegel's early commitment to Kant's Critical philosophy is evident in the definition of religion that he provides in the *Positivity.* He claims that the value of Christianity must be determined according to this fundamental judgment: "the aim and essence of all true religion, our religion included, is human morality" (W 1:105/P 68). He clarifies this further when he describes the "essence" of any true religion as "the establishment of human duties and their underlying motives in their purity and the use of the idea of God to show the possibility of the *summum bonum*" (W 1:124/P 86). If the aim of religion as such is the moral law, its universal means for achieving this end is the cultivation of "a certain attitude of mind [*Gesinnung*]" (W 1:138/P 98). Religion is of value to the extent that it cultivates the morality that is exposed in its philosophically rigorous form in Kant's moral philosophy. Yet Hegel is less concerned with engaging in a detailed examination of Kant's thought than he is with the more general priority given to morality and the place of reason as a means of determining moral action. Thus, he writes,

> once the church's system ignores reason [*Vernunft*] it can be nothing save a system which despises man. The powers of the human mind have a domain of their own, and Kant has separated off this domain for science. This salutary separation has not been made by the church in its legislative activity, and centuries have still to elapse before the European mind learns to make and recognize this distinction in practical life and in legislation, although the Greeks had been brought to this point of their own accord by their sound intuition. In Greek religion, or in any other whose underlying principle is a pure morality, the moral commands of reason, which are subjective, were not treated or set up as if they were the objective rules with which the understanding [*Verstand*] deals. (W 1:187–188/P 143, translation altered)

Hegel reveals both his allegiance to Kant's Critical project of delineating the proper domain of reason and his admiration for ancient Greece. Indeed, this admiration is articulated in Kantian terms: he understands the Greeks as having intuited the morality that Kant had to defend in philosophical form, for what was intuited and realized in practices in the ancient world can only be articulated in theory today. Hegel's self-assigned role is, then, defined more specifically: to determine how Kant's grounding of morality in pure practical reason can be made concrete, can be *lived* in a manner that approximates what he finds in ancient Greece. The fact that Hegel locates a point in history where practical reason permeated the full life of a culture means that the future return of such a culture is not extended, in principle, into what we can call an infinite future, one that necessarily recedes as quickly as we progress toward it. Its return could occur at a time that is tied to our own. Hegel does not, however, indulge in the stance of the apocalyptic prophet who heralds the imminent arrival of the kingdom of ends. He resists this stance and the dramatic tension that it entails. We should not expect this "return," he tells us, for hundreds of years. Thus, Hegel is thinking within an immanent sphere of temporality, one that not only lacks an infinite future but also an infinite past. Periclean Athens, with its immediate and free beauty, was, for Hegel, the temporal realization of this presence. The dictates of moral reason were fulfilled in concrete social life on the northern bank of the Mediterranean in the middle part of the fifth-century BCE, *not* in an immemorial past outside the continuum of history. Hegel's deployment of Greece as the manifestation of freedom and its possible "return" can be read, retrospectively, as a challenge to what he will attribute in his Jena essays to the Fichtean "moral world order," namely, the impossibility of ever realizing this order in practice. As we have seen, this challenge would extend to Kant as well, which raises the question: Can Kant make the journey back to Greece unscathed? Hegel's allegiance to Kant's moral philosophy in the *Positivity* is firm, but by positing Greece as the concrete manifestation of his moral idea, we can see (again, retrospectively) an inchoate challenge to the regulative character that Kant assigns to his idea. This prompts a further question: What exactly is the nature of a *future* "return" of the freedom once realized in ancient Greece?

In *The Future of Hegel*, Catherine Malabou argues that, for Hegel, time itself has a history. She holds that the idea of the future found in Hegel's later system is rendered well by the French *voir venir*, "to see (what is) coming."[25] This is a future that unites *anticipation*, and the continuity with the past that this entails, with *surprise*, and thus a discontinuity with the past. According to Malabou, *voir venir* is the synthesis of the Greek and modern modes of temporality, a synthesis that gives rise to a new temporal mode. This is a notion of temporality—specifically, futurity—that is both *beautiful* in that everything can happen and also *terrible* because everything already has. It is "the future understood as future within closure."[26] At this earlier stage in his thinking, in the *Positivity*, Hegel conceives the future as oriented by and tied to the Greek past; in this sense, it is an object of anticipation. The *when* of its return is not, however, dictated by a logic of historical necessity. Instead, Hegel simply projects it into the distant, if not infinite, future, and this lack of precision allows for a modicum of surprise. Of much greater interest, however, is the question of *what* will return. We can anticipate it to the extent that it will be a manifestation of an atemporal—thus, decidedly nondialectical—moral idea. The concrete character of its manifestation is far less certain. Will the future return of Greece in modernity, after the intervening history of Christianity, be a synthesis of Greece and Christian modernity? Is there something to salvage from the Christian legacy, or should it be rejected and abandoned outright, leaving only the task of translating Greek social and mythological forms into a different idiom? Although Hegel certainly does not pose the question of the future in anything like these terms in the *Positivity,* what is clear is his fidelity to an atemporal idea of morality that was manifest in Greece, articulated in theoretical form by Kant, and could be manifested again in the conceivable future. And this idea greatly diminishes the dimension of the future that surprises. It does not suggest the possibility of a future without precedence. At the end of "The Oldest Program," we find the author(s) heralding a new god: "A higher spirit, sent from heaven, will have to found this new religion among us; it will be the very last and the grandest of humanity's works" (OP 13). This openness is not found in the *Positivity.*

Secret Revolutions in Spirit

Instead of framing history in terms of the bad infinite of endless progress, the apocalyptic tension of an imminent return of past presence, or the arrival of a "higher spirit," Hegel conceives of history in the *Positivity* relative to an atemporal moral ideal that was realized in the past and will potentially be realized again in the future. Against this conceptual horizon, he addresses the historical question of why Christianity usurps paganism. His approach is grounded in his conviction that *secret* revolutions precede overt historical transformations: "Great revolutions which strike the eye at a glance must have been preceded by a still and secret revolution in the spirit of the age, a revolution not visible to every eye, especially imperceptible to contemporaries, and as hard to discern as to describe in words. It is the lack of acquaintance with this spiritual revolution which makes the resulting changes astonishing" (W 1:203 / P 152).[27] So an attunement to these subterranean revolutions presumably mitigates the element of surprise that would otherwise interrupt a sober, anticipatory relation to futurity. But to what should one be attuned? What are the tell-tale signs of an imminent shift in spirit? And once one is aware of the importance of these secret revolutions, is it possible to help precipitate one? If there are secret revolutions, are there also secret revolutionaries, and, if so, is it accurate to see Hegel as aspiring to this role? Or is he, instead, simply setting himself the task of bringing these prior revolutions to light? But perhaps this is a false opposition. Unearthing these previous revolts could be precisely the project appropriate to the untimely revolutionary who lives when the time is not yet ripe for the kind of overt revolution that strikes the eye immediately. Is the task of a spiritual revolutionary, then, to help "ripen" time?

Given Hegel's focus on Socrates and Jesus in his early writings, it is certainly tempting to think of them as spiritual revolutionaries of this kind. Yet Hegel introduces the concept of a secret revolution in spirit when accounting for how Christianity came to conquer paganism, and his analysis operates primarily at the structural level of political and economic class antagonism. Thus, when he provides an analysis of revolutions in spirit, the role that the individual plays is diminished. According to Hegel, Christianity succeeds paganism because the pagan world first turns against itself, thus inviting Christianity onto the historical stage. Despite the great importance that Hegel will come to place on the ideas that animate religions and cultures, his explanation of the self-destruction of the pagan world initially emphasizes its material causes:

> Fortunate campaigns, increase of wealth, and acquaintance with luxury and more and more of life's comforts created in Athens and Rome an aristocracy of wealth and military glory. The aristocrats then acquired a dominion and an influence over the masses and corrupted them by their deeds and still more by their riches. The masses had readily and willingly ceded power and preponderance in the state to the aristocrats, conscious as they were that they had given them their power and could take it away again at the first fit of bad temper. But gradually the masses ceased to deserve a reproof so often brought against them that they were ungrateful to their leaders. (W 1:205–206/P 155, translation altered)

In Hegel's account, the rise of luxury does not undermine the "city of sows," as Glaucon disparaged a city geared solely toward the sustenance of the most rudimentary level of natural existence (*Republic* 372d). Rather, the decadence of the aristocratic class undermines a political union that is, for Hegel, defined by freedom. The rule of the aristocracy is dependent on the acquiescence of those ruled, and Hegel attributes to the masses full consciousness of their power over the rulers.[28] Initially, the rule of the aristocracy was *freely* accepted because aristocrats were willing to die for the idea of the city, so criticisms leveled against the rulers could be deflected by the fact that the freedom of all was secured by the sacrifices that the aristocracy were willing to make. Eventually, however, criticisms of the excesses of luxury and power secured by the aristocracy could no longer be dismissed. In Book IV of the *Republic,* Plato warns against the birth of factions in the *polis* as a result of material inequality (see 421d), and Hegel's point here is a similar one.[29] The division that arises within the city as a result of the increase of wealth and acquaintance with luxury reaches such an extreme that the sacrifices made by the ruled are no longer justified. The inherent rationality of this historically specific social configuration is betrayed; consequently, the masses threaten to revolt against the aristocracy.

In light of this threat, the aristocracy who had once been given its power freely now imposes its rule by force; with this, the idea of the republican regime is shattered. The immediate identification with the city that allows for the possibility of a freely assumed sacrifice of one's life is lost.[30] What replaces this is the atomized state envisioned as a machine (*Staatsmaschine;* W 1:205/P 156) that unites the individual parts of the whole in a dead, positive manner. The individual is unable to perceive the relation it has to the whole, so the free association with the idea of the city is replaced by mere usefulness. With this reduction to usefulness, genuine political freedom vanishes, and the only rights that remain are those related to property. Hegel's analysis in the *Positivity* mirrors then, in broad strokes, the move in the *Phenomenology* from the plurality of city-states in Greece to the Roman Empire and the universal extension and domination of one city. The rise of the unipolar Roman Empire amounts to a *withdrawal* of the living city-states into a "soulless community which has ceased to be the substance—itself unconscious—of individuals" (PdG 316/PS 290).[31] Faced with a lifeless political union of this kind, where there is no shared collective end, what is left is a "sheer multiplicity of personal atoms" (PdG 318/PS 292). In the *Phenomenology,* then, Hegel conceives of Rome's empire in terms of an atomistic metaphysics. And, as in the *Positivity,* this is a dead order, immanence stripped of all transcendence. Individuated persons compelled by narrow self-interest knock against one another in a field secured by a minimal set of legal rights. The empire may afford to all its citizens equal formal rights, but what these amount to in practice is simply the protection of individual private property. The organizing principle, the caesar, is nothing more than an arbitrary elevation of one of these atoms over the other.[32] Thus, what Hegel calls "positivity" in his early writings characterizes the rigid, atomized individualities and abstract positive law of the Roman world as such.

Christianity's triumph over paganism is conditioned, then, by the division within paganism itself and its self-immolation. If we can speak of secret revolutionaries taking part in the silent revolutions that prefigure open revolt, we could imagine them being those who articulate and address the specific needs and contradictions of the times. This corresponds very closely with Hegel's portrayal of both Socrates and Jesus, and we will return to them below. At this point, however, we need only reemphasize that, although the concern with this spiritual revolution leads Hegel to focus most specifically on religious practice and its grounding in morality, his reflections on religion are inextricably tied to questions of politics and the *polis* generally. The Greeks are said to live in an immediate accord with pure morality because both their political system and religious practices were in harmony with it. Even when interpretations of Hegel's early texts draw attention to the crucial role that Greece plays in his early writings, there is still a danger of separating the religious from the political dimensions of his thought. Some studies of Hegel's pre-Jena writings emphasize and commend the thoroughly Christian character and orientation of his early thought. Wilhelm Dilthey and Theodor Haering are examples of this position. Others, like Lukács, laud his oppositional, even revolutionary stance toward the degraded German political and religious order.[33]

Hegel, then, is presented as either the theological student making his first tentative steps toward translating Christianity into the language of the concept or a political revolutionary tainted, perhaps, by idealist tendencies and a reactionary attachment to a mystical Greek ideal. The one interpretation implicitly subordinates Hegel's politico-philosophical work to his faith, while the other sees any appeal to religion as an offense to the purity of the dialectical science that he was in the process of developing. Yet if we read these early writings with an eye to the Greek ideal that animates and orients them, we see that a central assumption is precisely the intimate connection between religious and political unity. Hegel is unwilling to jettison either of these elements, and while he does not at this point come to relate the two in a dialectical manner, this attempt to understand their interrelation and interdependence assumes the idea of the *hen kai pan* intrinsic to the dialectical thinking that he will come to develop. Further, both the secret revolutions in the spirit of the age and the overt ones that these precede occur in this theologico-political space.

Volksreligionen

The arrival of Christianity onto the historical stage was, according to Hegel, premised on the internal material and spiritual conflicts within the pagan world itself. To better understand the contours of the life that was *lost* when this world turned on itself, we must consider in detail what Hegel calls a *Volksreligion.* This kind of engaged, "public" religion was thoroughly intertwined with the political, artistic, and philosophical aspects of Greek culture; as a result, it was crucial to securing the original harmony that was, in Hegel's mind, concretely manifested in fifth-century Athens.

The first sustained articulation of *Volksreligionen* occurs in a text that is known in German by its first words, *Religion ist eine . . . ,* and in English as *The Tübingen Essay* (although it was most likely written in Stuttgart in 1793).[34] If nothing else, the essay shows the degree to which Hegel's three years of theological study at the Tübingen Stift inspired the desire to confront the "positive" form of Christianity defended by Storr. The text draws a stark, uncompromising opposition between a subjective, living *Volksreligion* animated by moral feeling and an objective, private religion divorced from experience and anesthetized by dogmatism. Hegel correlates this opposition with the further distinction between the logic of *Vernunft,* which defines the living, public, and active quality of a *Volksreligion,* and *Verstand,* the calculative logic that guides a mechanical adherence to church law.[35] When Hegel personifies *Verstand,* it is as a courtier (*Hofmann;* W 1:21) because of its shrewdness: "It knows how to hunt up rationalizations for every passion, every venture" (W 1:21/TE 40). Ultimately, however, it does not put principles into actions but waits for orders from its master. Rather than setting its own ends, *Verstand* is in servitude to narrow self-interest. *Vernunft,* by contrast, is autonomous. It has the capacity for self-rule and, like love, the power to unify. As Hegel writes of love in *Religion ist eine . . . ,* "It finds itself in other people. Forgetting about itself, love is able to step outside of a given individual's existence and live, feel, and act no less fully in others—just as reason, the principle of universally valid laws, recognizes its own self in the shared citizenship each rational being has in an intelligible world" (W 1:30/TE 46). Although it is a pathological principle of action, love, like *Vernunft,* is not determined by self-interest: "It does not do the right thing merely because it has calculated that the satisfactions resulting from its course of action are purer and longer lasting than those resulting from sensuality or the gratification of some passion. This principle, then, is not refined self-love, in which the ego is in the end always the highest goal" (W 1:30/TE 47). The labor involved in carrying out a calculus of satisfactions is that of *Verstand. Vernunft,* fused with disinterested feeling, is the model of a concrete, unifying rationality beyond *Verstand.* It is thought united with, rather than dictated by, sensibility.[36]

The close allegiance between *Vernunft* and love is reflected in the intimate connection that Hegel finds in *Volksreligionen* between *Vernunft* and sensibility as such. For Hegel, a public, *Volksreligion* consists of three moments:

> I. Its teaching must be founded on universal reason [*Vernunft*].
> II. Imagination, the heart, and the senses must not go away empty-handed in the process.
> III. It must be so constituted that all of life's needs, including public and official transactions, are bound up with it. (W 1:33/TE 49)

The logical relation between these moments is as follows: (I) the rationality on which religion is based can (III) effectively shape the life and institutions of public life (II) only through the mediation of imagination, heart, and feeling. This was the great achievement of ancient Greek religion. However, it is only with the collapse of the *immediate* unity that Hegel ascribes to fifth-century Periclean Athens that an analytic account of the moments of a *Volksreligion* and their relation to one another becomes necessary. As he writes,

> A *Volksreligion*—engendering and nurturing, as it does, great and noble sentiments—goes hand in hand with freedom. But our religion would train people to be citizens of heaven, gazing ever upward, making our most human feelings seem alien. Indeed at the great Eucharist dressed in colors of mourning and with downcast eyes, even here, at what is supposed to be a celebration of human brotherhood, we fear we might contract venereal disease from the brother who drank out

> of the communal chalice before. . . . How different were the Greeks! They approached the altars of their friendly gods clad in the colors of joy, their faces open invitations to friendship and love, beaming with good cheer. (W 1:41–42/TE 56)

How different, indeed. In light of this stark contrast, the questions facing Hegel were the following: How does one go about recapturing the free, joyful spirit of the Greeks? How can the confluence of reason and the imagination that Hegel finds in Greece be translated into a contemporary context? And how were the Greeks themselves able to satiate "the imagination, the heart, and the sense" so as to engender such a free and noble people?

I will argue that, since the tragic poets play such a determinative role in forming and fulfilling the fifth-century imagination, tragedy provides a clue as to how the modern imagination might be reformed, thus, how we moderns might once again approach the altar in friendship rather than suspicion and fear. Yet, despite the fact that Hegel has already established the need for *Volksreligionen* in the 1793 *Religion ist eine . . .* essay, tragedy plays no significant role in *The Positivity of the Christian Religion.* The representative of Greece in the *Positivity* essay is Socrates, not Oedipus. Tragedy assumes greater prominence in a late fragment from the Bern period (mid-1796) titled *Jedes Volk hat ihm eigene Gegenstände,* and it truly comes to the fore in *The Spirit of Christianity.* The absence of tragedy can be explained, in part, by the overriding tenor of the essay. In the *Positivity,* Kant's second *Critique* provides the means of fulfilling the first moment of a *Volksreligion* ("Its teaching must be founded on universal reason [*Vernunft*]"), for it stands as the contemporary articulation of universal moral reason. As Hegel writes, "Reason sets up moral, necessary, and universally valid laws; Kant calls these 'objective,' though not in the same sense in which the rules of the understanding are objective. Now the problem is to make these laws subjective, to make them into maxims, to find motives for them" (W 1:188/P 143). Hegel's central concern, then, is with motivation, with how to put the dictates of pure practical reason into practice, a question that the second moment of the *Volksreligion* addresses. Yet, despite his proto-speculative description of love in the *Religion ist eine . . .* fragment and the role that he ascribes to *Volksreligionen,* Hegel follows Kant in the *Positivity* by claiming that "the sole moral motive, respect [*Achtung*] for the moral law, can be aroused only in a subject in whom the law is itself the legislator, from whose own inner consciousness this law proceeds" (W 1:189/P 144). The description of respect in the second *Critique* emphasizes its exclusivity as a feeling that can be known *a priori:*

> Since this law, however, is in itself positive, being the form of an intellectual causality, i.e., a form of freedom, it is at the same time an ob-

ject of respect, since, in conflict with its subjective antagonists (our inclinations), it weakens self-conceit. And as striking down, i.e., humiliating, self-conceit, it is an object of the greatest respect and thus the ground of a positive feeling which is not of empirical origin. This feeling, then, is one which can be known a priori. Respect for the moral law, therefore, is a feeling produced by an intellectual cause, and this feeling is the only one which we can know completely a priori and the necessity of which we can discern.[37]

We cannot respect what we are inclined to do. The feeling of respect is unique in that it is provoked by the ability of the will to command itself; with this *a priori* unity of reason and feeling, we find the realization of the stated aim of a *Volksreligion,* yet it is realized here in a way that appears to bypass the mediating role of the imagination. If we bear in mind that, for Kant, pain accompanies the curtailing of all inclinations (pain, that is, in the form of the humiliation that arises with frustrated inclination),[38] then the union of subject (feeling) and object (law) that is achieved through the negative activity of thwarting all inclination—and, thus, all self-love and conceit—is accompanied by the *coupling* of respect and pain. And it is only in this negative manner, through the resistance to sensuousness, that the pure practical law as a *drive* can be known. Our self-love fights back through scrutinizing the one for whom we feel respect. It does so with the hope of finding flaws that will relieve us of the burden of this moral feeling and of the sense of unworthiness that arises when our actions are not motivated by pure respect for our capacity to be autonomous. Yet the pain that accompanies respect is matched by a certain form of pleasure. When respect becomes our practical motivation, "we can never satisfy ourselves in contemplating the majesty of this law, and the soul believes itself to be elevated in proportion as it sees the holy law as elevated over it and its frail nature."[39] The logic of this elevation is familiar to readers of Hegel's later works. Hamacher describes it in this way: "The more bowed one's back, the higher one holds one's head; the fuller the conjunction of phenomenon and noumenon, the surer the bridge across the abyss of the rupture: this is the Kantian transition to speculative dialectics."[40]

If it is possible to find in Kant's analysis of respect, the sublation of the opposition between (moral) law and action *within* practical reason itself, what is the need for *Volksreligionen?* There is no simple answer to be found in the *Positivity,* precisely because this question points to a basic tension between Hegel's allegiances to the Kantian version of the Enlightenment project, as he understands it, and the idea that a public religion is necessary as an intermediary between the moral law and its manifestation. Hegel affirms that the sole moral motive is respect for the law, so he implicitly endorses the position that the moral law has the power to compel action out of itself, without relying on the imagination. Hegel's break with Kant will occur when he comes to recognize the Kantian moral law as an internal, *autocratic* force. In the *Positivity,* however, dominating power comes only from an external source. Hegel writes, "But the Christian religion proclaims that the moral law is something outside us and something given, and thus it must strive to create respect for it in some other way" (W 1:189/P 144). Thus, Hegel contrasts the sole moral motive of a respect for the law with the Christian attempt to find this motive outside oneself. He sees the latter leading to the positivity of a system of moral calculus that obscures the direct moral sense that would otherwise allow us to determine how to act without depending on this kind of code. The Christian proclamation that the moral law is given from outside also denies our capacity to give the law to ourselves through pure practical reasoning. This Christian codification of the moral law, then, takes the place of both the (Greek) moral imagination and pure practical reason.

Hegel's focus on Christianity and its history reaffirms the fact that his primary concern is with "collective subjectivities,"[41] not with the specific motivations of an individual moral agent and not with a mass of such agents reasoning together toward a kingdom of ends. This focus indicates, perhaps, an implicit recognition of the influence that the character of one's community has on one's ability to act autonomously. It is also an illustration of his organicist Greek ideal intruding on a broadly Kantian outlook. At this level of collectivity, the imagination is put in the service of realizing a moral world—the third moment of *Volksreligionen*. Producing a concrete social order that conforms to the moral law requires an engagement with sensibility and the imagination. As the historical manifestation of the moral law made substantial, the Greek *polis* required neither Kant's second *Critique* nor the obfuscating art of casuistry. An immediate grasping of the moral law was cultivated by the *Volksreligion* that fed the Athenian imagination. Given Hegel's Kantian tendencies concerning moral motivation, how exactly do the imagination and the feeling of respect relate? If, following Kant, respect is the proper motivational force for moral action, how can this unique feeling, a feeling that is provoked by a cognitive activity, be *cultivated?* And is this the feeling that the tragic poetry so central to the Greek *Volksreligion* attempted ultimately to evoke? Successful tragedies may elicit fear and pity and "accomplish the *katharsis* of such emotions,"[42] but in the service of what? Does the self-mutilation of Oedipus evoke respect for the autonomy of the hero, and does it present the model for a mythology that works to elevate through humiliation? Is this the way in which fifth-century Athenian religious and political life can complement late eighteenth-century Critical philosophy? If Kant's philosophy provides the means of ensuring that the first moment of a *Volksreli-*

gion is fulfilled, do Greek poetry and religious rituals provide the means of ensuring that the imagination, heart, and senses do not go away empty handed?

Greeks, Jews, and Christians

While I will return to the specific form and content of the Greek myths, I will note at this point that Hegel held the Greek ideal to be so intimately tied to the German present because the full scope of modern alienation, that is, its political tyranny and religious dogmatism, was only revealed by comparison with the absence in Athens of these manifestations of positivity. Their absence, that is, for Hegel[43]: the further question that we must raise concerns whether, from the vantage point of a dichotomous present, the imagination must assist in forming an ideal of this kind and whether this, in turn, threatens to degrade the present through producing a longing for the past, rather than a (Fichtean) longing directed toward the future. Although his early view of ancient Greece was undoubtedly an idealized one, Hegel's position toward the ideal cannot be reduced to nostalgic longing. For Hegel, the poetic imagination is not the explicit point of mediation between the German present and the Greek past; overcoming this fragmentation of the present is not simply a matter of translating the Greek myths into the German idiom. Instead, for Hegel, the historical period of political and religious fermentation taking place in and around first-century Jerusalem plays a crucial role in this mediation. He will interpret the transformation in religious thinking that he finds in the figure of Jesus as directed against everything that we have collected under the term "positivity." And his strategy for reading the New Testament will be to present the morality of Jesus as also grounded in *Vernunft,* not *Verstand.*

Thus, Hegel turns to the collective Greek subjectivity and its *Volksreligion* from out of the poverty of Christianity as it existed in his own time, yet he is not satisfied with simply positing Greece as a fallen ideal that must be held as a model for a contemporary rebirth. Instead, he judges the contemporary positive church against both the Athenian *polis* and the original doctrine of Jesus. While Hegel presents an historical account of the self-diremption and decline of the beautiful and free Greek *polis,* he does not, however, account for its birth. It arises in the *Positivity* fully formed. He does, by contrast, present Jesus as a figure of rebirth out of the reign of positivity, and the cultural and religious "personification" of this positivity is, according to Hegel, first-century Judaism. The intrinsic value of this spiritual reawakening is determined by comparing the doctrine and practices of the early Christians to both Kant's practical philosophy and the ancient Athenian *polis.* Hegel asks, in effect, is the community established in Jesus's name in accordance with the good *and* the beautiful?

Hegel's description of the origin of Christianity as a confrontation with the positivity of first-century Judaism and his account of its history as a fallback into a uniquely Christian form of positive religiosity reveals a specific *narrative* logic, one that structures this history as a *development*. This narrativizing is most clearly apparent when focusing on the names of the collective subjects that Hegel deploys. These subjectivities will later shed their proper names and be presented in their conceptual purity as shapes of consciousness, but, at this point, a distinctly historical constellation of peoples play a crucial role in structuring Hegel's thought. More concretely, "Greeks" and "Jews" come to operate as fixed extremes around which the only truly fluid subjectivity—that of the "Christians"—is situated. That is, Greek and Jewish cultures are presented in a reductive manner in part because they hold a specific structural role in the narrative of historical development that Hegel is constructing in order to draw out the essence of Christianity. Taken on its own, his characterization of Judaism, for example, would be of more value to a study of anti-Semitism than Judaism proper.[44] My concern at this point, however, is less with the manner in which he distorts Judaism and its history than with the need, from within his own project, for the kind of contrived counterpoint to Christianity that Judaism provides. Christianity is determined by comparing it to that out of which it arises and against which it defines itself—Judaism—and a past that stands as the possibility of bringing a truly autonomous moral society into existence—Greece.

The fixed, oppositional way in which Hegel deploys the Greeks and Jews is a product of *Verstand;* thus, it marks what we can see retrospectively as the distinctly undialectical character of the *Positivity.* (Emil Fackenheim argues that this absence of dialectical thinking extends into Hegel's later writings as well. While Hegel cannot but claim in, for example, his *Lectures on the Philosophy of Religion* that the historical condition for the birth of Christianity was the intermingling of Greco-Roman "Western" culture and religion with that of the Jewish "East," Fackenheim argues that Hegel's position is best understood as a product of his bias toward Hellenic culture.[45] He qualifies this conclusion, however, by applying it specifically to Hegel's mature thought.[46]) The thoroughly undialectical character of the *Positivity* is perhaps most evident if we consider how Hegel's accounts of fifth-century BCE Greece, as the historical embodiment of freedom, and first-century CE Judaism, as the embodiment of a positive religion, conform to the very logic of stark and entrenched opposition that defines positivity itself. Of particular interest in this regard is the way that Hegel's own analyses work, almost behind his own back, to dislodge the terms from this fixed positionality. Conceptual rigidity will be consistently challenged by the more concrete, historical analyses that Hegel embarks on in the *Positivity.*

To give one example of the "cunning of reason" operative in his own texts, Hegel often conflates Greek and Roman cultures in his early writings to the point where they seem to stand as a distinct conceptual unity.[47] In the *Phenomenology of*

Spirit, by contrast, the atomizing effect of the abstract Roman legal code is precisely what distinguishes Rome from ancient Athens. Yet Hegel's historical investigations into the decline of Greece force him to distinguish his Greek ideal from later manifestations of Greek culture, including the Roman Empire as it existed in the first century CE. Hegel's own Greek ideal will be dislodged in the same way when it becomes isolated from later Hellenistic culture, as will his distinctive comprehension of the essence of *morality* itself.[48] There is no denying that Kant's analysis of practical reason is used in the *Positivity* as the standard against which the Greek *polis,* Judaism, and Christianity are judged in order to determine whether they fulfill their proper aim of propagating morality. Yet it is precisely through Hegel's historical studies of these three collective subjectivities that his view of morality will be transformed. These studies will help reveal the possibility of a form of ethical thinking that both annuls and fulfills Kant's moral philosophy. Although this will entail relegating Kantian morality itself to the status of positivity, Hegel does not abandon the ideal status that he affords to ancient Athens, although he does change his view of the characteristics of this ideal.

Positivity Embodied

Hegel interprets the state of Judaism at the time of Jesus as a culture defined, like Hegel's own, by positivity. The most distinct sign of this is the relation it maintained to the law. Hegel claims that the original source of Jewish law was the "supreme wisdom [*Weisheit*] on high" (W 1:105 / P 68), but what this means is not entirely clear. He may be drawing attention to the fact that the Jews understood the origin of the law to be divine in nature and, thus, distinct from human beings. The source of the moral law, then, would not be practical reason. This may be the case. Yet Hegel also writes that "Jesus recalled to the memory of his people the moral principles in their sacred books" (W 1:106 / P 69). If we take this remark concerning the origin of the law in conjunction with the claim that genuine moral principles are the animating force of the sacred texts of Judaism, then we can assume that, whether the moral law is a divine gift or the product of practical reason, its content is that of universal morality. Hegel's supposition is that the basic principles found in these sacred texts are the same universal moral principles that he discovers operating in Greece and defended in Kant's practical philosophy. The contrast that he draws at the outset of his account of Judaism is between this original wisdom and the dominance of positivity that existed at the time of Jesus. The positivity of the law leads to a people who were "overwhelmed by a burden of statutory commands which pedantically prescribed a rule for every casual action of daily life and gave the whole people the look of a monastic order" (W 1:105 / P 68). To have the look of a monastic order means, for Hegel, living a life spent in "a monkish preoccupation with petty, mechanical, spiritless, and trivial practices" (W 1:106 / P 69). It means falling prey to the specific set of perversions that arise from a fetishization of the letter of the law, and this is, ultimately, a life of "mechanical slavery" (ibid.), a life void of the beauty and freedom found in Greece. Like the holy texts themselves, the religious practices of the time did not necessarily contradict the moral foundation of religion but came to stand *as* this foundation. The social effect was to instill a willingness to submit to an external authority—the letter of the law generally, a privileged priestly class more specifically, as well as national pride—and this sacrifice of self-determination provides a means to a complacent conscience. For Hegel, in the *Positivity*, Jesus's relation to Judaism can be reduced to these words from the Sermon on the Mount: "Think not that I have come to abolish the law and the prophets; I have come not to abolish them, but to fulfill them" (Matthew 5:17).[49] Beyond all forms of sterile legalism, Jesus introduces the "*complementum* of the law" (W 1:139/P 99) as a means of release from the external authority of positive commands.[50] The union of infinite and finite, the moral law and its concrete realization, requires the reawakening of the moral sense. Given Hegel's view that Jesus's highest moral principles were those found in the sacred Jewish texts, the fulfillment of the law could be understood as a reawakening of this true moral sense. Thus, Jesus confronts the positivity of his age by way of memory. Instead of establishing new moral laws, he aims to recall to memory the moral principles found in the sacred books of his people (W 1:106 / P 69). But if recollection is an integral part of fulfillment, does it involve a specific way of taking it up, of bringing it to the present? If it is more than a mere repetition of the past, what marks the difference? This is, as we have seen, as much of a problem for Hegel in his retrieval of Greek *Volksreligion* as it is for Jesus in his retrieval of the Jewish tradition.

Hegel will give a more detailed account of the history of Judaism in the later Frankfurt-era text *The Spirit of Christianity*, but, in the *Positivity*, Judaism is reduced to the purity of its sacred text, on the one hand, and the positivity of its culture at the time of Jesus, on the other. From within the logic of Hegel's text, there is, presumably, no need to furnish Judaism with an articulated past since it serves the limited function of drawing into relief the original meaning of Christianity. The question of how Jesus's attempt to fulfill the law relates to his own tradition must, therefore, be deferred. It is, however, important to stress that Hegel is attracted to the birth of Christianity because he sees in it a challenge to an ossified culture and religion. When he claims that Jesus's teaching was meant to free his followers from the "contagious sickness of his age" (W 1:106/P 69), it is not an overstatement to say that this kind of liberation is precisely what he thinks is necessary in his own time. He is drawn to the figure of the historical Jesus in particular because of the analogy that can be drawn between Jesus's epoch and his own. Both are defined in Hegel's mind by the reign of positivity, and we should note that Hegel, like Jesus, reacts to this by way of recollection. Hegel turns to the past from out of the most immediate concerns of the present, but he does not turn to the historical Jesus *solely* because of the contemporary relevance of this earlier challenge to positivity. Beyond this, the specific shape of the politico-religious regime that Hegel faced was, of course, very much determined by this original, Christian challenge. Hegel appropriates the gesture of Jesus in order to recollect and reawaken the spirit of Greece, but, at the same time, his detailed account of the path that Christianity takes, as it moves from its inception in the act of recollecting the moral law to its fall back into positivity, also stands as a *warning* to the present. From this historical analogy, Hegel is able to address the central question of the *Positivity* directly: How does a pure moral religion, grounded in a "free virtue springing from man's own being" (W 1:108/P 71), give rise to the positivity that it was originally attempting to ward off?

Quality, Quantity, and a Lack of Measure

Hegel divides the history of Christianity into three distinct stages: the time when Jesus and his disciples lived, the development of the many small sects that formed in the name of Christ, and, finally, its "triumph" as a state religion. Christianity's ascendancy to worldly power corresponds, however, to a spiritual degeneration. What Hegel calls "pure life," insofar as this exists at all, comes early to Christianity, and its historical trajectory is one of a long decline. This trajectory follows a logic where the more it expands—the more people join the Christian fold—the more positive it becomes. As it first grows beyond the living union of Jesus and his friends into small religious cults and then into a state religion, the original gospel of Jesus is betrayed.

A crucial section of the *Positivity* in this regard is titled "What Is Applicable in a Small Society [*Gesellschaft*] Is Unjust in a State" (W 1:124/P 86 ff.). If Hegel were here articulating a logic dictated by the unfolding of conceptual contradictions, then we could say that the problem being posed is that of how a qualitative change—a great leap backward—is spurred by an increase in quantity. He is, however, not yet engaged in an investigation into the immanent development of the concept. From the perspective of the historical progression of Hegel's own thought, this kind of logical investigation comes after the concrete historical analyses. Yet one sees, retrospectively, something like this self-determining logic at play: a contradiction in the very concept of a living community arises when it is expanded beyond a certain point. The betrayal of the original gospel of Jesus is *inevitable* to the extent that the expansion of the community is *inevitable*, for the fundamental principle on which Christianity is founded demands a degree of proximity and exclusivity. That is, a community grounded in friendship cannot be expanded indefinitely. What is lacking is a precise sense of the measure needed to secure its original, laudable quality. How, then, is the proper measure of a *living* religious community defined? Is it a group of friends? The congregation? If not the state, then the *polis?* Whatever it is, and I will return to this question of the proper measure, Hegel's contemporary Christianity has overstepped it, and this corresponds to its fall into positivity. The question to raise at this point is whether there is something internal in the teaching of Jesus that leads to this expansion and the consequences that follow from it or whether its fall into positivity is a historical accident. Is the germ of positivity present at the inception of Christianity itself? If this excessive expansion is *not* accidental, then Christianity and its tradition would be inimical to the *Volksreligion* that Hegel imagines, and we could suppose that what distinguishes the two is precisely the presence of a measure in the Greek religion and culture that is absent from Christianity.

Friendship

As Hegel charts the advance of Christianity's political influence and its simultaneous descent into positivity, he draws out the significance of the three stages it passes through by making reference to similar phenomena in Greek culture. The essential point of comparison is between Socrates and Jesus, although this is not based on the content of their doctrine, for the simple reason that they are, according to Hegel's universalist idea of morality, saying the same thing.[51] This similarity in the moral content of their discourse draws into relief the difference in their form of expression, and the context out of which each is writing ultimately determines the way in which this essential core is expressed. Hegel's comparison initially focuses on the way that the same doctrine comes to be translated into very different social worlds. He then turns to the kinds of communities that Socrates and Jesus form around themselves and their relation to the larger political order in which these are embedded. The community that each forms is based on *philia,* so the comparison ultimately rests on the differences between Greek and Christian friendship.

Notable for their humility, honesty, and dedication, the friends and disciples of Jesus—and the problem will be precisely this comingling of friend and disciple—were, nevertheless, lacking any "great store of spiritual energy" (W 1:119/P 81). Hegel portrays them as incapable of doing more than simply transmitting the doctrine of Jesus, and, because of their inability to add anything novel to it, their relation to his teaching exemplifies positivity. The fates of the common doctrines of Jesus and Socrates diverge at precisely this point. The mark of Socrates' friends, touched as they were by the "republican spirit" of Greece, was their *infidelity* to Socrates—or, more accurately, their fidelity through infidelity: "They had the capacity to work in their own heads on what they had learned and to give it the stamp of their own originality. Many of them founded schools of their own; in their own right they were men as great as Socrates" (W 1:120/P 82). We can take the example of Socrates' friends as a general imperative of interpretation and apply it to Hegel's own presentation of the Greeks. The vital challenge of a friend of Socrates was to *repeat* what is *unprecedented* and—*qua* unprecedented—unrepeatable. Alcibiades says of Socrates in the *Symposium* that what is most wondrous about him is his originality: "Perhaps he shares some of his specific accomplishments with others. But, on the whole, he is unique; he is unlike anyone else in the past and no one in the present."[52] Unlike the friends of Socrates, the followers of Jesus were not called on to engage in what Philippe Lacoue-Labarthe calls both "artistic *mimēsis*" and "producing *mimēsis*."[53] The life and teaching of Jesus do not inspire in his disciples an original repetition of an original. Instead, they are called on merely to repeat the words of Jesus, to practice what can be called, by contrast, "passive *mimēsis*."[54]

The friends of Socrates were citizens of a democratic republic; on this foundation, they were able to maintain their independence. Their friendship with Socrates did not interfere with their commitments to their family, and it allowed them to maintain active roles in political and military life. Both the way in which their different capacities were encouraged and their unwillingness to submit to the authority of a single person differentiated them from Jesus's disciples. While the Athenian friends could never sacrifice their investment in the state, the disciples are defined, for Hegel, by the sacrifice of all of their other interests. Belonging to a Christian sect meant withdrawing from many previous ties to kinship, office, and service. This sacrifice of the executive force of their reason and the loss of independence that this entails destroy the possibility of what Hegel saw as *genuine* sacrifice. They also destroy the possibility of the immortality gained through sacrificing oneself for the survival of the *polis*, that is, the immortality unique to a free people.

With this, we come to the heart of Hegel's conception of Greece in the Bern period. Hegel writes that, for the Greek republican, "The idea (*Idee*) of his country or of his state was the invisible and higher reality for which he strove, which impelled him to effort; it was the final end of *his* world or in his eyes the final end of *the* world. . . . Confronted by his idea, his own individuality vanished; it was only this idea's maintenance, life, and persistence that he asked for, and these were things which he himself could make realities" (W 1:205/P 154).[55] When comparing this account of the Greek *polis* with that of Greek ethical substance (*Sittlichkeit*) as presented in the *Phenomenology*, the Idea of freedom that the young Hegel attributes to the Greeks might seem misplaced. In the *Phenomenology*, the sacrifice of the son for the *polis* fulfills his role as a citizen (see PdG 296/PS 270), but the *role* that he fulfills is not self-determined. That is to say, in the terms of the *Phenomenology*, the ancient Greek *polis* lacks culture. As opposed to the immediacy of Greek *Sittlichkeit*, where gender and social roles were predetermined and naturalized, culture involves the self-forming of the self:

> It is therefore through culture that the individual acquires standing and actuality. His true *original nature* and substance is the alienation of himself as Spirit from *natural* being. This externalization is, therefore, both the purpose and the existence of the individual; it is at once the *means,* or the *transition,* both of the [mere] *thought-form of substance* into *actuality,* and, conversely, of the *specific individuality* into *essentiality.* This individuality *moulds* itself by culture into what it intrinsically is, and only by so doing is it an intrinsic being that has an actual existence; the measure of its culture is the measure of its actuality and power. (PdG 324/PS 298)

The dialectic of culture presents an aspect of the development of individual self-definition that is, for Hegel, determinative of spirit. Traces of this self-formation were already present in the Socratic philosopher and the community that surrounded him, but it was not reflective of the Greek *polis* as such. Thus, we find this Socratic shape of consciousness in the *Phenomenology* at the point of the demise of the immediacy attributed to Greek *Sittlichkeit.* The Greek tragedies can, in turn, be conceived as reflecting the waning power of these preestablished roles.

According to the Hegel of the *Positivity,* however, this willingness to self-sacrifice for the whole arises only among free citizens, those who obey laws they alone have given to themselves collectively, and this was achieved in the Greek *polis.* If the freedom of the Greeks consists of the fact that they only obey laws that they themselves have laid down, these laws are not presented in terms of a codified system that has been previously deduced, defended, and then transmitted. Hegel makes a point of saying that the maxims followed by a free people are not learned or taught but manifest themselves only through actions, and so his portrait of a free people describes a society that has yet to be disrupted by the rise of ethical self-consciousness. These Greeks embodied Kantian autonomy to the extent that they acted only according to self-given laws, but these laws were not determined according to the self-conscious exercise of practical reason. How is this lack of self-consciousness an attribute of a free people? Within Hegel's historical scheme that posits the Greek *polis* as the embodiment of life, we know that this lack cannot manifest itself in the kind of mechanical actions that characterize the adherents of positive religion. Rather than acting in this lifeless way, it would be more accurate to say that, for a free people, thought is so closely united with instinct that it is immediately translated into action. And this unification of thought, instinct, and action *is* the *polis.* Although the Idea that animates it is described as "the invisible, higher realm" (*das Unsichtbare, das Höhere*), it is, nevertheless, *immanent* to the concrete life of the *polis.* It is an Idea of an end which "[the free citizen] found manifest in the realities of his daily life or which he himself co-operated in manifesting and maintaining" (W 1:205 / P 154). The thought that such a unity could exist only in a "beyond" is inimical to a free people. With the individual vanishing into the concrete unfolding of the *polis,* it is not surprising then that there is also an absence of concern for the afterlife of individualized souls as well. Hegel writes, "It could never or hardly ever have struck him to ask or beg for persistence or eternal life for his own individuality" (W 1:205 / P 154–155).

The absence of this particular form of individuality does not come as an interruption born of the experience of a trauma that destroys the identity of the self-determining self. In the *System der Sittlichkeit,* produced in Jena between the winter of 1802 and the spring of 1803, Hegel describes "*absolute ethical life*" in a similar manner: "it does not appear as love for country and people and law, but as absolute life in one's country and for the people. It is the absolute truth, for untruth lies only in the fixation of something specific; but in the eternity of the people all individuality is superseded."[56] The Idea is always present in the same way that moral maxims are present, through action rather than as an explicit doctrine. The "vanishing" individuality of the free man both sustains the life of the Idea and allows for the persistence of the Idea alone as his sole, proper end. While almost inevitable, the adherence to this end is not without possible exception. Aberration comes with the surfacing of a purely self-regarding desire. Hegel's text betrays a certain ambiguity at this point. With the editor's assistance, it reads that it was "never or only [rarely]" (W 1:205 / P 154) the case that anyone would think in terms of his or her own individual immortality. The desire for eternal life would arise only in those moments of inactivity and indolence. Hegel's example of such an aberration, and the inactivity that gives rise to it, is telling. Only after the destruction of his republic does Cato turn to the *Phaedo* and thus take refuge in an order that transcends the state (see W 1:205 / P 155). This interruption, which exists as a moment of trauma, gives rise to an individuality that reflects the fragmentation of the *polis.*

Thus, Hegel affirms two aspects of the Greek *polis* in particular, the *immanent unity* that defines this free people and the *individual originality* that characterizes Socrates and his philosophical friendships. How do these two fit together? There is certainly a precedent for singling out these particular aspects. Friendship, as freely chosen, defines a relationship that is distinct from justice, and, according to Aristotle, more politically desirable. As he writes in Book VIII of the *Nicomachean Ethics,*

> Friendship also seems to keep cities together, and lawgivers seem to pay more attention to it than to justice. For like-mindedness seems to be similar, in a way, to friendship, and it is this that they aim most at achieving, while they aim most to eliminate faction, faction being

> enmity; and there is no need for rules of justice between people who are friends, whereas if they are just they still need friendship—and of what is just, the most just is thought to be what belongs to friendship.[57]

Acting virtuously with friends is automatic, in the sense that we desire to do what we ought to do, while relations defined by justice are more abstract duties. Yet the Socratic friendship that Hegel emphasizes is, of course, defined by self-reflexivity and is premised on everyone maintaining his or her autonomy. Perhaps the idea is that the groundedness of Socrates' friends in the free unity of the *polis* protected them from his wondrous originality (*Symposium* 221c), thus preserving the proper balance between individual and community. Perhaps, but Hegel does not explicitly address this in the *Positivity,* and the ambiguity concerning the role of mediation and immediacy at the heart of his portrait of the Greek *polis*—and, thus, his Idea of free life—again reveals the nondialectical character of his analysis. There is the harmonious and unreflective order of the *polis,* and there are complicating aberrations, but Hegel does not present the necessary interconnectedness of these two moments. In the *Phenomenology,* this immediate unity of thought, inclination, and action is what Hegel calls the "ethical life of a people which is Spirit in its immediate Truth" (PdG 290/PS 265). As unmediated, it is defined by beauty. At the same time, Hegel writes that "Spirit is, in its simple truth, consciousness, and forces its moments apart. *Action* divides it into substance and consciousness of substance" (PdG 290/PS 266). Action divides Spirit in its simple truth, so Spirit is always divided in that we have always already acted. The irony that changes, transforms, and perverts the life of the community is eternal (PdG 314/PS 288). This is to say, the *polis* is in itself contradictory, and, when its contradictory character becomes for itself, it loses its beautiful immediacy: "It [Spirit] must advance to the consciousness of what it is immediately, must leave behind it the beauty of ethical life" (PdG 290/PS 265). The free *polis* was a necessary condition for the cultivation of Socrates and a community of philosophical friendship, yet it was the great ironist's friend Plato who wrote the *Phaedo.*

The sign of the *decline* of the living union of the *polis,* then, and the desperation that this decline instills is the lure of individual transcendence. The form of individuality that is absent in the free *polis* and arises during its collapse is that of narrow self-interest—a form of individuation that Hegel also associates with the "bourgeois" individuality of modernity. As Hegel develops his analysis of Greece in the *Phenomenology,* the periodic and inevitable individuation within the *polis* that leads to isolated and potentially antagonistic factions means that "in order not to let them become rooted and set in this isolation, thereby breaking up the whole and letting the [communal] spirit evaporate, government has from time to time to shake them to their core by war" (PdG 298 / PS 272). In the *Positivity,* by contrast, the Greek *polis* is presented as a democratic republic of free citizens who face each other as equals. The chthonic realm of the Furies is seemingly absent. According to the logic of Hegel's analysis, this foundation ensured that the institutional legacy of Socrates was not a religion, but the development of philosophical schools. Jesus's oppositional stance, the disciples' renunciation of public life, their absolute adherence to his memory, if not his doctrine: all this follows from the lack of a comparable foundation in Jesus's time. Hegel's own future reconciliation with Christianity and its historical unfolding will require accepting the necessity of this oppositional stance. But when he is oriented by the Idea of Greece that we have just articulated, the relation between Jesus and his disciples stands in stark opposition to the unity that Hegel admires in the *polis.* As the movement founded in Jesus's name begins to expand and become institutionalized, the original positioning of the community continues to haunt the larger and more variegated forms that it takes.

Excursus on Measure in the Greek Republic

Since Hegel's model for a *philosophical* community is the one gathered around Socrates, we might turn briefly to how this is presented in Plato's dialogues. On the surface, Hegel describes these philosophical communities as if they function in a harmonious way within the larger Athenian society, but what exactly is the nature of this apparent harmony? Given Hegel's claims that Cato turned to the *Phaedo* and the consideration of personal salvation only when his own republic was collapsing, surely the life of Socrates and the events recounted in the *Phaedo* reflect similar conflict within fifth-century Athenian society. In the *Apology,* Socrates recounts how his *daimōn* warned him against pursuing a public role in the life of Athens, and he acknowledges that, if he had not heeded its warning, he would have died long ago (*Apology* 32c–d). For the most part, then, Socrates' questioning takes place outside the institutions of public power.

Within the Athenian context, we can presume that the confrontation of Socrates' private philosophical life and the public sphere, his trial and execution, were the preconditions for the development of the philosophical schools. Will the time ever be ripe for philosophy to venture out of the academy and into the political domain? In Book VI of the *Republic,* Socrates describes the difficulties and the inherent danger of this move from the private to the public sphere: "How a city can take philosophy in hand without being destroyed. For surely all great things carry with them the risk of a fall, and, really as the saying goes, fine things are hard" (*Republic* 497d). The danger exists because the potential philosophical ruler would have the same natural traits as the perfect tyrant (ibid., 491b). Nevertheless, if we assume that the philosophers could potentially come to power and that the *Republic* describes the extension of the philosophical "sect" outward to the level of the *polis,* there are a number of points in the dialogue where we find the arguments for a *measure* tied to quantitative limits. Perhaps the most explicit is Socrates' defense in Book IV of a poor but strong *polis,* one that will grow only to the point where it can maintain its unity. To expand beyond this proper measure would invite the kind of factionalism that will weaken and ultimately undermine the just *polis.* Socrates also argues that the philosopher is most suited to rule because he does not desire the post. Finally, the higher pleasure of thinking (581d) is one that does not inevitably provoke its opposite. As such, it serves to limit the desire for power and luxury and, with this, the will to the bad infinite of outward expansion.

The questions that this cursory discussion raises are multifold. Let us simply note that, while we have assumed that the *Republic* allows for the possibility of the ascendancy of the philosopher to political power, it is also possible to read the *Republic* as arguing for the *impossibility* of this ascent. In this case, there would be the need to return to the fourth best. Unlike a timocracy or oligarchy, democracy might at least tolerate philosophy.[58] And this was, of course, the position that Socrates found himself in. Philosophy, and philosophical friendship, could potentially maintain a place within the larger whole; as such, they could be seen as the model of the relation that Hegel describes between religion and the state: an internal, but ultimately beneficial, opposition.

As for Socratic philosophy being a symptom of decline, when Hegel addresses the *Republic* explicitly many years later, he concludes that this is both true and false. He remarks in the "Preface" to the *Philosophy of Right* that

> even Plato's *Republic,* a proverbial example of an *empty ideal,* is essentially the embodiment of nothing other than the nature of Greek ethics; and Plato, aware that the ethics of his time were being penetrated by a deeper principle [free infinite personality], which within this context could appear immediately only as an as yet unsatisfied longing and hence only as a destructive force, was obliged, in order to counteract it, to seek the help of that very longing itself. (PR 20)

Plato presents "the substance of ethical life in its ideal *beauty* and *truth,*" but rigorously excludes the rising principle of "self-sufficient particularity" by reducing it to mere arbitrary will (W 7:342/PR 222). In his Bern writings, Hegel, in effect, concurs with Plato's reduction of this first inkling of the modern principle of subjective freedom, a principle that, as Hegel writes, "arose in an inward form in the *Christian* religion" (W 7:342/PR 223).

Hegel does not engage the *Republic* in any sustained way in the extant fragments from this early period, although he makes clear reference to it in *Religion ist eine . . .* (see W 1:11). Yet, if we are right to say that tragedy is, in part, the *poetic* articulation of the penetration of the principle of subjective freedom into the substance of the Greek ethical life and the conflict that it subsequently provokes, then Hegel's turn to tragedy in *The Spirit of Christianity* can be read as a recognition of the need to engage this new principle in a way that does not simply amount to its exclusion. This also points to the tension with Kant, as a philosopher of this subjectivity, that we will see arising explicitly only in *The Spirit of Christianity.*

Sects

The first qualitative step in the expansion and institutionalization of the movement founded in Jesus's name is to the level of what Hegel calls "sects." He distinguishes three different kinds. The *first* is what he names a *positive* sect; it grounds its beliefs in a positive doctrine other than rationally defensible ethical principles and the indigenous myths of the community. As such, the positive sect is alien to both "thought" and the "national imagination" that arises from the indigenous tradition (W 1:111/P 74). Indeed, for the positive sect, a morality grounded in either of these is deemed to be sinful. The *second* is the polar opposite of the first, but it is not a nonpositive *religious* sect, but a *philosophical* one. It too is concerned with moral doctrine, but, as Hegel writes, "it connects damnation and unworthiness only with a deviation from ethical principles" (ibid.). Hegel clarifies this when he writes that a philosophical sect is one that "maintains religious doctrines but which recognizes no judge other than reason" (W 1:124/P 86). It follows from this that the imagery of popular belief is regarded as "unworthy of a thinking man," but, unlike the positive sect, the content of this popular, national imagination is not worthy of blame (W 1:111/P 74). If it is Kant's practical philosophy that shapes Hegel's understanding of morality, then the Greek schools of philosophy, as the model of a philosophical sect, represent Kantian moral thought put into practice as a living institution. A *third,* unnamed kind of sect stands as the middle point between these two extremes, since it is neither thoroughly determined by thought nor entirely at odds with it. It is grounded in a faith informed by traditional religious doctrine, yet it takes the essence of this faith to be "the commands of virtue" (W 1:111/P 75), rather than positive rituals and practices. The sects founded in Jesus's name are of this third kind, for Jesus's faith and gospel were grounded in both the Jewish tradition and "his own heart's living sense of right and duty" (ibid.).

As soon as Hegel distinguishes these three types of sects, he undermines the distinctions he has made. First, he is apprehensive about calling the philosophical community a sect at all because the term *sect* implies a position of contrariety and intolerance, and, as we have seen, Hegel understands the philosophical community as existing in a kind of harmony with the larger community. The point is clearly that these schools developed in a political atmosphere that could accommodate—for a time—the kind of philosophical questioning that Socrates inspired. Second, while Christian sects and the philosophical schools are modeled on friendship and have the same aim of furthering morality, the Christian sect *as* sect is unified by a force that the philosophical schools manage to avoid. In the latter, this unifying force is rational discourse and the freedom provided by the republic to which it belongs. A Christian community, by contrast, is held together in part by faith, and Hegel's aim is to show how ultimately it will become contaminated by the positive practices associated with it. As such, it loses its middle position between the philosophical community and positive sect and simply becomes positive itself. While it is clear that Hegel is fashioning Jesus as a kind of philosopher and not a messiah, Jesus is, nevertheless, dictated by his times to speak in a language other than that of pure reason. The decrees of religion are not adopted on the authority of one's own judgment alone. The aim of the early Christians was not "a free search for the truth . . . so much as the removal of doubt, the consolidation of faith, and the advance in Christian perfection which was most intimately connected with these" (W 1:143/P 103). Their aim could not be the uncovering of truth for the simple reason that the truth had already been given. The acceptance of truth as having already been imparted in full distinguishes these sects from a true philosophical community, and the rise of positivity in Christian sects follows, in part, from the unconditional obedience in faith and action. It also follows from the fact that these sects were not united solely by the desire to further morality but by the more immediate political commonality of their oppression.

The authority that is assumed by a Christian sect and the oppositional stance toward the larger political union comes to shape the character of friendship itself. Grounded in the contradictory notion of a "commanded belief" (W 1:140/P 100), Christian friendship is defined in terms of loyalty and is intimately tied to confession. A friend does not greet confession with "contempt or mortifying laughter" (W 1:142/P 102). Friendship guarantees "that, if I trust him with my secrets, I shall not feel betrayal; and that, in advising me for my own good, for my highest good, his motive will be an interest in my well-being and a respect rather for the right than for my material advantage. In short, before men can be united in this way, they must be friends" (ibid.). At the heart of this religious sect is the assumption grounding any friendship that entering and departing the group are entirely matters of free choice. Although compulsion is contrary to the concept of friendship and faith, freely entering this religious sect also entails "the unconditional obedience in faith and action which had to be vowed to the society." This trait, as Hegel says, "differentiates it *in toto* from a philosophical group" (W 1:144/P 104). When they subordinate reason to faith in this way, the early Christians, in effect, freely forfeit the seat of their freedom and, in so doing, would seem to undermine their very capacity to leave the sect freely. This forfeiture, however, is not absolute. It is conceived as a compromise, for, as we have seen, the early Christian sects assume a middle position between the explicit attack against positivity and an utter submission to it. The question that Hegel's text addresses is why the early Jesus movement develops in the direction of positivity rather than increased rationality. As it turns out, the most seductive fetish was Jesus himself.

As we noted at the outset of this chapter, Hegel's paradigmatic example of positivity is the temptation to ground the authority of Jesus's words on the force of his personality, rather than evaluating them according to the standard of reason alone or one's living sense of right and duty. What is important to note are those aspects of Jesus's own life that encourage this temptation. In the condemnation of the moral corruption of his time, Jesus must exemplify what he teaches, lest his words "fall from his lips dead and cold" (W 1:112/P 75). To avoid the fate of cold, dead words, Jesus must accommodate the language and customs of his particular social world. Yet this focus on the actions that animate and substantiate what he says has the effect of emphasizing the teacher himself, rather than what is being taught. There is an obvious need for consistency between word and deed, but, beyond this, Jesus is forced to turn away from reason as a means of persuasion because, as Hegel says, the people with whom he must communicate are themselves mired in positivity. While Jesus cannot, in the manner of Socrates, transfer authority away from himself and onto reason itself, he must recognize in others a natural sense for virtue and the divine (or, better, the divine as virtue). This is a "sense" that can be stirred by Jesus. If this were not the case, his efforts would be as futile as St. Anthony of Padua's zealous attempt to preach to the fish. In these early writings, Hegel will periodically return to St. Anthony as an exemplary figure of failed communication. The saint is not, however, an example of arch-positivity, for, like Jesus, St. Anthony too presumes, however erroneously, that the message can get through. Even if the sermon fails, assistance will come from a Being completely removed from this world and its laws. In his attempt to communicate with those around him, shaped as they are by the positive character of their language and culture, Jesus must assume a natural moral sensitivity in humans, if not in fish, but he must also avoid the use of reason alone if he wants to avoid the spectacle of Saint Anthony. He must adopt positive means of communicating but avoid the thoroughly positive view that he alone is able to grasp the good. As such, Jesus avoids embodying the "pure" position of positivity. This "pure" position is reached only when human and divine natures are so completely severed that, in Hegel's words, "no mediation between the two is conceded except in one isolated individual." In this case, "all of man's consciousness of the good and the divine is degraded to the dull and killing belief in a superior Being altogether alien to man" (W 1:225/P 176, translation altered). Can this tactical use of positive elements like miracles keep these elements contained, or is the slide into the deadly belief in an utter separation of human and divine nature inevitable? When concessions are made and positive elements tolerated, will these necessarily take the insidious form of the fetish that contaminates and overwhelms what remains pure (purely moral) in religious practices?[59]

The ambiguity of Hegel's view on these related questions is revealed by the description he gives of his own project in the *Positivity.* He claims that his focus is primarily on the intrinsic aspects of Jesus's thought that lead to positivity, but the reason that he continually gives for why Jesus adopts these aspects is that he must accommodate the prejudices of the time—must use miracles, make claims to being the messiah, and so forth—if he is to be heard at all. At the same time, Hegel's actual analysis shows that, regardless of how these prejudices originally came about, they become inextricably tied to Christianity as it exists in its historical unfolding.

Hegel will claim later in *The Spirit of Christianity* that, beyond this compromised form of communicating, *true* communication exists only when "spirit grasps and comprehends spirit" (W 1:372/SC 255). This describes a relation that involves both a prior readiness to hear Jesus's call to virtue and a role in eliciting the call itself. While Hegel makes very generalized reference in the *Positivity* to "the spirit of the times" (W 1:110/P 73) and the "spiritual state" (see W 1:104/P 145), there is no consistent idea of *Geist* operative in this text (he will also, on occasion, use "spirit" as synonymous with the "mystical" to describe what is most decadent in religious practices [see W 1:129/P 91]). In the *Positivity,* true communication is, essentially, grounded in reason and a self-conscious awareness of one's freedom.

The Circuitous Route

The threat to true communication arises with a submission to the authority of the dead. Yet, instead of the living communication of reason, Jesus confronts ecclesiastical power and its appeal to divine authority with similar appeals. His accommodations are made with the intent of smuggling his thought into this closed world of positivity, but this leads him to follow what Hegel calls a "circuitous route" (W 1:117/P 79) to the kingdom of God, one that leads from stories of miraculous deeds through faith in his person and only then to morality proper. While Hegel is clearly aware of the power of this indirect, meandering path, he ultimately condemns what Hölderlin's Hyperion describes as *"eine exzentrische Bahn."*[60] While planets may have eccentric orbits, they are most closely associated with the path of a comet. The eccentric path of the comet strays as much from the perfect circle as the straight line, yet it is not entirely arbitrary. For Hölderlin, there is no escaping this eccentricity: "We all traverse an eccentric path, and there is no other possible way from our childhood to the end" (FH 1:558).[61] In the *Positivity,* Hegel rejects this circuitous route precisely because he holds that there is a clear center—the moral law—and anything other than the most direct route from the particular to the universal and back again runs the risk of bypassing, or forgetting, this center.

The route that Hegel rejects is the one that travels through the imagination. Jesus's dramatic life and unjust death "riveted attention and captivated the imagination [*Einbildungskraft*]" of the disciples (W 1:115–116/P 78). While the roundabout way through the imagination courts the danger of "losing sight of the road" (W 1:117/P 79) and, thus, the homelessness of the wanderer, the real threat lies in its assault on the dignity of morality as such, for morality insists on being "self-sufficient and self-grounding" (ibid). Jesus's doctrine of virtue can be relayed only if those who hear it recognize the source of morality in themselves. The members of a community who have been brought to morality by way of this circuitous route must necessarily be humbled to such an extent that they forfeit the very possibility of recognizing the true source of morality and, thus, of fully grasping the significance of Jesus's words. This route is an offense to the dignity of morality because it amounts to a rejection of its source: the self-grounding freedom that they themselves are. Ultimately, this offense leads to a coup in the court of reason itself. It is stripped of its ability to legislate and reduced to a mere receptive capacity. Hegel extends his analysis by claiming that someone humbled in this way will be spurred to act only through the hope of salvation or, more likely, from the fear of punishment and damnation. The practical result is that this enslaved subject has no experience of a self-given law. This absence means that, even if it were to be emancipated from a purely positive religion, it would necessarily descend into immorality.

The consequences of this circuitous route are evident in the fate of the disciples. Instead of consciously shaping the doctrine of Jesus according to their own *Bildungstrieb*,[62] they simply repeat it, and this illustrates the reduction of reason to a mere receptive faculty. This faithful subservience, coupled with the break from both the traditional familial and political orders, leads Christianity to develop into a positive religion. A forceful expression of this break is found in Luke 14:26: "If any one comes to me and does not hate his own father and mother and wife and children and brothers and sisters, yes, and even his own life, he cannot be my disciple." As we have seen, this kind of rupture from the broader communal life is precisely what is absent from Hegel's account of the philosophical union of Socrates and his friends. The challenge to the "master" is essential to the philosophical schools inspired by Socrates.

Yet if Hegel faults the Christian sects for passing through the imagination on the way to the moral law, how do we reconcile this with his claim that—looking back to *Religion ist eine* . . . and forward to "The Oldest Program"—a sensuous *Volksreligion* requires the imagination? Is this simply an inconsistency, or is it an inevitable tension that arises with the attempt to conceptualize the rise of Christianity by way of both an idealized view of the ancient Greece *polis* and Kantian moral philosophy? By positing the unity of reason, imagination, and action as immediate, Hegel avoids the question of how this unity was initially achieved. This is, perhaps, to criticize him for not having written *The Birth of Tragedy*. The crucial point to reiterate, however, is that this tension in Hegel's text stems, in part, from what he will come to recognize as an inadequate representation of Greece in its role as origin. If his idealized view of Greece encourages him to avoid the question of how reason and the imagination come into harmony, he learns from the life of Jesus that, when confronting positive culture, we must resist the enticement of positive elements. How, then, do we avoid both the silence of resignation and the futility of St. Anthony's sermon? Is there another way through the imagination that does not lead to the sacrifice of self-determination? And what is open to us once the circuitous route *has already been taken*? What are we to do if merely avoiding this route is not an option? These last two questions are of vital importance to Hegel because, in late eighteenth-century Germany, he finds himself in precisely this position.

The question of the possibility of genuine communication within the Christian context is intimately related to the institution created in the name of the life and teaching of Jesus. Its urgency comes from the fact that, at least from Hegel's perspective at the time, the Christian church failed to navigate this transition successfully. This is perhaps the proper terrain of Paul of Tarsus, as much as of Jesus, but Hegel does not focus on the practical aspects of church building by the militant apostle.[63] Instead, he traces the legacy of Jesus's doctrine and the way his compromises with positivity govern the church to come. As mentioned above, for Hegel, this program is found in Jesus's Sermon on the Mount, but, before he turns to the sermon in any detail, he first recounts the history wrought in its name. Hegel is, as I have claimed, drawn to the historical Jesus and the early Christian community because of this confrontation with positivity. The aspect of Christianity that Hegel emphasizes at this point is separation, a separation that includes an essential political dimension. Yet what this generates in the friends of Jesus is an all-encompassing faith coupled with a passive intellect—a passivity that is essentially at odds with fulfilling the moral teachings of Jesus. As Hegel's analysis proceeds, he comes to see this as a recipe for fanaticism. By following the evolution of the church from cult to state, we see Hegel develop a logic of institutionalization, which, at this stage of his thought, is tantamount to the ascendency of positivity. When the moral core of Christianity becomes contaminated by positivity, the form it takes is an unbridled expansionist will. This marks the history of Christianity as Hegel recounts it, and it drives the movement beyond the level of sects to that of a state religion.

TWO

On Expansion

> Baby Suggs grew tired, went to bed and stayed there until her big heart quit. Except for an occasional request for color she said practically nothing—until the afternoon of the last day of her life when she got out of bed, skipped slowly to the door of the keeping room and announced to Sethe and Denver the lesson she had learned from her sixty years a slave and ten years free: that there was no bad luck in the world but whitepeople. "They don't know when to stop," she said, and returned to her bed, pulled up the quilt and left them to hold that thought forever.
>
> —Toni Morrison, *Beloved* [1]

Divided Jesus

The imperative to spread the word of the master comes after the Resurrection. The risen Jesus commands of his disciples,

> Go into all the world and preach the gospel to the whole creation. He who believes and is baptized will be saved; but he who does not believe will be condemned. And these signs will accompany those who believe: in my name they will cast out demons; they will speak in new tongues; they will take up serpents, and if they drink any deadly thing, it will not hurt them; they will lay their hands on the sick, and they will recover. (Mark 16:15–18)

With these words of the resurrected Jesus, the disciples are given their vocation: "So then the Lord Jesus, after he had spoken to them, was taken up into heaven, and sat at the right hand of God. And they went forth and preached everywhere, while the Lord worked with them and confirmed the message by the signs that attended it. Amen" (Mark 16:19–20).[2] According to Hegel, these words exemplify Jesus as a figure of positivity as much as the Sermon on the Mount and the scene of the Last Supper reveal him as a teacher of virtue. Rather than the imperative to spread the word, the teacher of virtue would, as Hegel imagines it, have said something along these lines: "Let every man do as much good as possible in the sphere of activity assigned to him by nature and Providence" (W 1:122/P 84). The difference between Jesus's parting words and Hegel's hypothetical gospel is a matter of faith and action. Positivity comes on the side of faith and virtue on the side of action, yet faith does not remain inactive, and action is circumscribed by nature and providence. Already in the *Positivity,* then, in Hegel's revision of the last words of Jesus, we find the attempted coupling of free, ethical action ("Let every man do as much good") within contextual limitations ("as possible in the sphere of activity assigned to him by nature and Providence").

I have argued that, in the *Positivity,* Hegel holds the substance of the moral teaching of Socrates, Jesus, and Kant to be the same; only their modes of expression differ. His revision of Jesus's last words can be understood as his rendering of Socrates' definition of justice in Book IV of the *Republic* ("one must practice one of the functions in the city, that one for which his nature made him naturally most fit" [433a]),[3] and it reflects what he admires in ancient Athens. Is this providentially determined place setting what conditions the actions of the free citizens of the *polis* and provides the harmony for which the Greeks are praised?[4] If so, then for Hegel the expansionism that derives from the injunction of the resurrected Jesus and that characterizes the historical unfolding of Christianity is not harmonized by a providential nature. Instead, it produces a political order determined by positivity. The social roles that arise as a result of this history should not be understood as natural assignments. Should we rest content, then, with our roles in the political order if this order is determined by mastery rather than citizenship—as was the case for both Jesus and Hegel? Or does Hegel recognize a kind of action that is neither the passive adherence to externally imposed laws nor the willing, self-reflexive adoption of naturally prescribed roles? Is there a third kind of action, born of a notion of individuality that does not melt away into the unity of the *polis,* that freely struggles *against* providence, rather than submitting to its limits? And is it the case that Hegel's two renderings of the last words of Jesus are necessarily at odds and ultimately irreconcilable?

One way of resolving this divided understanding of Jesus recalls Hegel's resolution to a potential conflict between individuality and collectivity in the Greek *polis.* In the same way that this conflict in Greece is avoided by the dissolution of one of the terms into the other (individuality vanishes, or in the case of Socrates, is contained), the apparent conflict between Jesus as moral teacher and the resurrected Jesus could be avoided by simply rejecting the figure who returns from the dead, along with his proselytizing mission. This is the route that Hegel takes in Bern, and we can see this most clearly in his "biographical" account of the life of Jesus. Completed in July 1795, so roughly contemporaneous with the composition of the *Positivity,* Hegel's *Life of Jesus* is the text from this period that reads most like a finished work. This characteristic is important because of its conclusion: Jesus is crucified, but he does not rise again. Thus, we can read Hegel's failure to present the resurrection of Jesus as a decision, and this follows not only from the fact that the text appears to be complete (his account of the Resurrection has not simply been lost to us) but also from the consistency with which he passes over all the miraculous episodes found in the gospel accounts of Jesus. Hegel's Jesus is, instead, presented as a brilliant teacher of what Kant articulates with full philosophical rigor as the moral law. Indeed, the proximity of Jesus and Kant is so close that at times the two are almost reduced to one. Hegel has Jesus say, for example, "'To act only on principles that you can will to become universal laws among men, laws no less binding on you than on them'—this is the fundamental law of morality, the sum and substance of all moral legislation and the sacred books of all people" (N 187/ LJ 116). It would be wrong, however, to present Hegel's Jesus as stripped of all divinity. He is divine to the extent that he harbors the moral law within himself and lives a life that exemplifies it. Divinity is, therefore, derived from a source shared by all humans: "Pure reason, transcending all limits, is divinity itself" (N 75 / LJ 104).[5] While Hegel's text assumes that Kant has presented an unassailable philosophical account of the autonomy of the moral law, he does not rest content. His *Life of Jesus* could certainly be read as an attempt to appeal to the imagination, since it presents an image of what a life lived according to the moral law would look like. It is, however, unlikely that his thoroughly humanized Jesus would be effective in feeding the imagination. The suggestion is clearly that modernity ought to contemplate the life of Jesus in a form stripped of the account of an immaculate conception, miracles, messianic proclamations, and the Resurrection. While a life lived according to the purity of the moral law leads to a clash with the established order and crucifixion, this conflict is visited on Jesus for extrinsic reasons. It does not develop as a necessary outcome from the essence that Jesus's life and his teaching embody; it is not, in other words, what Hegel will later call a *fate*.

In Hegel's portrait of Jesus, life and death maintain their distinct and exclusive domains. Hegel avoids the complication of these sovereign realms that a resurrection would introduce. Thus, the fixed (nondialectical) positioning of opposites like virtue and faith, morality and positivity, Greeks and Jews, extends to life and death as such. Although Hegel might simply want to edit out the resurrected Christ from the gospel, his historical account of Christianity must recount the effects of the conflict between the two competing interpretations of Jesus and the ultimate triumph of one over the other. In the *Positivity,* the history of Christianity *is* the unfolding of the opposition between two figures and two scenes—the teacher of virtue honored at the Last Supper and the resurrected Christ calling for an expansion of the faith. The question that must be asked concerns what happened in the space and time between these two scenes. What is it that gave birth to the imperative to expand? What happened in the underworld?

An anachronistic explanation of the origin of the will to expansion is that what takes place between Jesus's last supper and his return from the dead is the labor of *Aufhebung*, sublation. In the *Science of Logic*, Hegel presents the existence of opposed meanings within the German verb *aufheben* in the following way:

> it means to preserve, to maintain, and equally it also means to cause to cease, to put an end to. Even "to preserve" includes a negative element, namely, that something is removed from its immediacy and so from an existence which is open to external influences, in order to preserve it. Thus what is sublated [*das Aufgehobene*] is at the same time preserved; it has only lost its immediacy but is not on that account annihilated.[6]

The achievement of *aufheben* is that something enters into a unity with its apparent opposite and, as such, can be said to be lifted or raised up. When Hegel argues for a hierarchy of the three moments of Absolute Spirit (art, religion, and philosophy) in the *Encyclopaedia of Philosophical Sciences* (1817), he claims that the content of religion and philosophy may be the same, but their form of presentation differs: representation (*Vorstellung*) versus the Concept (*Begriff*)—"The three forms of the absolute spirit—art, religion, philosophy—represent the same Absolute. They differ only in the medium of expression."[7] Hegel holds that the highest form of religion is the revealed (*offenbare*) religion manifested in certain forms of Christianity; as such, its content should correspond to that of Hegel's own speculative philosophy. Given the centrality of *Aufhebung* in dialectical logic, and the various ways in which it expresses itself throughout the system,[8] the sacrifice of Jesus—his Crucifixion and Resurrection—can be conceived, in part, as a representation of the movement of *aufheben* within the religious domain. Yet, according to this logic, the call to expansion would not simply remain an unequivocal expression of positivity alone.

Hegel's philosophical articulation of the logic of *Aufhebung* is, however, still to come. Here we can only proceed by studying the historical unfolding of Christianity itself, and Hegel's historical analysis of Christianity shows that, insofar as the original Christian community was a living unity, when it overreaches itself, the quality of this community is not simply transformed but *reversed*. The logic of Hegel's argument assumes that, at this point of reversal, the living character of the community is lost. Positivity reigns at the expense of life. But to what extent *was* original Christianity a truly *living* community, and how does it compare to the ideal of the Greek *polis* that Hegel presents?[9]

In the competition for the place of the original historical embodiment of the Idea of a living, free community, Socrates and his friends represent for Hegel a more perfect union than that of Jesus and his followers, because everyone can maintain his own determinate identity—an identity that is tied to the larger community beyond one's smaller circle of friends. As the philosophical circle expands into schools, the rational orientation that these schools cultivate rejects the reduction of moral law to positive command. Within the context of a small religious sect, however, certain positive concessions are considered "expedient, appropriate and permissible" (W 1:121–122/P 86), although not without inherent danger. The climate of positivity necessitates finding a place for the elements of death within life. Thus, these positive elements assume the role of a *pharmakon,* and Jesus and his followers use them as an antidote insofar as they adopt an oppositional stance to the dominant, positivist religious and political community.[10] But when the small communities that are sustained by this balance between the moral and the positive are universalized and made "omnipresent throughout the state," these positive elements become immoral and politically oppressive. "Life" is unable to harbor this reversal within itself. It is not raised into a higher form that finds a place for death within itself. Rather, these elements now reveal themselves as death without qualification. The characteristics, then, that arise from this oppositional relation between life and death will be universalized as these sects unite and coalesce into an empire. For Hegel, preserving the oppositional stance of early Christians, even as Christianity ascends to the throne of worldly power, leads to the universalization of a contaminated rationality. Beyond this, Hegel describes what occurs when a political theology born of a marginalized community comes to be appropriated by the powerful in a later epoch.

The Comedy of Failed Sacrifices

This logic of reversal is not articulated by Hegel as a logic per se, but it can be detected in his account of the concrete, historical effects that develop when an uprising made in the name of moral purity nevertheless allows positive elements to hold an "expedient, appropriate, and permissible" role.

One example of these historical effects revolves around the role of property and the principle of equality. When opposing a dominant, positive culture, the retreat into a narrow circle of fellow believers is appropriate in that it allows for mutual encouragement in realizing their shared moral aims. It affords the space to found a community where property is owned communally, and this, in turn, allows for the fulfillment of the principles of equality and humility. Hegel's analysis of the expansion of the Christian community shows the way in which the original ideal of radical equality is transformed into its opposite when exposed to this expansionist drive. The principle of a community of material goods is telling in that it is rejected precisely *because* it is in conflict with the expansionist drive of Christianity, for the abolition of private property is most amenable to those who own nothing, so its abolition would likely limit those willing to join the movement.[11] The abandonment of this principle ultimately leads to the perverse situation of the laity's being encouraged to give freely to the priesthood with the result that these priests—"the poor and needy!" as Hegel remarks with incredulity—make "the rest of mankind beggars in order to enrich themselves" (W 1:126/P 88, translation altered). The farce continues when we move from the principle of material equality to moral equality. While the "slave is brother of his owner" (ibid.) and no one is to be valued over anyone else, the Christian principles of equality and humility are greatly altered when the supposition is made that this equality exists from the perspective of heaven alone. A false "beyond" is established so that inequality can be justified and maintained in the here and now. The result is that the "simple-minded" (*Einfältige,* W 1:127/P 89) are subjected to the contemptuous laughter of the prelate and gentry when they apply these principles to this world as well as the next.

Inadvertent comedy continues to define the result of these concrete reversals. Hegel gives the example of the annual rite of the prelate washing the feet of the poor. He locates the origin of the *pedilavium* ritual in the Jewish tradition of hospitality where washing the feet of visitors was a regular activity and a courtesy to guests (he does not mention at this point anointing feet in preparation for burial.)[12] While the contemporary continuation of the ritual is clearly meant to affirm the principles of equality and humility by illustrating the transience of temporal power and luxury that the prelate enjoys, the rite becomes a "comedy" (W 1:127/P 89) because the principles are realized in the symbolic realm of the prelate's gesture but nowhere else. The source of this farce is a society that needs, according to its own stated principles, to reconcile the extremes in material inequality that arise within it. These are represented by the privileged prelate and the simple-minded poor. The attempted reconciliation, however, involves two dissymmetrical sacrifices: the enduring material sacrifice of the poor and the symbolic, theatrical gesture of sacrifice made by the prelate.

The ritual is comic in that it has the effect of leaving everything as it was; or, more accurately, it is a sacrifice required in order that political and economic privileges remain in place. It is comic for the same reason that, from a disinterested perspective, so much hypocrisy and corruption are comic, for we laugh at the deflation of pretensions. As Henri Bergson writes, "any incident is comic that calls our attention to the physical in a person, when it is the moral side that is concerned"—he gives the example of a funeral oration where the deceased is described as "virtuous and plump."[13] Comedy brings us back to earth and to our bodily, material desires. The exalted religious ritual is revealed to be motivated by the most worldly concerns, and laughter accompanies the unmasking of these true motivations. This spectacle of the failed sacrifice is the source of the comedy here. Bergson provides another formulation of the comic imperative: what makes us laugh is "something mechanical encrusted in the living."[14] Life is fluid, mobile, elastic, filled with tension; anything that is inelastic, rigid, or repetitive—in other words, positive—is not as it should be, so we laugh at this distortion of life.

As a mock fulfillment of the law, the *pedilavium* ritual exemplifies the manner in which a positive state religion functions in general. The point, however, is not only the hypocrisy that the church falls prey to when it grows beyond a small sect into a state religion but the loss of the living character of the principle of equality. The act of washing the feet of the poor has no relation to what people actually do in late eighteenth-century Germany. That is, the grounding of the ritual in a tradition of hospitality has been lost. By extension, then, Hegel seems to be claiming that meaningful religious rituals must be grounded in the living social practices of the community, and, when this ground is lacking, the ritual becomes meaningless.[15] Comedy arises when principles that have been rendered meaningless in practice are still exploited to preserve—at least, in the case at hand—social divisions. To emphasize the point, Hegel gives a further example of the Chinese emperor who takes a turn at the plow once a year. While this ritual too has been reduced to the level of comedy, it nevertheless retains "a greater and a more direct significance for every onlooker, because the plowing must always be one of the chief occupations of his subjects" (W 1:127/P 89). Everything remains the same, so the spectacle is comic, but at least the ritual employs a living practice in a way that washing the feet of guests does not.[16] It should be noted that, ultimately, Hegel greets with disdain the spectacle of this transformation of equality and humility into their opposites. Any hint of the necessity of this failure is absent.

Die Mahle der geistlichen Liebe

The way in which the living meaning of religious practices is undermined when it is divorced from the source of this meaning is most striking in the case of the Last Supper. Hegel consistently refers to the feasts held to remember Jesus's last meal as *die Mahle der Liebe* (see W 1:129/P 90), and these feasts originally exemplified a rebirth out of positivity. What was originally being resurrected was the living event, the scene of virtuous union. When Hegel describes the historical Last Supper, he rigorously avoids imposing the symbolic meanings of subsequent Christian theology. *Das Mahl der Liebe* was simply a final gathering of Jesus with his friends and disciples. They shared a meal and conversation "about submission to . . . fate, about the way the virtuous man's consciousness of duty raised him above sorrows and injustices, about the love for all mankind by which alone obedience to God could be evinced" (W 1:128/P 89, translation altered). Yet for Hegel, as well as any sensitive reader uncorrupted by "the concepts of dogmatic theology," this gathering cannot but strike them as "sublime" (W 1:129/P 89). As a living event, it manages to transcend the deadening effect of positivity, but it does so without assuming a complete break from the past. Instead, it overcomes these effects by resuscitating an indigenous practice. *Das Mahl der Liebe* is a recollection of the Passover ritual, but a recollection that, at the same time, alters its meaning. Whenever the disciples enjoy bread and wine in the future, they will now be reminded of Jesus's bodily sacrifice; this imaginative union between the body and bread, blood and wine, is what Hegel calls "a sensuous symbol," *ein Sinnbild* (W 1:228/P 90). That is to say, it is more than a mere play on words or a metaphysical assertion. Body and bread, blood and wine are bound together in an immediate, "natural" way, and this grounds their sensuous, or lived, unity. This union is and should continue to be nothing other than the gathering of the disciples who meet to eat in friendship and remembrance. In Hegel's account of the history of Christianity, there is, it seems, a discrete moment of fulfillment in the Last Supper, but it takes place only at this very intimate level. (If this moment is achieved by both canceling and preserving elements of the Passover feast, it must also be noted that this concrete fulfillment is presented without reference to the Resurrection.)

As we leave this intimate realm, however, the meaning of *die Mahle der Liebe* as a sensuous symbol is undermined. When Christianity develops into a sect, the act of gathering to remember a teacher and friend is no longer a free act but becomes instead a religious obligation. It is transformed into a mysterious, divine ordinance. The mystification arises from the supposedly supernatural effects that such feasts, held in the name of Jesus, were promised to have *beyond* the satisfaction of hunger and the distinct pleasures of conversation that a shared feast naturally affords. Ultimately, the fall into positivity comes because the body is forgotten. This is the offense. As the Christian sects become even larger and more widespread, the reversal in meaning is complete and the body is abandoned entirely. The fraternity that constituted the true meaning of the Last Supper is transformed into the stark inequalities of rank. To the extent that, at the level of the sect, the rich helped the poor fulfill this duty, there was at least the semblance of fraternization, but, as Christianity became universalized, fraternity was rendered nonexistent. As Hegel notes, the charge raised in earlier times that *die Mahle der geistlichen Liebe* "degenerated into occasions and scenes of fleshly love" (W 1:129/P 90) was an increasingly distant concern as the satisfaction of the body became completely disassociated from the "spiritual" element (W 1:129/P 91). Far from the union of finite and infinite, *Geistlich* is here associated with what he calls the "mystical," and mystifying, reinterpretation of the Last Supper that forgets the natural, bodily aspect of the "sensuous symbol." When severed from its concrete, social, or "bodily" foundation, the ritual becomes empty. It is an emptiness that opens the way to autocracy.

The Drive Outward

The fall of Christianity into positivity is so intimately tied to its will to expansion that the fundamental problem facing Hegel's analysis becomes that of why Christianity must travel outside itself. Hegel does not, however, treat this outward movement as a simple adherence to the call to "Go into all the world and preach the gospel to the whole creation" (Mark 16:15). He interprets it instead as a drive to venture into what is foreign to it. Hegel's opposition to the will to expansion mirrors a criticism that has been raised against his own later, speculative philosophy itself. This is the criticism that the dialectical progression of reason is itself an incessant colonization of alterity. If the dialectic is the logical path of the endless subsumption of the other into the same, what are we to make of this early critique of expansionism? Will he reconcile himself with this history of expansion as the dialectical method becomes more fully articulated? To understand Hegel's critique of expansionism, we must turn to the origin of the will to expand itself.

When Hegel raises the question of the source of this expansionist drive, he is addressing within the delimited history of Christianity the same general issues that Herder, Kant, Schiller, and Fichte, among others, address in their reflections on "universal history." Hegel's question of the origin of a collective motivation to expand corresponds in the context of universal history to that of why we are driven to leave the state of "nature" in the first place. In his "Universal History with a Cosmopolitan Intent" (1784), Kant presents the thesis that an "unsocial sociability" provokes humanity to develop those capacities that remain dormant in its natural state.[17] His explanation relies on recourse to human nature, and his position is that we have both a "propensity for living in society" and a "great tendency to isolate ourselves."[18] The move out of the natural realm into a social order—from crooked wood to upright trees—is a development initially determined behind our collective backs. As Kant says, "Man wills concord; but nature better knows what is good for the species: she wills discord."[19] Through this conflict, the space in which human history unfolds is opened, and Kant postulates that this history is "the realization of a hidden plan of nature to bring about an internally . . . and externally perfect constitution."[20] While the negative drive toward unsociability is partially redeemed by nature itself, full redemption comes only when self-conscious reason has the courage to employ its understanding fully. The collective subject that Kant considers is the species itself and the trajectory that he would like to chart is one that leads toward this self-conscious, autonomous exercise of reason.

This is not the kind of path that one discovers in Hegel's studies of Christianity. The expression of moral reasoning that he finds in the individual figure of Jesus fails to flourish into a movement leading toward enlightenment. In an attempt to reconcile the project of "universal history" in its Kantian form with the seemingly less progressive view of history found in Hegel's early theologico-political writings, one might argue, for example, that Hegel's account of the development of Christianity ought to be understood as one distinct phase within a fully universal account of world history. The charge against Hegel would be that he fails to show how the cunning of unsocial sociability is, in fact, operating through the history of Christianity. One should not, however, underestimate Hegel's own suspicion of the concrete effects of historical Christianity and, thus, his distance from this hypothetical reconciliation with a progressive account of universal history. He considers, for example, the reaction of a philosopher who holds that moral action ought to be grounded in reason alone to a Christian who gives priority to the true element of his religion (that is, its moral core). The philosopher might acknowledge the virtue of this Christian, even if the latter were still committed to the positive dogma of his faith in order to inculcate "a false easiness of conscience" (W 1:130/ P 91). Nevertheless, when confronted by this contradiction between the Christian's head—the dogma—and heart, the philosopher will "marvel at the invincible might of the Ego which triumphs over an intellect full of morally destructive convictions and a memory packed with learned phrases" (ibid.). While the philosopher may marvel at this contradictory Christian figure, he also overlooks the Christian's adherence to positivist dogma insofar as he is ultimately guided by the true moral core of his religion. Yet there is no intimation in Hegel's description of this hypothetical encounter between philosopher and "righteous" Christian of how the latter might be the historical precondition of the former.

Beyond the different directionalities of the two histories (Kant's leading toward autonomy, Hegel's toward positivity), Hegel's focus on the origin of the will to expansion itself leads to the question of whether he too explains this outward drive by way of our unsocial sociability. The difficulty in responding to this stems from the fact that, instead of deducing an explanation for the Christian expansionist drive from an account of our human nature, Hegel's conclusions are drawn, in part, from the historical analyses he undertakes. Kant, by contrast, writes that "this capacity for social existence is clearly embedded in human nature," as is "the unsocial characteristic of wanting everything to go according to his own desires."[21] Hegel affirms a rational and moral dimension to human nature, but this does not help explain why a self-conscious attempt to revitalize this moral aspect of our nature leads to the opposite result.

Why, then, does Christianity expand? There is, as we have said, no suggestion of the cunning of reason at work behind the scenes. Instead, Hegel presents the drive outward, the will to proselytize, as the central trait of a positive sect, so, if Christianity is driven to expand, it is a consequence of its contamination by positivity. Thus, he is understandably disdainful of the line of thought that sees this expansionism as a product of its inherent and self-evident truth: 'Christianity has spread across the globe for the simple reason that it is true,' which is then bolstered by the circular claim that 'the fact that Christianity has spread across the globe *proves* that it is true,' and, finally, 'the inherent poverty of heathen mythologies, like that of the Greeks, only make the inevitable conversions easier' (see W 1:203/ P 153). In stark contrast to this type of self-satisfied position, the central conclusion of the *Positivity* is that what truth there is in Christianity is betrayed by its expansionist success. At the same time, we know from the moral core that Hegel finds in human nature that the concerns he raises with regard to expansionism do not indicate a privileging of the particular or the provincial. Thus, the members of an overgrown positive sect are compared negatively to both the adherents of a philosophical system *and* the "righteous" followers of any positive faith who see morality, or "purity of heart" (*Reinheit des Herzens;* W 1:131 / P 92), as the essence of faith. This is to reiterate that, at this point in his thinking, Hegel holds there to be one universal and static definition of morality against which any religion can be judged. As such, morality stands as a force that can unite across sectarian divides, whether philosophical or religious. Instead of being seized by the will to expand as an end in itself, a person whose positive faith is grounded in morality will embrace anyone who shares this grounding, regardless of his or her faith. To illustrate this purity of heart, Hegel cites an exchange from Lessing's *Nathan the Wise* between Nathan and a lay monk:

> Thou art a Christian: by God, thou art a Christian.
> A better Christian never was.

To which Nathan replies,

> 'Tis well for us! For what makes me for thee
> A Christian, makes thee for me a Jew. (Ibid.)

Given this affirmation of the Enlightenment position that presumes to find the same moral core in all true religions, it might be tempting to conclude that religious particularity ought to be excised altogether. Yet if it is the particularity of the idiom that threatens to obscure and usurp the universal moral law, Hegel concludes that, for Christianity, the reversal of its moral core and the subsequent fall into positivity takes place when the particularity of a religious community is disregarded. As we have seen, the comic spectacle of a prelate's washing the feet of the poor in Hegel's time is an example of positivity because the practice has no relation to the everyday customs of Germany at the end of the eighteenth century. The problem does not seem to be the historically or culturally specific rituals of this kind per se, but rituals severed from their grounding in lived experience. Is it the case, then, that the concessions to positivity that were made by early Christianity are relatively harmless when these communities remain small but destructive in larger communities without a robust common ground? To put this another way, could a perfectly rational religious sect—and it would be difficult to distinguish such a sect from a philosophical community—expand without this reversal taking place since its ground would be universal? Further, would a perfectly rational sect be driven to expand in the first place? Is reason inherently expansionist?

Resentment and the Imperial Will

Hegel does not take up the question of whether a community grounded in reason could expand its influence without betraying itself for the simple reason that this is not how he understands the historical expansion of Christianity. It derives from the universal extension of positive laws, rather than the moral law. As the positive elements of religion become increasingly dominant, they fuel and accelerate the will to expand, in part because the reaction toward those who are not part of the sect, toward "otherness" generally, takes the form of either pity or loathing. The absoluteness of faith, along with the intolerance that arises from it, is at the heart of both these reactions. To adhere to the positivity of a religious sect is to feel united with its doctrine to the point that any separation or deviation from it becomes almost unimaginable. What is lacking, or more accurately, what is actively banished, in this positive consciousness is the *negative* capacity of doubting that is constitutive of the Socratic figure of the philosopher. If this banishment is successful, "a sort of surprise comes over a sectary if he hears of men who are not of his faith, and this feeling of uneasiness which they create in him is very readily transformed into dislike of them and hatred" (W 1:132/P 93). From this positive perspective, facing someone who does not mirror one's own beliefs becomes a confrontation with what can only be understood as either ignorance or an evil will. The pity that the face of apparent ignorance evokes is one impetus for expanding the faith. "If he pities them, he will feel himself driven to indicate to the ignorant and unhappy the only way to the happiness he hopes to gain for himself. He will be especially inclined to do this if he has other reasons for loving them, and all the more because the means of finding this way seem so easy, so very easy" (W 1:131/P 92). If there is no reason to love them, however, then the reaction is a loathing that leads, in its extreme, to the *auto-da-fé* of the Inquisition, or, in a less incendiary form, the denial of civil rights by one ecclesiastical regime to the adherents of other faiths. Even the more temperate desire to further the honor of God by propagating a certain form of worship may initially be pursued by means of persuasion alone, yet it can quickly degenerate to the point where those who refuse to conform are slaughtered for this offense. Hegel initially mentions this slide from persuasion to murder in only the most cursory way (his example is the Spanish in America), but the fact that this degeneration begins from the moderate, if narrow-minded, position of pious duty indicates a logic of accelerating intensification, contamination, even frenzy. Unearthing its source discloses the core of expansionist zeal.

The condescension of pity and the violence that arises from intolerance are the expressions of positivity's unwillingness to entertain doubts. If reason is adopted at all and confrontation between reason and a positive doctrine arises, then positive faith is forced to rely on the kind of self-justification grounded in a logic of mere quantification: 'if my beliefs are shared by so many others, they must be true.' The hidden source of positivism's expansionist zeal is the fact that a consciousness whose imagination has been assaulted to the point of being "faced with the very terrors of hell" (W 1:133 / P 93) will find perverse consolation in the thought of all the others who will be sharing in this fate: "The yoke of faith, like any other, becomes more tolerable the more associates we have in bearing it, and when we attempt to make a proselyte, our secret reason is often our resentment that another should be free from chains which we carry ourselves and which we lack the strength to lose" (W 1:133 / P 93–94). If the direct cause is a pedagogy that operates by terrorizing the imagination, the secret reason for this expansion is *resentment*. Resentment comes with the failure fully to suppress the doubts that arise when the force of indoctrination lapses. It is the haunting suspicion that the sacrifices we have made are in vain and that, no matter how coercive the means by which faith has been imposed, there has nevertheless been a degree of willing participation in serving it. Thus, submission to church doctrine affords only a "false tranquility" (W 1:185 / P 140). The surfacing doubt that Hegel describes is the recognition of our freedom and the complicity in suppressing this aspect of our nature. When this occurs, faith is indeed experienced as a yoke. But the moment of recognition is fleeting. Rather than self-consciousness and a more intensified, inward movement, it leads to a lashing outward at those who do not conform and who, in doing so, disrupt the unanimity of the sacrifice. The imagery of self-enslavement to faith that Hegel employs presumes that the object of disdain is someone who has assumed the position of "life," and, according to Hegel, within this Christian tradition, the figure of life is Jesus himself. Those united by sacrifice resent the living and the free, and this resentment is driven by the desire that all be made to sacrifice and submit to the yolk. Beneath the universal call to spread the good word, to enlighten, baptize, and save, is obedience, self-sacrifice, confrontation, and resentment.

In the typology of communal structures that Hegel is implicitly presenting, Greece is the model of a philosophical community of pure reason embedded within a larger democratic society of free citizens. The Judaism of Jesus's time is described as a community grounded in duty. With the early Christian sect, the community is characterized by *philia* and dissent. As Christianity expands in scope, it becomes, according to Hegel, defined by resentment instead. This last type, with its drive to impose on others the letter of its own faith, offends the right that everyone has to his or her own convictions, a right that Hegel thinks is the very condition of virtue itself. More concretely, the will to proselytize leads to a fundamental contradiction inherent in the logic of the early Christian communities because the drive to expand undermines the relation of friendship that Hegel recognizes as one of their most valuable qualities. Once Christianity has been widely disseminated, the ideal of friendship is stretched to the point where the love—and Hegel uses the term here in the *Positivity* (see W 1:143/P 103)—that defines the community of Christians becomes nothing more than a façade.

Internal Expansion

For the young Hegel, the global spread of Christianity provides evidence not of its truth but of the power of this expansionist drive itself. He then continues by drawing out the following reversal: as Christian theologians boast about the number of conversions that have been made, the very success of this mission has the effect of diminishing the zeal for further proselytizing. The expansion of Christianity may have been fuelled by the existence of those who, by the very absence of their Christian faith, posed a challenge to the conviction of absolute belief, but a reversal occurs when this external affront is subdued. When the resentful subject faces a world that reflects itself, no meaningful external threats exist, so it turns against *internal* enemies. Hegel writes that, from the point of view of positive Christianity, "the most dangerous enemies of Christianity are internal ones, and so much preparation and labor are needed in dealing with these that little thought can be given to the salvation of Turks or Samoyeds" (W 1:134/P 95, translation altered). To diagnose fully the diremption that characterizes Hegel's own time, we must track this internalized expansion of positivity. Hegel does not initially explain who these internal enemies are. They could be religious figures like Martin Luther, but it is also tempting, more generally, to see in this self-reflexive, inward turn the logic of internalization at the heart of Christianity itself.[22] Hegel has already described the reactive stance that the early Christians adopted because of their outcast status. This, in turn, leads to a withdrawal into themselves, a withdrawal manifested in the monastic tradition of separation. George Bataille writes of how "totalitarian monasticism answers the need to stop the growth of a closed system"[23]; it accommodates the drive to expand when the possibility, and challenge, of outward growth ceases. I will argue, however, that the true internal enemies of the positive church are the thoughts of the faithful themselves. The asceticism of the church becomes the internalized form of positivity such that the aggression that was unleashed externally is now directed toward the self.

The Modern *Complementum* of the Law

Immediately upon raising the specter of enemies within, Hegel turns to the contemporary church and its relation to the state. Instead of pursuing the internalization of positivity, he considers what a proper balance might be in modernity between religious and political orders, and he does so in light of their present autocratic nature. The disruption of the appropriate relation between morality and legality—virtue and positivity—has guided Hegel's account of Judaism and early Christianity from the beginning, and he has charted in some detail the manner in which the moral principles that guide religion change into their opposite when adhered to with excessive zeal. There must, therefore, be limits placed on the domain of both church and state. Indeed, autocratic rule arises precisely when the proper limits determining these separate domains are transgressed. After recounting Christianity's extraordinary expansion and its decline into positivity, Hegel is now in the position to consider a question raised above, namely, how is it possible to restore balance in the wake of this decline? He will attempt to orchestrate what existed immediately in Greece. It is going too far to claim that, for Hegel, the move beyond the immediacy of ancient Greek unity was of inherent value or even, for that matter, necessary. Greece is not an undeveloped—"undeveloped" in the sense of lacking freedom—natural origin. Nevertheless, Hegel's analysis implies that any "return" to the Greek ideal of freedom, any attempted *mimēsis* of it, cannot ignore the long, intervening historical reality. It cannot ignore the qualitative change born of quantitative growth.

The burgeoning modernity that Hegel confronts in his own time is the product of the history that he has just recounted, and one of the consequences of this history is a conflict between church and state. He enlists reason as a means of determining a proper relation between these domains, although whether this is reason as *Vernunft* or *Verstand* is not immediately apparent. He affirms the necessity of limiting the power of religion and containing its outward drive within the state, that is, within the proper sphere of legality. In the same way, however, that he is critical of legalism when it takes the form of religious positivity (especially in the extreme case where the state becomes entirely subsumed by religious authority), Hegel is equally concerned with the state's becoming an exclusive form of authority. The state must be supplemented by a moral sphere, and Hegel's task, or rather the task of reason, is to orchestrate an allegiance of two universals. The first universal is the law of the state, and the second is the particularized expression of a moral universal that must be harbored within the first. Historically, with the dominance of religious positivity, the church has consistently appropriated the power of the state, so reason must now contend with the situation that resentment has produced. Thus, when Hegel returns to the present day after engaging in historical studies of the institutions that populate his contemporary world, he develops an argument based on the nature of right and duty, an argument that defends harmonizing the institutions of the church and state by way of their separation.

Hegel's defense of a separation of church and state can be understood as a necessary but unfortunate compromise forced on modernity by the history that gave birth to it. Since the scope of modern, eighteenth-century institutions precludes the kind of unity found in ancient Greece, this separation, if properly negotiated, will allow for the possibility of accord between these two domains; but this accord is, *qua* Greece, of a secondary, diminished order. Because of historical necessities, we are forced to accept the second best. The Greek ideal looms over modernity in such a way that it seems as if the contemporary world can never escape from the shadow it casts. At the same time, Hegel's understanding of ancient Greece allows for the sort of separation that he prescribes for the present, albeit on a much more intimate scale. The circle of friends around Socrates, the philosophical schools that are developed from the example that he provides, the familial and political structures that the philosopher never withdraws from in the way that the Christian disciples do: these distinct institutions and the balance that is achieved among them within the higher unity of the Athenian *polis* provide an example of a union that remains so despite being divided within itself. It is an intimation of the concept of the concrete universal and the speculative principle of "the identity of identity and non-identity."[24] Although Hegel's early historical analyses begin the work of showing the full extent to which the present is mediated, the *unity* of Greece is, nevertheless, posited immediately. The present, then, is mediated, which is to say, *oriented*, by an original point of immediacy. Lukács argues that Hegel's early writings are both constantly moving toward the articulation of the dialectic at the same time that they are littered with what he calls "mystical" moments of immediacy.[25] This is one of them. Looking ahead, *The Spirit of Christianity* considers the consequences that arise when this original point of immediacy—Greece, as a figure of the origin—is itself understood as mediated. But this original displacement has yet to occur.

Hegel's remedy for the divided state of modern society entails determining the proper rights that define the spheres of church and state, and he proceeds by distinguishing three types of duties: *civic, moral,* and *religious.*[26] The first concerns questions of justice. The rights of a civil society are those founded on the rights of others. If I choose not to follow the laws made to enforce these rights, the state treats me with force and, thus, as a natural object. These are essentially the rights to life and property, and they apply to the individual citizens of the temporal state. The example that Hegel provides of the second kind of duty is the obligation to give charity. This moral duty cannot be demanded of an individual citizen *qua* individual, although it can exist as a general duty demanded of citizens *en masse.* While the state has no right to demand that an individual fulfill this duty, those who do act according to the moral law are what Hegel calls the true adherents of a philosophical sect, the citizens of the moral realm and members of the "invisible church" (W 1:144/P 100). They adopt only the duties that they give to themselves. The third class of duties, those that apply to a religious sect, are grounded neither in the rights of others nor in rights of humanity as such. Duties of this kind, like the confession of sins, are assumed voluntarily, and they must not override those imposed by the state, for, if they did, this would mean that there is a power within the state that is both distinct and of greater authority. Since these religious duties are grounded neither in the rights of another nor in the moral law, they can be renounced with the same freedom with which they were adopted. So the freedom to enter and leave the Christian community, which corresponds to the freedom inherent in the idea of friendship, would now be codified within the proper legal structure of the modern state.

Harmonizing morality and civil law with the help of religion as the third note in the chord consists in recognizing the constraints that exist on the state, as a body whose proper concern is legality, to *impose* morality. Since the ideal of moral perfection cannot be the aim of civil legislation, any disregard for these results would be a kind of comedy or farce; it would be "improper, contradictory, and laughable" (W 1:137/P 98). The body would be putting on false airs. Civil laws work through coercion; as such, they function outside the realm of morality, for moral action, according to its idea, is based on laws that are entirely self-determined and freely chosen. By encouraging the adoption of the third kind of duty, religious institutions can be beneficial to a state, *if* these duties aid in steering people toward moral action. Yet just as the state cannot enforce moral duties, it would also be overstepping its proper bounds if it were to enforce religious duties. Religious institutions exist as the embodiment of belief; as such, they cannot be founded on a *contract,* as long as we understand this to be a means of social unification that is necessarily accompanied by the sort of coercion sanctioned by civil law. "In matters of faith there is in strictness no social contract" (W 1:166/P 123). All contracts are based on a calculating will, but "a will to believe is an impossibility" (ibid.). Unlike the binding force of a contract, faith is something that, by its very nature, is alterable; and since faith cannot be constrained or determined by external force, the church is, by extension, always underway. Hegel goes as far as to say that "the most sacrosanct right of every individual and every society [is], namely, the right to change one's opinions" (W 1:166/P 124), and he concurs with the "great men" who claimed that "the fundamental meaning of 'Protestant' is a man or a church which has not bound itself to certain unalterable [*unveränderliche*] standards of faith" (W 1:170–171/P 128).

This defense of the negative character of faith is very much in the spirit of a text like Kant's "What Is Enlightenment?" (1784), which stands as a strategy for passing from a theoretical defense of human autonomy to its concrete, institutional manifestation. When Hegel speaks of "fixed symbols" (*bestimmte Symbole;* W 1:176/P 133) and the danger to this sacrosanct right that they pose, it is reminiscent of the following lines from Kant's essay:

> But would a society of pastors, perhaps a church assembly or venerable presbytery (as those among the Dutch call themselves), not be justified in binding itself by oath to a certain unalterable symbol [*unveränderliche Symbol*] in order to secure a constant guardianship over each of its members and through them over the people, and this for all time: I say that this is wholly impossible. Such a contract, whose intention is to preclude forever all further enlightenment of the human race, is absolutely null and void.[27]

A conclusion that Kant draws from this position is that a strict division must initially be drawn between the public and private use of reason. The former involves thinking freely in terms of ends and presenting the conclusions publicly, while the latter refers to the instrumental reason that one adopts when fulfilling one's duties within a given institution. Thus, the priest uses his reason privately when he deliberates about the best way to convey church dogma in his sermon on Sunday morning, and he reasons publicly when he nails his reasoned objections to that dogma to the church door on the following day. The Enlightenment imperative of *Sapere Aude!* ("have the courage, the audacity, to know"[28]) leads to the conclusion that one must "*Argue* as much as you want about what you want, *but obey!*" with the added condition that an enlightened monarch fulfills "*his* duty to prescribe nothing."[29] Kant's veiled threat to Friedrich the Great amounts to saying that, given the spirit of the times, if the monarch wants to avoid revolt and keep his title, he must agree to curb his will. This compromise on the side of the citizens—"*Argue* as much as you like . . . , but *obey!*"—opens the space for the infinite progression toward the kingdom of ends and the ostensible collapse of the divide between public and private reason. Public discourse will be able to reform a manner of thinking freely, as Kant reasons (publicly), in a way that a *revolution* that overthrows "autocratic despotism and profiteering or power-grabbing oppression" cannot.[30]

I have shown how Hegel will come to condemn this kind of Enlightenment position in the Jena-era *Faith and Knowledge* essay as the moralism of a false "beyond," a moralism that has, as its correlate, the production of the divided modern subject. This divided subject is very much the one who may argue but must obey. Can we conclude, then, that Hegel's solution to the historical legacy of religious positivity (unifying the different institutions by way of properly circumscribing them) is able to avoid the divide that we find in Kant's compromise? As a means of responding, I propose looking to the formation of the mediating institution of the church. Hegel contrasts a religious community that determines its faith through the vote and the will of the majority with one that arises *automatically* (*von selbst;* W 1:161/P 118) out of a common view of faith and purpose. The "automatic" church organizes itself around maintaining its faith and worship and reproducing the ideal of perfection it holds. A church that determines its dogma through a vote is not necessarily submitting itself to an unalterable symbol in that another vote is always able to transform it, but this approach lacks the pure correspondence between all particular worshippers and the "universal"—the latter being the church dogma. Thus, Hegel maintains the idea of pure correspondence as the basis of a true moral union. He affirms an immediate, quasi-organic community, although it is fundamentally nonpolitical and, thus, dissimilar in this regard to what he finds in Greece. The immediacy that Hegel posits in the ancient *polis,* however, is transferred in modernity to the distinctly religious realm.

The logical necessity of keeping the sphere of faith and politics separate follows from the freedom inherent in joining a religious institution. Coupled with this is the right reserved by a religious institution to expel those who do not follow the religious duties that is has determined. When the distinction between church and state collapses, a contradiction, or, as Hegel says, a "collision" (*Kollision,* W 1:105 / P P146), arises because a justifiable exclusion from an ecclesiastical society would entail the exclusion from the state as well. *Structurally,* this is an irreconcilable contradiction between two types of duties and rights—the civic and religious. *Historically,* this has meant that, instead of the competing rights existing together in a reconciled way with one another, the rights proper to the state have been sacrificed. The concrete result is the unjustified exclusion of dissenters and the curtailing of religious freedom, because, now, leaving the national church also entails severing ties to one's country and civil rights. Beyond this inherent contradiction, Hegel observes that a church that has previously been the object of suffering and discrimination forgets this and becomes intolerant if it is able to assume power.

In carving out the proper spheres for these different kinds of rights, Hegel is making room for a set of religious duties that are in the service of the state but distinct from civil law. He again describes the proper balance at the national level in terms of Jesus's claim that he is introducing a "moral sense" (W 1:138 / P 99) that stands as the "*complementum* of the law" (W 1:139 / P 99). Through this, one earns full citizenship in the kingdom of God or the "invisible church." The subject of God's kingdom is simply another name for the citizen of the moral realm. Hegel's earlier criticisms of the fetishism of the image were made by way of contrast with the purity of philosophical "sects" (philosophical circles regard "the imagery of popular belief as unworthy of a thinking man but not as worthy of blame" [W 1:111 / P 74, translation altered]). From this perspective, the circuitous route through the positive elements of a religion carries with it the inherent dangers we have discussed. Despite these concerns, however, Hegel appears willing to tolerate in modernity an intermediary between the legal duties of the state and the moral duties that are imposed by reason alone. Beyond tolerance, however, is there a *need* for such an intermediary? Does the invisible church need the visible one? If so, how do we reconcile the call for an extramoral supplement with Hegel's concern about the circuitous route that strays away from the straight path of reason?

Positivity as Asceticism

Hegel's responses to these questions turn on the power of the imagination generally and the role of the imagination in religious life more specifically. As we have seen, alongside resentment, a terrorized imagination is central to Hegel's explanation of positivist expansion. Religion and the imagination are so intimately united that Hegel will even claim that a religion is commendable if it sets about cultivating the imagination in a moral way and should be condemned if it proceeds to terrorize it (see W 1:138/P 98). Thus, it is not only the products of the imagination—mythologies, popular stories, and so on—that act as a *pharmakon,* but religion does as well, to the extent that it works to shape the imagination. As this ambivalent intermediary, religion may play a role in a potential modern reconciliation of civil and moral law, state legality and individual moral deliberation, which is to say that it can be seen as a potential element of the *complementum* of the law. It remains, however, a threat if it interferes with the proper distinction between the different forms of duties. As both potential poison and remedy, the quality of religion depends on an adherence to its proper measure. Hegel's description of the holy will as "unifying into a single concept what truly pious men have in common with vagrants, lunatics, and scoundrels" (W 1:141/P 101) provides evidence of this proximity of extremes in the Christian ideal. When the proper spheres of influence are not maintained, the moral condition that accompanies that political despotism is *asceticism.*

Hegel is not yet in line with the substance of "The Oldest Program" insofar as his Kantian Enlightenment sympathies exist in an uneasy tension with the call for the philosophers to be sensuous. Nevertheless, the trajectory of his thinking appears to lead him to the point where the imagination cannot simply be discounted but must be engaged. This shift occurs when the question changes from that of the political-moral ideal of manifest freedom to that of the best tactics to be employed when confronted by a political-historical situation mired in positivity. That is, it occurs when the circuitous route through the positive *has already been taken.* The positivity of Jesus's time eventually becomes the asceticism that arises when the scope of the Christian church expands to the point that it has subsumed the domain of civil duty into itself. This historical progression may initially appear to be simply a reversion to what Hegel ascribes to the Judaism of Jesus's time, namely, a bondage to the law characterized by the rule of *Verstand,* rather than *Vernunft.* According to this initial impression, we would then conclude that the message of

Jesus, now distorted into a form of asceticism, has been forgotten, and religious duties are once again mere commandments enforced by fear. But Hegel argues that the terror inflicted on the imagination goes much deeper in Christianity, for whereas the Jews are said to have satisfied God through performing external ceremonies, the most intimate thought of the Christian, indeed, his very "disposition [*Gesinnung*] is prescribed for him in every detail" (W 1:184/P 140, translation altered). This clarifies Hegel's earlier remark that, once the monumental project of external expansion had, by virtue of its own success, lost its vitality, the force of fear and loathing was directed inward. This campaign against the inevitable internal enemy of piety is the insidious effect of the internalization of the expansionist drive. The work of asceticism is the colonization of the interior realm of consciousness through its regulation by an impossibly intricate system of rules. Hegel describes this reduction of morality to casuistry in the following way:

> This [casuistic] arithmetic is so extensive and the multitude of duties is consequentially so infinitely enlarged that little is left to free choice. What in itself is neither commanded nor forbidden as a duty finally becomes important in the asceticism which leaves free no thoughts however private, leaves uncontrolled no action, no involuntary glance, no enjoyment of whatever kind, whether joy, love, friendship, or sociability. It lays claim to every psychical emotion, every association of thought, every idea which flits through the mind from moment to moment, every sense of well-being. It deduces duties by a calculation like that employed in eudaemonism, and it knows how to deduce dangers by a long string of syllogisms. It also prescribes a mass of exercises by which the soul is supposed to be developed. It is a comprehensive science of tactics which teaches artful and regular maneuvers both against every enemy of piety which lurks in everyone's bosom and which may be created out of any situation and any thought, and also especially against the invisible enemy in hell. (W 1:179–180/P 136)

When morality is reduced in this way to a calculus, legalistic thinking fully infiltrates and undercuts that of morality. Asceticism is positivity revisited, but its scope is far greater. Beyond actions alone being commanded, the church presumes to command feelings as well. The effect is that this usurps the freedom grounding genuine morality and imposes a kind of mechanical mode of being.

With this, we reach the source of the divided consciousness that Hegel diagnoses in modernity, for the effect of asceticism is to drive apart reason and feeling, thought and action. This destructive effect is understood in relation to what he refers to in the *Positivity* as an unmediated "true and natural feelings" (W 1:185/P 140). It is clear that Hegel understands this moral feeling as an immediacy that becomes disrupted by a casuistry that dictates how we ought to feel. Hegel writes, "we are supposed to feel more grief at the death of our relatives than we ever really do, and the external signs of this feeling are governed not so much by what we really feel, as by what we are supposed to feel, and in this matter convention has even gone so far as to fix the feeling's strength and duration" (W 1:183/P 139, translation altered). Even if it does not manifest itself in hair shirts and ritual self-flagellation, the ascetic church works to strip feelings of their natural quality. Hegel makes the point that the very idea of a commanded feeling is contradictory precisely because of the immediacy of feelings (see W 1:184/P 140). The effect of this contradictory injunction on the subject whose "natural" instincts have been turned against him- or herself is not merely self-division, but a much more radical kind of self-deception. A structural analogy can be drawn between the effects of external and internal positivity: the destruction that comes with the colonization of foreign lands by the externalized positive drive mirrors the kind of civil war, the anarchy of the senses, that is produced when it is internalized. The perverse logic of colonial self-justification mirrors the self-deception that takes one's own feelings as actually corresponding to those prescribed by the church. While it is possible that these artificial feelings—manufactured, as Hegel writes, in a "spiritual hothouse" [*geistliche Treibhaus*]—may instill a sense of ease, it is a false, unstable tranquility because it is not grounded in "true and natural feeling" (W 1:185/P 140). One can glimpse the way in which Hegel understands the concrete manifestation of this divided consciousness when he describes the feelings that are denied by the asceticism of the modern Christian church as those of the ordinary man. The everyday life of trade and commerce is severed from the spiritual self that appears on Sunday, and the culmination of this separation is the utter lack of exchange between these two selves: "the ordinary self goes on acting as before alongside the spiritual self and is at best dressed up by the latter with rhetorical phraseology and external gestures" (W 1:185/P 141). The divide can become so complete that it would be imprecise to level charges of hypocrisy, since this assumes a unified self that is divided into these two contradictory stances. With the false tranquility that Hegel is describing, there is simply no consciousness of the glaring contradiction that exists between what is professed on Sunday and performed during the rest of the week. When this occurs, religious rituals assume the same role as the false sacrifice of the Chinese emperor who takes his turn at the plow once a year. They act as a kind of empty release that allows everything to remain as it previously was.

This false tranquility can, however, be interrupted. Hegel allows that someone might come to recognize the self-deception obscuring the contradiction between what one ought to feel and what is actually felt. The result, however, would not be the easy satisfaction of the newly enlightened subject relieved of the burden of error. When the tranquility of misrecognition is shattered, the self, in Hegel's words, "sinks into helplessness, *Angst,* and self-distrust, a psychological state which often develops into madness" (W 1:185 / P 141, translation altered). In this instance, *Angst* arises when the self-deception of the Christian subject is recognized directly, when the two aspects of the self and their discontinuity are exposed as such. Yet it can also occur when religious aspirations become dominant at the exclusion of everything else. In this case, the false tranquility is shattered by the awareness that one's feelings always fall short of the heights that are required of them, despite one's best efforts and intentions. In the religious realm, when natural feelings have been uprooted, there is no proper measure by which to orient oneself. One is, in effect, always already guilty. This unhappy consciousness is left in a state devoid of strength and resolve; the only refuge left is submission to the mercy of God. But as a *measure,* this is a desperate one. As Hegel writes, "It takes only a slight increase in the tension [*Spannung*] of the imagination to turn this condition too into frenzied madness" (ibid., translation altered). This refuge is a product of the imagination and is at the same time threatened *by* the imagination. The fulfilled Christian Idea takes the concrete shape of the madness of fanaticism, and, if the Christian subject snaps, it is the result of an excessively stimulated, "overly tense" imagination.

The intimate connection between imagination, art, and Idea is evident in a short fragment that Herman Nohl includes among Hegel's early "Entwürfe." While in Bern, Hegel wrote the following remark:

> The pious Christian who dedicates himself to his ideal [*Ideal*] is a mystical fanatic. If his ideal fills him to the exclusion of all else, if he can not divide his energies between this and his secular life, if all strength goes in one direction, a Mme de Guyon will be the result [that is, a mysticism of extreme quietism]—The need to contemplate the ideal will satisfy the overly-tense imagination [*überspannte Einbildungskraft*], and even the senses will exert their rights; examples are the countless nuns and monks who dallied with Jesus and dreamed of embracing him. (N 366)[31]

These observations follow an excerpt that Hegel made from German Jacobin Georg Forster about ancient and modern art. In his comments on this excerpt, Hegel's central point is to draw out the concrete consequences that follow from these different Ideas. He writes, in conclusion, "The idea of the [ancient Greek] Republican is of the sort that enables his noblest energies to find satisfaction in true labor, while that of the fanatic is a mere figment of the imagination" (ibid.). Hegel does not comment on how Greek art functions in relation to this republican Idea; still less does he consider how tragic narratives in particular might have functioned in this context. Nevertheless, Hegel's account of the *Angst* that greets the recognition of the truth of a positivist existence (rather than the experience of *Angst* that arises from the idea of religion) provides perhaps the most direct evidence of his tragic sensibility as it is found in the *Positivity.* A clear-eyed, enlightened gaze is simply not enough to break the spell of positivity and then reorient oneself once this demystification has occurred. Beyond the limitation of the power of reflective thinking, we can glimpse in this the need for the imagination to assume a position other than reason's understudy.

Given this, Hegel's analyses in the *Positivity* lead to the conclusion that the imagination provides the stage and setting without which reason could not perform (at least in his own time). Hegel might continue to maintain that a true religion is one based on pure morality, a morality grounded in the commands of pure practical reason and the autonomy of the will; and he does claim, as I have stressed, that the "sole moral motive, respect [*Achtung*] for the law, can be aroused in a subject in whom the law is itself the legislator" (W 1:188/P 144). *Yet,* with an eye to the historical situation, when the imagination has been terrorized in the way that Hegel describes, it leaves such an impression that cogent reasoning alone cannot reverse it, precisely because the educational regime that wields the imagination in this way takes aim at the faculty of reason itself. Even if the imagination is not controlled through fear outright, it is blunted through brute repetition. Asceticism reduces education to rote learning, which instills a sense of "anxious scrupulosity" (*Ängstlichkeit und Vorsicht*) and obedience, rather than the virtues of "courage, resolve, strength" (W 1:181/P 137). Ultimately, the manipulation of the imagination is instrumental in producing a politics of domination and despotism:

> The church has taught men to despise civil and political freedom as dung [*Kot*] in comparison with heavenly blessings and the enjoyment of eternal life. Just as a lack of the means to satisfy physical needs robs us, as animals, of life, so too, if we are robbed of the power to enjoy freedom of mind, our reason dies, and once we are in that position we no more feel the lack of it or a longing for it than the dead body longs for food and drink. (W 1:182/P 138)

An education that makes of this world a wasteland has not only banished the question of freedom but also produced a situation in which the question itself has been forgotten. Through its method of education, the church enslaves rather than frees its citizens.

Reason is not enough to recover from the "trauma" of positivity, for such a recovery requires revamping precisely what caused the damage, namely, the imagination. But would the imagination be necessary even if this trauma had not occurred? If so, would it simply assume the role of a pedagogical tool in the service of reason, or is the imagination so intimately connected to reason that the latter is *always* rendered powerless without it? And, finally, is this trauma unique to Christianity, or is it, in fact, constitutive of *reasoning* itself? If the latter were the case, the trauma of separation would not be caused by the imagination per se, but it could potentially help resolve it.

A German Theseus?

Hegel argues in the *Positivity* that the power of the imagination to control through fear leads to the suppression of reason and, ultimately, to resignation. How, then, can it be rehabilitated and used to form a social unity that embodies freedom? While Hegel's initial account of the rise of positivity in Christianity is dominated by the figure of Kant, the Greeks take center stage when Hegel turns explicitly to the imagination as a necessary correlate to *Vernunft*—necessary, that is, given the times and the history that gave rise to them. This is Hegel's focus in the fragment *Jedes Volk hat ihm eigene Gegendstände,* written in 1796, a short while after the *Positivity,* and it can be interpreted as a shift in emphasis to what he calls the second moment of a *Volksreligion* in *Religion ist eine . . .* (W 1:145).[32] If the Greek Idea of freedom is one that Hegel shares, the Greeks in conjunction with the mytho-poetic images that he ascribes to them assume the place of Hegel's Ideal.[33] At once religious and political, these images filled "[Greek] souls with great resolve on festal occasions" and animated the "sacred groves where these deities drew nearer to them" (W 1:197/P 146).[34] Hegel's lament is that, while Christianity has succeeded in controlling young minds through fear, it is unable to provide the kind of genuine religious and political festivals that might spark the imagination rather than terrorize it. Instead, Christianity has

> emptied Valhalla, felled the sacred groves, extirpated the national imagery as a shameful superstition, as a devilish poison, and given us instead the imagery of a nation whose climate, law, culture and interests are strange to us and whose history has no connection whatever with our own. A David or Solomon lives in our popular imagination, but our country's own heroes slumber in learned history books, and, for scholars who write them, Alexander or Caesar is as interesting as the story of Charlemagne or Frederick Barbarossa. What heroes could we have had, we who were never a nation? (Ibid.)

Unlike Hegel's contemporary world, where class differences are reflected in the different figures that animate the imagination of the upper classes and the common people, all Athenian inhabitants—rich, poor, and enslaved—were aware of who Oedipus was when "Sophocles or Euripides brought him out on stage" (W 1:199/P 148). And, as Hegel writes, "Anyone who did not know the history of the city, the culture, and the laws of Athens could almost have learned them from the festivals if he had lived a year within its gates" (W 1:199/P 147). The Athenian imagination was unified in this way by the tragedians, just as Shakespeare gave the material for a national imagination to the English. Hegel develops this line of thinking in "The Religion of Art" section of the *Phenomenology* when he presents epic poetry as the precondition of tragedy. The Homeric epics functioned, in part, to draw together the distinct and often-warring city-states of the Greek world. The implication is that what unites a people as a people, as an ethnicity, is neither blood nor a common language (nor, in the *Phenomenology,* Kantian practical reasoning). It is, instead, a narrative of how they came to be a people through a "common undertaking" (PdG 474/PS 439). The rhapsode's retelling of the *Illiad* and the *Odyssey* worked to unite the Greeks as Greeks, and not merely as Thebans, Athenian, and Spartans. Thus, a common history of the archaic past unites the Greeks in the present.[35] As part of Greek religious life, the tragic performances helped provide the imaginative substance necessary to unify a people as a people, for, of course, they use much of the same raw material found in epics. Tragedies, however, also come to play a protophilosophical role in that they present the conflicts and contradictions inherent in the *polis.*

The construction of a unified and unifying collective imagination had not occurred in Hegel's own culture; for this reason, he could claim that the Germans were never "*eine Nation*" (W 1:197/P 146). It is not even certain they are a "people." As he writes, "every people [*Volk*] has its own imagery, its gods, angels, devils, or saints" (ibid.); but, beyond these "creatures," the collective imagination of a people, especially a *free* people, can also be populated by the ancient political heroes, founders, and liberators of their state. These heroes must be remembered and linked with "public festivals, national games, with many of the state's domestic institutions or foreign affairs, with well-known houses and districts, with public memorials and temples" (W 1:197/P 145–146). A "people" either has its own religion and polity, or it can make "wholly its own any part of the religion and culture it has acquired from foreign nations" (W 1:197/P 146). Yet Hegel's concern is that the Germans lack precisely the kind of indigenous or appropriated imagery that populates the collective imagination of a people. In light of this, those who were never a nation must ask, as Hegel does, "[W]ho could be our Theseus, who founded a state [*Staat*] and was its legislator? Where are our Harmodius and Aristogiton to whom we could sing scolia as the liberators of our land?" (ibid.).

This tells us something about the content of a unified imagination. The heroes of the Athenian democracy are its mythic founders and more recent tyrannicides. Whether there was an actual historical figure who existed behind the mythic account of Theseus is, it seems, of little concern. As the person who is said to have brought about the unification of the different Attic communities into one state, he clearly represents a point of origin; as such, he functions, or the act of recollecting him functions, to maintain the unity of the Athenian *polis.* Harmodius and

Aristogiton certainly existed at the level of historical record, but they too exemplify the often tenuous link between historical fact and the kind of political mythologizing that Hegel evokes. While the two did manage to kill Hippias's brother Hipparchus, the tyrant himself survived the assassination attempt. Nevertheless, they came to be honored to such an extent that they continued to receive credit for ending tyrannical rule in Athens, despite the attempts made by both Herodotus and Thucydides to attribute the expulsion of Hippias to its proper source, the Alcmaeonidae and Spartans.[36]

When Hegel asks about a German Theseus, he is looking backward and forward at once. He looks back to Greece as an example of a unified *polis* that is related to the present by way of a still vague historical, if not mythic, narrative.[37] As for a specifically *German* Theseus, he offers local possibilities from its more recent history, namely, Martin Luther and those who fought in the Reformation. However, according to Hegel, these events failed to operate as a unifying force, for, in stark contrast to the kind of festivals celebrated in Greece, they have only ever been memorialized by tedious sermons and somber readings of the Augsburg Confession. One could argue that Luther's rise was largely conditioned on assigning to *Jesus* the role of Theseus.[38] This is a strategy that we will see Hegel employ in *The Spirit of Christianity* when he scripts Jesus as a tragic hero. In the *Positivity,* however, he argues against the efficacy of employing an "oriental" founding father. He maintains that far from offering potential material for a national imagination, Christianity has destroyed the native resources—Valhalla has been emptied, the national gods conquered—that are necessary to *sustain* the achievements of a Theseus.[39]

The paucity of local material forces the question of a *future* Theseus. To what extent is Hegel also looking *forward* to the one who will bring Germany its unity and law? (This anticipatory perspective could itself be read as anticipating, at the national level, the final lines of the "The Oldest Program": "a higher spirit, sent from heaven, will have to found this new religion among us; it will be the very last and the grandest of humanity's works" [OP 13]). To ask about a future Theseus is to ask about the initial conditions that allowed for the achievements attributed to the original Theseus. There can be little doubt that Hegel is looking ahead to a future transformation of the present, for his very concern with the relation between reason and imagination is grounded in this. His position appears to be that any possibility of future change, any possible success of a future lawgiver, depends on a proper imaginative "infrastructure." What is needed is the kind of secret revolution that prepares the way for this political change. The necessity for this can be gleaned from Hegel's claim that, without a stock of native images, it becomes "totally impossible to . . . refine the imagination and sensibility of the common people" (W 1:198 / P 147). And, for Hegel, the *lack* of this unified imagination has accompanied the reign of autocracy in Germany: "The wars which have engulfed millions of Germans were wars waged by princes out of ambition or for their own independence; the people were only tools, and even if they fought with rage and exasperation, they still could only ask in the end, 'Why?' or 'What have we gained?'" (W 1:198/P 146). But if the dilemma facing the nonnation of Germany is the lack of a native mythology, how is one to be attained? This is ultimately to ask how a *people* is created. Hegel allows that a people must either have its own religion and polity, *or* it must be able to appropriate wholly what it has received from other nations.[40] Can the mythology of a people—the content of its imaginary—be *appropriated?* The problem facing Socrates' friends of effecting an original repetition of originality now returns at the communal level. If the condition for Socrates' friends becoming philosophers in their own right was the free republic they inhabited, how is this free political organization originally established? Does it depend on the revolutionary gesture of relegating the entirety of the past to the status of a dream? At the very least, we know that the project of the self-production of the self must make use of the art of myth-making.

Hegel both praises the Greeks for the unifying power of their artistic production and criticizes his contemporaries for submission to a mythology born of what he calls the "Orient." Is the point of contention, then, the submission to *any* nonindigenous mythology, in this case, that of Judea? If the danger is imposing foreign images, surely an equally submissive appropriation of Greek mythology would warrant similar condemnation. Since archipelagos and olive groves are as foreign to the German landscape as deserts and plane trees, is there something beyond the concrete imagery that makes one mythology more worthy of appropriation than another? Is Hegel praising, uniformly, the revolutionary gesture of indigenous self-formation that we can apparently find at the outset of both the Greek and Jewish traditions—and perhaps in the life of Jesus as well? Or beyond this crucial gesture, is it the case that by virtue of its *content,* one culture is worthy of imitation while another is not?

Excursus on Hölderlin's *Death of Empedocles*

Hegel shared the questions of historical appropriation and the proper relation between ancient Greece and modernity with his friend Hölderlin. The poet's unfinished play *The Death of Empedocles* was modeled on Greek tragedy, and it can be read as an attempt to shape the kind of new, unifying mythology that Hegel thought was absent from the contemporary German social and political world. As such, it works well as a foil to Hegel's own analyses of these same issues. I will return periodically to Hölderlin's tragedy, as well as the theoretical texts that he wrote concerning tragedy, to understand Hegel's own project better.

For some three years, roughly a quarter of his most fertile writing life, Hölderlin was engaged in writing a modern tragedy based on the philosopher-poet-physician Empedocles.[41] Why would a late eighteenth-century Swabian poet choose Empedocles as the subject for such an endeavor? In a short, dense theoretical text titled *Die Tragische Ode . . .*, written in the summer of 1799 (it is also known as *Der Grund zum Empedokles*), Hölderlin attempts to explain the relation of the subject matter of his tragedy to the present: the tragic drama is meant to express the poet's experience of "a more profound intensity [*die tiefste Innigkeit*], a more infinite divinity" (FH 1:866).[42] His answer is that the poet's experience can only be presented by translating it into a foreign context—in this case, fifth-century BCE Agrigentum:

> A different world, foreign surroundings and characters are called for, and yet, as with every likeness of a bolder sort, all these things must be adapted to the underlying material [*Grundstoff*] all the more intensely; they are heterogeneous only in the extrinsic configuration, for if this intense affinity of the likeness to the material, that is, the characteristic intensity that lies at the basis of the image, were not visible its displacement or foreign configuration could not itself be explained. (Ibid.)[43]

By expressing, and protecting, his own *tiefste Innigkeit* through the life of Empedocles, Hölderlin is inscribing what is very much a religious sentiment into a non-Christian context (although it would be more accurate to say that it is something that cannot be judged according to the opposition of the secular and religious).

On this point, there is a risk of misinterpretation. Hölderlin is certainly not driven by the intention of presenting his own most intense experience of the unity of subject and object as the ground of a religious movement that he intends to construct. Rather, the poet-playwright assumes a position that is both Greek and fundamentally "modern" at once. The divine is made to speak through the words of the poet, and these are always up for revision. Hölderlin is a "modern" to the extent that the point of reference is to an opposition between subject and object, something he cannot simply ignore. Yet the material through which this is to be presented is decidedly not modern. Pre-Socratic Greece is foreign but not otherworldly. The foreign character of the raw material raises the question of why a nonindigenous text like the Old Testament cannot work in a similar manner to Empedocles' Agrigentum. Is it not foreign enough to late eighteenth-century Swabia as a result of the historical prevalence of Christianity?

Truth for the Imagination

The central position that Hölderlin affords to subjective experience in his theory of historical and poetic appropriation is also obliquely present in Hegel's own engagement with this issue. It arises in the role that Greek mythology plays in his contemporary world. Despite the dominance of the Judeo-Christian tradition, Hegel acknowledges the seductiveness of the Greek myths to certain educated people in his society, and this reveals how the ideas represented by these myths are more "self-sufficient," which is to say, "more independent of the intellect [*Verstand*]" (W 1:200 / P 148–149). Hegel's point is that the *significance* of these mythic images and narratives rests in the self-sufficiency that they embody, but, because they come from such a foreign time and place, they would seem, from the perspective of *Verstand,* to have only a limited and ultimately superficial connection to present concerns. However, the fact that they are *enjoyed* by this educated class shows at least an intuitive, imaginative leap beyond the limits of the modern intellect. There were those like Friedrich Gottlieb Klopstock, by contrast, who rejected the attempt to find an origin for contemporary German mythology in Greece ("Is Achaea, then, the Teuton's fatherland?" he asks). Yet, for Hegel, Teutonic mythology is as distant as that of Ossian or India. Furthermore, as presented by Klopstock, any "native" mythology has been so thoroughly infused with the catechism that it leads Hegel to echo Klopstock's own criticism of a return to Greece: "Is Judaea, then, the Teutons' fatherland?" (W 1:200 / P 149)

The emphasis on the "native" stems from Hegel's view that the imagination is drawn to solidity. This sense of solidity is provided by reference to familiar places. What captivates the imagination is the kind of localized mythologies the Athenians created for themselves. This is the source of the unity that Hegel attributes to the Greek imagination. As for the Bible, what is properly called "history"—that is, for Hegel, much of the Old Testament—provides the potential raw material that might be appropriated as content for the popular imagination. The New Testament, by contrast, is a text that it is "strictly our duty to believe" (W 1:201 / P 150), a curious remark, given his discussion concerning the inherent freedom of belief. Is *eine Glaubenspflicht,* a duty to believe, imposed by reason? Is it a *moral* obligation or *religious* duty that Hegel assumes by freely submitting to the order of the church? Does the object of belief in this case mean the Resurrection? In any event, it is not fodder for the imagination. From Hegel's perspective, the New Testament will stand up to intellectual scrutiny. The Enlightenment intellect will find in the New Testament a narrativized form of what it finds in itself. This is not the case with the Old Testament, despite its "occasional references to universal human nature" (ibid.). The New Testament is not the historical saga of a people in the way that the Old Testament and Greek religious texts are. It lacks this epic quality. The Old Testament *as history* is, however, too foreign. It not only fails to seize the popular European imagination of the late eighteenth century, but it is also unable to satisfy those who are beginning to reach a level of consciousness that demands universality. From the latter perspective, that of the modern *Verstand,* the Old Testament is read purely as edification. From this Enlightenment perspective, the imagination is *necessary* solely in order that the "vulgar" can be accommodated. The Old Testament aids those with a "holy simplicity" (*heilige Einfalt,* ibid.), those who accept that everything it describes could have been experienced as such (that is, a literal understanding). It is also useful to those who do not stoop to judging this kind of material from the perspective of *Verstand,* but judge it only in terms of what Hegel calls its *truth for the imagination.* One can begin to grasp this appeal to a form of truth that exceeds the universality of *Verstand* if one recalls that both *Vernunft* and the imagination extend beyond the thought that incessantly divides the whole into fixed, opposing terms. Works of and for the imagination, including national mythologies, are not ethical primers for children and the unenlightened; nor is their sole function to awaken in the enlightened consciousness "an obscure feeling of saintliness (because he is now occupied with ideas about God)" (W 1:202/P 151). Rather, they allow for the possibility of cultivating a unified, free nation. Establishing this ground after it has been assaulted by a long "positive" tradition requires an ability to read the Bible, or the Greek tragedies, with an eye to this imaginative truth.

In a densely written footnote, Hegel builds on these distinctions. In doing so, he goes some way toward providing a typology of the different ways in which to read a saga like that of Moses seeing God on Mount Sinai. *First,* the "ordinary Christian," the Templar in Lessing's *Nathan the Wise,* would understand Moses to have perceived God and perceived him as an *object.* Moses would have grasped God as "objective," as located in space and time. This means, in effect, that the senses and the *Verstand* alone are attributed to him. The ordinary Christian ascribes to Moses both "subjective" and "objective" truth, which is to say that Moses *thought* he saw God as an object standing before him and God really *was* an object standing before him. According to this approach, we would have to accept that everything happened in the Bible as described, and we would, thus, be confronted with the problem that, from the perspective of *Verstand,* not all the myths found in the sacred texts of Christianity accord with the first canon of a *Volksreligion.* That is, taken literally, they do not accord with the tenets of practical reason. *Second,* the "reflective" view of Lessing's Racha is that of *Verstand* alone. This enlightened perspective denies the possibility that Moses could have actually perceived God but holds that "he stood before God wherever he stood" (W 1:201n/P 150n). Although God is not an empirical object, he is truly objective in the sense that he is always present, even when Moses is not thinking of him. If Moses were to claim that God was visibly present to him, Racha would not attribute *Sinne* and *Verstand* to Moses, but *Phantasie* alone. A *third* and final view reads the story of Moses in terms of its *truth for the imagination.* There is no equivalent to be found for this in *Nathan* because, as Hegel claims in the *Religion ist eine . . .* (see W 1:21–22), Lessing's text exemplifies the Enlightenment logic of *Verstand.* The different characters in the play portray (*darstellen,* W 1:21) these various religious principles in their purity; but, as we know, *Verstand* does not put principles into action, but only takes orders.[44] This third way of reading the saga does not do so in terms of discursive, theological principles. It holds that Moses *felt* the presence of God, and this feeling is *true,* in the same way that *whatever* we feel is subjectively true. From this perspective, Moses makes no dogmatic assertions about the existential quality of God. In the moment that Moses feels God, God is present to him, but, otherwise, he is not. His subjective feeling of the presence of God is, at the same time, the momentary "objective" presence of God. Subject and object unite, although within the larger subjective context of feeling. This same unity is found between the reader and the text. The text-object opens with perfect transparency to the reader-subject, or, as Hegel writes, "the *spirit* of Moses speaks directly to his *spirit;* it is revealed to him" (W 1:201n/P 150n, emphasis added). This third interpretation follows the logic of *Vernunft* because, when the reader learns of Moses' experience, he or she is not presented with a new ontological truth. Rather, the subjective experience of Moses is grasped only because it corresponds with something already present in the reader: a similar feeling of the presence of God. This is conveyed through the imaginative elements of the story, the image of the burning bush, which both locates Moses' encounter at a particular place and conveys the intensity of the presence of God to the reader.[45]

Imaginative readers are not concerned with the objectivity of the events of the Old Testament, but rather with the way in which they satisfy our imaginations. By describing this typology of reading, Hegel is, in effect, describing the manner in which Greek culture ought to be appropriated. He writes of Shakespeare that he "delineates his characters so truly that, quite apart from the fact that many of them are familiar historical figures, they have been deeply impressed on the English people and have formed for them a group of imaginative pictures that are wholly their own" (W 1:199/P 148). Shakespeare read the history of Rome with an eye to its truth for the imagination. Surely, for Hegel, the tragedians appropriated their own mythological tradition with this same eye, and this is the way that Greek literature must be read as well.

The religious sagas of the Greeks were, as Hegel writes, "almost exclusively for the purpose of having gods to whom they could devote their gratitude, build altars, and offer sacrifices" (W 1:202/P 151). This has to be understood in direct contrast to the modern approach to sacred history, which attempts to uncover, among a myriad of other things, the source of moral truths. But as Hegel points out, "discovering" these truths is, in practice, simply a matter of reading a previously held moral view back into the myth. The effect of this nonimaginative reading is unappetizing: misconceived holy zeal, a pious pride in one's edifying contemplation of God, and, ultimately, "lethargic submission" (ibid.). The degree to which Hegel admires the Greeks' nonmoralistic views of the gods is revealed in the way he ridicules the sense of self-satisfaction that Christians achieve when they compare themselves to the "heathens." This is a self-satisfaction that is coupled with a patronizing concern for the despair that the heathens must experience because their religion denies them both the promise of forgiveness and faith in a wise and benign providence. Such a thorough misunderstanding of the "heathen" Greeks is clearly born of *non*imaginative reading. The absurdity of the Greek gods cavorting in heaven and on earth is also an easy target for Enlightenment mockery; but to this Hegel counters, in no uncertain terms, that "the heathens too had understanding [*Verstand*], and that in everything great, beautiful, noble, and free they are so far our superiors that we can hardly make them our examples but must rather look up to them as a different species at whose achievements we can only marvel" (W 1:204/P 153). The concrete evidence of these achievements is found in their political life. Hegel states his thesis in this regard bluntly: "Greek and Roman religion was a religion for free peoples only" (W 1:204/P 154). It is of no use to those states that have been conquered and that no longer obey laws that they have given to themselves.

Hegel's presentation of Greece is a challenge to the easy moralism of the Christianity of his day, for, if the Greeks lacked the comforts that modern religion provides, they had no need for them. The needs fulfilled by the Christian faith, as well as the postulates of pure practical reason, stem from the separation between reason and sensibility, thought and being, mind and nature, and this is precisely what, for Hegel, did not exist in Greece. The unity that he finds there—the absence of a will turned against itself—is intimately related to their gods being less than benign and thus *worthy* of blame for our mortal sufferings. As Nietzsche remarks in *On the Genealogy of Morals,* "For the longest time these Greeks used their gods precisely so as to ward off the 'bad conscience,' so as to be able to rejoice in their freedom of soul. . . . In this way the gods served in those days to justify man to a certain extent even in his wickedness, they served as the originator of evil—in those days they took upon themselves, not the punishment but, what is *nobler,* the guilt."[46]

The Flight of the Gods and the Loss of Immanence

The guiding question of the *Positivity* proper is that of how the religious tradition founded in Jesus's name came to betray his moral teachings. "Imaginative reading," as Hegel presents it, works in the service, ultimately, of revitalizing the moribund sociopolitical world that has been shaped so fundamentally by this tradition. It works, that is, to reveal the vitality harbored in distant but foundational cultures like that of Greece. While this vitality is conceived in terms of morality, it also has the protospeculative quality of uniting the divide between rationality and sensibility, a divide that, for Hegel, defines the contemporary world. Grasping the source of this vitality through imaginative reading promises insight into how best to confront this present divide. Grasping what takes place when this vitality is *lost* will also help confront this divide, for Christianity in its inception was one response to a loss of this kind.

In the fragment that we have been considering (*Jedes Volk hat ihm eigene Gegendstände*), Hegel addresses the question of how the sacred status and joy once found in the "heathen" festivals of the Greeks were lost, how the faith in gods that had woven itself so thoroughly into the fabric of social life could be torn from it. I have shown how Hegel explains the disruption of Greek *political* unity in terms of the class conflict that comes as the result of its economic expansion and success. Hegel is not, however, a thoroughgoing materialist. What is the source of the flight of the gods, the disappearing of belief, the ruination of temples, altars, and rites of worship? Hegel continues to afford a prominent place to concrete political realities and relations of domination when explaining both the flight of the Greek gods and what comes after they have gone. Yet he also describes the way in which this flight corresponds to the separation born of the development of self-consciousness. The degree to which the rites and festivals of native Greek religions shaped the social and political customs, and, ultimately, the very instincts that defined the times, attests to the truly rending force at the heart of this transformation. When the pagan gods leave, *immanence,* the quality of a religion that fulfilled the imagination and heart of its adherents, is lost.

Before their flight, the Greek gods' domain was nature and their work was characterized by strong passions. They offered counsel as a gift but did not impose divine commands. Thus, the mortal will was free to obey its own law, and, because of this freedom, they could set themselves over and against these "lords of nature" (W 1:205 / P 155). Hegel does not elaborate on why such a conflict would arise and what the outcome might be. By describing the Greeks' relation to their gods before their flight in terms of a portrait of freedom confronting the necessity of nature, we find Hegel approaching the terrain of what has been called the "speculative" theory of tragedy.

Peter Szondi has argued that Schelling, in his *Philosophical Letters on Dogmatism and Criticism* (1795), was the first to propose such a theory because he read Greek tragedy as, above all else, a conflict between humans and destiny.[47] Schelling's central question in this text concerned how "the reason of Greece [was] able to bear the contradictions inherent in its tragedy."[48] He understands this tragic contradiction as an *aporia* of fate and freedom: "A mortal—pushed by fate into becoming a criminal, himself fighting *against* fate, and nevertheless punished frightfully for the crime which was itself the doing of fate!"[49] This model of tragic contradiction is the *aporia* presented by the story of Oedipus. Oedipus commits crimes against the very foundation of human society, but he commits them unintentionally. He assumes the role of the exemplary tragic hero initially by struggling to outrun what fate has prescribed; he *fulfills* it when the discovery of who he is and what he has done brings him to poke out his eyes with the brooches of his dead mother. He fully adopts this role to the extent that he freely assumes the responsibility for a crime that he was fated to commit. The solution to the antagonism between freedom and necessity is found in the *dis*solution of the hero. In Sophocles' play, this comes with the blinding of Oedipus, the empty moment of self-consciousness marking the reversal in his station from king to exiled wanderer. In Schelling's interpretation, we see an illustration of a necessity of degree: the hero is at once sacrificed of necessity and freely self-sacrificing. The necessity of the sacrifice is realized only through its affirmation, so the voluntary acceptance of what cannot be controlled becomes the ultimate sign of freedom. The theory is "speculative," or philosophical, because, as Françoise Dastur writes, Schelling

> gives an interpretation of drama itself and not only, as had been the case since the *Poetics* of Aristotle, an interpretation of the cathartic effect of the representation of tragedy in the soul of the spectator. Schelling understands tragedy as the representation of a conflict between man and destiny. Tragedy shows the reconciliation of necessity and freedom, finitude and infinity, subject and object. It is then understood in terms of a dialectical phenomenon.[50]

Lacoue-Labarthe puts the point in this way: "The negative, here, converts itself into the positive; the struggle (be it ever so vain or futile) is in itself *productive*. . . . The Oedipal scenario therefore implicitly contains the speculative solution."[51]

Hegel does not explicitly defend a tragic logic of this kind in the Bern period, although when presenting the living relation that the Greeks had with their gods, he refers to *Antigone* by name: "His [a Greek's] will was free and obeyed its own laws; he knew no divine command, or, if he called the moral law a divine command, the command was nowhere given in words but ruled him invisibly (*Antigone*)" (W 1:205 / P 155). If the destruction of Cato's republic leads him to a reading of the *Phaedo* and the promise of individual immortality as a refuge beyond the state, then Sophocles' play acts as a kind of anti-*Phaedo*. The unwritten, "divine" law guiding Antigone is equated with the moral law, and Hegel refers to her conflict as simply an indication of the Greek unwillingness to submit to any external authority. *Antigone* is not presented as the conflict between two perfectly incommensurable laws. It is not seen as a dramatization of one form of *dikē* in conflict with another. Further, Hegel does not find in *Antigone* the conflict that arises with the *distancing* of the Greek consciousness from the archaic figures that populate its tragedies, a distancing without detachment that is reveled by the fact that the tragedians take great license with this archaic, religious material at the same time that they see the need to engage it in debate. In other words, *Antigone* does not give expression to that unique point where, as Jean-Pierre Vernant writes, "the human and divine levels are sufficiently distinct for them to be opposed while still appearing to be inseparable."[52] The implied fate of a clash with the gods is not overtly tragic, and it does not signal their imminent departure. Instead, Hegel cites *Antigone* in the context of a portrait of the Greeks that praises their autonomy. The freedom to set oneself against the lords of nature is interpreted as a sign that the Greeks acknowledged their right to have a will of their own. With this challenge to an absolute law, one that would be imposed by an external force, the Greeks offer, through *Antigone,* an affirmation of the Kantian prohibition against fixed symbols.

Sophocles' play, then, corresponds historically and conceptually to Greece at its republican heights, before the free, native, immemorial religion of the Greeks is usurped by a foreign one. When this usurpation takes place, the political effect is the rise of what Hegel calls a *Staatsmaschine:* associations within the society are based on mere usefulness, and rights are reduced to those of property. Only when the state becomes a means of safeguarding property alone, and when private property becomes the individual's entire world, does the full weight of mortality impose itself. The security of the individual's private property is offered at the expense of the security that the republic provided to the republican's soul when it was seen to receive immortality through the longevity of the republic itself. The loss of the specific form of immortality associated with the free state, and the decline of tragedy as religious expression, brings a new, suffocating seriousness. The individual and incomplete nature of the Greek deities exhibited human weaknesses and temptations, and this allowed the Greeks and Romans, as Hegel writes, to "tolerate the mockery of their gods on the stage, because to mock them could never be to mock holiness" (W 1:207/P 157). They could make the gods the subject of comedy precisely because holiness—the eternal (*das Ewige*) and self-subsistent (*das Selbständige*)—resided not in the gods but within themselves. The self-subsistence of a universality of this kind that was one with the universal ideal of the free republic made the very thought of looking to the gods as a measure of duty foreign and absurd.[53] When the slave in Terence's comedy *The Eunuch* justifies his actions with reference to the gods—"If Jupiter the most high does this, why should I, a manikin, not do the same"—the laughter comes because of the absurdity of the remark.[54] Christianity kills the joke. The need to posit a (moral) God as an ideal only arises with the destruction of the old democracy and the loss of the joy (*Freude;* W 1:207/P 157) once experienced by its citizens at the festivals of the city. The only ideological force that the Greek master has in justifying his superiority over a slave is his freedom and independence, and Hegel readily admits that the slave might very well have greater natural capacity and education than his lord. With the loss of freedom, this justification is lost as well, and the slave is ripe for a religion like Christianity that is adapted to his needs.[55]

The Greek versus Christian Imagination

What, then, are the needs that Christianity fulfills in the wake of the flight of the Greek gods? Given Hegel's claim that Greek religion was "a religion for free peoples only" (W 1:204/P 154), it should come as no surprise that these needs reflect the experience of the absence of freedom. Hegel draws attention in this regard to the fact that, as Christianity develops, the moral Idea could no longer be willed into existence. It became simply the object of a wish. That is, we find in a nascent form Hegel's later critique of Fichte. Or, reciprocally, we see the way in which Fichte's thought reflects this characteristic of Christianity. The correlate of positing the Idea in this way is the passivity found in the followers of Christianity. They await with monumental patience a "universal revolution" (W 1:208/P 158) to be effected by a divine being. Initially, their anticipation is intense. However, with their sense of hope continually disappointed, the future arrival of presence is deferred to a time immemorial. As the sacrifices made by Christians become more severe, compensation takes the form of the increasingly elaborate character of the object of hope. The nature of the reward comes to be adorned by everything that, as Hegel describes it, "an enthusiastic oriental imagination" (W 1:208/P 158) could fathom. What stands, then, as the difference between the Greco-Roman imagination and that of the Orient? Hegel says less about the actual content than he does about the status of what is imagined. In the case of the Christian imagination, the object hoped for, the product of the imagination, was "not a fantasy but something expected to be actual" (ibid.). By extension, the free imagination, one born of a spirit that has not been rendered passive by the promise of an afterlife, would not confuse the line that divided the products of the imagination from what could possibly become present. This difference can be explained with reference to the temporal dimension assumed by Hegel's analysis. The free citizens of Greece may imagine a transcendent future, but this future is recognized *as* a product of the imagination. Further, this imagined future does not interrupt the internal coherence of the three moments of temporality. Past, present, and future remain united through the continuity of the state. By contrast, the Christian imagination assumes a future that *does* interrupt the internal coherence of these three moments. As such, it challenges the status of what can be called the extended present—the immanent flow of past, present, and future—*as* present. By introducing a transcendent future of this kind, it initially challenges its status, but then rejects it; the result is that a product of the imagination comes to forget its origin.

The different characters of the Greek and Judeo-Christian imaginations are ultimately explained by the political situation of the people exercising their imaginations. Hegel claims, for example, that, as long as the Jewish state was able to maintain its independence, there was no need for "recourse to the expectation of a Messiah" (W 1:208/P 158). During times when the Jews were dominated, the consolation of such expectations became more attractive, although politically ineffectual. These messianic hopes were again abandoned, and they were, as Hegel notes approvingly, replaced by armed struggle. Within the pagan world, the reaction to political subjugation was not messianism, but the *lamentations* of Lucian and Longinus, as well as the *thought* of Porphyry and Iamblichus (the later assigns to God the wealth that once belonged to human beings; God then smuggles this back to humans in the form of a gift). But Hegel's strongest rebuke is reserved for the response that willingly adopts "the doctrine of the corruptness of human nature":

> For one thing, it [this doctrine] corresponded with experience; for another, it satisfied their pride by exculpating them and giving them a reason for pride even in the feeling of degradation; it gave honor to what is disgraceful, since it sanctified and perpetuated every kind of weakness by turning any possible belief in human potentialities into a sin. (W 1:209/P 159–160, translation altered)

This logic of resentment stems from the apparent increased proximity of the human to the divine that, nevertheless, conceals an inseparable distance growing between them. The pagan gods were once thought of as the animating force of nature alone, and they were confined to this domain. As they come to extend their reach, like a foreign conqueror, over "the free world of spirits" (W 1:210/P 160), they helped usher in the Christian God. But the expansion of God's domain is not a homecoming. Hegel claims that the transfer of power—indeed, the transfer of *everything* of value to God—means that all that is good comes from a transcendent God with whom we share nothing in common. It does not come from the divine within us.

This divorce means that morality is effectively cast into oblivion. For Hegel in Bern, morality is determined as the true divinity, and, when this has been stripped from the image of humanity that Christians give to themselves, the image of the divine that *reflects* this image of humanity will also lack true divinity. Excluded from the possibility of morality, human nature can only be conceived as an object of nature; thus, the image of God that is reflected back to a people that defines itself in this way will certainly be an ideal of perfection, but one that mirrors the same categories used to comprehend a natural object. That is, rather than understanding God in terms of action, God is understood theoretically, by way of the mathematical rather than dynamic categories.[56] Action severed from morality leads to the despotism that arises within Christianity as it penetrates into what Hegel calls "the upper and more corrupt classes" (W 1:210/P 160). It also leads to the slaughters committed in the name of theoretical controversies over this mathematically defined ideal of perfection. Hegel is unambiguous about the effects of interpreting God through so many theoretically determined formulas: it is a counterpart to the corruption and slavery of the human being, thus, a "manifestation of the spirit of the age" (W 1:212/P 163). The consequences of understanding God as being so distant from us is that we can hope to gain access to him only through begging or conjuring. Humans have made of themselves *and* their God a *Nicht-Ich* (ibid.).

Hegel's own response to this situation was a call for a *theoretical* attack: "It has been reserved in the main for our epoch to vindicate at least in theory the human ownership of the treasures formerly squandered on heaven" (W 1:209/P 159). Yet the strategy is endangered by a lack of certainty regarding the possibility of humanity's being able to reclaim what it has squandered. Thus, Hegel asks, "What age will have the strength to validate this right in practice and make itself its possessor?" (ibid.). This perspective stands in stark contrast to the view that the present stands as the vindication for past injustices. As I have argued, Hegel's critique of the present is not based on a negative comparison with the wealth of an imagined future harmony beyond immanent temporality. This would be to repeat the logic of Christianity that has played such a central role in the creation of his present. Given, however, that his evaluation is based on a transhistorical moral point of view (the present is found lacking when compared to the practical Idea articulated by Socrates, Jesus, and Kant), it is tempting to see Hegel as depending on what he is attacking. Yet there is already the intimation of a logic at work in Hegel's analysis that points beyond such a reliance. After describing the theoretical debates that raged over how best to subject an infinite object to ideas derived from sense-perception (origin, creation, engendering), he continues by claiming that "such a perversion [*Umkehrung*] of nature could only entail a most frightful revenge" (W 1:211/P 162). Why does the error of comprehending God according to the categories of physical objects entail revenge? Who is exacting this revenge, and what does it look like?

Turning to the last question first, God is already severed from the world's *moral* goal and becomes simply an authority used to advance the particular interests of a small group of individuals. Hegel distinguishes this, however, from a popular contemporary view of providence, a "eudaemonism" (*Glückseligkeitslehre*) that he refers to sarcastically as "a picturesque and comforting theory" (W 1:211/P 162) born of more prosperous times. The God of earlier Christianity could never sustain such a view because the situation these Christians found themselves in was far too unhappy. This unhappy consciousness, again, learns to "despise the mundane joys and earthly blessings they had to forgo and found ample compensation in heaven" (ibid.). Understood politically, the church now takes the place of both a fatherland and a free state, yet, as an institution devoid of freedom, it must compensate for this by audacious claims regarding its proximity to heaven. Thus, "heaven stood so closely to the cycle of Christian feelings that the renunciation of all joys and goods could seem no sacrifice at all, and only to those spectators of martyrdom who did not know this sense of heaven's nearness was it bound to appear extraordinary" (ibid.). For early Christians, the *agent* of revenge took the form of an objective, transcendent Being, but, when *Hegel* writes of "the perversion of nature" being "avenged," he is clearly appealing to a moral force that is neither the reassuring design of providence nor a tutelary God. There is the intimation of agency without a particular, transcendent agent. If we can understand this perversity in terms of a natural community, the "revenge" takes the form of immanent contradiction. A community of friendship cannot increase in size without, at the same time, transforming its essential quality. But this contradiction is not resolved through its intensification. As Christianity continues to expand—and thus intensify the source of the original contradiction—it gives rise to the collapse of the distinction between church and state and their accompanying rights and duties. This is what we have seen: the interests of the state are usurped by those of religious institutions, and, with this acquiescence by the state, the possibility of a genuine *complementum* of the law is undermined. The traits found in a community of friends seeking truth or moral improvement are also present in universal Christianity (the church that is now a state), but their essence becomes, as Hegel writes, "disfigured, . . . contradictory [*Widersprüchen*] and unjust" (W 1:144/P 104). The teachings of Jesus become *disfigured* because the right to choose one's authorities—an essential element of a free society—is lost. As a result, one's confessor is no longer a friend but an official, and confession itself becomes a duty, rather than something voluntary. The aim becomes *surveillance*. Positivity is internalized such that thoughts themselves become the perceived enemy.

Regardless of how one judges Hegel's later system, and his later philosophy of religion more specifically, it is difficult to deny the vehemence of his early criticisms of the suffocating, ascetic systems produced by medieval and modern Christianity. In a later emendation to the *Positivity*, circa April 1796 (W 1:187–188), he considers resistance to this asceticism in greater depth. Even after the rise of positivity has become so predominant that it seems as if human freedom has been blotted out almost entirely, there will still be those who listen to what Hegel calls "healthy common sense" and "their own hearts" (W 1:187/P 142). Resistance by Christian sects throughout the Middle and modern ages occurs because the "beautiful spark of reason" (W 1:190/P 145) proclaims in these moments that "the right to legislate for one's self, to be responsible to one's self alone for administering one's own law, is one which no one may renounce, for that would be to cease to be human altogether" (ibid., translation altered). New sects arise because certain individuals *sense* their right to legislate themselves. Nevertheless, as soon as these new sects begin to expand, it is "inevitable" that the source of the laws for the adherents of the sects is no longer freedom but ecclesiastical statutes. "This brought with it new sects once more, and so on indefinitely" (ibid.). This cycle will repeat itself as long as, from the side of the state, it improperly limits itself and either allows a dominant church to arise or goes into partnership with such a church. From the side of the church, positivity will inevitably arise if it continues to discount our faculty of reason. In this cycle, Hegel witnesses the "remarkable *fate*" (the lone appearance of *Schicksal* in the *Positivity,* W 1:189/P 144) that, while all human arts have improved with succeeding generations, human morality alone has not visibly advanced.

If the spark that incites a rupture in the reign of positivity does not catch fire, it is because "in uncivilized times, or in men born in a social class condemned to barbarism by its rulers, the principle of such a legislation was generally a fevered, wild, and disordered imagination" (W 1:190/P 145). With this reference to *eine erhitzte, verwilderte und unordentliche Phantasie,* we return to a central question that weaves its way through the *Positivity.* To effect the social, political, and religious change that Hegel envisions, one must ask if it is necessary to cultivate the opposite kind of imagination—one that is not fevered, wild, and disordered. *Or* is it the case that, as Hegel himself states, "the sole moral motive, respect for the moral law, can be aroused only in a subject in whom the law is itself the legislator, from one whose inner consciousness this law proceeds"? (W 1:189/P 144). In the *Positivity,* as we have seen, the answer is both yes and no. When the imagination has been stormed so forcefully by positive religiosity, it leaves such an impression that cogent reasoning alone cannot reverse it, and it cannot do so precisely because the regime that wields the imagination in this way takes aim at the faculty of reason itself.

> Schreckfeuer aufgesteckt auf hohen Türmen
> Die Phantasie des Träumers zu erstürmen,
> Wo des Gesetzes Fackel dunkel brennt.

[Terrifying fire blazed from the high steeples,
The dreamer's imagination stormed,
Where the torch of the law burns dim.][57]

In *The Spirit of Christianity and Its Fate,* to which I will now turn, Hegel concludes that *respect for the law* is the modern legacy of asceticism. The break with Kant is accomplished by scripting Jesus as a tragic hero, rather than an apostle of pure practical reason. The question, then, is whether the tragic affront to positivity requires the paradoxical *cultivation* of a fevered, wild, *un*cultivated imagination.

PART 2

The Spirit of Withdrawal

THREE

The Idea of Freedom as Independence

> Dialectic thought is an attempt to break through the coercion of logic by its own means. But since it must use these means, it is at every moment in danger of itself acquiring a coercive character: the ruse of reason would like to hold sway over the dialectic too.
>
> —Adorno, *Minima Moralia*

Baptismos

With *The Spirit of Christianity and Its Fate* fragments, Hegel begins again.[1] He traverses much of the same terrain as he did in *The Positivity of the Christian Religion,* but now he does so in such a way that the full force of dialectic thinking becomes evident. As we will see, when the unity of Periclean Athens, as the historical proof of the possible concrete existence of the moral law, is disrupted, a shift occurs in Hegel's thinking. This shift in thought accompanies the move to Frankfurt in January 1797 and the reunion with his friend Hölderlin, and it is expressed through a reorientation of some of the central terms I have been charting in the *Positivity:*

1. Greece, while still an ideal of *beauty,* is no longer understood primarily in terms of *moral* beauty but as an explicitly *tragic* form of it. Beauty of this kind does not belong solely to nature and life but to their demise as well.[2] I have already shown that, in the *Phenomenology of Spirit,* the pre-Socratic Greek *polis* is aligned with beauty (see the "Friendship" section in chapter 1). In Hegel's *Philosophy of History,* this alignment continues as the Greek character is described as that of "*Individuality conditioned by Beauty*" (W 12:293). More specifically, Hegel writes of the "vital freedom" of Athens and of "the spectacle of a state whose existence was essentially directed to realizing the Beautiful" (W 12:319/PH 261). In this context, the *subjective* freedom that was introduced by the Sophists—they "first introduced subjective reflection and the new doctrine that each man should act according to his own conviction" (W 12:309/PH 253)—could only manifest itself in Greece as a destructive element. Indeed, it "plunged the Greek world into ruin" (ibid.). As Hegel writes, the "perfect bloom" of Athens lasts only about sixty years (from the Per-

sian Wars [492 BCE] to the Peloponnesian War [431 BCE]), but the principle of subjective freedom, as a "germ of corruption," was "*inevitably* introduced" (W 12:323, emphasis added). Thus, the "germ" that engendered the fall of the Greek world was inherent in the idea of beautiful individuality and its self-realization (see W 12:195 / PH 239).

2. Jesus is no longer conflated with Kant but is now portrayed as a tragic hero. This point entails that the historical consequences of Jesus's doctrine can no longer be isolated from the fundamental Idea that it articulates. This is to say, Jesus and the movement founded in his name are *fated*.
3. Kant's moral philosophy is relegated to the status of positivity.

In the *Positivity,* Hegel describes historical change in general as conditioned by "a still and secret revolution in the spirit of the age" (W 1:203 / P 152). There is a kind of secret revolution in Hegel's own thought when he concludes that Christianity cannot be reduced to a pure moral core. With the insistence that Jesus's doctrine be judged *along with* its historical consequences, Hegel is not simply affirming heteronomy. There is, instead, an immanent and inevitable connection between the doctrine and its history. In *The Spirit of Christianity,* the Idea that plays itself out through the history of Christianity is still described as the fulfillment of the law, but now fulfillment takes place by way of *withdrawal* (*zurückziehen*[3]), a necessary retreat from the impurity of positive law into the full intensity of love. But this is a love that cannot sustain differentiation; ultimately, it reveals itself to be an empty interiority. Or to put this another way, the gesture of withdrawal, as the attempt to lift oneself above fate entirely, calls into being the greatest and most colossal fate. Hegel writes of *fate* that it is "the consciousness of oneself as an enemy" (W 1:346, under erasure), and the enemy of this most colossal fate is the world itself. To the extent that Hegel's investigation into the history of Christianity acts as a *warning,* it is ultimately a warning against repeating the fate born of an attempt to avoid all fate. While Hegel does not write of "absolute freedom" in these words in *The Spirit of Christianity,* the need for thinking freedom together with fate, or necessity, presents itself.[4]

The development of these two concepts—spirit and fate—measures the distance that Hegel has traveled from Bern to Frankfurt. Although it is difficult to deny a shift in tone between *The Positivity* and *The Spirit of Christianity,* the extent of the transformation in Hegel's thinking is a point of contention among those who read these texts closely, as is the extent of the influence of Hölderlin. To point to the high-water marks, Dieter Henrich claims that "before his encounter with Hölderlin in Frankfurt, Hegel was a critic of the church and a historical and political analyst with connections to the Gironde. Only in relation to Hölderlin, and by the latter's influence on him, was he to become the philosopher of the age."[5] Lukács has also argued along these lines, seeing an almost unfathomable distance between the two texts in style and logic. He writes of the "extraordinarily abrupt, unmediated, unprepared transition" occurring with the move to Frankfurt.[6] Harris is convinced by Hölderlin's "Seyn, Urtheil, Modalität" that the poet was a catalyst in Hegel's thinking on the role of *Vereinigung* and a love beyond domination and reason; he, nevertheless, rejects the interpretation of a revolution in Hegel's thought and makes the case that it develops according to an immanent progression.[7] On this point, Hamacher balances the two positions. In a reading that attempts to unsettle the possibility of any pure reconciliation of opposites, Hamacher argues that it overstates the case to say that Hölderlin's encounter with Hegel leads to an "incomprehensible rupture" in Hegel's thinking.[8] He concludes that "Hölderlin's influence on Hegel, then, however great it might have been, is reworked to such an extent in Hegel's Frankfurt texts that it no longer represents the incursion of an 'entirely different' theoretical conception, but a dialectical rupture with positions whose fragility had already been intimated."[9]

The conceptual apparatus operative in the *Positivity is* fragile. How does one think together Kantian moral philosophy and its form of Enlightenment politics with the (Greek) imperative for a unified collective imagination that makes self-reflective moral reasoning unnecessary? If these two strains—Greek and modern—simply coexist uncomfortably in the *Positivity,* Hegel attempts, in effect, to synthesize the two in *The Spirit of Christianity.*

The transformation of Hegel's interpretation of baptism is emblematic of the move from Bern to Frankfurt, from the concern with the corrosive effects of positivity on a moral religion to Christianity's fated spirit. In Matthew's gospel, the last words of the risen Jesus to his disciples amount to an expansionist call to baptize all nations, and Jesus does this from a position where he is most withdrawn from worldly demands. He says this as a ghost[10]: "Go therefore and make disciples of all nations, baptizing them in the name of the Father and of the Son and of the Holy Spirit, teaching them to observe all that I have commanded you; and lo, I am with you always, to the close of the age" (Matthew 28:19–20). In the *Positivity,* these words of the resurrected Jesus are interpreted as being very much at the heart of the inauguration of the positivist tradition within Christianity. The ritual of cleansing and rebirth is simply dismissed as a dead, "external sign" (W 1:122/P 84), a contract forced on infants who are then, as Hegel describes it, subtly coerced into confirming it when they have reached their teenage years (he is referencing certain Protestant rites). Thus, it is unambiguously a law that is externally imposed. As we have seen in the *Positivity,* the law that Jesus, as a moral teacher, introduces is both old and new, or, more accurately, it is eternal and only "new" to his own time. One can debate whether Jesus, as presented in the *Positivity,* was a reformist or revolutionary in his aims and methods, but the fulfillment of the law is not revolutionary in the sense that it does not call for the introduction of something utterly unprecedented. Instead, its fulfillment entails a rebirth into a living relation that was proclaimed in the sacred books of Judaism long before Jesus's arrival (W 1:105/SC 69) and in Kant's second *Critique* long afterward. As it is presented in *The Spirit of Christianity,* to be reborn into the "holy spirit" *is* a kind of *recollection,* but of Greek tragedy and not the moral law. As Hegel shifts to interpreting Jesus through Aeschylus and Sophocles, rather than Kant, the *effects* of his life become more properly revolutionary. Despite the reference to Greek tragedy, Jesus's life and teaching inaugurate an Ideal of subjectivity and a relation between universality and particularity that is *not* found in the Greek world. Considered retrospectively, Jesus's life stands as an inaugural moment of a distinctly *modern* subjectivity. In *The Spirit of Christianity,* however, Jesus's gesture of *rebirth* and the novel form of subjectivity that he manifests is interpreted as failing to repeat the tragic Greek precedent.

Hegel says of John the Baptist that he was "not the light [*phōs,* which Hegel equates with truth, *Wahrheit,* earlier in the text]; he only bore witness to it; he had a sense of the one whole, but it came home to his consciousness not in its purity but only in a restricted way, in specific relations. He believed in it, but his consciousness was not equivalent to life" (W 1:374/SC 258). John was not the agent of radical rebirth, and he was aware of this: "I baptize you with water; but he who is mightier than I is coming, the thong of whose sandals I am not worthy to untie; he will baptize you with the Holy Spirit and with fire" (Luke 3:16). If John only bore witness to the light, Jesus was "the light individuated as man" (W 1:384/SC 268). While a baptism of fire is the revolutionary fulfillment of John's ritual of immersion into water, Hegel, nevertheless, sees genuine value in John's practice. This comes from the natural union of experience with symbolic meaning, and it provides a figure for the reconciliation that Jesus will introduce:

> No feeling is so homogenous with the desire for the infinite, the longing [*Sehnen*] to merge into the infinite, as the desire to immerse one's self in the sea. To plunge into it is to be confronted by an alien element which at once flows round us on every side and which is felt at every point of the body. We are taken away from the world and the world from us. We are nothing but felt water which touches us where we are, and we are only where we feel it. In the sea there is no gap, no restriction, no multiplicity, nothing specific. The feeling of it is the simplest, the least broken up. (W 1:391/SC 275)

This immersion into a foreign element, as a forgetfulness of the world, is a withdrawal (*Entnehmen,* W 1:391 / SC 275) from the past in its entirety. It is the loss of self. Resurfacing, as a return from this immersion, is the rebirth into the multiplicity of the world. Hegel continues:

> After immersion a man comes up into the air again, separates himself from the water, is at once free from it and yet it still drips from him everywhere. So soon as the water leaves him, the world around him takes on specific characteristics again, and he comes back strengthened to the consciousness of multiplicity. When we look out into a cloudless sky and into the simple, shapeless, plain of an eastern horizon, we have no sense of the surrounding air, and the play of our thoughts is something different from mere gazing. In immersion there is only one feeling, there is only forgetfulness of the world, a solitude which has repelled everything, withdrawn [*entwinden*] itself from everything. The baptism of Jesus appears in Mark's account [1:9ff] as such a withdrawal [*Entnehmen*] from the entire past, as an inspiring consecration into a world in which reality floats before the new spirit in a form in which there is no distinction between reality and dream. . . . In coming out of the water he is filled with the highest inspiration [*höchste Begeisterung*], and this prevents him from remaining in the world and drives him into the wilderness. At that point the working of his spirit had not yet detached itself from the consciousness of everyday affairs. To this detachment he was fully awakened only after forty days, and thereafter he enters the world with confidence but in firm opposition to it. (W 1:391–392 / SC 275–276)

The dialectic of this progression is striking. Resurfacing from the immersion in the element of water means being reborn into a new world. The "highest inspiration" that accompanies this new spirit is figured by the heavens opening and a voice proclaiming Jesus to be the beloved Son of God. But inspiration, the immediate union of finite and infinite, also drives Jesus into the wilderness. As Jesus follows John, the fire of the desert sun follows the water of purification.

Hegel's phenomenological account of baptism exposes a logic of interruption. The immersion into undifferentiated Being is a result of being drawn to John the Baptist—or Jesus—out of the customary life of the times, and it entails the abandonment of all differentiation. The subsequent interruption, a sustained forty-day detachment from the everyday, is a trial against temptation, but, at the elemental level, it is an experience of exposure. When he returns to the world, it is in strict *opposition* to it. Hegel's description of this movement of interruption, inspiration, withdrawal, exposure, and confidence amounts to a revival of the ritual of baptism, but it also presents a fundamental problem that will come to define Christianity, namely, the divide between itself and the world. Is there an imperative to overcome this opposition, and, if so, is the fact that baptism, as Hegel describes it, leaves one alienated from the world evidence of its failure? Or is there a complementary ritual that leads the Christian self back to the world?

Hegel's answer in *The Spirit of Christianity* is that there is such an imperative. He describes a reconciliation with the world that the rituals and mythology of a religion are meant to achieve in a way that corresponds closely with "The Oldest Program": "The need to unite subject with object, to unite feeling [*Empfindung*], and feeling's demand for objects, with the intellect [*Verstand*], to unite them in something beautiful, in a god, by means of the imagination [*Phantasie*], is the supreme need of the human spirit and the urge of religion" (W 1:406/SC 289). Fulfilling this need was the great achievement of the Greeks. Their religious practices embodied a union of subject and object *in beauty;* as such, they provide the model for a *Volksreligion.* As a ritual of purification, by water and fire, we can draw a correlation between the Christian practice of baptism and the Greek tragic theater—at least as Aristotle conceives of the latter. While it goes without saying that the catharsis achieved through ancient tragedy is intimately tied to imagination and spectacle, the role that these play in Christian rites, including baptism, is less evident. In the *Phenomenology,* the move from Greek "religion of art" to early Christian "revealed religion" involves the God who was presented in the Greek tragedies removing his mask and walking off the stage and into the audience.[11] When this occurs, the former relation between spectacle and spectator is uprooted. Logically, this is a precondition for the development of Christian consciousness: the divine is not on a stage before us but walks among us instead. Yet, according to Hegel, the possibility of Christianity fulfilling the "supreme need of the human spirit and the urge of religion" in modernity depends on the character of the Christian imaginary. In the *Positivity,* we have seen the imagination terrorized. Can Christian imagery be enlisted to unite feeling and intellect in beauty? Who corresponds to Aeschylus and Sophocles in the Christian world, and through what means will they engage the imagination?

The logic inherent in Hegel's description of baptism—the interruption of the world of multiplicity through submersion, followed by an experience of undifferentiated unity that leads to a position of stark opposition—is not entirely foreign to the *Positivity.* It is prefigured in the implicit logic at play in Christianity's fall into positivity. According to the earlier text, Jesus attempts to fulfill the moral law that had become obscured in his own time, but, through the expanded influence of his name, the moral core of his message is subverted. Thus, an attack on positivity becomes the vehicle for the spread of positivity itself. In formal terms, when a position is pushed consistently to its extreme, it is transformed into its opposite. This movement, which intimates an essential characteristic of the later dialectic, follows what can be called a logic of excess. More to the point, it exhibits the logic of an excess of *fidelity.* Hegel writes of the disciples in the *Positivity,* "their ambition was to grasp and keep this doctrine [that of Jesus] faithfully and to transmit it equally faithfully to others without any addition, without letting it acquire any variations in detail by working on it themselves" (W 1:119/P 81). Taking a principle to its extreme, exhibiting an unwavering faithfulness to its letter, leads to the transformation into its opposite. The historical account that Hegel gives in the *Positivity* of the reversals that characterize the descent of Christianity into the tyranny of a positive state illustrates this logic. If the sources of this reversal are to be found in Jesus's life and doctrine, these were, however, inessential additions to the true meaning of his life and teaching. As we have seen, Hegel argues that they are concessions dictated by the "spirit of the times" (W 1:110/P 73). Jesus adopts the stance of a miracle worker and employs messianic language because he would not have been heard otherwise. If he had expressed himself in the language of pure practical reason, he would have relegated himself to the obscurity one would expect to befall a first-century laborer living in the eastern reaches of the Roman Empire. Jesus was in a double bind imposed by virtue of his relation with history, and, because Hegel attributes it to extraneous conditions, the immanent nature of the logic of this movement is left undeveloped.

In *The Positivity,* this logic of excess is not for itself. In *The Spirit of Christianity,* it is. *Fidelity* is a claim to immanence: the reversal does not come from an outside intervention. The gesture that Jesus adheres to with such fidelity is that of *withdrawal,* a gesture prefigured in the account of his baptism. One returns to the same world that was temporarily left behind with the immersion into the infinity of the sea. For Hegel, the promise of Christianity is that, through this extreme gesture of *distancing* and *passivity,* a novel form of *engagement* and *activity* will arise. Looking back from the vantage point of the later system and appealing to the central categories in the "Doctrine of Being" in the *Science of Logic,* this form of activity could be seen to hold the place of the *measure* that unites quality and quantity.[12] The measure as Nemesis or *fate* imposes itself when a position is taken to excess, and the effect is its reversal. Thus, Hegel writes in the *Encyclopaedia Logic,* "In the religious consciousness of the Greeks we find the divinity of measure represented, with special reference to the ethical order, by *Nemesis.* Nemesis involves the general notion that everything human—wealth, honor, power, and similarly joy, sorrow, etc.—has its definite measure, the transgression of which leads to undoing and ruin."[13] In the corresponding section of the *Science of Logic,* Hegel emphasizes the necessity and rigorous reversal inherent in this undoing and ruin: "Measure in its more developed, more reflected form is necessary; fate [*Schicksal*], Nemesis, was restricted in general to the specific nature of measure, namely, that what is presumptuous, what makes itself too great, too high, is reduced to the other extreme of being brought to nothing, so that the mean of measure [*die Mitte des Maßes*], mediocrity [*Mittelmäßigkeit*] is restored."[14] When presented in terms of religion and not the science of logic, the force of fate comes by way of the imagination.

What occurs with the move from Bern to Frankfurt is that the conceptual foundation of the *Positivity,* which is grounded in the fixed oppositions between morality and positivity, life and death, truth and falsity, become unhinged as the nature of each term is seen to exist only through intercourse with its opposite.[15] The movement from one extreme to the other follows the path of self-negation through strict fidelity. Yet if this appears to exhibit the form of an excessive, revolutionary logic, it is without revolutionary fulfillment. The promise that Jesus makes to fulfill the law through adhering to it is not borne out by Christianity. Hegel's description of this failure will guide my reading *The Spirit of Christianity.*[16]

A Typology of Responses to Nature's Infidelity

By beginning my reading of *The Spirit of Christianity* with Hegel's phenomenological description of baptism as a ritual of revolutionary interruption and rebirth, I am setting out from the point where the text itself concludes. *The Spirit of Christianity* beings with another event, another point of interruption. It does not begin with an image of the withdrawal of Jesus into the unity of Being but with the original diremption of nature itself. The point of pure and immediate unity is no longer Greece as it was in the *Positivity.* Fifth-century Athens does not stand as an *immediate* fixed point of beauty and freedom. Although Greece is still distinguished by these characteristics, its spirit is no longer simply given as such but is presented, to a degree, as an achievement. In their role as anti-Greeks, the Jews continue to exemplify a lack of beauty and freedom, but they are no longer presented as a static point of opposition either. In *The Spirit of Christianity,* Judaism is set in motion. While the opposition between Greeks and Jews remains, Christians are no longer the sole collective subjectivity to be represented as fluid. Hegel presents both the Greeks and the Jews as developing from a historicized essence, or Idea, that each has chosen for itself. They too have a "spirit" and a "fate." In the Bern writings, Christianity is born at a particular historical point, and the concrete doctrine that Jesus presents is developed in relation to this historical context. The positivity that arises, however, within the Christian sects leads to the formulation of an Idea of perfection that is, as Hegel writes, "extremely confused and defective" (W 1:141 / P 101). This confused Idea stands in stark contrast to the Idea of autonomy embodied in Greece. The manifestation of this Greek Idea was the gods of nature, and they were, as Hegel describes it, *confronted* by free mortal wills. Yet, in the *Positivity,* the conflict between the necessity of nature and mortal freedom was not presented as a tragic conflict (see "The Flight of the Gods and the Loss of Immanence" section in chapter 2). The descent from the unified life of the Greeks was accounted for primarily by the social disharmony that arises through material inequality. Bad decisions were made, and disharmony followed. In other words, it does not arise from within the Idea of freedom itself. When Hegel begins to make use of the tragic concept of *fate,* he is indicating that collective subjectivities can no longer be thought of as embodying immobile essences; rather, they are determined by the specific Ideas that they adopt, and their histories are, in turn, presented as the unfolding of the contradictions inherent in these Ideas.

Before turning to the immanent contradictions in the Ideas that define Greeks, Jews, and Christians, we must begin, as Hegel does, with the original birth of these Ideas out of nature's violence.[17] His account of the development of these spirits is located within the "development of the human race" as such, and this overarching history begins with a rupture in an original state of unity between human beings and nature (W 1:274/SC 182). Later in *The Spirit of Christianity,* Hegel refers to what he calls "pure life" or "being" (see, for example, W 1:372/SC 255), and it is tempting to see this as the state that existed prior to the initial rupture within nature. I will return, as Hegel does, to the question of pure life. At this point, however, it is crucial to note that the destruction of this unity throws humanity into a state of barbarism. This barbarous state is brought on, in part, by the experience of the violence of nature: "The impression made on men's hearts by the flood in the time of Noah must have been a deep distraction and it must have caused the most monstrous disbelief [*ungeheureste Unglaube*] in nature" (ibid.). But it is not a product of this violence alone. More precisely, barbarism arises because nature initially revealed itself as friendly or tranquil. Since there was an initial harmony or balance amongst its elements, when it unleashed its *indiscriminate* fury, it was seen as a betrayal. As Hegel writes, nature's force made "none of the distinctions which love might have made" (ibid.). Instead, it savaged everything. Thus, the rupture that gives rise to this barbarous state and the need for a development of the human race result from an experience of *infidelity.*

Hegel's account of this inaugural separation is brought into relief by comparing it to another description of the relation between nature and humanity. Hegel begins with a presumed unity and proceeds from there to separation. In the notes that Hölderlin wrote after translating Sophocles' *Oedipus Rex,* his *Anmerkungen zum Oedipus* (1803), he presents the *union* of God and humanity, "pure life," in this way:

> The presentation of the tragic is mainly based on this, that what is monstrous and terrible in the coupling of God and man, in the fusion of Nature with the innermost of man, so that they are one at the moment of wrath, shall be made intelligible by showing how this total fusion into one is purged by their total separation. (FH 2:315)

The object of tragedy is this limit between human beings and God. It can only be experienced through its attempted transgression, and it is made intelligible by showing how this monstrous union is purged by the radical separation of the divine and the human. The purgation, or catharsis, of this experience of transgression, coupling, and wrath is a radical separation that is expressed by *both* God and human beings as an "all-forgetting form of infidelity" (FH 2:316). As Dastur writes, "infidelity and forgetfulness [are] more profound than fidelity and memory in the sense that they institute the limit between man and the divine."[18] This *reciprocal* betrayal is absent from Hegel's account of the origin of the separation of human beings and God. While God's violent withdrawal is experienced as a betrayal, any account of *hubris* on the side of humanity is missing. And if there is a tragic moment in Hegel *qua* the relation of God and human beings, it is in their separation, not in their coupling. How, then, does Hegel conceive of the harmony that nature's monstrous infidelity interrupts? He writes that nature acts with "none of the distinctions which love might have made" (W 1:274/SC 182): did love exist prior to the unleashing of nature's devastating force? Or, in accordance with Aristophanic *erōs,* does love come only in the wake of the *interruption* of pure life?[19] Does it only make sense to speak of love as a *mending* of a preexisting divide? Is then the state of pure life something other than love, or is that which existed prior to nature's betrayal something other than pure life?

For Hegel, nature's betrayal not only spurs a "monstrous disbelief," but it also gives birth to a being that is then conceived as existing in opposition to it. John Sallis writes regarding Nietzsche's account of the origin of tragedy that this kind of monstrous opposition (*ein ungeheurer Gegensatz*), and the *monstrous* as such, is "at once natural and unnatural, a certain divergence from nature within nature."[20] The drive beyond nature to what it is not—call this "culture," "art," "human history"—arises from within nature itself. The emergence of the division between human self-consciousness and nature, subject and object, is an aberration, a monstrosity.[21] Hegel interprets the accounts of the flood in the time of Noah as providing an intimation of this rupture and betrayal, but the earliest steps leading out of barbarism and toward a state of unity with nature remain for us only in the form of "dark traces" (W 1:274/SC 182). Despite their oblique nature, the ways in which Noah, Nimrod, Deucalion, and Pyrrha respond to this monstrous infidelity provide a typology of possible responses to the need for unity necessitated by the self-division of nature. These, in turn, harbor nascent philosophical orientations. I have noted that Hegel will later write in his *Differenzschrift* essay that the need for philosophy arises as a result of the combination of a division of the whole and the recognition of this division. Reformulating this with an eye to *The Spirit of Christianity,* the need for *religion* arises when nature is revealed as hostile or foreign to us. The need, then, is to reunite the sphere of nature with that which has been alienated from it.

A first response to the violence of the flood was the attempt to *master* nature. When the whole that nature represents becomes severed, it can only be divided into Idea and reality. As a result, "the supreme unity of mastery" arises either in something "thought" (*Gedachte*) or in something "real" (*Wirklich,* W 1:275 / SC 183). Noah opts for the former, but, because it is the thought of a *being* that is used to mend the divided whole, everything else assumes the status of a thought. In other words, what *we* see, looking back to this early stage in the development out of barbarism, as merely a *thought* of unity—the God of Noah—is understood by Noah himself as a *being,* as the *real*. For Noah, his God stands above nature and ensures that all of its potentially dangerous elements can be reduced to something merely thought and, thus, mastered. The God of Noah promises that the elements will not rise up again. Nature will be subdued; there will not be another flood, as long as human beings subjugate themselves to the law. More specifically, they must not kill one another. As Hegel presents it, Noah's thought works according to the logic of exchange found in legal covenants. Human submission before God's law prohibiting homicide is offset by humanity's dominion over the natural world.

Nimrod exemplifies a second potential response to nature's betrayal. He does not turn to the *thought* of a being who contains the power to subjugate nature and who extends a certain degree of this power to human beings. Potential unity resides in human beings alone; thus, we assume in its entirety the task of making "the other realities into thoughts, i.e., to kill and master them" (W 1:276 / SC 184). What is mastered by thought is killed. That which is subject to the power of judgment—*Ur-teil*—is not united but exposed to what Hölderlin calls, in a fragment from 1795, the "original separation," *die ursprüngliche Trennung,* of subject and object.[22] Nature is subdued by our human ingenuity, and the symbol of this response is, of course, the tower that was built, according to Alexander Polyhistor, to stand above the highest point of any subsequent floods.[23] Nimrod was able to unify those who had become estranged from one another into a social order, but this unity was void of any thought of a being higher than the human being, and the outcome was despotism. Thus, Nimrod's strategy of overcoming the divide between human beings and nature through technical cunning and force determines the character of his attempt to unify a divided people as well. The Tower of Babel illustrates the futility of any attempt to heal the wound between human beings and nature through the force of will alone. The society based on these foundations will not enable Nimrod's people to revert to a "cheerful social life in which they trusted nature and one another" (ibid.). It does not "dissolve in spirit's being at home with itself everything 'positive,' everything estranged and alien."[24]

These Old Testament solutions are limited in that "both made a peace of *necessity* with the enemy [*Feind,* the figure of fate] and thus perpetuated the hostility" (W 1:276/SC 184, translation altered). Both the priority that Noah gives to thought and the priority of the human will found in Nimrod provide, at best, only a temporary truce. What, then, would a genuine peace, one where the stain of necessity is absent, entail? One can gain a clearer sense of what a freely assumed peace might look like by considering a third way of negotiating this same terrain. It should come as no surprise that the example is Greek and that Hegel describes it as exemplary of a genuine reconciliation with nature. He turns to the son of Prometheus, Deucalion, and the daughter of Epimetheus, Pyrrha, because this "more beautiful pair" (ibid.) are the only two survivors of the flood sent by Zeus to cleanse the earth of the sins of the Bronze Age.[25] In Ovid's account in the *Metamorphoses,* the flood is not simply a sign of nature's infidelity but is provoked by the wickedness of man. Nevertheless, it instills the same distrust in the son of "forethought" and daughter of "afterthought": "Yet even now our lives are scarce assured, / And still the clouds strike terror in my heart."[26] But from the position of betrayal and mistrust, Deucalion and Pyrrha do not set out to dominate the natural world in the manner of Nimrod. Prostrate before the temple of Themis, they won the pity of the goddess of law and justice with their prayers, and, thus, she revealed to them the way in which the human race could be regenerated: "The goddess, pitying, gave her answer: 'Leave / My temple, veil your heads, loosen your robes, / And cast behind you your great mother's bones.'"[27] Although, as Ovid writes, "distrust oppressed them both," they overcame this to the point of having enough trust in both the oracular word (Deucalion: "oracles are holy and will never counsel crime"[28]) and their ability to interpret it (the bones of their mother being the scattered stones of the earth) that they followed its advice. The stones they tossed behind them softened and began to assume shape with "a gentler nature's touch."[29] Hegel describes this reconciliation between nature and the human race as a union forged by *love:*

> after the flood, in their time, [Deucalion and Pyrrha] invited men once again to friendship with the world, to nature, made them forget their need and their hostility in joy and pleasure, made a peace of *love,* were the progenitors of more beautiful peoples, and made of their age the

mother of a new-born natural life which maintained its bloom of youth. (W 1:276–277/SC 185)

Once again, the Greek response to the violence of nature stands as an Idea of reconciliation against which Hegel will compare both the spirits of Judaism and Christianity. Regardless of the mythic character of this trace, what is important to note is that Hegel chooses to describe this Greek union defined by love as an achievement. The Greeks that Hegel admires neither lived in a preestablished harmony with nature nor were shielded from the hostility that it could unleash. They too experienced the force of its betrayal and were, presumably, also threatened by the most monstrous disbelief that follows in its wake.

In *The Spirit of Christianity,* then, Hegel at least considers the question of the *origin* of Greek social harmony. Yet his cursory account of this origin does not defuse the charge that he offers an idealized view of the Greeks, an idealization that exposes both a nostalgia for the beauty of a unified "natural" existence and the hidden need that is being fulfilled by this nostalgia. The charge could be raised, and it would no doubt be warranted, but I will not pursue it here.[30] Let us wait instead for Hegel to level it against himself, if only implicitly, as he comes to revise his portrayal of the Greeks. What is of interest is simply the character of Hegel's presentation of this Idea of unity and the narrative of an original unity, fall, and potential reconciliation in which it is embedded. The reconciliation with nature that the Greeks enjoy is not an immediate, unconscious one. According to Hegel, Deucalion and Pyrrha *invite* the Greeks to make peace, and it is in this peace, achieved through love, that their greater beauty lies. The relation of mastery that Hegel ascribes to both Noah and Nimrod is absent. And the beauty that he ascribes to the Greek pair is conditioned by this absence. Certainly, their interpretation of the oracle on which the repopulation of the earth depends is itself a form of mastery, but, if we are to reconcile Hegel's and Ovid's characterization of the Greek reunion of humanity and nature, then perhaps Deucalion and Pyrrha's invitation to live outside the ties of domination is a repetition of the invitation that the oracle itself is. Through the oracle, Themis opens the possibility of reconciliation, rather than one-sided mastery, because the gift of these "baffling words"[31] can only be received by shedding an oppressive distrust. The mastery of interpretation is then grounded on a prior moment of groundless trust. With this, the clouds will no longer strike terror in the hearts of Deucalion, Pyrrha, and their descendents.

The Abrahamic Tear

The inauguration of the *spirit* of Judaism is found in neither Noah nor Nimrod. Their different ways of responding to the betrayal of nature are not the same as founding a spirit or a people. A "spirit" begins as an original, groundless *choice,* whereas Noah and Nimrod were simply reacting to nature understood as a transcendent force. The spirit and history of the Jews begin, instead, with Abraham: "his [Abraham's] spirit is the unity, the soul, regulating the entire fate [*Schicksal*] of his posterity" (W 1:274/SC 182).[32] *Geschichte, Geist, Schicksal:* Hegel deploys these three interdependent terms in a precise sense that was lacking in his Bern writings, and, at the outset of the Frankfurt text, he provides a first sketch of their meaning in relation to Abraham.

Who, then, is Abraham? And in what sense can we say that the spirit he inaugurates is self-generating? His relation, in this regard, to Noah and Nimrod is ambiguous. The defining element of mastery uniting both Noah and Nimrod will also be central in Abraham, yet, as Hegel states, Abraham founds an entirely *new* spirit. Neither Noah nor Nimrod participates in it, nor, for that matter, does Abraham's own father. Spirit is not a matter of lineage. Instead, Hegel presents the spirit that Abraham initiates as a break from his family (see Genesis 12:1). He is said to prize *independence* above all else, including, most importantly, independence from "the bonds of love" that found the "beautiful" relationships of community (W 1:277/SC 185). Thus, instead of interpreting Abraham's willingness to sacrifice Isaac in terms of faith, Hegel reads it through the prism of independence. As such, it is a triumph over love: "his heart is quieted only through the certainty of the feeling that this love [for Isaac] was not so strong as to render him unable to slay his beloved son with his own hand" (W 1:279/SC 187).[33] The Greeks, then, are defined according to love, friendship, communal life, and the continuity that this entails, but Abraham, by contrast, according to mastery, independence, and rupture. Again, the contrast is not simply between the Greek and Abrahamic spirit but between Abraham and his own society. As corroboration, Hegel cites Joshua relaying the words of the God of Israel: "Your fathers lived of old beyond the Euphrates, Terah, the father of Abraham and of Nahor; and they served other gods" (Joshua 24:2). In an earlier draft of Hegel's text concerning the spirit of Judaism, he writes that Abraham, in his youth, had a relation with nature that was animated by the imagination (*Einbildungskraft*), but his renunciation of these gods led to an estrangement from nature, so that he became "a stranger on earth."[34] When Hegel refers to a community that is able to foster these kinds of beautiful relations through its religious imagination, it cannot but evoke his idea of a *Volksreligion,* and, regardless of the plausibility of this association between the religious worlds of Abraham's youth and the Greeks, it is of interest because of the way in which his account of a figure like Abraham actively disrupts a prior harmonious way of life and the imaginative landscape that helped secure this harmony.

As a figure ruled by the will to achieve complete independence and self-subsistence, Abraham could not be the spiritual descendent of Noah and Nimrod. Instead, his ancestors had to share with the Greeks an imaginative religion and the communal life that was based on it. Only in this way can Abraham be presented as making a radical break with all that he had known, and only in this way can Abraham's independence be seen to rest on a unique and determinable sacrifice. For Hegel, this sacrifice of love marks the distinct origin of the spirit of his people, yet this origin is as ambiguous as the apparent self-subsistence that it inaugurates. Despite the different incentives for their actions, the logic that Abraham embodies appears to be one that he shares with Noah and Nimrod, at least to the extent that Abraham's position assumes a strict opposition to all that is. Relations exist only between hostile entities and are, thus, defined by mastery. The difference between them lies in part in the form that mastery takes. Abraham does not presume to master nature. Instead, he remains nomadic. He maintains a relation of distance from the world and does not attempt to control it through cultivation: "With his herds Abraham wandered here and there over a boundless territory without bringing parts of it any nearer to him by cultivating and improving them" (W 1:278/SC 186, translation altered). Abraham is defined by an aloofness, a willful separation, that is distinct from direct mastery.

Unlike the Greeks who were able to achieve a genuine reconciliation with nature, Noah and Nimrod, defined by mastery, simply reach a truce with an enemy that still stands opposed to them. They make a kind of peace with nature out of necessity. Is the relation of distance that Abraham establishes also born of necessity? For Hegel, any peace that Abraham makes cannot be gained through love because his very gesture of independence is premised on its rejection. As such, any apparent peace or reconciliation that Abraham achieves will only incite further hostility. Thus, Abraham's actions have the same *effect* as Noah's necessary peace. If there is, in fact, a substantial difference between the two, if this point of origin of a spirit has not simply been arbitrarily decided, it would have to be a difference in the perceived need to achieve peace in the first place. The violence that gave rise to this need in the case of Noah was external: it was the force of nature turning on its children. Unlike Noah, Nimrod, Deucalion, and Pyrrha, Abraham is not defined by way of an externally imposed diremption from a prior unity with nature. Hegel does not understand Abraham's actions as essentially determined by nature's infidelity. Instead, Hegel makes it clear that it was not an external necessity that drove Abraham to break with the communal bonds of life and love: he "tore himself" (*reißen sich*) from his family "in order to be a wholly self-subsistent and independent man, to be an overlord himself" (W 1:277/SC 185). Hegel continues: "He did this without having injured or disowned, without grief which after a wrong or an outrage signifies love's enduring need, when love, injured indeed but not lost, goes in quest of a new fatherland in order to flourish and enjoy itself" (ibid.). Abraham's decision to tear himself away from his family, in what Hegel calls "the first act," establishes him as the progenitor of a people. If this is the case, the foundation of a spirit has the status of an origin born solely of a free action; in light of this, we can differentiate Abraham from Noah. The will to struggle against nature—to dominate it through thought and submission, as in the case of Noah, or physical force, as with Nimrod—is freedom subordinate to an external power. It is reactive since, according to Hegel's presentation, the flood comes from outside. It is not conceived as a response to the sins of the human race, which is to say that it is not an act of cleansing. For precisely this reason, it is experienced as a monstrous infidelity, and, as Hegel interprets it, this is not as much the betrayal of a prior transcendent God as it is the occasion, at least in the case of Noah, for the creation of one. With this, God is separated and made distinct from nature. Unlike the reaction to a betrayal by nature, Abraham's *act* betrays the unity that nature represents.

The independence that makes Abraham a stranger on earth determines both his spirit and his fate. Abraham's *spirit* is that of independence as a negative act of rupture. For Hegel, this spirit will appear in various forms at different points in the history of the Jews and the form it takes will depend on whether it battles its enemies or whether it succumbs through force or seduction to the will of an alien power. The *fate* of the Jews as a people is regulated by the spirit embodied in Abraham, but this fate arises at those points in their history where they submit to the "fetters of the stronger" (W 1:274/SC 182). When they confront opposing forces with arms and conflict, this is *not* designated as fate. One can see in this general way that, for Hegel, the *fate* of the Jews is *dependence.*

Moving, for the moment, from Hegel's interpretation of the history of the Jews to the fate of Hegel's own early idea of Judaism as it manifests itself in his later thought, we find that his ideas themselves turn out to be somewhat nomadic. In his *Lectures on the Philosophy of Religion,* for example, the place that Hegel assigns to Judaism varies over the decade that he offered the course (the last ten years of his life, 1821–1831). In Hegel's 1821 manuscript of the *Lectures,* Judaism—"The Religion of Sublimity"—is determined solely by its covenant, which he describes as "a bond conditional on fear and service" (LPR 2:157). As there is no conceivable relation with God, there is no immortality: "the servant [is] only a temporal being, and the servant's rewards are in time" (LPR 1:160). In the 1824 *Lectures,* Judaism is presented as the first religion of freedom. While both accounts (1821 and 1824) see the negative moment of Judaism as fear, this is understood in 1824 as the fear "of the invisible, i.e., of the absolute power" (LPR 2:442), rather than of any earthly authority. There is in this a release from all contingency and an elevation to pure thought: "Hence it [this fear] is the absolute negativity, it elevates us to the level of pure thought, which surrenders all else and has before itself nothing but this pure thought, remains this free element, wills only this. This fear of the Lord, we are then told, is the beginning of wisdom" (LPR 2:443).[35] Hegel continues, "The fear of the Lord is this absolute negativity that is the one essential aspect of freedom; it is not the bad kind of fear that is afraid of something, but the fear that lets everything go, gives everything up. . . . This fear of the Lord sublates all dependence" (LPR 2:443–444).

This is a potentially revolutionary position. In the master/slave dialectic of the *Phenomenology,* the fear of that which cannot be named is *Angst:*

> For this [the future slave] consciousness has been fearful, not of this or that particular thing or just at odd moments, but its whole being has been seized with dread [*Angst*]; for it has experienced the fear of death, the absolute Lord. In that experience it has become quite unmanned, has trembled in every fibre of its being, and everything solid and stable has been shaken to its foundations. But this pure universal movement, the absolute melting-away of everything stable, is the simple, essential nature of self-consciousness, absolute negativity, *pure being-for-self.* (PdG 134/PS 117)

The slave's intimation of mortality amounts to the experience, if not the self-conscious recognition, that the spiritual desire for recognition is empty without the preservation of our physical being. Both spiritual fulfillment (recognition) and physical well-being are needed. But the immediate effect of this experiential recognition is submission, not to the master *qua* human master but to what the master threatens—death.

In *The Spirit of Christianity,* Hegel does not presume to account for the experiential origins of Abraham's break from the past. There is no mention of *Angst.* Hegel simply describes it as being in the name of independence. While the origin of this spirit is posited as a revolutionary break with the past, its future, as a *fate,* is a return, in part, of that which was revolted against. As such, Hegel's account of the Abrahamic spirit and its distinct fate offers a preliminary way into his development in *The Spirit of Christianity* of the concepts of spirit and fate as such.

Abraham's act inaugurates an original spirit, and, as such, a point of true commencement, but he implements the principle of independence that defines this spirit *excessively.* His independence is too radical, and his fate arises as a result of this excess. Why? A nomadic existence, as the extreme extension of the will to independence, is based on separation (*Trennung*), and this becomes, in practice, an unwavering *opposition* to everything. This oppositional stance, and the logic of opposition as such, will, for Hegel, define the spirit of Abraham and its fate. Independence can be beautiful, but, when oppositional, it becomes subservient. By following the desire for independence to its extreme, that is, by exhibiting a pure fidelity to this principle, Abraham falls prey to the opposite condition. In this way, dependence is his fate: "His urge for independence was strictly an urge to dependence on something his own" (W 1:293–294/SC 201). The urges are the same: the urge to independence (the spirit) is the urge to dependence (its fate), although it is not recognized as such.

Associated with Abraham's original rejection of communal life is the rejection of the natural world, and this, too, will return as a fate. Although sustained by God as its master, nature was thought to have no part in God, and it is reduced to the status of *matter,* "a stuff, loveless, with no rights, something accursed" (W 1:280/SC 188). God and matter form a dualism that is radical in that the two share nothing in common. This radicality, however, does not define the relation of *opposition* that exists between *Abraham* and the natural world. To be *opposed* to something means existing on the same plane as that which is being opposed, so that both terms in the opposition are subordinated to the same power. As Hegel writes, "Abraham, as the opposite [*Entgegengesetzt*] of the whole world, could have had no higher mode of being than that of the other term in the opposition, and thus he likewise was supported by God" (W 1:279/SC 187). Human beings, then, are seen as existing on the same plane as matter and are, thus, separated from God in the same way. In the competition between equally subjugated opposites, Abraham's God (his Ideal) places the world under Abraham's control. While this mediated relation provides Abraham with the gift of security, "love alone was beyond his power" (W 1:279/SC 187).

This logic of spirit and fate determines Hegel's account of Christianity as well as that of Judaism, and there is a formal similarity between the fate endured by Jesus and Abraham. Both of their fates are the opposite of the intentions that shape their respective spirits. Is Jesus, in his break from the spirit of Judaism, merely repeating the break that Abraham himself enacts? Hegel's position will be that Jesus effects a repetition of the gesture of rupture, of beginning anew, but in order to instill love. The question that will help guide my reading of *The Spirit of Christianity,* then, concerns how the original act of *separation* (opposition) that establishes Abraham as the father of a spirit compares with Jesus's act of *withdrawal.*

Mastery, Imagination, and Fate

Abraham sets himself in opposition to "community," which means, for Hegel, in opposition to relationships grounded in love, whether these are understood as a communion with God, nature, or other people. The *spirit* that he inaugurates is that of freedom-as-independence, and this assumes an oppositional stance toward that from which he is independent. This oppositionality is, in turn, defined by the will to mastery. Hegel writes,

> Mastery was the only possible relationship in which Abraham could stand to the infinite world opposed to him; but he was unable himself to make this mastery actual, and it therefore remained ceded to his Ideal. He himself also stood under the domination of his Ideal, but the Idea was present in his mind, he served the Idea, and so he enjoyed the favor of his Ideal. (W 1:279/SC 187)

Abraham's Idea, then, is independence, and his Ideal is the being that conforms to this Idea. This being, however, is not Abraham himself since Abraham is unable to fulfill the Idea of mastering the world that opposes him. Thus, he assumes a being in *thought* who is able to do so, or, more accurately, Hegel understands Abraham's Ideal of mastery as being merely a thought. But if Hegel is practicing the critical use of theoretical reasoning by limiting its scope in relation to claims concerning the existence and character of God, is Abraham doing the same? Given that he is said to enjoy the favor of his Ideal, the implication is that Abraham, in serving the Idea of mastery, is unable to grasp the "subjective" origin of his Ideal. Abraham is unwittingly mastered by his own Idea of mastery.

In this discussion, Hegel is, in effect, charting the terrain of what will later go under the name of "externalization." As Lukács writes, "externalization" (*Entäusserung*) designates for Hegel in his later system, "the entire problem of the nature of objects [*Gegenständlichkeit*] in thought, nature, and in history."[36] The characterization of the objective world that arises as the fate of the Abrahamic spirit is a product of the founding Idea of this spirit, although, of course, Hegel thinks that Abraham misunderstands the status of this Idea. Abraham's "contempt for the whole world" and his own privileged status are based on his understanding of the Ideal (God as *Lord*) that he serves. In the service of his Ideal, he sacrifices all pleasure that might arise from this relation. He also sacrifices before his God all other tutelary deities and national gods. In this lies the crucial difference between the spirit of Abraham and that of Greece and Rome. There is an exclusionary gesture inherent in establishing the national gods found in Greek and Roman religion, but Hegel argues that these gods of family and nation concede the existence of other such gods and do not make an exclusive claim to what is "immeasurable" (*Unermeßliche;* W 1:280/SC 188). By contrast, "in the jealous God of Abraham and his posterity there lay the horrible claim that He alone was God and that this nation was the only one to have a god" (ibid.). From Hegel's perspective, Abraham's Ideal is only a symptom of the Idea to which he has subjected himself, as is his contempt for the whole of the material world. As Hegel's thought is increasingly oriented by his own Idea, that of the *hen kai pan,* he will see in such claims to exclusivity a blindness to the necessary dependence on what has been excluded. Abraham's stance of radical independence is freely chosen, yet his intentional act of striving for independence entails the attempt to reject what will ultimately refuse to remain in exile. Or, at least, this is what Hegel will attempt to show. The one who makes claims to exclusivity will endure the weight of what has been excluded, which is to say that what Abraham excludes will return to the very heart of the sphere of what is his own. This, again, will be his fate. As the enduring presence of what has been rejected, it takes the form of a return of the repressed, and what will return is *matter.* Thus, the pure cut is only a fiction; castration becomes circumcision. As Hamacher writes, more broadly, "The kingdom of the Jews is the kingdom of the universal fiction of castration." And he adds, the pure cut is "a fiction without which there could be no truth."[37]

Abraham founds a people through his initial act of separation, but the understanding of this act is amended, such that its origin rests not with his act but with God. That is, the Idea, which is the subjective origin of the imaginary production of the Ideal, is assumed to have objective reality; it is externalized; thus, it is seen to play a causal role in the world. For Hegel, this is the result of a confusion concerning the role of the imagination and the understanding, and it is reflected in the history of Abraham's people. Thus, when the king of Egypt succumbs to the demand of Moses to permit the departure of the Jews, this is not explained with recourse to the understanding (the king's fear) but the imagination (God intervened). The imagination places one of its creations at the origin of a causal chain, and then the role that the imagination has played is forgotten. Thus, for Hegel, the Jews are left with a false view of their liberation that denies their agency: "for the Jews a great thing was *done,* but *they* do not inaugurate it with heroic deeds of their own" (W 1:282/SC 190).[38] From the perspective of *Verstand,* Moses was a heroic figure who led his people to freedom, and, if the imagination were to be used in the service of these heroic actions, it would present these deeds in a suitable manner—Moses as the Theseus, or perhaps Solon and Lycurgus, of the Jews. In this case, the imagination would not lead to falsification. Instead, it would work in the service of *Verstand,* but in such a way that its subordinate status and the irreality of its products would not be forgotten, at least not by those who wield it.

Hegel claims, as we have seen, that the beautiful life of the Greeks, as well as that of the young Abraham and his ancestors, existed as a result of their adherence to a *Volksreligion* and the imagination that animated it, but, in these cases, the imagination does not simply function as the propagandist of the *Verstand.* The imagination works for nothing less than the deification of the image in the enjoyment of beauty—as well as the "lover's intuition" (*Anschauung der Liebe,* W 1:284/SC 192)—and this acts as an intermediary between human beings and God. To cite, again, Hegel's guiding principle in *The Spirit of Christianity:* "The need . . . to unite feeling [*Empfindung*], and feeling's demand for objects, with the intellect [*Verstand*], to unite them in something beautiful, in a god, by means of the imagination, is the supreme need of the human spirit and the urge of religion" (W 1:406/SC 289). Without the imagination as a mediating element, there would be an insurmountable distance separating the finite and infinite, and this distance is inimical to Hegel's Idea of freedom. Here, the image provides a point of focus, a directionality but, beyond this, also a concrete shape. Judaism again provides the negative illustration of this. Moses initially offered fire and smoke as an image of God, but these fail as mediating images because they offer no fixed form. The eye is kept occupied by endless transformations, but this is no more than visual sophistry. Yet, for Hegel, the problem has less to do with the *content* of the image as with the Idea that is associated with it. When Moses settles on the Holy of Holies of the Tabernacle and, ultimately, the Temple itself as this image, it is, *qua* the Jewish Idea, the perfect presentation of the insurmountable difference between human beings and God. Hegel recounts Pompey's surprise when he enters the Holy of Holies and finds nothing but an empty room. The invisibility of a God made infinite subject and, thus, untainted by any objectivity is, as such, wholly alien. As an illustration of the Idea, this contentless content is much better in this regard than the indeterminacy of fire and smoke. From Hegel's perspective, however, it cannot act as the mediation between finite and infinite because it entails the rejection of all concrete shape.

What, then, distinguishes the erroneous exercise of the imagination from its vital use? More specifically, how would the Exodus be figured in accordance with *Vernunft?* Would this be the presentation in figurative form of the mutual self-production of Jewish and Egyptian identity as a unity of self and other? Or, at the level of the Jewish fate generally, would it be the presentation of the Ideal as *both* self-produced *and* determinative of this fate? In the case of the Holy of Holies, one could argue that the imagination is not being employed erroneously but is simply being denied altogether. (In 1798, Hegel does not interpret the rejection of all concrete shape as an initial elevation to the level of pure thought, as will be the case in the 1824 version of his *Lectures on the Philosophy of Religion* [LPR 2: 443].[39]) Yet Hegel holds that an act of the imagination is responsible for giving *content* to the thing-in-itself in the form of an Idea, and it is when the origin of this Ideal is denied, or "repressed," that a fate is called forth. Thus, a mere imaginative act returns to dominate Abraham and his descendents, robbing them of the independence that drove Abraham in his founding act of separation. If the Holy of Holies is the proper presentation of a God of absolute distance, Greek *tragedy,* for Hegel, is the model for the imaginative correlate of *Vernunft*. As such, it is a presentation of beauty in division. For this reason, Jesus is figured as a tragic hero in *The Spirit of Christianity,* rather than the Kantian moralist we find in the *Life of Jesus* and the *Positivity.* The reverence appropriate to the moral law is deemed to be insufficient to traverse the distance between human beings and God. We revere only what lords over us, only what humiliates our self-conceit, and, since the aim of the beautiful image is what annuls all relationality determined by mastery, Hegel would have to say that we do not *revere* the beautiful. As Aristotle argues, the tragic hero cannot be too far removed from us, for we feel pity for someone only when he or she is sufficiently like ourselves.[40] But if Jesus is to be figured as a tragic hero, he must embody the beauty of the *Greek* tragic hero, for, as Hegel informs us, there is another kind of tragedy:

> The great tragedy of the Jewish people is no Greek tragedy; it can rouse neither fear [*Furcht*] nor pity [*Mitleid*], for both of these arise only out of the fate which follows from the inevitable slip of a beautiful character; it can arouse horror [*Abscheu*] alone. The fate of the Jewish people is the fate of Macbeth who stepped out of nature itself, clung to alien Beings, and so in their service had to trample and slay everything holy in human nature, had at last to be forsaken by his gods (since these were objects and he their slave) and be dashed to pieces on his faith itself. (W 1:297/SC 204–205)

The tragic fate of the Jews—a tragedy marked by sublimity—is that of domination by an alien law, which now means, for Hegel, that it is also the tragedy of Kantian moral philosophy.[41]

How, then, does the sublimely tragic fate of Abraham unfold? I have shown that Abraham's spirit is defined by independence as opposition and his fate is the adventure of the failed struggle against succumbing to dependence of any kind. More concretely, the fate of the founding gesture of separation is reached when this nomadic people becomes a settled, agrarian nation. Yet far from being a fulfillment, when this fate manifests itself, Hegel claims that the Jewish national *daimōn,* the spirit that unites them, continues to play itself out "all the mightier and more frightful" (W 1:287/SC 194). Why? There is a lack of fulfillment because the sublime tragedy of the Jews, in their servitude to "alien Beings," is played out as their history. Abraham's God, as the source of all activity, renders his adherents passive. The empty space of the tabernacle presents, in its emptiness, the truth of a God who is understood as the "sole infinite subject" and the "sum of all truth and all relations" (W 1:283/SC 191). This God is the "sole synthesis" and "the antitheses are the Jewish nation, on the one hand, and, on the other, the world, along with the rest of the human race" (ibid.). It would be wrong to say God's antitheses are dead, for they are, as Hegel explains, "a something only in so far as [the sole infinite subject = God] makes them something, i.e., makes them not something that *is,* but something *made* which on its own account has no life, no rights, no love" (ibid.). Indeed, this is the case whenever the Ideal takes the form of an infinite subject. The Greek figure of this is Cybele, the absolutely unknowable. As Hegel writes in a footnote, this "sublime godhead which is all that is, was, and is to be, and their veils no mortal has unveiled—her priests were castrated, unmanned in body and spirit" (W 1:283n/SC 191n). Whoever worships such a sublime god, whether they be the Jews or the priests of Cybele, are, according to Hegel, stripped of their fecundity and made—by contrast to this infinite subjectivity—"genuine pure objects" (W 1:283/SC 191). The fate of the spirit of radical independence is to be made matter. Matter denotes passivity, and it would be contradictory for a passive people to give the law to itself. The gift of the law on Sinai is only a further indication of the fact that, for the Jews, "the holy was always outside them, unseen and unfelt" (W 1:285/SC 193). The distance that the holy assumes reveals itself not only as the empty space of the Holy of Holies but also the "empty time" (W 1:286/SC 193) of a seventh day of rest, a day Hegel interprets as a day of idleness.

Empty time and space, the pure conditions of phenomenality: Hölderlin writes in his *Anmerkungen zum Oedipus* that it is precisely in the properly *tragic* moment of *der kategorische Umkehr,* the moment of categorical *reversal* or *volte-face,*[42] that is, the moment of "the utmost suffering," that "there exists nothing but the conditions of time and space" (FH 316). Deleuze translates *der kategorische Umkehr* as the "categorical abduction," and he does so in the context of an analysis of Hölderlin's privileged relation to Kantianism. As such, Deleuze effectively correlates the insurmountable opposition between God and humanity that Hegel attributes to Judaism with the opposition between the *cogito* and the empirical self:

> Rather than being concerned with what happens before and after Kant (which amounts to the same thing), we should be concerned with a precise moment within Kantianism, a furtive and explosive moment which is not even continued by Kant, much less post-Kantianism—except perhaps, by Hölderlin in the experience and the idea of a "categorical abduction." For when Kant puts rational theology in question, *in the same stroke* he introduces a kind of disequilibrium, a fissure or crack in the pure Self of the "I think," an alienation in principle, insurmountable in principle: the subject can henceforth represent its own spontaneity only as that of an Other, and in so doing invoke a mysterious coherence in the last instance which excludes its own.[43]

There is, then, the Greek tragedy that follows the slip of a beautiful character, and then there is the tragic experience of the categorical abduction and the insurmountable diremption of the self. Which form of tragedy does the life of Jesus embody? To develop an answer to this question, I will initially consider the conceptual significance of Hegel's description of the spirit and fate of Judaism, because the tragic portrayal of Jesus that he offers is ultimately framed by Jesus's relation to this spirit.

Human Nature and Its Perversion

What has Hegel given us in his account of Judaism and its history but a litany of some of the basest stereotypes leveled against the Jews? His interpretation of Judaism is clearly prejudicial, and the role that cultural and theological preconceptions play in this kind of simplification and denigration is evident.[44] His treatment is especially violent when he presumes to be accounting for the spirit of Judaism as such, and not simply a particular moment in the history of Judaism. Hegel's explanation in the *Positivity* of the imperial will that cannot tolerate those who reside outside its sphere of direct influence goes some way toward explaining the cultural basis of his own analysis.[45] To what degree, however, can we understand Hegel's position as more than simply the expression of the prejudices of his own culture? Despite his deeply reductive account of Judaism, to what degree is Hegel following the imperative of universal philosophical reason to examine all religions in light of the supreme human need for unity—"the need to unite subject with object . . . in something beautiful, in a god" (W 1:406/SC 289)?[46] Interpreting Hegel's engagement with Judaism simply in terms of Christian cultural presuppositions is complicated somewhat by the fact that it is as yet unclear what Hegel's relation to Christianity is. It is no doubt correct to say that, as in the *Positivity,* Hegel's real interest is not Judaism per se, but Christianity and its spirit, and I will turn to the way in which he presents Christianity as the attempted fulfillment of Judaism. Ultimately, his judgment is that Christianity fails in this regard and, thus, fails to fulfill the supreme need for unity in beauty. When reconstructing Hegel's analysis of this failure, however, I will focus in particular on the way that the philosophical project of which he is a part is not simply confronted by its perceived opposite (Judaism as the spirit of freedom as independence) but is responsible for its construction.

According to Hegel, before Judaism sets the stage for the arrival of Christianity, it stands as the negation of all that is embodied in the name of Greece, and this opposition is now framed in terms of two different forms of tragedy. As opposed to the beauty that grounds Greek tragedy, the "great tragedy of the Jewish people" is defined by domination and servitude. Yet Hegel's account of Judaism is not based on a negative comparison with Greece alone but is ultimately grounded in the existence of an original human essence that Greece embodies. Thus, he writes, in relation to the spirit of the Jews, "even here the honor of human nature is still partly preserved in the fact that, even if its innermost spirit is perverted and turned to hatred, human nature still does not wholly disavow its original essence [*ursprüngliche Wesen*], and its perversion [*Verkehrtheit*] is not wholly consistent, is not carried through to the end" (W 1:287/SC 194–195). This original human essence is presented as static, atemporal, and inalienable in nature. It is conceived according to the metaphysics of substance, and not the substance that is equally subject. As such, it appears at odds with the restlessness of the later Hegelian subject that succeeds in dissolving every instance "capable of coming to rest in itself and taking undivided enjoyment in its mastery and property."[47] Individual nations, or spirits, are *chosen,* even if, as in the case of Abraham, this choice comes to be concealed; but presumably the choice is either to affirm our prior nature or stray from it. Yet why exactly were the Greeks able to realize the spirit of freedom while others are not? Is it a matter of an original decision that founds a spirit, or does this apparent decision mask a deeper necessity? Although Hegel appeals to an original, universal *human* essence, does he, in the end, also assume an ahistorical essence of the Greeks and the Jews, thus, a human essence that is divided within itself?

Hegel's text is ambiguous on this point. There is an *ursprüngliches Wesen,* a necessary, universal human essence, to be found in the Greeks, Abraham's ancestors, and his descendents. At the same time, Hegel presents an essence, as spirit, that is *chosen,* and, at least in the case of Abraham, this choice is not limited by any reference to a prior conditionality. If we focus on this latter understanding of *Wesen,* and the understanding of objectivity as *Entäusserung* (externalization) that accompanies it, is it possible to escape one's fate? Given that Abraham's original separation from his ancestral community was freely assumed, is it possible to shake off the weight of objectivity born of this original act? Does Hegel allow for a return from what is most foreign—the perversion of our innermost spirit—to what is most properly our own, namely, our "original essence," or *life?* If such a return were possible, it would have to be the return of the original choice *as choice,* not simply the particular decision Abraham makes to sever all ties to his community. And this "second" choice could not be made in abstraction from the original choice that it was meant to redress. That is, its historical position *as* a return and repetition of an original choice would have to be acknowledged.

In the "Introduction" to the *Lectures on the Philosophy of World History* (*Wintersemester* 1822–1823), the essence of humanity is conceived as *freedom,* and freedom, in turn, conceived *qua* historicity. In the context of discussing the general concept of world history, Hegel writes the following: "For freedom in itself carries with it the infinite necessity of attaining consciousness—for freedom, by definition, is self-knowledge—and hence of realising itself: it is itself the end of its own operation, and the sole end of the spirit" (W 12:33/LWH 55).[48] As for the means of realizing this spirit of freedom, he states,

> what we have hitherto called the principle, or ultimate end, or destiny [*Bestimmung*], or the nature and concept of the spirit *in itself,* is purely *universal and abstract.* A principle, fundamental rule, or law is some-

> thing universal and implicit, and as such, it has not attained complete reality, however true it may be in itself. . . . In other words, that which exists only *in itself* is a possibility or potentiality which has not yet emerged into existence. A second moment is necessary before it can attain reality—that of actuation or realisation; and its principle is the will, the activity of mankind in the world at large. It is only by means of this activity that the original concepts or implicit determinations are realised and actualised. (W 12:36/LWH 69–70)

As the nature and concept of spirit, freedom *is* precisely what I have been calling a self-actualizing "essence." However, the activity of the will in the realization of the idea of freedom is always limited or one-sided, and the full extent of how an act works to realize this end can be grasped only retrospectively. The "cunning of reason" is revealed only after the fact (W 12:49/LWH 89). Although Hegel does not make use of the language of "in-itself," "for-itself," "realization," or "actualization" in *The Spirit of Christianity*, the question remains, is the philosophy of history presented in the *Lectures* operative at an inchoate level in this earlier text? Is the "original human essence" that Hegel refers to in the Frankfurt-era text *static*, or is it *self-producing*? And was this human essence already realized through the activity of the ancient Greeks, or is its realization still to come?

The status of Hegel's idea of an "original human essence" is significant to his account of the history of the Jews precisely because it is guided by the question of whether another beginning, similar in form if not content to the one that Abraham achieved, can take place. Can a second beginning be achieved that would cancel the distinct form of tragedy that Hegel attributes to their spirit, and, in doing so, can it effect a "return" to this original essence (whatever it might be)? Hegel's commentary on the history of the Jewish nation describes its attempts to overcome servility and follow the way of more "friendly *daimōnes*" (W 1:293/SC 201). With these attempts, the Jews forge relations with other peoples and simultaneously desert their spirit, which means, according to Hegel, they are unable to overcome their tragic fate. Thus, I will turn to the explanation that Hegel gives for why these attempts to follow more "friendly *daimōnes*" fail, and I will do so with the broader question of Jesus's relation to Jewish spirit and its fate in mind. Since this history is, for Hegel, leading toward the birth of Christianity, will Jesus bring about a catharsis of the horror that defines this tragic history?

When the fate of the Jews brought them into a settled relation with nature, the prosperity that followed made them amenable to serving foreign gods. Hegel describes the construction of a common life with other nations through friendship and marriage in the following idyllic way:

> Together they enjoyed the sun, together they gazed at the moon and the stars, or, when they reflected on their own feelings, they found ties and feelings in which they were united with others. Through these heavenly bodies, together with their union in them (i.e., together with the image of the feeling in which they were one), the Jews represented to themselves something living, and in this way they acquired gods. (W 1:293 / SC 201, translation altered)

When the Jews practice the imaginative religion that Hegel praises as the source of a free community, when they adopt these new gods and achieve "a more beautiful union" (ibid.), they do so at the expense of the sacrifice of their own God. This sacrifice allows for the "shaking off [*abschütteln*] of their whole fate" (W 1:292 / SC 201), and Hegel equates it with the capability of experiencing the "pure feeling" that demonstrates a return to full humanity. Yet, according to Hegel, they are only able to shake off their fate by joining temporarily in a more friendly union with others. This is the true fate of the false understanding of freedom as independence. It takes the form of an unshakeable contradiction inherent in the spirit of Abraham and the tragedy associated with it: as the Jews become "humanized"—become more Greek—"their vigor [*Kraft*] declined" (ibid.). This vigor is directed toward their independence, but this urge for independence was "an urge to dependence on something their own" (W 1:293–294 / SC 201). While Hegel allows that the Jews can reach the beautiful union characterizing the full humanity of the Greeks, it is only by betraying their God. They are free to turn away from their *daimōn*, but, at the same time, their fate ("an infinite power which they set over against themselves") will return. Hegel does not entertain the possibility of their oppression coming from the outside. Instead, the force that drives them from this beautiful union back to their prior *daimōn* is presented as a logical inevitability. Any possible reconciliation with their fate is necessarily a fleeting one. Indeed, Hegel makes a point of emphasizing the *acceleration* and *velocity* of this oscillation between the state of independence and union. Changes that would take other nations millennia are experienced with increasing rapidity, and the character of this movement is a product of excess: they are *too* opposed to nature (see W 1:294 / SC 202).

This quality of *excess* characterizing the spirit of independence shapes the unique form of tragedy that defines its fate. It is the tragedy of a fate that cannot be conquered, and it plays itself out as a violent oscillation between dependence and independence. More concretely, it is the inability to make true sacrifices. Hegel's position is based on the view that a fulfilled humanity is "realized" with the possibility of sacrificing one's life; this, in turn, is based on a possible relation with the eternal. As we saw in the *Positivity,* this relation existed for the Greeks because the eternal was nothing other than the concrete, living whole of their republic. If the Greeks were equal because "all were free and self-subsistent," the Jews are a community of equals because "all were incapable of self-subsistence" (W 1:290/SC 198).[49] All are equally dependent on an invisible ruler with whom they share nothing in common, and this lack of self-subsistence precludes everything that stands as exemplary in the Greek republic. All that is left is an economy of exchange and following the logic inherent in such an economy faithfully would make entering into military service irrational. The sacrifice that transcends this economy depends on a qualitative leap. As Hegel writes, "It is contradictory to stake *this* property and *this* existence for property and existence as such; if one thing is sacrificed for another, both must be heterogeneous—property and existence only for honor, for freedom or beauty, for something eternal. But the Jews had no share in anything eternal" (W 1:287/SC 195).[50] Hegel interprets this inability to make true sacrifices as a consequence of the false Ideal of a God defined by absolute separation, and, if the sacrifice is a necessary moment for overcoming fate, then the inability of the Jews to overcome their fate is tantamount to the tragic impossibility of returning to a universal human essence.

According to this view, then, Abraham has called forth a fate that can never be completely "shaken off." Judaism is judged according to the standard of an "original human essence" and found to be lacking. It does not "unite subject with object, to unite feeling, and feeling's demand for objects, with the intellect, to unite them in something beautiful" (W 1:406/SC 289). Against Hegel, one might object that he has erroneously elevated his Greek ideal to the status of original human essence and, in doing so, is guilty of precisely the misunderstanding that he attributes to Abraham and his descendants. That is, he has misunderstood the ontological status of his Ideal and attributed to his *image* of the Greeks the status of a being. If this is the case, then Hegel would be guilty of following a logic that posits the Jews as the source of the perversion of an original, harmonious community that never existed.

Poetic History

Tragic beauty and the unification of subject and object that is associated with it are ultimately related to sacrifice. Hegel's view is that the tragedy of the Jews, as the embodiment of the spirit of independence, is born of a perversion of human nature that precludes genuine sacrifice, and, for this reason, he denies to the Jews the status of a *Greek* tragedy. This view follows from a definition of tragedy that is framed by Aristotelean criteria, broadly conceived: only the "necessary slips" (*notwendige Fehltritt*) of a beautiful character can evoke the emotions of fear and pity (W 1:297/SC 204–205).[51] Because Hegel thinks that the Jews lack the requisite beauty, the tragedy they suffer through inspires horror, rather than fear or pity. Their fate, again, is that of Macbeth, the one "who stepped out of nature itself, clung to alien Beings, and so in their service had to trample and slay everything holy in human nature, had at last to be forsaken by his gods (since these were objects and he their slave) and be dashed to pieces on his faith itself" (W 1:297/SC 205).[52] When tragedy is conceived according to Aristotle's criteria, the failure to evoke fear and pity would seem to entail the failure of the proper aim of tragedy, namely, the catharsis of these emotions. Yet, is the tragic spectacle that evokes horror, rather than fear and pity, simply a failed tragedy, or is it a tragedy of another (modern) order? Can the audience of a spectacle of this kind experience a catharsis of *horror,* and, if *not,* what stands in the place of catharsis in the tragedy of Macbeth? Does the violent, and seemingly unending, oscillation that Hegel presents as the fate of the spirit of independence provoke *despair,* the "despair" (*Verzweiflung;* PdG 61/PS 49) that Hegel associates in the *Phenomenology of Spirit* with the loss of self that natural consciousness experiences through the unfolding of its history?[53] In the *Phenomenology,* what comes to relieve the experience of this history of despair is the philosopher's presentation of the cunning of reason that, despite appearances, structures history itself. In *The Spirit of Christianity,* what comes to relieve this seemingly unending oscillation born of the spirit of independence is Christianity. Does Hegel, then, think of Christianity as something like a catharsis of horror? Or does the relief intrinsic to this non-Greek tragedy take another form? A response to these questions has to first take into consideration the way in which Hegel understands the relation between *history* and *dramatic narrative.*[54] That is, a response must consider the fact that Hegel understands the history of a people, and *our* experience of this history, in terms of tragic, poetic categories.

Despite the cursory nature of Hegel's reference to the *Poetics,* it is clear that he is adopting Aristotle's account of tragedy as a ritual purification, or *katharmos,* of the emotions of fear and pity, and it also seems that he interprets catharsis in a "subjective" manner. This is an interpretation that emphasizes the "subjective" effect of a play (or a history) on the spectator, rather than an "objective" account that would interpret tragedy as the *mimēsis* of a catharsis that the tragic characters themselves undergo.[55] When Hegel writes that the tragedies of the Greeks rouse fear and pity, he seems to be referring to the reaction of those who observe the slips of beautiful characters on stage. Given this subjective perspective, then, who exactly is the spectator when Hegel claims that the tragedy of the Jews provokes neither fear nor pity but horror? The complexity of the question arises from the fact that the unfolding of history itself, not its poetic retelling, is presented as tragic. When Hegel structures historical analyses according to the categories of tragic theater, the action of the play, the plot or *mūthos,* would consist of objective history as such. That is, his account of the "great tragedy" of the Jews consists of the actual development of a people. Sophocles' *Oedipus Rex* is a retelling of a kind of *mythic* history, but this is not the material of the historian's narrative. According to Aristotle's explanation of these different practices, "poetry is more philosophical and more elevated than history, since poetry relates more of the universal, while history relates particulars"—history tells us what happened, while poetry presents the sort of things that happen "according to the laws of probability or necessity."[56] Given this, can we apply the categories of poetics to the discipline of history? Can we apply those categories that concern the sphere of universality to what relates particulars? Can we speak, for example, of a subject of history in the sense that today we speak of a literary hero or protagonist? (This series of questions provoked by *The Spirit of Christianity* anticipates the need for the thoroughgoing *speculative* theory of tragedy mentioned above [see the section titled "The Flight of the Gods and the Loss of Immanence," chapter 2]. That is, it points to a theory in which tragedy is not simply understood in terms of "the kathartic effect of the representation of tragedy in the soul of the spectator."[57] Instead, the idea of tragedy, in the words of Dennis Schmidt, "presents a conception of *life* as torn, conflicted, and agonized."[58])

In the sublime tragedy of the Jews, the "subject" is the Jewish people, not Abraham alone. Yet, for Hegel, a "people" is itself the development of the particular spirit founded by an originary act—that of Abraham in the case of the Jews and Jesus in the case of Christians. One can imagine a tragic poet taking the life of Abraham and Jesus as the material for a *mimēsis* that is, to use Aristotle's description, "whole" and consisting of "sufficient amplitude to allow a probable or necessary succession of particular actions to produce a change from bad to good or from good to bad fortune."[59] But the historian who is attuned to the tragic dimension of the unfolding of history is also limited by the particularity of historical events and does not have the same liberty as the poet. In effect, Hegel's conceptualization of historical unfolding in terms of "spirit" and "fate" is a hybrid of the universality of poetry and the particularity that Aristotle finds in the writings of historians. So in Hegel's Frankfurt-era account of the life of the historical Jesus, he is presented as a tragic hero and the history that he inaugurates is also conceived on the model of tragedy. Yet, Hegel does not attempt to write of Jesus as Hölderlin writes of Empedocles in *Death of Empedocles*. Obviously he does not write a play based on the life of Jesus. While Jesus is conceived according to the more universal categories of poetics, Hegel's presentation of Jesus is not a "whole" action, with, as Aristotle writes, "a beginning, middle, and end."[60]

The fragmentary character of *The Spirit of Christianity and Its Fate* precludes the possibility that his presentation of the life of Jesus will evoke the experience of catharsis as Aristotle understood it. At most, Hegel is making the case for whether certain peoples in their historical unfolding are the proper stuff of tragic narrative. But the limitations of Hegel's text aside, when is a history conceived *qua* tragic narrative capable of evoking the experience of catharsis? Can the history of a people in its down-going be recounted in such a way that it has the same effect on its readers as the plays of Sophocles had on their ancient Greek audience? And if so, *who* would experience it as such? Is it enough to say that the historical unfolding of a people is only experienced *as* tragic retrospectively? Or, returning to our earlier question, does blurring the distinction between tragic drama and the writing of history mean that the catharsis of fear and pity is experienced both "subjectively" by the viewer/reader and "objectively" by the "characters" themselves, that is, those internal to the history/play? If so, does the historian reconstruct the *cathartic experience* of a people in their role as the subject/hero of a tragic history? And can a *people* be such a subject at all? For Hegel, there is some historical material that does not provide the proper substance to provoke the tragic effect of catharsis, whether this is experienced from the perspective of those living through the history or those looking back at it. If the history of the Jews fails on this account and that of the Christians remains an open question for us, how do the *Greeks* fare *as a people?* In *The Spirit of Christianity,* Hegel does not elaborate on the history of the Greeks that he provided in the *Positivity,* but, in the *Phenomenology of Spirit,* he does conceive of a particular period of Greek history in terms of tragedy. For if one considers the hybrid of poetic universality and historical particularity found in *The Spirit of Christianity* from the perspective of the *Phenomenology,* it can be seen to anticipate the phenomenological reconstruction found in the later text. The fate of what appears to be a unified and internally coherent spirit of a people is the coming to presence of the latent contradictions that both make it what it is and lead to its demise. Shorn of the proper names "Greek," "Jew," and "Christian," this is the protodialectical unfolding of shapes of consciousness.

Hegel begins the "Spirit" chapter of the *Phenomenology* by presenting the historical shape of Greek consciousness through the lens of *Antigone.* The play presents in poetic form and through the archaic figures of Teiresias, Antigone, Ismene, Creon, and Haemon the conflicts plaguing Athens in Sophocles' own time. The "simple substance" (*einfache Substanz*) of the living ethical world of the Greeks "splits itself up into an [inwardly] distinguished ethical essence, into human and divine law" (PdG 290).[61] Antigone and Creon are the dramatic figures of these two distinct laws. Hegel states this most directly in his *Lectures on Fine Art* when he writes, "Antigone honours the bond of kinship, the gods of the underworld, while Creon honours Zeus alone, the dominating power over public life and social welfare" (W 15:544/LFA 1213). Contrary to modern tragic drama, which rests on individual will, character, and accidental circumstances, both Antigone and Creon are driven by an individual pathos that acts as an ethical justification precisely because each manifests an ethical position found in the Greek ethical substance.[62] Hegel stresses the distance of these figures from modern characters:

> The individuals animated by this "pathos" are not what we call "characters" in the modern sense of the word, but neither are they mere abstractions. They occupy a vital central position between both, because they are firm figures who simply are what they are, without any inner conflict, without any hesitating recognition of someone else's "pathos," and therefore (the opposite of our contemporary "irony") lofty, absolutely determinate individuals, although this determinacy of theirs is based on and is representative of a particular ethical power. (W 15:540/LFA 1209–1210)

The extreme one-sidedness of the pathos leads to the conflict, and this one-sidedness can be canceled only with the sacrifice of the *individual*. The sacrifice is, ultimately, based on a misperception, for, as Hegel writes, both Antigone and Creon reflect the totality of the one Greek ethical substance. As a citizen of Thebes and the daughter of a king, Antigone ought to be obedient to the royal command, as Ismene advises. Creon, in turn, ought to respect the sacred ties of blood, as his son Haemon urges. Thus, Hegel can conclude that there is "immanent in both Antigone and Creon something that in their own way they attack, so that they are gripped and shattered by something intrinsic to their own actual being" (W 15:49/LFA 1217–1218).

Vernant makes this same general point about tragedy being an articulation of conflicts within the Greek world itself. Beginning with Solon walking out of an early theatrical performance and ending with Aristotle's *Poetics,* tragedy was born, rose to its apex, and then exhausted itself over a span of about one hundred years. According to Vernant, this tragic age corresponds to a turning point in Greek history itself. The relation between history and art is not arbitrary, for the tragic age begins when the presentation of the heroic past is felt to be too near and too threatening to the new form of legality, and it plays itself out when it is no longer experienced as a threat. (According to this analysis, then, Plato's combative relation to tragedy found in Book X of the *Republic* would indicate that the tragic spirit was still breathing. Aristotle's defense of tragedy in the idiom of philosophy would signal its demise.) During this one-hundred-year period, a division exists at the very core of Greek social experience: "It is wide enough for the oppositions between legal and political thought on the one hand and the mythical and heroic traditions on the other to stand out quite clearly. Yet it is narrow enough for the conflict in values to still be a painful one and for the clash to continue to take place."[63] This is to say that a tragic sense of responsibility arises when human action becomes the object of reflection and debate while still not being regarded as sufficiently autonomous to be fully self-sufficient. The particular domain of tragedy lies in this border zone where human actions hinge on divine powers and where their true meaning, unsuspected by even those who initiated them and take responsibility for them, is only revealed when it becomes a part of an order that is beyond man and escapes him.[64]

Bringing Aristotle and Vernant together, the power of Sophocles' *Antigone* to arouse fear and pity depends on the way in which the conflict between Creon and Antigone reflects a conflict that exists for the spectator. Whether or not the spectator happens to be Greek is not essential. What is of importance is that the laws guiding human action are both self-determined *and* dictated by divine power. If a division exists between the written, civil law and the unwritten, divine law, then Sophocles' play will potentially provoke these emotions. The conflict between Creon and Antigone would at best be understood in an abstract way. *Katharsis* requires an investedness in the play that goes beyond the theoretical recognition that Antigone represents "x" and Creon represents "y." It requires that we live for a time with the tragic hero. We feel pity for the hero when we remain distinct from her, and we fear for ourselves insofar as we are her. What allows us to live with another in this way? Aristotle holds that true friendship is not a matter of Heraclitus's talk of "hostility bringing together,"[65] but of like drawn to like. Sophocles' *beautiful* tragedy could reflect, and reflect on, the historical unfolding of Greece because Greece itself was beautiful—*beautiful* in the distinctly tragic sense of a unified whole, freely determined but divided against itself. Beauty depends on an Idea that is defined by the absence of relations of domination, yet, as presented in the *Phenomenology,* it does not require the harmony associated with life alone, but also its destruction as a result of the conflict inherent in this Idea.[66] This conflict is found, for example, in the gender roles prescribed by Greek ethical life. The structural exclusion of women from the public sphere limits the scope of the recognition that they can hope to achieve. The awareness of this structural limit in the Idea of the Greek *polis* manifests itself as "the everlasting irony of the community" (PdG 314/PS 288). This irony is an indication of the contradictions internal to the *polis* despite the temporary stability that it has achieved. The Greek Ideal is divided within itself.

Tragic Sacrifice and World Historical Individuals

In order for Sophocles' *Antigone* to provoke a catharsis of fear and pity in an audience, we spectators must also live in a historical period that is determined by the clash between written and unwritten law, or, more concretely, a clash arising from discriminatory gender roles. The particularities of both the tragic death of a young woman with an unnerving family tree and the archaic Greek history in which it is set speak across history in part because of the universality of these ethical contradictions. How can the particularity of the tragic hero as the embodiment of more general conflicts inherent in a people be translated from the sphere of tragic drama to that of history?

In his later philosophy of history, Hegel develops the idea of the "world-historical individual" as the sacrificial harbinger of new life. This is a historical figure who stands as the union of the particular and universal, but, because this union is, to recall Hölderlin's description of Empedocles, *premature* (*vorzeitig*), this individual becomes a sacrifice to world history, or fate (*Schiksal*).[67] Hegel not only invests a particular historical individual with a universal spiritual significance, but he also employs categories in describing him that are culled from the poetics of tragedy. The world-historical individual is a hero who is driven by pathos and is fated to go down. As such, the marriage of the particularity of factual history and the universality of the mytho-poetic historical narrativizing is raised to the level of a properly philosophical history.[68]

In the "Introduction" of the *Lectures on the Philosophy of World History*, nations are conceived, in all their varying forms, as the manifestation of "one original reason," and it is the "concrete spiritual principle in the life of nations" that is the concern of philosophical history (LWH 28, 30). As he writes in the 1822–1823 manuscript, for the course "In world history . . . the individuals we are concerned with are nations [*Völker*], totalities, states" (LWH 36). At the same time, Hegel calls the great individuals of world history *"heroes"* in that they "realise the end appropriate to the higher concept of the spirit" (LWH 83). Great individuals arrive on the stage of world history at times of great conflict, when collisions arise "between established and acknowledged duties, laws, and rights, on the one hand, and new possibilities which conflict with the existing system and violate it or even destroy its very foundations and continued existence on the other" (W 12:45 / LWH 82). While the dramatic heroes of ancient Greek tragedy, like Agamemnon, Orestes, Oedipus, and Antigone, were scripted by Aeschylus and Sophocles to reflect the essential conflicts that existed in the era of the tragic poets, the philosopher of world history locates those historical figures like Alexander the Great, Caesar, and Napoleon who can be seen *qua* the retrospective philosophical gaze to both embody and anticipate the essential conflicts of their own times. According to Hegel, the inspiration driving these world-historical heroes comes from a hidden spirit that has not yet come into existence. They have the character of being far-sighted, which means that they *sense* what is necessary and timely. And unlike Hölderlin's Empedocles, who lived at a time that did not demand "true action" (FH 1:872), these are men of *praxis*. As such, they *will* what is both universal and necessary for the times and what is only able to emerge in its universality when the "time is ripe." Thus, world-historical individuals are heroes who are both timely in their actions and ahead of their times, anticipatory. They will the desires of their contemporaries before their contemporaries have explicitly articulated these desires to themselves. Through their actions, they bring the inner soul of their contemporaries into the light of day, yet they are also used up by their vocation. When these world-historical individuals have fulfilled their end, "they fall aside like empty husks" (W 12:47/LWH 85). Alexander dies young, Caesar is murdered, and Napoleon ends his life in exile.

Like the characters of ancient tragedy, world-historical individuals are defined by their pathos. They are dictated by a great passion that verges, as Hegel says, on animal instinct, yet it is coupled with a capacity for circumspection that helps explain their far-sightedness: "if such zeal is genuine, it remains cool and reflecting; the theoretical faculty retains a clear view of the means by which its true ends can be realised" (W 12:47/LWH 86). Although they have, as in the case of Caesar, a correct *Vorstellung* of their contemporary context and its failures, they are not aware of the universal Idea itself. Caesar is said to have developed accurate "impressions" of the Roman Republic, but only impressions, and these are ultimately in the service of obtaining satisfaction for himself. Hegel writes, "it is not the universal Idea which enters into opposition, conflict, and danger; it keeps itself in the background, untouched and unharmed, and sends forth the particular interests of passion to fight and wear themselves out in its stead. It is what we may call the *cunning of reason* that it sets the passion to work in its service, so that the agents by which it gives itself existence must pay the penalty and suffer the loss" (W 12:49/LWH 89). This is the sacrifice of Caesar at the hands of the Idea, and, at the same time, despite the cunning of reason, it is his own *self*-sacrifice.

Hegel contrasts the heroes of world history with the moralizing schoolmaster who reveals his own lack of pathos by condemning that of Alexander or Caesar. World-historical individuals offend their psychological valets because they disregard accepted values, which is to say, that they disregard precisely the standards by which moralists make their judgment. The actions of these exceptional individuals extend beyond contemporary legal and moral norms. To use Hegel's language, "the spirit's inward development has outgrown the world it inhabits" (W 12:46/LWH 84). We find ourselves at a point like that of fifth-century Athens where fundamentally contradictory laws can become articulated *as* contradictory, while also remaining intertwined so that their clash is felt with acute intensity. The effect of the collision is not simply the ill-fatedness of the hero but is evident in Hegel's notorious remark that "[a] mighty figure must trample many an innocent flower underfoot, and destroys much that lies in its path" (W 12:49/LWH 89). The value of the hero's suspension of the ethical can only be determined retrospectively.[69] The "purification" of the contradictions inherent in a historically determined ethical substance amounts to the realization of a higher concept of the Spirit, and it is achieved through the transgressions and ultimate sacrifice of the world-historical individual. A history informed by the categories of tragic poetry, then, does not appear to recount the cathartic experiences of concrete historical figures but presents instead moments of historical intensification and violent conflict, the true significance of which is only determined by speculative reason after the fact.

Jesus in the First and Final Act

Like the world-historical individual, Jesus too lived at a time of "inner fermentation." He is, of course, not a political figure in the same way that Alexander, Caesar, and Napoleon were; but Hegel's presentation of Jesus as both timely and untimely, as the progenitor of a new spirit and as a sacrifice, coincides in this limited way with his later description of the world-historical individual. When describing the tempestuous historical period out of which Jesus arose, Hegel writes that the "fermentation of the multifold elements in the Jewish fate" preceded what he calls the "last act" (W 1:317/SC 205) of the Jewish nation. This final act requires concentrating these warring elements into a whole. Thus, the last act in the un-Hellenic tragedy of the Jews is a scene of opposition, namely, the open conflict with Rome. This is the stage on which Christianity arises, the scene of its first act.[70]

As Hegel comes to understand the development of a people in terms of its *spirit,* specifically a spirit that is determined as a reaction to a preceding one, is he also introducing a suprahistorical narrative structure that serves to unify these different spirits into one overarching development? If so, what is the implicit historical logic that structures this narrative? Hegel's later writings on Christianity, and religion more generally, certainly invite the expectation that the final act in the tragedy of the Jews will set the stage for a higher phase of development that we can see, retrospectively, was dependent on the limitations or contradictions inherent in the preceding one. Yet a development of this kind—the arrival of a new "universal" in the language of the *Lectures on the Philosophy of World History*—seems improbable when the tragedy that constitutes this previous stage is, as Hegel insists, un-Hellenic. The "great tragedy" of the Jews does not appear to be the precursor to the cathartic leap from one historical stage to the next. Hegel's description implies instead that it simply leads to a historical deadend, like Macbeth "dashed to pieces on his faith itself" (W 1:297/SC 205).

The question I will now pose to Hegel's presentation of the spirit of Christianity is whether the tragedy of the life of Jesus is capable of calling forth fear and pity. This is to ask, is the life of Jesus the stuff of tragic beauty? And given that, for the young Hegel, calling something beautiful reveals its affinity to the Greeks, to what extent is Jesus a Greek? Or to put it negatively, to what extent must Jesus be dissociated from the spirit of Abraham? Does the spirit of withdrawal that is so central to Hegel's understanding of Jesus follow from Abraham's separation and nomadism, or is it nonoppositional and, thus, distinct from the Abrahamic tear? Is, then, Christianity ultimately a religion of beauty or sublimity? Is Jesus's analogon Oedipus or Macbeth, or is this figure who steps out of the *world,* and not *nature,* distinct from both the beautiful and the sublime?

FOUR

Withdrawal and Exile

> To be a subject is to be a power of unending withdrawal, an ability always to find oneself behind what happens to one.
>
> —Emmanuel Levinas, *Existence and Existents*

Separation from Separation

In the time of fermentation that leads up to the Jewish revolt against Rome, there were those who were able to grasp the fate of the Jews but only in a partial manner—"men of commoner soul, though of strong passions" (W 1:317/SC 205). They lacked the inner vision that Hegel will later attribute to world-historical individuals. As such, they were "not calm enough either to let its waves carry them along passively and unconsciously and so just to swim with the tide, or alternatively, to await the further development necessary before a stronger power could be associated with their efforts. The result was that they overran the fermentation of the whole and fell without honor and without achievement" (ibid.). According to Hegel, Jesus distinguishes himself from these commoner souls by setting himself against the whole of this fate, such that his doctrine was aligned with none of its elements. In a gesture reminiscent of Abraham's initial act, and, thus, a gesture that recalls the act that founded the spirit of independence itself, Jesus is said to break with the fate of this spirit in a similarly all-encompassing manner. What most clearly distinguishes Jesus's original gesture from that of Abraham is what each is reacting against. According to Hegel, Abraham separated himself from a community of love, while Jesus separated himself from a nation suffering the fate of the rejection of love. Hegel presents Jesus's own fate concisely: "But the enmities like those he sought to transcend can be overcome [*aufheben*[1]] only by valor; they cannot be reconciled [*versöhnen*] by love. Even his *sublime* effort to overcome the whole of the Jewish fate must therefore have failed with his people, and he was bound to become its victim himself" (W 1:317/SC 205–206, emphasis added). On its face, then, Hegel's account of the movement from Judaism to Christianity does not appear to embody the internal "progress of the consciousness of freedom" (W 12:32/LWH 54) that he will later find in world history. The spirit of Christianity is born as an attempt to overcome the spirit of Judaism, but it is not explicitly presented as surmounting its contradictions, and there is no clear indication that we are progressing toward freedom as "the sole end of the spirit" (ibid.). Rather, it is scripted, at least in this passage, as a sublime but failed attempt to achieve this end. Yet despite Jesus's failure to mediate *fully* the separation opened by Judaism, can his sublime effort still be conceived as a moment within a broader progression toward genuine reconciliation (the union of feeling and the intellect "in something beautiful, in a god, by means of the imagination"), even if it is not this final fulfillment itself?

The answer rests with the status of *withdrawal,* for, as Hegel presents it in *The Spirit of Christianity,* this is a defining gesture of Jesus and the spirit that he inaugurates. Indeed, it gives birth to an entirely novel sphere that Hegel calls the "subjective": "Against purely objective commands Jesus sets something totally foreign to them, namely, the subjective in general" (W 1:225 / SC 209). It is rooted in Jesus's attempt to separate himself from another spirit in a way that is not oppositional. Yet if Hegel defines Judaism as an excess of objectivism, he presents Christianity, in turn, as an extreme of subjectivism. Thus, we can reframe our question in the following way: Does the position of Christianity stand as an advancement over its predecessor, or is the move from one to the other simply an oscillation from one point of opposition to the next, void of any overarching directionality? Is it an oscillation between genuine *opposites,* an alternation that precludes the possibility of rising to a mode of being that is higher than that shared by the opposed positions? Or is this an early and oblique recognition that there is no reconciliation beyond finite opposition, that, in other words, "the Absolute is *nothing but* the movement of self-sublation of these finite determinations"?[2] What can be said with certainty is that, in *The Spirit of Christianity,* in the winter of 1798–1799, reconciliation or fulfillment is the proper aim of religious practice, which Hegel describes as "the most holy, the most beautiful, of all things." And, he adds, if the "spirit of beauty be lacking in religious actions, they are the most empty of all" (W 1:318 / SC 206). The question, then, *a propos* Jesus and Christianity becomes whether he, in his sublime effort to overcome his fate, is precluded from *beauty.*

Religious practice is *beautiful* in its endeavor "to unify the discords necessitated by our development" (W 1:318 / SC 206) and by doing so through an Ideal that is fully existent and so not opposed to reality. The source of beauty is determined, in part, by the origin of religious practice. That is, its proper source is a human need, rather than external command. What is this need? I have drawn specific attention to Hegel's claim in *The Spirit of Christianity* that uniting subject with object in a beauty that has been forged by the imagination is the supreme need of the human spirit. However, let me descend from these abstract heights. As early as his *Life of Jesus* (1795), Hegel uses the story of the disciples picking ears of corn on the Sabbath to show that Jesus condones the transgression of this law in the name of a *physical* need (Matthew 12:1; see LJ 118). The source of religion, and the source of the sacrifices associated with it, is internal to human nature and human needs. Hegel is committed to this view to such an extent that he claims that "the satisfaction of the commonest human need rises superior to these [actions originating from external commands], because there lies directly in such a need the sensing or the preserving of a human being, no matter how empty his being may be" (W 1:318 / SC 207). Hegel concedes, however, that need, even the highest need, will necessarily profane what is sacrosanct since need always arises from a state of disruption. Religious beauty reconciles disruption and discord, while need makes either a human being or nature into a (foreign) "object" (*Objekt,* ibid.). In the most extreme case of objectification, when someone destroys temples and alters in a fit of pious zeal, the zealot profanes not only the particular sanctuaries that have been destroyed but *all* communal sanctuaries. In the name of overcoming discord, then, is Jesus guilty of this extreme crime of objectification when he sets himself against the Judaism of his time so thoroughly? Hegel qualifies his previous remark. To profane a sacred object or command that is based on utter renunciation and servitude is justified in that one is only reappropriating one's rights. In this case, there is nothing genuinely *communal* to profane, nothing that properly belongs to all alike, and so Jesus's rejection of his tradition is nothing more than the disturbance that any community would experience when one of its members leaves and reappropriates his or her property. If the point of contention between one member of the community and the whole is slight, then the self-restraint guiding the relation of friendship would ensure no disruption in it. However, the situation is different between Jesus and his community because he dismisses the whole life of his people. Thus, the restraint governing the relation between friends is renounced. Instead of *tearing* himself from his community, however, Jesus *withdraws* from it.

For Hegel, the difference between Abraham and Jesus is understood in terms of the distinction, then, between separation as a tearing (*reißen*) and separation as withdrawal (*heraustreten;* W 1:319 / SC 207). The former involves renunciation, the later only a rejection of bondage and objective commands. The break Jesus makes with his tradition is a separation from separation. This leads to the heart of Hegel's defense of the spirit that Jesus inaugurates; on this basis, Hegel justifies the series of transgressions of Jewish law that Jesus undertakes. Returning to the example of the disciples picking corn on the Sabbath, Jesus's point is simply that the most basic human need trumps artificial, "objective" commands: "Nature is holier than the temple" and "need abolishes guilt" (W 1:320 / SC 208). But does this confrontation with the objective law entail its abolition? I have claimed that, for Hegel, Jesus's proclamation that he has come not to abolish but to fulfill the law is at the very core of his teaching. Yet given his utter rejection of the spirit and fate of Abraham, how are we to understand *plērōma,* as distinct from *katalusis,* dissolution? In the *Positivity,* Hegel interpreted *complementum* in terms of the move from positive law to the moral law as articulated by Kant. The novelty of the interpretation that Hegel develops in Frankfurt stems from the central place that the categories of tragedy assume in his thought, and it shapes his reassessment of Kant. In the *Life of Jesus* and the *Positivity,* the authority of Jesus comes from his recognition of the moral law that resides within us and that transcends positivity. In both of these texts Jesus is essentially a Kantian, and, although a subtle rift between Hegel and Kant can be detected beneath the surface, it is only when *need* is elevated above the law that the position held by Hegel—and Hegel's Jesus—comes into direct and explicit conflict with that of Kant. This occurs most decisively in the Sermon on the Mount, and Hegel will explicate it in terms of a spiritual need that is higher than the command of law. He will use it as a means of dethroning the moral disposition, defined by reverence of the law, and, in doing so, he relegates Kant to a figure of positivity. In a letter to his brother on New Year's Day 1799, Hölderlin calls Kant the Moses of the German people—the one who will lead them "out of the Egyptian apathy into the free, solitary desert of his speculation" (FH 2:726).[3] For Hegel, there is a danger that those who stand in reverence before the law revere their oppressor.

The Shaman of Königsberg

Hegel's theoretical articulation of Jesus's spiritual revolution amounts to an attack on the law as *command:*

> Since it is natural relations which these [moral and civil laws] express in the form of commands, it is perverse to make them wholly or partly objective. Since laws are unifications of opposites in a concept [*Begriff*], which thus leaves them as opposites while it exists itself in opposition to reality, it follows that the concept expresses an *ought.* (W 1:225/ SC 209)

It is possible for the unification of opposites to arise naturally, whether what is opposed are the needs of two people (thus, a civil concern) or whether the opposition is between reason and desire within oneself (a moral one). However, the unification is artificial when it is effected through the imposition of a *law* that mediates the conflict between two opposing needs or the antagonism between reason and desire. To function as laws, the opposing forces must be understood; for this to occur, they must exist as *concepts.* As such, practical laws express an *ought,* and, for Hegel, this means that they stand opposed to reality for the simple reason that one does not necessarily have to follow them. Practical laws *as concepts* hold the status of an imperative alone, and the example of Jesus's disciples picking corn on the Sabbath illustrates their conditional character. Hegel explains the difference between *moral* and *civil* laws in a manner that clearly follows Kant's own analysis. The binding force of moral laws arises from the form of the law alone and is, thus, *subjective,* while the force of civil laws is asserted by an external power. In further explicating the difference, Hegel argues that, because the authority of civil laws is imposed by external force, they are necessarily *positive.* Moral laws must be differentiated from civil laws because an external authority can never command that one act morally. It is a contradiction to be coerced into following the moral law. Jesus's aim is to overcome the positivism that understands the law solely in terms of an external command.

One might expect that Jesus would confront the positivity, or objectivity, of civil law by simply rejecting the *form* of civil law and concentrating instead on the form of the law that corresponds to moral imperatives: 'Do not incur debts that you promise to repay, even though you know this will be impossible, because, if you do, you will be punished by the state' *versus* 'The universality of a law that states that everyone ought to make a promise with the intention of not keeping it would contradict the act of promising as such, for this "would make the promise and the end one might have in itself impossible, since no one would believe what was promised him but would laugh at all such expressions as vain pretenses."'[4] A *civil* law, which is to say, a *positive* one, can be annulled (*Aufhebung;* W 1:322 / SC 210) if the matter of the law—its content—is also moral and its authority is no longer taken to arise externally, but from a reverence for duty alone. This broadly Kantian approach could also be extended to a type of command that comes neither from an external, civil authority nor from the form of the concept itself, but is conceived as both alien and subjective at the same time. This occurs when the moral law is thought to be imposed by God directly rather than by the practical rationality of the law itself. This law could also be canceled if it too—like civil law—was judged by the form of its concept alone. As Kant says in the *Groundwork,* "Even the Holy One of the Gospel must first be compared with our ideal of moral perfection before he is cognized as such."[5] One might expect that, when confronted by the problem of how to cancel the positivity inherent in civil and religious laws, Jesus would bring these before the court of pure practical reason. Those laws that pass this court's judgment would then be maintained and the others rejected. This was very much the strategy that Hegel attributes to Jesus in the *Positivity.* In this earlier text, Jesus teaches his friends and disciples to cultivate their capacity for moral reasoning so that they no longer need the threat of external coercion to act in conformity with the moral law.

As Hegel presents him in *The Spirit of Christianity,* Jesus could have chosen this Kantian path, but he does not, and this is to his credit. Appealing to the autonomy of the human will alone removes positivity only partially:

> Between the Shaman of the Tungus, the European prelate who rules church and state, the Voguls, and the Puritans, on the one hand, and the man who listens to his own command of duty, on the other, the difference is not that the former make slaves of themselves, while the latter is free, but that the former have their lord outside themselves, while the latter carries his lord in himself, yet at the same time is his own slave. (W 1:323/SC 211)[6]

While Kant criticizes the submission to external authority in *Religion within the Limits of Reason Alone,* Hegel extends the criticism to the attempts made by Kant to exorcise, in the name of an alien and objective universality, the particularity of impulses, inclinations, pathological love, and sensuous experience as such. The universality of the *moral* law is objective, which is to say that it is still mired in an "indestructible positivity" (ibid.), to the extent that the content of the law (for example, "don't make false promises") is a specific, "restricted" duty. One is thus confronted by the contradiction of a duty that is both restricted and universal at the same time; for Hegel, relying on the universality of form alone cannot mend this rift. This will not allow for the achievement of his aim—an aim that he sees himself sharing with Jesus—to "restore man's humanity in its entirety" (W 1:324/SC 212). If this contradictory concept of duty is used to guide our relations with others, Hegel's conclusion is that it will lead us to either exclude or dominate them, and his thesis regarding Jesus is that his spirit, "a spirit raised above morality [*Moralität*]" (ibid.), is opposed, *avant la lettre,* to this tyrannical effect of pure practical reason. The sham resolution to the *aporia* between particular and universal that is supposedly achieved through simply excluding the particular (imperatives, inclinations, and so on) marks the obdurate one-sidedness of Kantian formalism. Hegel's Jesus is unwilling to accept this opposition between the "ought" of the moral law and "reality," and, as I have shown in the earlier discussion of the Jena-era *Faith and Knowledge* text, this is a central point in Hegel's own critique of Kantian moralism. Speaking anachronistically, Hegel's Jesus refuses to accept the gap between the regulative ideal of unification and its realization, a gap that extends to (a bad) infinity and that, as such, will never be bridged.

The Kantian subject is a divided one, severed into rational and sensual parts; for Hegel, the spirit of Jesus offers a way of overcoming this division born of *Moralität.* The character and extent of this divide can be grasped more fully if one considers Kant's defense against Schiller's charge of moral "rigorism." Kant argues that morality exists as such only *qua* freedom. Given this, we must admit that all choices (*Willkür*), if they are to be judged by the standards of morality, involve *either* subordinating the law of self-love to the moral law and thus following the moral law for its own sake *or* subordinating the moral law to self-love.[7] In the former case, one is *good* and, in the latter, Kant tells us, *evil*. Beyond this, there is a propensity toward evil in human beings, or, as he puts it at one point, "man is evil by nature."[8] As Kant argues in the first book of his *Religion within the Limits of Reason Alone* ("Concerning the Indwelling of the Evil Principle with the Good, or, On the Radical Evil in Human Nature"), "radical evil" is the grounds of the possibility of moral evil, which is to say that it is the possibility of following a maxim that is opposed to the moral law: "We call a man evil . . . not because he performs actions that are evil (contrary to the law) but because these actions are of such a nature that we may infer from them the presence in him of evil maxims."[9] Insofar as Kant equates freedom of the will (*Wille*) with acting according to the moral law, one cannot both act against it and be free. To claim that we can be good or evil but nowhere in between reveals to Schiller an overly monastic cast of mind. There appears to be no room for grace, and Schiller argues that its absence would give rise to a fear-ridden and dejected temperament.[10]

In defense of his position, Kant claims that, while the idea of duty, with its claim to necessity, does not allow for the possibility of grace, its *dignity* spares it from this dour, monastic fate. Courage and joy, rather than fear and dejection, define the temperament of someone who has a firmly grounded disposition to fulfill his or her duties. For Kant, the fearful, slavish frame of mind can never occur without a hidden *hatred* of the law. Of dignity, Kant writes,

> The majesty of the moral law (as of the law on Sinai) instills awe [*Ehrfurcht*] (not dread, which repels, nor yet charm, which invites familiarity); and in this instance, since the ruler resides within us, this *respect,* as of a subject toward his ruler, awakens a *sense of sublimity* of our own destiny which enraptures us more than any beauty.[11]

Reading this in the context of his criticism of Kant, Hegel remains, in effect, unconvinced that the discovery of this foreign element within us should provoke awe and not dread. Further along in his analysis of radical evil, Kant remarks that we cannot help but experience the "highest wonder" (*Verwunderung*) toward this foreign element in us.[12] For Kant, this sense of wonder gives rise to a question—the inaugural question of philosophy, if, as both Plato and Aristotle claim, philosophy begins with wondering (*thaumazein*):

> What is it in us . . . whereby we, beings ever dependent upon nature through so many needs, are at the same time raised so far above these needs by the idea of an original predisposition (in us) that we count them all as nothing, and ourselves as unworthy of existence, if we cater to their satisfaction (though this alone can make life worth de-

> siring) in opposition to the law—a law by virtue of which reason commands us potently, yet without making either promises or threats?[13]

What is it indeed? This sublime "object" is *in* us at the same time that it is radically distinct *from* us. It is *distinct* in the way that a ruler is separate from the ruled, in much the same way as Noah's submission to his Ideal allows him then to dominate the natural world. Our submission to a law that we discover within ourselves provides us with the authority to then dominate our "natural" self. Thus, the objectivizing and self-alienating character of the moral law works to divide the subject against itself.

"I was once alive apart from the law"

Can the spirit of Jesus, raised above *Moralität,* overcome this divide subject? In his Sermon on the Mount, Jesus confronts the positivity that Hegel finds in both the spirit of Judaism and Kantian moral philosophy by "strip[ping] the law of its legal form" (W 1:324/SC 212). Jesus refuses to face the law with the sense of "reverence" (*Achtung,* ibid.) that Kant will claim is inalienable. In doing so, he desanctifies it. Rather than accepting the sublime status of the law, Jesus reveals, instead, "that which fulfills [*erfüllen*] the law but annuls [*aufheben*] it as a law" (ibid.; see Matthew 5:17). *Fulfillment, plērōma,* is also an annihilation because in the higher union of inclination and the law these two opposing terms lose their distinct referents. Once a law beyond the law—that is, a law fulfilled—is present, then a law that commands and, thus, tames otherwise errant inclinations becomes superfluous. On this account, we can see the degree to which, for Hegel, Paul's declaration of the interdependence of law and desire follows from the spirit of Jesus. Paul describes the condition that gives rise to the *need* for fulfillment in Romans 7:7–11:

> What then shall we say? That the law is sin? By no means! Yet, if it had not been for the law, I should not have known sin. I should not have known what it is to covet if the law had not said, "You shall not covet." But sin, finding opportunity in the commandment wrought in me all kinds of covetousness. I was once alive apart from the law, but when the commandment came, sin revived and I died; the very command which promised life proved to be death to me. For sin, finding opportunity in the commandment, deceived me and by it killed me.

There is the potential for the law and desire to provoke each other endlessly and to do so according to a logic of acceleration and velocity: the greater the force of the law is—or, to put it another way, the greater the sense of reverence one has for the law—the greater the desire to transgress it becomes. This is the cycle that follows from a relation based on dominance and submission.

Kant, for his part, distinguishes the letter and the spirit of the law in the following way: The man of good morals (*bene moratus*) follows the *letter* of the law so that his actions conform to what the moral law commands, but the law itself is not his supreme incentive; the morally good man (*moraliter bonus*) obeys the *spirit* of the law in that "the law is sufficient in itself as an incentive."[14] To follow the spirit of the law is, for Kant, still to obey, whereas the true spirit of Jesus is freedom from mastery as such and, thus, freedom from any authority that must be obeyed. To bring forth that which is higher than the law would be to fulfill (*erfüllen*) and cancel (*aufheben*) this antagonism, which means cancelling/fulfilling the divided existence that Jesus saw in his people and that Hegel saw in both Kant specifically and late eighteenth-century Germany more generally. How is this possible? Hegel argues as follows:

> Since the commands of duty presuppose a cleavage and since the domination of the concept declares itself in an "ought," that which is raised above [*erheben*] this cleavage is by contrast an *is* [*ein Sein*], a modification of life, one which is exclusive and therefore restricted only if looked at in reference to the object since the exclusiveness is given only through the restrictedness of the object and only concerns the object. (W 1:324/SC 212, translation altered)

The division between *reason* telling us to love our enemy and the *inclination* to do so—that is, the immediate, *unconscious* desire to love—is an inherent part of law as command. The law, as a *concept,* as a command, as an *ought,* binds reason and inclination together artificially, in "opposition to reality," as Hegel says (W 1:321/SC 209). To cancel this cleavage is to reach a point where reason *is* inclination, where inclination conforms to reason *immediately.* We desire doing what we are supposed to do. This is *love*—a modification of *life,* or life *qua* praxis. *Life* continues to be Hegel's word for the *hen kai pan,* and, as *eine Modifikation des Lebens,* this *point* of reconciliation—love—*is.* Unlike the law, which is made real only in an infinite future, love is present. It is not something that, by virtue of its very structure, is always deferred. As *ein Sein,* love *is* "the synthesis of subject and object, in which subject and object have lost their opposition" (W 1:326/SC 214). Instead of Kant's false resolution of the opposition between particularity and universality, which amounts to the mastery of the particular by the universal, Jesus presents a reconciliation as love in which objective law loses its universality and the subject its particularity. And as love is a modification of life, so the virtues are modifications of love. They are "virtues without lordship and without submission" (W 1:359/SC 244). In Aristotle's words, "The man who does not enjoy doing noble actions is not a good man at all: no one would call a man just if he did not like acting justly, nor liberal if he did not like doing liberal things, and similarly with the other virtues."[15] Fulfilling a virtue means, for Aristotle too, desiring what one ought to do and desiring this consistently over time to the point where it becomes a second nature.[16] For Hegel, in turn, Jesus set virtue, as a loving disposition, against moral commands. Love is "the sole principle of virtue," and, if this were not the case, "every virtue would be at the same time a vice" (W 1:359/SC 244–245). This alternation of virtue into vice, and of noble intentions into their opposite, has fueled Hegel's investigations into the history of Christianity, as has his desire to find an antidote to these kinds of alternations.

The fatal limitation of Kantianism is that it has no means of harmonizing the different restricted duties that arise in any lived situation. Love, by contrast, unifies the multiplicity of virtues in a way that avoids the inevitable conflicts that would arise, given the complexity of human relations, if every virtue were taken to be absolute in itself (one must always be courageous, always open-handed, always just, and so on). Thus, Hegel's attack is based on distinguishing the living unity fostered by love from a *principle.* As universal, a principle is also a concept, and a concept can neither cancel multiplicity nor unify the various virtues that are in play in any situation. "You shall not kill" (Matthew 5:21–22) works as a universal law prescribed by pure practical reason, but, according to the teachings of Jesus, this command is fulfilled by the "higher genius of reconcilability" (W 1:327/SC 215), which renders the command redundant. The content of the command—"You shall not kill"—is so limited that it permits all manner of transgressions other than the specific one it has outlawed. It follows, then, that Hegel would affirm the effort that Jesus, as the embodiment of the reconciling power of love, makes to emphasize the relative severity of calling someone a "fool" (*Narren*), as opposed to a "scoundrel" (*Schurken*) (see Matthew 5:22; W 1:138/SC 216). Anger, as the feeling of being oppressed coupled with the desire to oppress in return, could very well be the motivation behind both of these insults, yet, when you call someone a scoundrel, there is at least an implicit recognition that you share something with the person you are insulting. There is a greater degree of contempt implied by calling someone a fool because this insult denies "all equality, all community of essence," and, thus, it entails demoting the other to the status of "a non-being" (*ein Nichts,* ibid.). Both of these judgments may have the same motivation as murder, that is, anger, yet the command "You shall not kill" will outlaw murder but leave anger alone. Jesus's point is that anger itself in any of its modifications can be a crime, but focusing only on laws addressing these modifications is a fool's errand. By contrast to the attempted mastery of the situation *qua* principle, and ultimately *qua* thought itself, the living unity of virtues in love may be modified in an endless number of ways. In this, it mirrors the complexity of life itself. This living unity will never be manifested in the same way twice. Thus, "its expression will never be able to afford a rule, since it never has the force of a universal *opposed* to a particular" (W 1:362/SC 246, emphasis added). As the expression of a union of the universal and the particular that can never be captured by a rule or algorithm, it is akin to a work of artistic genius, insofar as this is understood, with Kant, as a work that embodies a lawfulness without law.[17]

The sacrifice of a strict *universality* of the law is, in fact, an "infinite gain on account of the wealth of living relations with the individuals (perhaps few) with whom it comes into connection" (W 1:327/SC 215). It is not an accident that at this point Hegel writes of a properly *living* relation of men and that he does so in terms of "friendship." Thus, he renders John 13:34–35 as, "A new command give I unto you, that you love one another: thereby shall men know that you are my friends [*Freunde*]" (W 1:394/SC 278, translation altered). When translating *mathātai* here, Hegel does not choose *Jünger*, "disciples," but opts for *Freunde* instead. (Elsewhere, Hegel employs both *Jünger* [see W 1:121/P 83; W 1:398/SC 282] and *Schüler* [see W 1:118/P 81].[18]) The love binding a more intimate group is deemed an infinite gain over the empty abstraction of a "universal" union based on the notion of respect, or a "universal philanthropy" (*die Menschenliebe*, W 1:362/SC 246). The latter is an ideal command that may stand as an exalted "conceptual object" but that lacks any real achievement. As Hegel writes, "a thought cannot be loved" (W 1:362/SC 247). In contrast to the poverty of such empty ideals, *life* appears to thrive in the absence of theoretical reflexivity.

Married Life

The unity that defines love as the *plērōma* of the law is exposed through its disruption. In his reading of the Sermon on the Mount (Matthew 23–24), Hegel presents the unity of lovers in marriage by way of the absurdity of a *duty* to fidelity. A duty of this kind does not take into consideration the logic that guides desire toward someone other than one's wife. According to Paul, a *duty* to fidelity will only spur wandering lust. As the fulfillment of the law against divorce, and of *law* in general, love takes care of this oversight by instilling the sanctity that will redirect roaming eyes to their proper object. Hegel can write that "love cancels the leave to divorce" (W 1:329/SC 217), but the matrimonial union is not based on the law that divorce counteracts. Taking a lover outside marriage is ultimately seen, from the perspective of love, as an offense against the whole, where the "whole" is the human essence realized in the union of lovers. Love is both the *feeling* of this whole and that which cancels anything that might threaten it. An offense *against* love is not met by any punishment associated with the law but by a *fate*. Fate comes to avenge an act that one has *not* intended and that is, therefore, outside the purview of the morality of the good will. The husband who falls out of love with his wife does not choose to do so: "To cease loving a wife who still loves compels *love* to sin" (ibid., emphasis added). When love falters, it is not the lover but love itself that "sins" precisely because it is beyond the control of the lover. Thus, one should avoid understanding and condemning the lover's transgression as simply an offense against the law or the authority on which the law is based. One should avoid this, in part, because it was an unintentional act, but more importantly because love, in fulfilling the law, deprives the law of any meaningful domain. At the same time, there is no possibility of hiding from this offense, for when love "sins" the union is inwardly sundered.

What form does the dissolution of the whole take? Do we descend in this case back to the sphere of legality? To enter the legal realm and deploy a *right* to divorce in this context is, for Hegel, a brutal offence, "an outrage to the wife's love" (ibid.). Reducing a relation of love to that of legality denies the tragic nature of the *aporia*. An internally severed love calls forth a fate that no amount of alimony can pacify. The sole exception that Jesus offers is telling. It is an exception that Hegel acknowledges but without elaboration. Love sanctions the right to divorce—the right to an exit from the whole—when the wife gives *her* love to someone else, but not when the husband does the same. The fact that the parts of the whole are determined as "husband" and "wife" reveals the extent to which love, as fulfillment, is corrupted by legal relations—as is the fact that the two can be treated so differently. If love fulfills the legality of marriage as such, to the point where the law loses its referents, why should the legal categories of husband and wife remain, and what is their status? Is the configuration of this union as one between a man and a woman a remnant of an irreversible law of nature or, to put a sharper point on it, a biological necessity?[19] If the "whole," as love, as the union of husband and wife, stands as the prototype of the speculative "identity of identity and non-identity,"[20] how do we accommodate this residue of legality, let alone its thoroughgoing incorporation into Hegel's own logic of *plērōma?*

A Different Genius

Love is a modification of life, and life, as being, is unconscious or, at least, unreflective: "When life is conceived in thought or given expression, it acquires a form alien to it, a conceptual form" (W 1:325 / SC 213). Like Hölderlin's insight that to judge (*urteilen*) is always already to draw a separation from (*Ur-teil*) what is being judged, to reflect (*reflektieren*) is inevitably to distort life. When we desire to do what we ought to do, then reflection is unnecessary. The extent to which this is the case is evident in Hegel's account of another modification of love, *charity* or *compassion* (*eleēmosunē;* see Matthew 6:1–4). The *duty* to charity can be seen as impure if something alien taints the action. This alien element can be an ulterior motive, such as the desire to gain recognition, but, beyond that, even the self-satisfaction that one might take in giving charity corrupts the act and renders it impure. The proper fulfillment of the virtue of charity requires that we "banish even the consciousness of the action as a duty fulfilled" (W 1:331/SC 219). Finding the completion of the law in the purity of unconsciousness indicates a fear of the "intrusion of something foreign" (ibid.). The fear of the foreign that exists at the core of love is the self-awareness that would grasp charity as charity, as a duty fulfilled. Reflection contaminates the purity of this virtue because it does not belong to the action itself. So the self-satisfied person of good conscience (Hegel mentions the Pharisee of Luke 18:9) judges himself only by way of individual virtues that are not properly united by love; thus, his good conscience rests on mistaking these individual virtues for the whole. It also allows him to claim universality for his action, and inherent in this claim is a sense of superiority over others. Hegel goes as far as to draw a direct parallel between the mere self-consciousness of a fulfilled duty and the applause of a crowd publicly honoring someone's moral deeds. The consciousness of a duty fulfilled is understood as a victory of the universal moral law over the particular. This victory allows the self-consciously dutiful individual to claim universality for himself, and, as he makes this claim to universality, particularity—*mere* particularity from the perspective of the universal—will be assigned to all others. At moments like these, Hegel's Jesus is an acute analyst of the hidden needs behind supposedly pious activities like prayer and fasting. As such, he unmasks the pretense of those who would claim, to themselves or others, to follow duty for duty's sake alone.

If the consciousness of the Christian is free of thoughts of right and duty, what, then, is its content? The lack of consciousness of rights and duties is, as I will argue, a crucial aspect of the gesture of withdrawal, but how far does withdrawal extend? In this context, Jesus can claim to those listening to his Sermon on the Mount that he is introducing "something wholly foreign, a different genius, a different world" (W 1:325/SC 214, translation altered). The "new region of life" (ibid.) that he is introducing is, of course, *new* only to those accustomed to understanding the law as something of foreign origin. That is, pure life is foreign to reflective moral consciousness. However, if fulfillment entails the withdrawal from this form of reflectivity, surely this includes the language of reflection as well. The Sermon on the Mount, then, must address the possibility of a language that is able to give voice to that which is, by its very nature, distorted by reflection. Thus, Hegel comes to focus on this problem of *expression*. At the very least, a mode of speaking that attempts to express pure life would be empty of moral judgments and the division that they introduce. "Judge not," says Jesus, for all judgments of this kind involve a mastery of their subject through the concept. Through judgment, we divide and conquer, which means that we force those whom we judge to conform to our own moral critique; we take them for what we think they ought to be rather than what they are. As a result, we dominate those we judge *in thought* when we are unable to dominate them in other ways. Yet in judging another, we presume the authority of the law and then subject ourselves to the mastery of this same law in turn. The judge, in the form of righteousness, sets a Lord above himself. This is a Lord against whom he is powerless yet through whom he gains the pretense to command others by the force of indignation—an indignation based on his own submission. This is by now a familiar logic: the production of a "beyond"—of a God who shares nothing with his subjects—is harbored within the very structure of judgment itself.

Jesus, then, embodies a spirit raised above *Moralität,* in part because he rejects the righteousness of judgmental consciousness and the associated language of judgment. Indeed, the Platonic view that understands moral deliberation as striving to uncover the Idea of the Good through rational deliberation would appear to be foreign to the "new region of life" that Jesus presents. Instead of righteousness and love coming from a transcendent law, they are, as Hegel says, "issued from life" (W 1:352/SC 237). They are immanent to life itself. Although he had spoken of it as a "higher" sphere, Jesus must avoid presenting life as a realm that is in opposition to the law. According to a *logical* order of priority, life is *prior* to law and the concept. When Jesus cancels/fulfills the moral law, he is not giving birth to an entirely new and unprecedented being. He is only exposing what has been covered over by thought itself. The emphasis on immanence that Hegel's rejection of a false "beyond" entails is also evident in this description of reconciliation as a withdrawal from false divisions.

Instead of a realm that is higher than that of the law, what Jesus ultimately describes (Matthew 7:6–29) is an "expression of life in its beautiful free region" (W 1:335/SC 223). This is a region that is not expressed through the language of judgment; it is also not one in which sworn statements or promises are necessary. The structural need to postulate a transcendent God that is inherent in judgments is even more apparent in the linguistic act of swearing to keep a promise. No matter what we swear on when we give our word, we are ultimately always swearing to God. Whatever we swear on is a proxy for this Being that grounds and unites word and deed. That is to say, this linkage is grounded in an external authority, rather than the person making the promise. In the sworn promise, Being must be enlisted to act as the guarantor of the future fulfillment of the promise because there is a perceived *lack* of unity between duty and desire. Being is envisaged and represented after the fact, so to speak, to fill in the gap between the promise and its fulfillment. A potential consequence of this is that, if what was promised is not fulfilled, the Being on which the promise was made is denied as well. When we swear to God, then, there is always the risk that we are also swearing at him. Thus, Jesus rejects the need for making oaths as they are deemed to be superfluous;[21] a living unification of *word*—a promise of fidelity offered—and *deed*—fidelity realized—must not rest in an external Being but must reside instead only in the person making the promise.[22]

Life in its full beauty and freedom involves neither judgment nor sworn statements but rather, as Hegel says, "a unification of men in asking, giving, and receiving" (W 1:335/SC 223; see Matthew 7:7–11). How is this unification that is defined by an abundance that transcends the narrow logic of utilitarian calculation and exchange to be adequately expressed? According to Hegel, Jesus's attempts to do so fall short. They amount to nothing more than "inadequate parables" (W 1:335/SC 223). In light of this failure, we might turn to Shakespeare for a clue as to what Hegel has in mind by his trinity of verbs (asking, giving, and receiving). In a fragment on *Love* that is roughly contemporaneous with *The Spirit of Christianity,* Hegel cites these lines from *Romeo and Juliet:* "the more I give to thee, / The more I have" (W 1:248/L 307).[23] He adds, "The lover who takes is not thereby made richer than the other; he is enriched indeed, but only so much as the other is. So too the giver does not make himself poorer; by giving to the other he has at the same time and to the same extent enhanced his own treasure" (W 1:248/L 367). This account of unified life is framed in terms of love, but, given the lack of elaboration, it is unclear as to whether it ought to be understood by way of *philia, erōs,* or *agapē.* Regardless, this logic of love stands in stark contrast to a logic of exchange that can be summarized in this way: "the more profit you make, the more you want."[24] Or, translated into the moral opposition between duty and desire, "the more you obey the [law's] command, the guiltier you are."[25]

Remaining within the framework offered by *The Spirit of Christianity,* Greek tragedy also offers a way of clarifying what Hegel might mean when he describes the "beautiful free region" of life as a unification in "asking, giving and receiving." This is the case because, for Hegel, "beauty" and "freedom" are intimately related to his idea of Greece, and tragic poetry is a privileged form of Greek self-expression. The question of whether ancient Greek tragedy expresses this other beautiful world, however, raises another pressing question: *Who* exactly needs to achieve this reunion? Is it a need shared by all humanity? Is the opposition between (i) the *logical* priority that places life before law, unity before separation, and (ii) the *phenomenological* order of law before life, separation before unity, a structural truth of human being as such? According to Hegel, the need for reunion is present for us moderns, and it is, of course, also shared by Jesus and his contemporaries. Do the Greeks also need to rejoin the living, or have they been spared this separation from pure life? If they have been spared, then it is difficult to see how tragic drama could stand as the expression of life in its beautiful free region, for it is unclear why such an expression would be needed in this case. If, however, tragedy is interpreted as the expression of a separation that undermines the illusion of a Greek unity untouched by division, and if it is, indeed, the case that tragedy defines the spirit of the Greeks, then what is true for us moderns and the early Christians is also true for the ancient Greeks. Life may be *logically* "prior" to law, from the perspective of thought and reflection, but alienation, as the *experience* of a separation from unity, is "prior" to this unified life. If, as I have claimed, tragic beauty does not belong to nature and life alone, but also to their demise, then Greek tragic drama could plausibly stand as an expression of "the beautiful free region" that Hegel finds in the Sermon on the Mount. Tragedy would express the return from a state of alienation to the proper unity of life, yet this unity of life would never have been *consciously* experienced before. Finally, if Greek tragedy and tragic beauty are interpreted in this way, then, for Greeks, Christians, and moderns alike, unity is, *qua* experience, always a *re*conciliation. Given this continuity, it is tempting to extend it universally and claim that, *qua* the *phenomenological* order, the experience of separation is always already prior to that of unity. This is to say that, despite Hegel's many appeals to "human nature" as a seemingly original experience of unity, the logic of his text seems to lead to the position that the experiential priority of law before life, separation before unity, is a structural truth of human being as such.

Hölderlin corroborates this vision of tragedy in some of his early theoretical texts. *Über das Gesetz der Freiheit (Es giebt einen Naturzustand . . .)* and *Über den Begriff der Straffe* (1794/1795), for example, concern precisely this issue of a *return* to life and the scope of the division that necessitates this return. He sketches the idea that a primordial unity of "the sensuous with the sacred" (FH 2:46)[26] is only revealed retrospectively ("analeptically"[27]), after it has been transgressed and after that transgression has been punished. It is revealed, then, only after it has been lost. Further, this original transgression is the *inevitable* disrupting of Being.[28] Any attempt to know primordial Being means inevitably shattering the essence of Being *as* unified. Only an intellectual intuition after the fact allows for the mediation between sensuousness and the sacred. Tragedy is, in turn, a *metaphor* for this retroactive intellectual intuition: "The tragic, in appearance heroic poem, is idealistic in its significance. It is the metaphor of an intellectual intuition."[29] Primordial Being, therefore, is only ever known in its withdrawal. Art, in its highest form, does not realize a unification of subject and object, but, as a tragic *metaphor,* it presents the impossibility of philosophy, insofar as philosophy is realized through intellectual intuition.

One can argue that Hegel in effect agrees with Hölderlin that, *qua* experience, we are inevitably separated from life. Given this, and given that love, as a modification of life, marks the Christian fulfillment of the law, it follows that when Hegel attempts to grasp Jesus's expression of a return to pure life, it takes the form of a fulfillment that follows from an inevitable *transgression* of the law. It should not surprise us that he does so by way of a meditation on tragedy and that, in this context, tragedy finds its way to center stage. What is so striking is that Hegel does not think of tragedy as foreign to the life and teaching of Jesus. The beauty that Jesus attempts to introduce—indeed, the beauty of Jesus himself—does not ignore the dissolution of life but incorporates it as a necessary element. As if in pursuit of the beauty of Greek tragedy, Hegel's Jesus attempts to live the troubling intimacy of God and human beings.

Plērōma

Hegel faces the challenge of expressing the specific movement that tragedy depicts with an array of verbs: in addition to *zurückziehen,* he calls upon *aufheben, erheben, erfüllen,* and *ausfüllen.* He employs these to capture the movement through transgression to this intimate region of "life in its beautiful free region" (W 1:355/ SC 223). What is the move to an utterly foreign spirit if not a revolution? If it is, however, this revolution would best be described in terms of *immanent transcendence,* beauty in dissolution—that is, *beauty* and *not* sublimity. I will return to the Idea of an immanent transcendence, but I can say at this point that it characterizes the spiritual revolution that, according to Hegel, Jesus presents in the Sermon on the Mount. Hegel clarifies the nature of this movement when he says that what Jesus shows his listeners is "not the dissolution [*Auflösung*] of the laws, but that they must be fulfilled [*erfüllen*] through a new kind of righteousness, in which there is more than is in the righteousness of the sons of duty and which is more complete because it is a filling out [*Ausfüllung*] of the deficiency in the laws" (W 1:326/SC 214, translation altered). This passage ought to be read in relation to Hegel's earlier account of "opposites" (*Entgegengesetzt;* see W 1:279/SC 187 and W 1:321/SC 209). To be *opposed* to something both assumes a higher being *and* precludes the possibility of being higher than what is being opposed. Rather than a logic of opposition, then, we have one of *Ausfüllung.* The old law is not broken up or dissolved but must be fulfilled, and in this act of fulfilling—defined by the unification of inclination and law—the *law* "loses its form as law" (ibid.). While the earlier form is maintained to some degree and not simply dissolved, the law *as* law becomes thoroughly superfluous when judged according to the criterion of life. This logic beyond opposition is not present in an explicit form in either the *Positivity* or *Life of Jesus;* it arises through a conceptualization of Jesus that is framed by Greek tragedy, rather than Kantian moral philosophy.

Above all else, Jesus signifies for the young Hegel the birth of the subjectivity that is missing in the one who simply follows the law through habituation or because of a sense of duty. The world that Jesus introduces is a subjectivity that establishes itself through an extreme flight from all objectivity. It emerges as a confrontation of the subject with itself, and it reveals that any limitations that might be confronted are its own creation, as are any virtues to which it might hold itself.

The objectivity that is considered to be foreign is, in fact, an extension of the self. Freedom is *not* the self-alienation that is inherent in submitting to the moral law. For Hegel, this would simply be the positivity that he locates at the heart of Kant's moral thought. It would be the submission to an alien element that is somehow *in* the self but *other* than it. For Hegel, *freedom* is the possibility of drawing the distinction between virtue, as a modification of love, and vice, such that, if virtue is actual, then it is only a possibility. Freedom is "the 'or' in 'virtue or vice'" (W 1:337/SC 225). Indeed, the distinction between virtue and vice is a *product* of human freedom. As Hegel writes, "In the opposition [*Entgegensetzung*] of the law to nature, of the universal to the particular, both opposites are posited, are actual; the one cannot exist without the other" (W 1:337/SC 225, translation altered). If a moral action is defined *qua* universality at the exclusion of the particular, which is how Hegel understands Kantian morality, then the action is impossible, since universality *is* only *qua* particular. If freedom is defined as reason overcoming desire, then, without desire, there can be no freedom. Freedom, as the origin of the possibility of dividing law from nature, universal from particular, presupposes the originary *union* and codependence of these opposites. Any division of this whole is secondary, a product of thought or judgment. Tragedy expresses the inevitable break with this union and the impossibility of mending it through the domination of the particular by the universal. It is crucial to Hegel's analysis of Jesus and the movement to "life in its beautiful free region" that Jesus embodies and attempts to express because it presents the catharsis of transgressions against this life. That is, it presents the catharsis of these transgressions, rather than a judge's moralizing condemnation and retaliation.

On Crime and Punishment

Instead of the domination of inclination by the law, the opposition between law and inclination is unified through the modifications of love that Hegel calls the *virtues*. To the extent that law can be said to oppose love, it is at the level of *form* alone. That is, this formal "opposition" can take place despite the fact that both Jesus, guided by love, and someone of a positivist disposition, guided by law alone, might agree with the *content* of, for example, the injunction "You shall not kill." Although Hegel does indeed call this an *opposition* (*Gegensatz*) of form, love does not so much oppose law as take it up into itself (*aufnehmen*, W 1:338/SC 225). In contrast to a simple opposition, the incorporation of the law by love results in the law's losing its shape (*Gestalt*, ibid.), such that it is no longer simply opposed to inclination. A *criminal* act, however, opposes the law at the level of *content*. When a theft occurs and the command of pure, practical reason goes unheeded, the crime excludes (*ausschließen*, ibid.) the law, yet its opposite, that which it attempts to destroy (the law), remains. The law and the crime that breaks it are both actual and, thus, not mutually exclusive in the way that virtue and vice are. In other words, when a theft is committed, the law itself is not abolished but simply transgressed. A thief may both know the law and disregard it. Hegel defines crime as "a destruction of nature," and, because nature, as another name in this instance for *life,* is *one,* "there is as much destruction in what destroys as in what is destroyed" (ibid.). To attack nature is to attack oneself. This is another way of saying that there is no "outside"; any transgression is always a transgression against oneself. *Here one confronts, in the full light of day, the central Idea guiding Hegel's early thought—life, the* hen kai pan*—and the way in which it grounds the ethics that he opposes to Kant's submission to the moral law.* Indeed, it is unthinkable apart from it. Drawing out the consequences of this Idea, the question arises of what ethics would look like if any pretense to an "outside" were rejected and the absolute boundary between criminal and victim, prosecutor and defense, was lost. As a means of addressing these questions, I will initially consider how the law retaliates against transgression and then turn to the proper fulfillment of the opposition between transgression and legal retaliation.

The law that attempts to mend the whole that has been divided by crime is *penal.* Whereas positive law commands what is just, the penal law that arises when the command has been disobeyed punishes. In punishing the transgression of a positive command, penal law presumes to mend the divide between transgressor and transgressed. But given Hegel's understanding of crime as an offense against the unconscious unity of nature, this kind by penal justice will be futile, for now the content and the form of penal law are opposed to nature. The penal law as *law* only exists in contradistinction to nature, and its content is a further division of it. With the "fulfillment" (*Aufhebung,* W 1:338/SC 225) of positive law by the virtues, only the *form* of the law vanishes, since the *content* of law and the *content* of virtue are not necessarily opposed. Penal justice, however, requires the fulfillment of both form and content; thus, it poses a much more daunting challenge.

To elucidate, consider not a single murderer but a family of murderers. A son who commits an act of murder goes against the content of the moral law ("You shall not kill"); as such, the murderer loses the rights associated with the law. "The trespasser has forfeited the same right which his trespass has injured in another" (W 1:338/SC 225). But since the law and the rights associated with it only exist as thought, the law must be "linked to life and clothed with might" (W 1:339/SC 226). It must be put into action. And to the extent that the law continues in its "fearful majesty" (ibid.), there is no possibility of escaping the need for punishment because, if the law were merciful, it would cancel *itself* out. That is, the universality of the law would lose its authority. "Justice," as Hegel says, "is unbending" (ibid.). Or, as the Furies say of their prey, Orestes, in Aeschylus' *Eumenides,* "Let him hide under the ground, he shall never go free."[30] Thus, universality as the *form* of the law remains, even if the content of the law ("You shall not kill") has been canceled by the murder. The law pursues the murderer ("keep on, / keep on, as the unspeaking accuser tells us, by / whose sense, like hounds after a bleeding fawn, we trail / our quarry by the splash and drip of blood"[31]), and in the figure of the executioner, "the right which he has canceled [in another] is canceled [*aufgehoben*] in him" (W 1:339/SC 226). The problem arises with the fact that the judge, or the avenger, and the executioner are not simply abstract tools of justice but living beings. While the punishment itself is, *qua* universality of the law, invariably deserved, its fulfillment becomes contingent. Orestes is pursued by the Furies because he himself had assumed the role of avenger of his father's murder, but,when he did so, he had to contend with his mother's pleas—"Oh, take pity, child, before this breast / where many a time, a drowsing baby you would feed."[32] And he hesitated: "What shall I do, Pylades? Be shamed to kill my mother?"[33] When the Furies subsequently avenge Orestes' act of matricide, they too are subject to the force of persuasion. With Athena's invocation of Peitho, the Furies turn from threatening to savage the city that has sided against them to asking, almost humbly, "Lady Athena, what is this place you say is mine?"[34]

When the avenging law bends in its practical execution, a contradiction arises between (i) the universal and unbending *thought* of justice and punishment, which calls for the sacrifice of the individual to the universal, and (ii) their *reality*. The contradiction exists because the person who presumes to judge and assign punishment can surrender the role of judge and forgive. Hegel would say that the pardon marks the end of the role of the judge because the judge is subservient to the law and the law is unwavering: one is either innocent or guilty. A pardon, then, leaves justice unfulfilled, for *qua* the *thought* of justice, punishment follows transgression indissolubly; execution will inevitably follow murder. Given the law's universality, a crime can never be undone. There is no possibility of reconciliation, *not even through suffering punishment*. Certainly the *law* is "satisfied" (*befriedigen*) when, as Hegel writes, "the reality of the criminal is cancelled" (W 1:340/SC 227); but this satisfaction is not reciprocal, for the universality of the law is *necessarily* alien to the particularity of the murderer. For him, as a condemned man hunted by Erinyes, the law's calculations, judgment, and punishment will always be experienced as foreign, regardless of whether the Furies take the form of a god, the state, a wife, son, or the internal weight of bad conscience. As Nietzsche observes, "it is precisely among criminals and convicts that the sting of conscience is extremely rare; prisons and penitentiaries are not the kind of hotbed in which this species of gnawing worm is likely to flourish."[35] After the punishment has been leveled against the transgressor, the "alien power which the trespasser has created and armed against itself" lets go, but it only "withdraws [*zurückziehen*] to a threatening attitude; it has not lost its shape or been made friendly" (W 1:340/SC 227). Even if the punishment is self-imposed, even if one has judged oneself according to the law, the self-condemned criminal still looks on himself with loathing, as the reality of his crime persists. When the Furies, or the reality of a crime, merely withdraw, there is no true reconciliation. The proper fulfillment of the *penal* law comes only when the misrecognition of the alien power as *alien* is overcome. Hegel writes that bad conscience—"a consciousness of self in opposition to self"—always presupposes "an ideal over against a reality which fails to correspond with the ideal, and the ideal is in man, a consciousness of his own whole nature" (W 1:335/SC 241). The consciousness of the criminal who is pursued by the internalized *law* will remain divided because of the oppositional form that the law takes, so the division between the reality of the self and the ideal unity is sustained.[36]

Grace, Fate, Catharsis

Plagued by the intangible threat of this withdrawn, judging power (or, in another register, the grief of a bad conscience), the transgressor is condemned to a state of *Angst* that, as Hegel writes, can only be quelled by the thought of *grace. Angst* arises as the *combined* effect of "the terrifying reality of evil and the immutability of the law" (W 1:341/SC 227). The majesty of the law, then, from the perspective of the one who transgresses it provokes terror, not reverence. This is precisely what the law, figured as the Erinyes, signifies. It represents a mercilessly symmetrical force, taking from the criminal the right that the criminal originally took from the victim. Yet to the one who transgresses it, the law appears thoroughly asymmetrical. It is an unbending, distant force, and as such, it is experienced as a *disruption* in life. Thus, the *Angst* that Hegel describes arises when the moral law is understood as a foreign element, even if it is "internalized." We do not give ourselves the law; instead, we submit before its majesty, and because of this separation from the law, the punishment that it inflicts is also always experienced as a foreign imposition. *Angst,* then, arises with the experience of being condemned for a crime for which one does not assume responsibility and punished by a law that is not one's own.

It follows that, when the terrible majesty of the law renders passive those who acknowledge it, even as they transgress it, the only possible relief would come in the form of grace. Thus, in the same way that the law punishes from on high, forgiveness is also handed down from above when it is understood in this manner. For Hegel, then, grace is a *symptom* of a subject rendered powerless by the terror of a withdrawn and immutable law. As such, it stands as a false means of reconciliation. There is at least a structural connection, however, between grace and catharsis. Both confront a guilt that exists outside the moral equilibrium that would presume to correlate, in a seamless manner, transgression with punishment and obedience with reward. The challenge that Hegel faces is to determine the means of escaping from this state of *Angst* without relying on the kind of outside intervention that grace assumes. It is precisely in this attempt to mend the damage inflicted by a transcendent law that Hegel depends most heavily on the categories of tragic drama.

This graceless escape is equated with the cancellation of punishment and a return to a unity of consciousness, a return deemed impossible as long as punishment is understood as unconditional. Hegel writes, "Law and punishment cannot be reconciled, but they can be cancelled/fulfilled [*aufgehoben*] if *fate* can be reconciled" (W 1:341/SC 228, translation altered, emphasis added). The difficulty of achieving reconciliation involves cancelling/fulfilling both the law and punishment, which can only be achieved through conceiving punishment as *fate*. I have shown in an abstract manner that the spirit of a people is saddled with a fate, that this fate is internal to its original spirit, and that it amounts in content to the reversal of this spirit (dependence is the fate of the spirit of independence). But what exactly is fate in *this* context? It is initially premised on a necessary *misunderstanding*, based on the false belief that we can escape from the law by transgressing its content. The "matter" of a command like "You shall not kill" is smashed by an act of murder because, through contradicting the command, the murderer has apparently shown himself to be the master of a law that is ultimately transient. Yet the *universality* of the law remains, and it continues to harbor the resources to mete out punishment. Thus, Hegel writes, "Punishment is the effect of a transgressed law from which the transgressor has torn himself free but on which he still depends; he cannot escape from the law or from the punishment or from what he has done" (ibid.). Hegel distinguishes *punishment* and *fate* succinctly when he writes that "the former comes from outside, from somewhere independent, the latter is fixed by your nature, and even if it is something now hostile, still it is set up not above you, but against you" (W 1:353/SC 238). An act of murder assumes the erroneous belief in an outside. The murderer assumes that, when she kills, she kills another and not herself. The correlate of this false assumption is the misconception of punishment as a foreign imposition coming from on high.

As love is the fulfillment of law, so fate is the fulfillment of punishment. Breaking with the law is not a *break* at all, but its "*perversion*" (*Verkehrtheit;* W 1:341/SC 228), and the laws' perversion has the effect of rendering the content of the law into the *opposite* of what it was. Thus, when it is adhered to with full rigor, the law ("You shall not kill," the law that the murderer presumes to have overpowered) acquires a content that is the direct opposite of its former injunction ("Kill"). The killer *ought* to be killed. This is no longer an abstract injunction, but a concrete action reproducing the murderer's transgression that, nevertheless, assumes the status of universality ("You shall not kill those who transgress the prohibition against murder"). Far from being simply opposed to the law, punishment, as the law's perversion, is utterly dependent on it. The movement of cancellation/fulfillment—of *aufheben*—consists in presenting punishment not as the inevitable outcome of a transgressed law but as fate. Like love, fate is a concept of *Vernunft,* of *reconciliation,* not a category of *Verstand,* of *division.* Like love, fate too is the union of the universality of the command and the particularity of its execution, but, instead of a benevolent force, it is a hostile power. As a concept of *Vernunft,* fate is thought in terms of the totality of what Hegel has been calling *life,* where *life* is conceived as *being* prior to the judgment that fixes the opposition between the universal and particular. Thinking in this way avoids the hypostasis of any particular moments of life and society but attempts instead to grasp the whole process of their self-destruction and regeneration. This is not to say, of course, that the particular has been forgotten. Through the movement of life, the universal is contained in the particular and the particular embodies the universal. The individual representing the particular does not participate in the universal only through subordination to the moral law. For Hegel, the relation between the universal and the particular is thought in terms of *conflict* rather than subordination.

This presentation of life emphasizes immanence. If the murderer learns that the law is inescapable, this is because there is no outside to life. The question of *plērōma* becomes that of how the movement of transcendence as fulfillment is achieved within this immanent sphere. This "immanent transcendence" takes the form, *qua* fate, of a "cancellation of annihilation" (W 1:343/SC 230), and precisely at this crucial point Hegel refers to both ancient Greek and Shakespearean tragedy. Hegel's conceptualization of law, crime, punishment, life, and fate is, in part, a commentary on the texts of the *Eumenides* and *Macbeth.* The punishment that cannot be outrun is explicitly presented by way of the Furies:

> Only through a departure from that united life which is neither regulated by law nor at variance with law, only through the killing of life, is something alien produced. Destruction of life is not the nullification of life but its diremption [*Trennung*], and the destruction consists in its transformation into an enemy. It is immortal, and, if slain, it appears as its terrifying ghost which vindicates every branch of life and lets loose its Eumenides. The illusion of trespass, its belief that it destroys the other's life and thinks itself enlarged thereby, is dissipated by the fact that the disembodied spirit of the injured life comes on the scene against the trespass, just as Banquo who came as a friend to Macbeth was not blotted out when he was murdered but immediately thereafter took his seat, not as the guest at the feast, but as an evil spirit. The trespasser *intended* to have to do with another's life, but he has only destroyed his own, for life is not different from life, since life

dwells in the single Godhead. In his arrogance he has destroyed indeed, but only the friendliness of life; he has perverted [*verkehren*] life into an enemy. It is the deed itself which has created a law whose domination now comes on the scene. (W 1:342–343 / SC 229, emphasis added)

Hegel labors to avoid the mistake of interpreting the Furies as the personification of the universality of the laws. It is certainly the case that, after his act of matricide, Orestes experiences the Furies as foreign, antagonistic entities: "No! / Women who serve this house, they come like Gorgons, they / wear robes of black, and they are wreathed in a tangle / of snakes. I can no longer stay."[37] Yet, properly understood, the law is a lord, while fate is (merely) an enemy. The Furies do not represent the absolute quality of the law reigning over and rendering passive the particular transgressor, even if this is the way that they may be perceived. As the *fulfillment* of the penal law, the Erinyes are closer than the law, for, above the law, there is nothing, not even God, who only administers the law. At least, this how it looks from within the orbit of the law. The fulfillment of punishment as *fate* is not the judgment of a master on a slave or jury on the condemned but the effect that arises with an assault on life—*life* being, again, that which contains within any one of its parts the whole of itself. Hegel's claim that "[i]t is the deed which has created the law" means, most importantly, that the original deed *creates* the division in immortal life that the law then presumes to mend. So the punishment that the law unleashes loses its absolute and unbending quality, for the enemy is a living being. Because it is of the same ontological order, it shares something with the transgressor, and this alone allows for the possibility of reconciliation. Seeing the other as an enemy, as someone standing *against* oneself rather than a lord who stands *above,* invites the possibility of genuine struggle, one that takes place on an equal plane. A struggle with fate is not a rebellion or an act of indignation by a subject against a ruler; it is not, as Hegel says, "the slave's flight from his master, liberation from subservience, a revivification out of a dead situation, for the man is alive, and before he acts there is no cleavage, no opposition, much less mastery" (W 1:342/SC 229). From the perspective of the authority reflected in the existing law of the time, the 1789 uprising in France would have seemed like a rebellion and an act of indignation, but it could occur only when those who rose up no longer saw themselves as subordinate to the law. It could occur when the majesty of the law has been deflated and revealed as a disruption of life. Similarly, the proletarian uprising that Karl Marx anticipated could be interpreted as an act of liberation from the perspective of the moral law. Qua *fate,* however, the sharp distinction between oppressor and oppressed becomes blurred. The proletariat exists as such only because of the concentration of laborers in cities and factories, and they are exploited only to the extent that they respect the law that secures bourgeois private property. The owning classes exist only because of the labor of the proletariat and the surplus value that it produces. Marx's famous conclusion that "what the bourgeoisie, therefore, produces, above all, is its own grave-diggers"[38] is the materialist way of saying that fate is the consciousness of oneself as another. The antagonists, bourgeois and proletariat, oppressor and oppressed, depend on each other for their existence, and, ultimately, they share the same mode of existence. Maurice Blanchot articulates this well when he writes,

> this toolness, this relation of use between men, gives men the value of things; this is as clear for the slave as it is for any man who hires out his work—his time—to another, but it is also clear for the master. The person who treats another as a thing—even without knowing it, and perhaps especially then—through the unseen detour of economic relations treats himself like a thing, accepts the fact that he belongs to a world in which men are things, gives himself the reality and figure of a thing, not only breaks off communication with one who is similar or dissimilar to him but breaks off communication with himself.[39]

For Marx, of course, the bourgeoisie, in its role as Macbeth, would be more than merely haunted by the ghost of capital. The tragic dimension in this case comes with the recognition that the possibility of struggling against fate requires an intensification of suffering through an intensification of ever starker class divisions. "Reconciliation" comes on the other side of "open revolution."[40]

All destruction of life is avenged, and the Furies represent this unavoidable response in a way that resists relying on an overarching, withdrawn law that looks down in judgment. Furthermore, all life is stained by transgression insofar as we *act*. *Qua* fate, the equilibrium of justice is thrown out of joint. As Nietzsche wrote of the Aeschylean world, "All that exists is just and unjust and equally justified in both."[41] And as Hegel claims in his *Lectures on Fine Art*, "in considering all these tragic conflicts we must above all reject the false idea that they have anything to do with guilt or innocence. The tragic heroes are just as much innocent as guilty" (W 15:545 / LFA 1214). Orestes is bound by an obligation to Agamemnon, as Clytemnestra was bound by an obligation to Iphigenia, as Agamemnon was bound by obligations to his *polis* and his family. All are innocent and guilty at one and the same time. Orestes is hounded by the Furies because his matricidal act constitutes the destruction of a particular moment of life. Within the unfolding of the fate of the house of Atreus, however, Clytemnestra's death at the hands of her son does not call forth the Furies alone but only serves to spur them further. They represent, after all, the principle that all destruction of life will be avenged. As Aristotle notes, the best tragedies recount the stories of "only a few families,"[42] and, within the insular world of these unfortunate families, the reversal inherent in transgression is made blindingly clear. The one who intends to murder another destroys his or her own life. This counters the view that interprets punishment as the reaction of an utterly foreign and irrepressible master; for punishment as fate is self-destruction. If the world of Kantian practical philosophy is characterized by the apparent distance of a universal moral law on high, Hegel's is a more claustrophobic world. In *Hamlet,* the prince voices this thought when he says, "To die, to sleep; / To sleep: perchance to dream: ay, there's the rub" (3.1.64–65). As Levinas writes, "Hamlet recoils before the 'not to be' because he has a foreboding of the return of being."[43] As for Macbeth, far from "blotting out" Banquo, his murder calls forth an evil spirit, or as Levinas writes, the ghost of Banquo returns "through the fissures through which one has driven it."[44]

What is it, then, to struggle against this fate? Hegel offers both the Furies that chase Orestes and the ghost of Banquo that haunts the feast of Macbeth as illustrations of fate, yet he also claims that, as tragic heroes, there is a difference between the beauty of the Greek Orestes and the sublimity of Macbeth. Where does Jesus fall in relation to these two? As the one who sets himself against the whole of a sublime fate, his spirit stands as the distinctly Christian attempt at reconciliation. Does it, however, give rise to a beauty akin to that of Greek tragedy?

The Empty Site of the Law

According to Hegel's interpretation, Jesus attempts to negate this negation of life through a reconciliation of fate as such. I have spoken of this negation as an initial transgression or crime against life, but the effect of an act against life is less a transgression than a wounding. That is, what exists in the regime of law and punishment as a crime exists within the fuller domain of life as a wound: "And life can heal its wounds again; the severed hostile life can return into itself again . . . and annul the law and punishment" (W 1:342/SC 230). The healing, or reconciliation, that Jesus is thought to undertake would annul not only the punishment but the law as well. The wound itself can exist as a result of the suffering caused by an externally imposed punishment. It can also exist as the awareness of oneself as disrupted, and a wound of this kind takes the form of bad conscience. In either case, it gives rise to the workings of fate. Fate is first manifested as a *feeling,* and "this feeling of life disrupted must become a longing [*Sehnsucht*] for what has been lost" (W 1:344/SC 230). While this longing may initially be sensed as something like nostalgia,[45] it is only when it becomes intensified to the point that it "springs from the deepest recesses of his soul" (W 1:345/SC 232) that the longing for lost life becomes a distinct awareness of the extreme disruption of life and the immutability of the law. Only when Orestes has followed the Apollinian law to its extreme and killed Clytemnestra and Aegisthus does the horrible limitation of law and punishment *qua* law arise. At this point, the awareness of life takes the form of *Angst.* The *lack* of life is experienced as being a part of the one who has transgressed the law but in the form of the awareness of an absence. It is the intimation that there should be something in the transgressor that is not present. Something is missing, and it is now sensed *as* missing. "This lack," Hegel stresses, "is not a *Nicht-Sein,* but life known and felt as *nicht-seiend"* (W 1:344/SC 231).

To see the distance that Hegel has traveled, compare this experience with that of the moral law as described in his *Life of Jesus:* "Pure reason, transcending all limits, is divinity itself" (N 75/LJ 104). In the earlier text, the moral law that pure reason reveals is precisely what those who are reawakened by John the Baptist's teaching "should be able to find within, in their true selves" (ibid.). It must be distinct from the self at the same time that it is within us, for we cannot revere what is not above us. While an alienation from the law would allow us the distance to recognize this "spark of divinity" (ibid.), pure reason, as a foreign element reigning within the proper sphere of the self, is the sign of a divided consciousness—a wounded or disrupted self. In *The Spirit of Christianity,* this foreign element has left the scene; nevertheless, the place that it once held remains. As I have stressed, for Kant the emotion proper to the experience of the immutability of the moral law is reverence, and the phenomenal manifestation of this is the sublime object. When this sense of majesty is lost, the feeling that replaces it—the feeling that arises with the awareness of the possibility of fate—is a unique kind of fear. It is neither the fear of a concrete punishment nor the fear of what is alien, but the fear of separation as such, an awe (*Scheu,* W 1:344/SC 231) before one's self. When the law is absent but the site of the law remains, awe replaces the respect (*Achtung,* ibid.) that is said to come from doing duty for the sake of duty alone.

Achtung versus *Scheu:* according to Hegel, the moral thinking that endorses the feeling of respect for the law leads to submission, and, when this foreign law takes the form of punishment, it ultimately comes to be resented. Thus, punishment makes nothing better, for it is only "a feeling of impotence in the face of the lord" (W 1:344/SC 231). The experience of awe is different. When we "submit" to fate, it does not amount to surrendering before a foreign lord but is rather a reversion and approach to oneself. Even the most severe acts of pilgrims, walking barefoot in hair shirts on hot sand, arise from some intimation of a lost unity. Even those acts spurred by a conviction in an original sin, a conviction that ensures we are all criminals before an absolute law, arise from this intimation. True penance must be opposed to acts performed in the name of duty, and the need for it must be seen as the disruption of life, rather than the transgression of a law. As is clear from the *Positivity,* ascetics are Hegel's figure for the living dead. The self-sacrifices they make only prolong their consciousness of being evil ("the more you obey the [law's] command, the guiltier you are"). Yet even in these most extreme cases, a longing for reunion can still surface, and because what is opposed to the longing consciousness (its "enemy") is felt as life and not something infinitely removed, reconciliation is deemed possible.

According to Hegel, when the oblique sense of life that fuels the penitence of the ascetic is recognized as such, it is revealed as love: "In love, fate is reconciled" (W 1:346/SC 232). Love produces a reconciliation that consists in neither the destruction nor subjugation of what is alien. It is also unmarred by any distance between the human being as concept and the human as reality, which is to say that this reconciliation is not structured by either messianic hope or teleological projection. Fate fulfilled by love does not exist as a promise and the temporal separation inherent in promise making. It is not determined by the *command,* arising from the noncoincidence of reason and inclination and the *sacrifice* that this noncoincidence necessarily entails (one follows the law only with the sacrifice of the pleasure of inclination). Through love what was perceived as alien is grasped retroactively as a part of what is one's own. This initial sensing of life "recognizes what has been lost as life, as what was once its friend" (W 1:344/SC 231). Whereas the transgression of a law is an offense against something existing *outside* the sphere of one's own, the wounding of life reveals the whole. The transgressor's deed reveals the whole as *divided,* but as a *whole* nevertheless. Once this has been exposed, "the pricks of conscience have become blunt, since the deed's evil spirit has been chased away; there is no longer anything hostile in the man, and the deed remains at most as a soulless carcass lying in the charnel-house of actualities, in memories" (W 1:346/SC 232). That which haunts us is our own doing. The criminal senses in the suffering he experiences through his punishment the same life that he originally harmed through his crime. And Hegel tells us that, with this, *justice* is satisfied. *Love* is what he calls the power that is able to lay past crimes to rest. Are we secure, however, in putting our fear of their future return to rest as well?

The reconciliation that law provides operates within a moral economy of intention and culpability. Yet moral concerns do not always begin with good and bad intention; they do not begin with self-conscious reference to an Idea of the Good. Guilt can certainly arise when we willfully commit a crime, but what Hegel calls the most *"exalted"* (W 1:347/SC 233) form of guilt arises when we are entirely *innocent.* As Schelling writes of ancient Greek tragedy, "It was a sublime thought, to suffer punishment willingly even for an inevitable crime, and so to prove one's freedom by the very loss of this freedom, and to go down with a declaration of free will."[46]

Punishment suffered for an inevitable crime: Hegel does not evade the problem that the life of Oedipus poses for the sake of tidy resolutions. He has indicated that, beyond judgment, action *as such* divides life, and, given this, fate is as unbounded as life itself: "Where life is injured, be it ever so rightly, even if no dissatisfaction is felt, there fate appears, and one may therefore say 'never has innocence suffered; every suffering is guilt'" (W 1:347/SC 233). (Hegel reiterates this sentiment in the *Phenomenology* when paraphrasing Sophocles' Antigone: "Because we suffer, we acknowledge that we have erred" [PdG 310/PS 284].) Just as there is no absolute guilt, one that can be thrown into the charnel house with no fear of return, there is no absolute innocence. Injuring life is inevitable. Upon Agamemnon's death, the chorus asks, "Now to this man the blessed ones have given / Priam's city to be captured / and return in the gods' honor. / Must he give blood for generations gone, / die for those slain and in death pile up / more death to come for the blood shed, / what mortal else who hears shall claim / he was born clear of the dark angel?"[47] As Vernant notes, the line translated as "Must he give blood for generations gone" is ambiguous. It could mean that Agamemnon must pay for the blood that his ancestors have shed, but it could also mean the blood that he himself has shed. Aeschylus's Agamemnon is both the casualty of an ancestral crime over which he has no control and guilty of acts for which he is directly responsible. Thus, he is caught between "the ancient religious concept of crime-defilement, *hamartia,* . . . the delirium sent by the gods that necessarily engenders crime, and . . . the new concept in which the guilty one, *hamartōn* and, above all, *adikōn,* is defined as one who, under no compulsion, has deliberately chosen to commit a crime."[48]

Beauty in Withdrawal

The tragic outlook considers action and culpability from a perspective that extends beyond the interiority of the intending subject. Hegel offers as an example the reaction a victim might have to an unprovoked attack. Let us take Oedipus at his word when he describes his meeting with Laius at the crossroads as just such an attack:

> Making my way toward this triple crossroad
> I began to see a herald, then a brace of colts
> drawing a wagon, and mounted on the bench . . . a man,
> just as you've described him, coming face-to-face,
> and the one in the lead and the old man himself
> were about to thrust me off the road—brute force—
> and the one shouldering me aside, the driver,
> I strike him in anger!—and the old man, watching me
> coming up along his wheels—he brings down

> his prod, two prongs straight at my head!
> I paid him back with interest![49]

The assault by Laius and his men may be the occasion that gives rise to a fate, but the manner in which Oedipus reacts to another's deed—by fighting back or submitting—will determine its character. As Hegel says, "it is with his reaction . . . that his guilt, his fate, begins" (W 1:347/SC 233). What is striking here is both the direct association of guilt and fate and the apparent freedom Oedipus has in determining his fate. As the association reveals, however, this freedom is a limited one, for he is free only to assume a specific attitude toward an outcome that is itself predetermined. The oracle at Delphi tells Oedipus his fate *and* Oedipus chooses the road leading to Thebes, Laius, and Jocasta, rather than the one heading back to Corinth, Polybus, and Merope.

When we are at a crossroads, called to "choose" within the broader confines of a fate, Hegel claims that courage and the struggle against an adversary are the better path to follow because, on entering the fray, we are forced to recognize that, if we lose, we are responsible. The way of submission is much more susceptible to avoiding this responsibility. But Oedipus not only enters the fray; he also triumphs, "I killed them all—every mother's son!"[50] His culpability, however, depends solely on the singularity of the victim. The next line reads, "Oh, but if there is any blood-tie / between Laius and this stranger . . . / what man alive more miserable than I?"[51] For Hegel, this confrontation is opposed to life in itself, in that it entails a conflict between the concept of right, as a thought, and its realization; we can see that the scenario he has in mind is a properly aporetic one in that it is based on the combatants' conflicting claims to right. Thus, we have the impossible situation of two universals: "both are right, both are at war. And this gives them both the right to self-defense. . . . Life is in conflict with life" (W 1:348/SC 234). This confrontation could simply lead to the reduction of right to might and the inherent danger that, with right and reality remaining at odds, the former would become dependent on the latter. Oedipus kills Laius; therefore, he is right. A second alternative involves submitting to the alien authority of a judge. The combatants would then have to renounce their own mastery of the actual and surrender their claim to the right that they were defending in the first place.

Jesus offers a third alternative to this rudimentary political deadlock. It is, indeed, the truth of these two opposed and one-sided responses—courage and struggle or the submission before an external legal authority—and it is realized as "beauty of soul":

> The truth of both opposites, courage and passivity, is so unified in beauty of soul [*Schönheit der Seele*] that the life in the former remains though opposition falls away, while the loss of right in the latter re-

mains, but the grief vanishes. There thus arises a cancellation [*Aufhebung*] of right without suffering, a living free elevation [*Erhebung*] above the loss of right and above struggle. (W 1:349 / SC 234–235)

This resolution of activity and passivity anticipates, up to a point, a shape of consciousness found in the "Conscience" section of the *Phenomenology*, on the cusp of the transition from "Spirit" to "Religion." Of particular interest is that the "Conscience" section as a whole stands as the dialectical fulfillment of the Kantian moral view of the world in that it brings together the universality of the Kantian moral imperative with an attunement to the unavoidable singularity of the situation to which the imperative is applied. In broad strokes, the dialectic of conscience unfolds in such a way as to pit the extremes of the active, "evil" consciousness and the inactive, hard-hearted judging consciousness against each other (see PdG 437, 440 / PS 404, 407). The first *acts* and is guided by self-interest masked as a universal good. The second *judges* and maintains the purity of its position by never acting. The two sides are reconciled insofar as they both recognize their guilt retrospectively. They can fulfill the aim of spirit by mutually confessing and receiving forgiveness from the other. The "evil" consciousness, then, reflects the deadlocks of conscience on the side of actions, pathos, and impurity. The fate of purity and inaction, however, passes not only through the judgmental consciousness but also the "so-called 'beautiful soul'" (PdG 433 / PS 400). This particular shape of consciousness

> lives in dread of besmirching the splendor of its inner being by action and an existence; and, in order to preserve the purity of its heart, it flees from contact with the actual world. . . . Its activity is a yearning which merely loses itself as consciousness becomes an object devoid of substance, and, rising above this loss, and falling back on itself, finds itself only as a lost soul. In this transparent purity of its moments . . . its light dies away within it, and it vanishes like a shapeless vapor that dissolves into thin air. (Ibid.)

Looking back from the "Conscience" section of the *Phenomenology*, a question arises: How does the beauty of soul that Hegel attributes to Jesus in *The Spirit of Christianity* and the gesture of withdrawal that is so intimately related to this beauty avoid the danger of vanishing into thin air? If Jesus achieves a "living free elevation" (W 1:349 / SC 234–235) above the opposition between acting and judging consciousness, how does he manifest beauty of soul without withdrawing to the point of losing himself?

Transcending both the anger of Oedipus at the crossroads and the grief that comes with submission before an alien authority, Jesus introduces a beauty related to the subject, rather than substance. The fulfillment that he effects is through *with-*

drawing (*zurückziehen;* W 1:349/SC 235) from any engagement with the other. If someone approaches what we consider to be ours in a hostile way, then we avoid an assault on our rights by the hostile other or an alien judge by simply giving up what the other has claimed. Initially, this can be understood as renouncing the right we have over something like a mundane piece of property. But if the object or relation being threatened is more dear to us, it must be renounced with greater intensity: "If any side of him is touched, he withdraws himself therefrom. . . . To renounce [*Aufhebung*] his relationships [to both property and other people] in this way is to abstract from himself, but this process has no fixed limits" (ibid.). Indeed, to avoid being contaminated by the violence of the other, the beautiful soul must break with all relations, even the most vital ones—those of friendship and family. According to this logic of withdrawal,

> every grief which thus results to him is so far just and is now his unhappy fate, a fate which he himself has consciously wrought; and it is his distinction to suffer unjustly, because he is raised so far above these rights that he *willed* to have them for enemies. Moreover, since this fate is rooted in himself, he can endure it, face it, because his griefs are not a pure passivity, the predominance of an alien being, but are produced by himself. (W 1:349–350/SC 235)

An unhappy fate is wholly his own doing, not visited on him from an alien being, so all suffering can be tolerated because his nemesis, whatever form it might take, has been produced by his own will. Thus, the beautiful soul is reconciled with his fate through *self-sacrifice* alone:

> To save himself, the man kills himself; to avoid seeing his own being in another's power, he no longer calls it his own, and so he annihilates himself in wishing to maintain himself, since anything in another's power would no longer be the man himself, and there is nothing in him which could not be attacked and sacrificed [*aufgegeben*]. (W 1:349/SC 235)

The will to recapture life is so intense that this beautiful soul is driven to renounce it and renounce it to such a degree that he "must withdraw into the void altogether" (W 1:350/SC 236). What ultimately defines this soul is the radical, inward flight from life, yet this most extreme passivity achieves what eludes other modes of activity:

> By himself setting an absolutely total fate over against himself, the man has *eo ipso* lifted himself above fate entirely. Life has become untrue to him, not he to life. He has fled from life but done no injury to

> it. He may long for it as for an absent friend, but it cannot pursue him like an enemy. On no side is he vulnerable; like a sensitive plant, he withdraws into himself when touched. (Ibid.)

The description of the movement of withdrawal that Hegel gives in *The Spirit of Christianity* provides a striking contrast to the similar account of the break from prior relations found in the *Positivity* (see W 1:120/P 82). In the earlier text, Hegel evokes Luke 14:26 ("If any one comes to me and does not hate his own father and mother and wife and children and brothers and sisters, yes, and even his own life, he cannot be my disciple"), but he does so in the service of emphasizing the rupture from the social world that Jesus required of his disciples, as well as a sacrifice of their free will. This was a rupture that Hegel placed in direct contrast to the Greek philosophical communities that were sustained by the *polis*. That Jesus was forced to adopt positive elements was deemed by Hegel to be a concession to his time. The occasion for the withdrawal that Hegel describes in *The Spirit of Christianity* is still external, but it is an affirmation of freedom that does not engender resentment but manages to circumvent it.

One way of interpreting this presentation of Jesus in terms of "beauty of soul" is that he represents the form of subjectivity that is required in the wake of the collapse of the unified life of a free *polis*. Yet, again, has this collapse always already occurred? It is tempting to draw this conclusion from Hegel's choice in *The Spirit of Christianity* to represent Greece by way of Orestes, Oedipus, and Antigone, and not, as was the case in the *Positivity*, by the philosophical sects that he understood as harmoniously embedded within the democratic *polis*. Perhaps Hegel is coming to recognize the great labor that is necessary so that the critical self-reflectivity that he associated with Greek philosophers and a free political order can coexist harmoniously. That is to say, any beauty that Greece can claim for itself was won *through confrontation with fate*. When Hegel is scripting the life of Jesus on the model of Greek tragedy, then, is the beauty of soul that defines the essential gesture of Jesus also found in Greece? Did the "different genius" presented in the Sermon on the Mount exist in ancient Athens? If Oedipus reacts out of anger when confronted by Laius, has he become a figure of withdrawal when, at the end of the play, he grasps Jocasta's broaches in his hands? To pose these questions in a broader way, is *withdrawal* an unfortunate and doomed stance necessitated by historical contingency, or is it a necessary moment in the development of subjectivity as such? Hegel's response will determine the status he affords to Christianity. It is either necessary in order to bolster a genuinely free, self-determining society, or, despite its best intentions, it is—tragically—fated to be inimical to realizing this "expression of life in its beautiful free region" (W 1:335/SC 223).

FIVE

Dialectic of Love

> The dead body resting there in the interminable decomposition of relics, the spirit never raises itself high enough, it is retained as a kind effluvium, of gas fermenting above the corpse.
>
> —Jacques Derrida, *Glas*

Beauty as Love Objectified

The beauty found in the beautiful soul is attributed to the subject rather than the social "substance" as a whole. Indeed, it marks a rupture that opens the subjective sphere of interiority.[1] For Hegel, the withdrawal characterizing this beauty of the soul is an essential aspect of the figure of Jesus, and the fate of the beautiful soul is that of Christianity in general. This is the figure in whom, as Hegel writes, "the supreme guilt is compatible with supreme innocence; the most wretched fate with elevation above all fate" (W 1:351/SC 236, translation altered). The purging of all hostile feelings, all sense of pride, all demands on another is necessary because the possibility of reconciliation and the rebirth of friendship and love depends on having done no harm to life. The soul that has detached itself from all objectivity is open to reconciliation. Only with the "cancellation" (*Aufhebung*, ibid.) of the hostile fate that the beautiful soul has brought into being against itself can the possibility of forgiveness arise. As an inevitable transgression against life, the original act that gave rise to the fate subsists, but "only as something past, as a fragment, as a corpse" (W 1:354/SC 239), not, presumably, as a ghost that continues to haunts the conscience. If properly buried, it will not return. Indeed, Hegel speaks of a reconciliation that conquers fate to the point where it is "dissolved into the airs of night" (W 1:351/SC 237), like a wound that heals without a trace.[2] By way of forgiveness, "life has severed itself from itself and united itself again" (W 1:354/SC 239). Who participates in *forgiveness*? The short answer is Mary Magdalene, but a fuller response requires clarifying the proper relations among forgiveness, faith, and withdrawal.

Hegel describes the one who does not offend life, who withdraws to the level of a plant, in terms of *faith*. Faith, in turn, is characterized by the relation of "like *knowing* like": "Faith is a knowledge [*Erkenntnis*] of spirit through spirit" (W 1:355/SC 239).[3] But this is a curious kind of knowledge, neither the emissary of theoretical reason nor knowledge as judgment. It is not a relation of mastery but, instead, the discovery of the beauty in another that can only be sensed by one who also possesses this beauty. (Hegel will later claim that "love is a sensing [*Gefühl*] of a life similar to one's own" [W 1:363/SC 247].) Jesus and those who have faith in him are not related as lord and servant. Indeed, the form of knowledge based on the reconciliation of *Vernunft* is the *Aufhebung* of lordship generally. They meet not so much as equals, for equality is an abstract relation of legality. This is a *thought*, and, as Hegel writes, "a thought cannot be loved" (ibid.). When Peter recognizes the beauty in Jesus (see Matthew 16:16), he can do so only on the condition that he too has a comparable soul, even if he is blind to this beauty in himself. As one who carries within himself the "whole of human nature" (W 1:354/SC 240), the awareness that Jesus has of the beauty in others is an *immediate* knowledge that is consistent with the nonjudgmental status that Hegel attributes to him: "An integrated nature penetrates the feeling of another in a moment and senses the other's harmony or disharmony" (W 1:355/SC 240). For Peter to recognize the divinity of Jesus properly, he too would have to be aware of the "whole depth of man" (W 1:357/SC 242) in himself. In other words, he would have to be aware that human beings are the children of God. If withdrawal defines the specific form of revolution that Jesus embodies, it is to this end. The proper awareness of this divinity entails recognizing in others the belief that would free them of all remaining fate, thus raising them above all domination and law. This is the end of the movement of immanent transcendence. To be united with God, so to speak, *is* to be possessed of a heart free from all guilt and fate. Once Peter recognizes the divinity in this particular man, in Jesus, he should be able to see it in others, including himself, but he does not. He was conscious of God united with *one* man, Jesus, but not all human beings.

While Hegel initially provides this sketch of Peter as a concrete example of forgiveness, the true presentation of "spirit knowing spirit" is the relation between Jesus and the "famous and beautiful sinner" (*berühmte schöne Sünderin*, W 1:357/SC 242), Mary Magdalene. Her relation with Jesus embodies the Idea of love most fully; as such, it provides the model for spiritual reconciliation. Hegel identifies Mary Magdalene with the unnamed "sinner" of Luke 7:36–50 and Mary of Bethany (see John 12:1–8), and his description of her encounter with Jesus is based on this identification. As it stands, it is almost breathless in its admiration for the shy, proud, self-sufficient young woman. The grieving sinner, kissing and anointing the feet of Jesus, must offer "all the riches of her loving heart so that she can drown her consciousness in this fervent joy" (W 1:358/SC 243). Drowning consciousness in the tears of despair and the feet of Jesus in kisses, she extinguishes all guilt in this "bliss of love, drinking reconciliation from its effusion" (W 1:358/SC 243). The beauty in this scene is marked by excess in that it transcends all the categories of reflective consciousness. The baptismal fluid now comes in the form of tears, and this form of externalization stands in sharp contrast not only to the spoken word but also to the internalization of the meal that Mary Magdalene has interrupted. Beauty is this excessive externalization, and, in the case of Mary Magdalene, it cancels the guilt of a guilty consciousness, bringing her to "the most beautiful consciousness" (W 1:359/SC 244). In the words of Werner Hamacher, "Mary Magdalene's act initiates the aesthetic revolution within Christianity" and the scene "—one where the prostitute becomes as devout [*fromm*] as Hegel's mother Maria Magdalena Fromme—is a primal scene of speculative ontology."[4] As one who has, traditionally, been so closely associated with the physicality of *erōs* and the reduction of love to the equivalency of commercial exchange, her previous relations would seem to have been the very antithesis of the one that Mary Magdalene forms with Jesus.[5] Yet, precisely this excessiveness, through her sin and her exclusion from the righteous, conditions this reversal. Because of the extreme reduction of the act of love to the physical and her separation from those who live righteously under the law, she avoids the limits placed on the power of forgiveness that we have mentioned above, namely, the sin of the adulteress. Had Mary Magdalene been bound in marriage, her act would be unforgivable. As Jesus will never be a husband, she will never be a wife.[6]

Hegel enumerates the responses that the righteous give to this scene of forgiveness and reconciliation. Before Mary's "beautiful work,"[7] Jesus's disciples are consumed by utilitarian calculations: the ointment was expensive and could have been better used if it were sold and the proceeds given to the poor (see Matthew 26: 6–9).[8] In contrast to the disciples, Simon the Pharisee can only judge (see Luke 7:36–39). He knows this woman to be a sinner and infers that, if Jesus does not recognize this, he is not the seer he claims to be. Thus, Simon says of Mary Magdalene what Kantian moral thought says of that which lies outside the moral law: "Woe to the human relations which are not unquestionably founded in the concept of duty" (W 1:323/SC 212). By *not* withdrawing from the claims of right and duty, Simon is left open to the anger of the righteous. He is not offended by crimes committed against him individually but by a crime against the universality of duty, against the concepts he uses to forge an artificial unity with the conflicting elements of desire and duty. The righteousness of Simon is grounded in the kind of conviction that ties it to the severe limitations that Hegel uncovers in Kantian moral theory. A theory of this kind attempts to unify the many-sidedness of human relations and the multiplicity of virtues that arises in any specific moral context by way of a principle, and this, in turn, can only lead to "despair" (*Verzweiflung;* W 1:361/SC 245). Beyond the utilitarian calculations of the disciples and Simon the Pharisee's moralizing judgments, the beauty of Mary Magdalene's gesture flows from its excessive nature, as does the inevitable sin of one with a beautiful heart who refuses to live as an automaton (*ein Automat,* W 1:359/SC 244). While Hegel criticizes those who witness this scene as automata, from the perspective of those on the outside looking in, the *union* of Jesus and Mary Magdalene itself cannot but appear automatic. It would seem at best to be a kind of mystical reconciliation and, as such, effervescent. Is her loving act of the premature preparation of the body for burial a scene of *tragic* beauty and *tragic* fulfillment? Is the purification through love of Mary Magdalene's prior sins also the catharsis of fear and pity? And is the *mimēsis* of the scene potentially the stuff of a future *Volksreligion* and its rituals? Hegel's answer appears to be "no." If Mary Magdalene's act *initiates* the "aesthetic revolution within Christianity," her beautiful deed falls short of religion. Religion cannot be based on the excessive gesture of Mary Magdalene and the immediate, radically *subjective* union of spirit *sensing* spirit. The wound may be healed without the trace of a scar but only when no flesh remains. More generally, the union grounded in love, like Jesus's encounter with Mary Magdalene, cannot sustain its institutionalization.

Last Supper Revisited

How, then, will the unity of forgiveness be made objective? What will stand in for the festival of Dionysus? From the perspective of the law, the expression of Mary Magdalene's love—anointing the feet of Jesus—is the ritual preparation for death. Jesus's departure from his friends is another expression of love but one more closely aligned with *philia.* Like the scene of Mary Magdalene's forgiveness, however, this feast will also lack objectivity, and it too reveals the limitations of an exclusively subjective reconciliation of fate. As Hegel writes, "Love is less than religion," or more precisely, love alone does not qualify as religion because "only a unification in love, made objective by imagination, can be the object of religious veneration" (W 1:364/SC 248). Religion *is* the *plērōma* of love: "it is reflection [*Reflexion*] and love united, bound together in thought [*denken*]" (W 1:369/SC 253). In this union, the imagination must not be sent away empty handed, for it is the means of attaining objectivity. The Last Supper, which Hegel continues to refer to as *das Mahl der Liebe,* is an expression of emotion alone and not an objective presentation—an image—of love. It is not the unity of feeling and its objectification through the imagination. Thus, it lacks substantiality. Yet if objectivity does not come in the form of an image, the Last Supper is still more than the immediate sensing of like spirits. Objectivity *does* exist as the food shared by the friends at the table:

> in *das Mahl der Liebe* there is also something objective in evidence, to which feeling is linked but which is not yet united in an image. Hence, eating hovers [*schweben*] between a common table of friendship and

> a religious act, and this hovering makes the clear interpretation of its spirit difficult. (W 1:364/SC 248, translation altered)

Hegel clarifies this indeterminate union of the subjectivity of friendship and the objectivity of religious ritual by referring to the significance that Arabs place in sharing a cup of coffee with a stranger, an act that is said to unite the two in a bond of friendship. The unity produced through this act of sharing is not realized as a mere "symbol" (*Zeichen;* W 1:364/SC 248). In the connection forged between the symbol and what is symbolized, the union is dependent on a third, alien thing—a broken ring or *astragalos.*[9] Thus, this union exists only in thought. Beyond this kind of symbolic union, the felt union of the *act* of sharing a meal or wine is a truly living, spiritual union because, as Hegel explains, "it runs counter to natural human feeling to drink a glass of wine with an enemy; the sense of community in this action would contradict the attitude of the parties to one another at other times" (W 1:364/SC 248). The nonsymbolic, felt union does not require a third, alien thing to bind the act and its significance. Although the Last Supper should not be understood as a symbol, it nevertheless remains the kind of indeterminate and unfulfilled union that Hegel characterized by the phenomenon of *hovering.*

The idea of *plērōma* that will include the objectivity necessary for religion proper is, initially, modeled on eating. As Hamacher writes, "Eating does not merely mean, but *is.*"[10] For Hegel, the unification of the subject and object as the proper aim of religion takes place in immediate experience. This is the significance of a nonsymbolic, felt union. But beyond this immediate feeling of unity, Jesus also *speaks:* "Take, eat; this is my body" (Matthew 26:27). I have shown that to enter into the domain of language, to name, is to leave the purely subjective realm of feeling. With the combination of the natural feeling associated with a shared meal and this declaration, the *feeling* of unity is now, as Hegel says, "partially objective." As such, it is described as a "mystical action" (W 1:366/SC 249). Like Mary Magdalene's deed, it is qualified as such, in part, because of its *excessiveness.* It is something more than mere utility: the act of two friends each taking half of a broken ring so that they can identify each other in the future is, from the outside, merely breaking something useful. The sacrifice of a useful object, indeed, the sacrifice of the body and blood, cannot be assimilated into a logic of exchange. This excess is something that can be grasped only by those *within* the community of friends: "Objectively considered, bread is just bread, the wine is just wine; yet both are something *more*" (W 1:365–366/SC 249). What makes a piece of bone more than a bone and bread more than bread cannot be explained with reference to allegory or parable, for, in both of these figures of speech, difference remains. As I have demonstrated above, Hegel considers the parables in Jesus's Sermon on the Mount to be insufficient to the task of expressing *plērōma*. They are unable to express "life in its beautiful free region" (W 1:335/SC 223).[11] With the "mystical" union of the blood of Jesus and wine, body and bread, all difference falls away and seemingly heterogeneous things are intimately united. It marks a unity that the *Verstand* cannot corral into a concept. The union of the friends in their shared feeling of love *is* itself the spirit of Jesus made objective. As such, it is an *objective* feeling. But the spirit made objective cannot be sustained: "the love made objective, this subjective element become a *thing*, reverts once more to its nature, becomes subjective again in the eating" (W 1:367/SC 251). As the host passes through the lips, as it is internalized and digested, the "mystical" union disappears and so reveals itself to be again less than a religious act. In consumption, the quality of excess, of being more than bread alone, is reigned in.

For Hegel, in Frankfurt, Christianity will never proceed any further toward the unity of (subjective) feeling and (objective) expression than the kind of fleeing fulfillment experienced in this meal. *If there is a form of tragedy proper to Christianity, it is grounded in the fact that this disappearing union is always experienced in its full fragility.* The vanishing objectivity of the "mystical" union is comparable to the transience of reading and the ostensibly permanent written word. It would be like the moment when a thought, objectified in writing, is read and thus resurrected, *if* the written words, the objectification of thought, were to vanish as they were being read. It would be comparable *if*, that is, the reading eyes consumed the letters they passed over. The objectivization of this "mystical" union is like the perfect translation of a meaning from author to reader by way of the vanishing mediator of the word—no misunderstanding, no remainder. But, of course, words do not vanish in this way. The impossibility of such a translation marks the melancholia of reading.[12] Reading aims to close the divide between the black marks on the page and the thought they are meant to convey, but instead it only *produces* the divide. The inevitable regret that Hegel sees arising after the completion of Christian religious rituals follows from the separation between feeling and objective expression. The experience that arises when sensing this "contradiction" (*Widerspruch*) is like "the sadness [*Traurigkeit*] accompanying the idea of living forces and the incompatibility between them and the corpse" (W 1:369/SC 252). Rather than the properly religious experience of the whole soul at peace—*plērōma* as *Friede* and *Befriedigung*, peace and fulfillment—the most that the Christian can hope to feel in the communion rite is a "melancholy serenity" (*wehmütige Heiterkeit*): "something divine was promised and it melted away in the mouth" (W 1:369/SC 253).

The dissolution inherent in *das Mahl der Liebe* is an expression of the tragic fate of the spirit of withdrawal, and it stands in marked contrast to the Greek religious experience: "When lovers sacrifice before the altar of the goddess of love and the prayerful breath of their emotion fans their emotion to a white-hot flame, the goddess herself has entered their hearts, yet the marble statue remains standing in front of them. In the love-feast [*das Mahl der Liebe*], on the other hand, the corporeal vanishes and only living feeling is present" (W 1:368 / SC 251). Eating the divine is a union unmediated by the imagination. Love is not made sufficiently objective; thus, nothing remains standing. Any trace of substantiality vanishes because the imagination cannot render bread and wine into an image that could possibly evoke the experience of love. Thought contradicts feeling; the *thought* of the bread and wine cannot be unified with the *feeling* of love, so the possibility of their unification is denied: "There is nothing for the imagination (in which intellect and feeling are both present and yet canceled [*aufgehoben*]) to do; here it cannot provide any image in which seeing and feeling would be united" (W 1:369 / SC 252). What exactly is missing such that the imagination is left so empty handed? It is the beauty of the *shape* of a statue of Venus: "in looking at the shape [*Gestalt*]," Hegel writes, "we are permeated with the sense of love and eternal youth" (ibid.). In a properly religious act, the subjective feeling of the divine and its objective form are united through the imagination that produces the statue of Venus. Destroying the image, grinding Venus into dust, undermines the unity that the beautiful shape provides. The unity of subject and object is severed. Devotion may still occur, but it has lost the sense of direction that it once had and lost this in the most literal sense. It has nowhere to turn, for it cannot worship dust. For Hegel, this must be distinguished from the emptiness of the Holy of Holies, in that the emptiness at the heart of the temple does not signify the disappearance of the living image but the glorification of this emptiness. There is no experience of loss and the emergence of longing that can give rise to an intimation of a prior totality. When faced with the ruins of such living images, one is, again, beset by the sadness that accompanies the contradiction between the corpse and the life that once dwelt in it.[13]

When viewed from enough distance, the experience of these ruins can be accompanied by what Hegel calls in his *Lectures on World History* "disinterested sorrow": "It seems that all must perish and that nothing endures. Every traveler has experienced this melancholy [*Trauer*]. Who has stood among the ruins of Carthage, Palmyra, Persepolis or Rome without being moved to reflect on the transience of empires and men, to mourn the loss of the rich and vigorous life of bygone ages? It is not a sorrow like that which we experience at the graves of those dear to us" (LWH 32). This disinterested sorrow should be distinguished from the experience of the flight of the living gods themselves. The loss and regret tied to this latter experience correspond to the flight inherent in the structure of the Christian communion. Ruination is an inextricable part of it. Conflict and separation, experienced as regret, inevitably contaminate the moment of *plērōma*. The original feast, and its ritual repetition, cannot help but instill this sense of flight and the dissolution that follows. For Hegel, this is the failure of Christianity *qua* religion, which he, again, defines as the *plērōma* of love ("[religion] is reflection and love united, bound together in thought" [W 1:362/SC 253]). Thus,

> after the supper the disciples began to be sorrowful because of the impending loss of their master, but after a genuinely religious action the whole soul is at peace. And, after enjoying the supper, Christians today feel a reverent wonder either without serenity or else with a melancholy serenity, because feeling's intensity was separated from the intellect and both were one-sided, because worship was incomplete. (W 1:369/SC 252–253)

This is not unlike the poet who affirms the speculative drive toward the *hen kai pan,* for he, like Empedocles, is an enemy of all one-sided existence, yet precisely because he is so invested in the speculative project, he experiences its failure most acutely.

The Proper Vessel of the Infinite

I have been reading Hegel's text with an eye to the rational progression of various Ideas in their unfolding as concrete religious and social practices. The emerging logic of this unfolding is distinctly dialectical, although, at this point, it exists in-itself and not for-itself. It is "dialectical" in the sense that a specific orientation toward the world becomes contradictory when it is radicalized.[14] Let us retrace our steps. The lack of objectivity that we have just been describing in *das Mahl der Liebe* is born of the transience of love. The limitations of love mark the limits of Jesus's teaching generally: "Morality cancels [*aufheben*] domination within the sphere of consciousness; love cancels the barriers in the sphere of morality; but love itself is still incomplete in nature" (W 1:362/SC 253). Kantian morality, grounded in reverence for the moral law, cancels/fulfills the position (exemplified by Judaism in Hegel's analysis) that posits a fearful *external* authority as the guarantor of morality. Yet by positing a corresponding *internal* authority, it alienates a part of human nature from itself. Love, in turn, cancels/fulfills the self-diremption inherent in Kantian morality by uniting reflection and feeling, but it does so in only a fleeting way. It too falls short of a genuine reconciliation of objectivity and subjectivity, since, in love, there is no room for objectivity. Put another way, if the aim in the religious sphere is the identity of a living objectivity with subjectivity, love has the tendency to isolate, and its attempts to extend beyond transient fulfillment fail.[15] As it stands in the teaching of Jesus, love provides an intuition of completeness, but it cannot sustain reflection, for, as we have seen, reflection cancels love. Thus, Hegel understands the inability of love to reflect upon itself as its fundamental limitation, and this is a limitation of *love,* not reflection. The "contradiction" is that, "intuition [*Anschauung*], representative thinking [*Vorstellung*], is something restrictive, something receptive only of something restricted; but here the intuited object would be something infinite. The infinite cannot be carried in this vessel" (W 1:370/SC 253). Religion, as the union of reflection and love, is held to be the cancelation/fulfillment of love. The guiding question, then, with regard to Jesus's *religious* teaching, in contradistinction to his moral teachings, is ultimately how to convey the infinite? How is it to be made *objective?* If the Last Supper is insufficient, what is its proper vessel? With these questions, occasioned by the failure of Christian love to unite subject and object, finite and infinite, we pose once again Hegel's guiding concern: what religious form, or in the terms of "The Oldest Program," what new mythology, will allow for "universal freedom and equality of spirits [to] prevail"? (OP 13). Can that which is founded on the gesture of withdrawal ground such a mythology? Can it ground that which is necessary to bring together subject and object in an immanent, substantial union? Can this attempt to withdraw from all fate work to fulfill the idea of the *hen kai pan?* Or will the attempt to withdraw from fate, from objectivity as such, provoke fate in turn?

If it is, indeed, the case that for Hegel, in *The Spirit of Christianity,* the form of tragedy distinct to Christianity is marked by the fragility of a communion that only ever exists in its disappearance, then Christianity *fails* to fulfill the proper aim of religion as he defines it. The flight from fate does, in actuality, *provoke* a fate. In the wake of his account of the failure of the Last Supper to make love objective, Hegel nevertheless continues to investigate the question of how the infinite might be presented so that it achieves objectivity. His investigation revives the question of language *and* his position that Jesus's parables in, for example, the Sermon on the Mount are insufficient to express a living union of the finite and the infinite. It also leads him both to clarify the Idea of pure life as love *and* articulate most starkly the inherent insufficiency of it. Finally, it brings him to the Crucifixion and the presentation of the Resurrection. Beyond feeling and intuition, how is what Hegel calls alternatively the infinite, pure life, being, and the divine to be *communicated?*[16] And why does the articulation of the Crucifixion and its aftermath, as an expression of withdrawal in the service of love, only reaffirm for Hegel the fragility of the Christian union of finite and infinite?

The divine cannot be grasped by the expressions of reflection—"command, teach, learn, see, recognize, make, will, come into the Kingdom of Heaven, go"—but can only be spoken of through *inspired* terms (*Begeisterung,* W 1:372/SC 255). From the perspective of reflection, such a "spirited" language is contradictory. Of the four canonical gospels, John's comes closest to this inspired language. "In the beginning was the *logos*" (John 1:1): this is not reflective language because the predicates are not concepts or universals but something "living" (W 1:373/SC 256) or, by the time of the *Phenomenology of Spirit,* "speculative." When Hegel insists that "only spirit grasps and includes spirit" (W 1:372/SC 255), this means, in the present context, that language cannot be assimilated passively.[17] The spiritual sense of the text is grasped only to the degree that "the relationships of life and the opposition of life and death have come into consciousness" (W 1:373/SC 256–257). Life, then, is the organic whole: "each part [of life], to which the whole is external, is yet a whole, a life" (W 1:374/SC 258). This can only be comprehended when the whole comes into self-consciousness in such a way that "consciousness" is not reduced to the analytic activity of reflection that creates distinction but is equivalent to life. Jesus *is* nature coming to self-consciousness. He is *logos,* which is to say *God* or, more precisely, "God and the Logos are only different in that God is matter in the form of Logos: the Logos itself is with God; both are one" (W 1:374/SC 257–258).

While, for the most part, John describes the living connections between God and world using what Hegel calls, in a derogatory way, "mystical speech" (W 1:375/SC 259), there are also a few "natural expressions" (*Naturlaute,* W 1:375/SC 260) to be found in his gospel. The most striking and successful example of a natural expression is the description of the relation between God and Jesus as father and son. Rather than an abstract, conceptual connection, or the autocratic relation of lord to subject, father and son are simply modifications of the same life. Extended to a wider community, the corresponding natural, living union describes the union of any free people, and, to illustrate the point, Hegel turns for a second time to the Arabs.[18] This is a union where the relation of the individual to the community is not understood in terms of what Hegel calls a mere *collection* (*Versammlung,* W 1:393/SC 278). An aggregation of this kind is a conceptual unity reserved for lifeless objects. In *communion* (*Gemeinschaft,* W 1:394/SC 278), as a unity *qua* life, the whole does not lie outside the individual; rather, "he himself is just the whole which the entire tribe is" (ibid). With a genuinely free people, the individual is a part and at the same time a whole. This "natural, undivided people" is not to be found among modern Europeans who are said to be bound together through the abstract concept of shared rights. Against the *concept* (*Begriff*) and the relation in which each individual in a whole maintains its status as a "one," Hegel affirms *essence* (*Wesen,* ibid.). *Essence* entails *being,* which is to say, *life.* As Hegel writes, "Living things . . . are essences, even if they are separate, and their unity is still a unity of essence. What is a contradiction in the realm of the dead is not one in the realm of life" (W 1:376/SC 261). Referring to Kant's "Observations" in *Religion within the Limits of Reason Alone,* Hegel writes that *life,* as the connection of finite and infinite, is a "holy mystery" to reflective thinking, which can partition life in this way but cannot fathom how the parts are one.[19] How the ideal of humanity could also be an actual human being poses such a problem to the reflective thought of the enlightened mind because this kind of thinking takes abstract definitions, that is, an abstract universal of "humanity," as absolute.[20] Like all "positive" relations, reflective thought and the concept inhabit the realm of what is fixed rather than what is alive, and, as *movement,* life can withstand contradictory attributes. Life *is* "the union of union and disunion."[21] The image that Hegel chooses to express what is at once a living unity in both the political and religious spheres is an overtly organic one: "A tree which has three branches makes up with them one tree; but every 'son' of the tree, every branch (and also its other 'children,' leaves and blossoms) is itself a tree. The fibers bringing sap to the branch from the stem are of the same nature as the roots. . . . And it is just as true to say that there is only one tree here as to say that there are three" (W 1:376–377/SC 261). The unity of essence between father and son is this living union of "sons," and, for this reason, the "vessel" for conveying the union of finite and infinite that Hegel singles out is the language of organic generation. Yet this mode of expression will never take hold when the concept achieves a position of dominance and dismisses the image as the mere untruthful play of the imagination. When the life of the image is dismissed in this way by reflective thinking, we are condemned to a world populated by mere *Objekte* alone. In this context, withdrawal would be a retreat from *Verstand,* from the consciousness that divides the world into distinct, fixed, opposing *Objekte.*

Beyond Faith

If a fulfilled religion is "reflection and love united, bound together in thought" (W 1:362/SC 253), the New Testament, and the gospel of John more specifically, offers some "natural expressions" that begin to bring this thought to language. As the same time, even these will fall on deaf ears if the reader is not ready to hear them. What these expressions attempt to convey is nothing less than the essence of Jesus (that is to say, the living relation with God that he achieves by way of withdrawal), and this can only be "grasped" (*auffassen;* W 1:382/SC 266) by faith. Given that "only spirit grasps [*fassen*] and comprehends [*einschließen*] spirit" (W 1:372/SC 255), it follows that faith, which has the divine as its object (*Gegenstand,* rather than *Objekt,* W 1:382/SC 266), is only possible if the believers themselves have within them a divine element. But the "grasping" proper to faith is a "feeling of harmony," and this feeling is itself only an "inkling" (*Ahnen*) of the divine (ibid.).[22] Thus, faith remains a middle state of *desire for* union with the divine, rather than its fulfillment. It falls short of the wholly divine life, which Hegel defines as that point where the divinity has "pervaded all the threads of one's consciousness, directed all of one's relations with the world, and breathes throughout one's being" (ibid.). Thus, there is a progression from an abstract understanding of Jesus to an initial relation with him through faith. This is followed by the move beyond faith to a "living union" (*lebendige Vereinigung,* W 1:384/SC 268) that amounts to the overcoming of alienation and the realization of pure life. It is, however, only when Jesus departs that the disciples can move beyond faith. The danger for Jesus's followers is that they will assume that he alone is divine. Thus, the *culmination* of faith, which is more than a mere middle state or an "inkling," can only be achieved through the *downfall* of Jesus, and, for Hegel, Jesus was aware that it was "necessary for his individual self to perish" (W 1:388/SC 272).

One can think in this regard of the conflict that Jesus courted in his final days in Jerusalem.[23] Hegel distinguishes this act of withdrawal as self-sacrifice from renunciation. The withdrawal that ultimately leads to Jesus's arrest, trial, and crucifixion is not simply a rejection of the world as such but the attempt to avoid being contaminated by a world that is unnatural and corrupt. Only by forcing a confrontation in Jerusalem with the full expectation of defeat does the possibility of a return to pure life arise, for only the death of Jesus can prove irrefutably that no ontological difference exists between Jesus and those who have faith in him. Leo Steinberg argues that, for those who care to look, the conspicuous depiction of Jesus's genitalia throughout Renaissance painting illustrates the desire to show his thorough "humanation."[24] The perceived need to emphasize Jesus's *human* nature only arises at the point where there is overwhelming confidence in his *divinity.* The more fully *human* Jesus is shown to be, the greater is the testimony to God's power: "The rendering of the incarnate Christ ever more unmistakably [as] flesh and blood is a religious enterprise because it testifies to God's greatest achievement."[25] For Hegel, the "humanation," or incarnation, of God is only fully revealed to the disciples with his death. The humanity that he embodies is not unique but is precisely what all can share, and Jesus's struggle against those who would attribute a divine personality to him and him alone is a struggle against *all* thought of a difference in essence between Jesus and those whose faith has been fulfilled. As Hegel says in his short fragment *Love,* written in late 1797 or early 1798, "True union, or love proper, exists only between living beings who are alike in power and thus in one another's eyes living beings from every point of view; in no respect is either dead for the other" (W 1:245–246/L 304). The recognition of this similarity in essence is not an article of faith, and fulfillment is more than faith: it is pure life. According to Hegel, Jesus's crucifixion, as an act of self-sacrificial withdrawal, was in the service of leading the disciples to this state.

Pure Life

Although they indicate the unity of essence, Jesus's suffering and death pose the most profound challenge to his disciples. Thus, Peter is struck with terror at the thought of Jesus's parting, and his terror is a sign of the distance his faith stands from its culmination. Faith fulfilled—"pure life"—is expressed as the child's purity (see Matthew 18:1–3), and, by recognizing this purity, we can capture a glimpse of the essence of the spirit of Jesus. What is "happily unified" in the figure of the child is "unconsciousness [*Bewußtlose*], undeveloped unity, being and life in God" (W 1:386/SC 269). But coupled with this purity is, once again, its inevitable loss. Hegel laments, "Oh! the grievous necessity of such violations of the holy! The deepest, holiest sorrow of a beautiful soul, its most incomprehensible riddle, is that its nature has to be disrupted, its holiness sullied" (W 1:385/SC 269). If the most incomprehensible thing for the *Verstand* is the divine *unity* with God, this inevitable alienation from pure life is what is most incomprehensible for the "noble heart" (ibid.). As long as the child lives in this state, he or she knows nothing of it. Alienation is always a retroactive grasping of a lost unity that had not previously been recognized as such.

The purity of the origin and the image of an eternal seeing bring Hegel back to the Greeks, but he now refers to their *violation* of pure and unrestricted life. His reference is not to the tragic age but to Plato. The philosopher is said to provide a vision of the divine, yet, to draw out spirit as such, untainted by restrictions, "Plato separates the entity which is pure life from the restricted entity by a difference of time" (W 1:385/SC 270). The pure spirits that have lived within the "sight of the divine" maintain their purity in later life, although "they have only a darkened consciousness of that heavenly vision" (ibid.). Although Hegel does not cite a specific dialogue at this point, living in "sight of the divine" recalls the description in the *Phaedrus* of a "recent initiate who has seen much in heaven when he sees a godlike face or bodily form that has captured Beauty well": "first he shudders and a fear comes over him like those he felt at the earlier time [when he saw the form of Beauty itself]; then he gazes at him with the reverence due a god."[26] If it is the *Phaedrus* that Hegel has in mind, Socrates explains in this dialogue that, of all the Ideas, Beauty alone has the privilege of shining most clearly through sight. If grasped on earth through the senses, wisdom and all the other Ideas would arouse a "terrible love" (*Phaedrus* 250d), one that could not be endured.[27] The image of beauty (the beloved), as the trace of Beauty itself, acts as an interruption that first exposes the world of mere appearance *as* the world of mere appearance. This interruption, in turn, provokes a *yearning* for what Socrates calls "the joys of that *other time*" (*Phaedrus* 250c, emphasis added), and this "other time" is figured as the feast and banquet of the gods held on the outer surface of heaven (*Phaedrus* 247c). If it is the *Republic* that Hegel has in mind and not the *Phaedrus,* we might recall that, in the Myth of Er, the soul that has laid eyes on the divine is distinguished from its "restricted" life by the voyage across the river Lethe.

Hegel's point seems to be that, while the immortal may linger in the restricted life that is experienced after this crossing, when the divine is seen as such, all particularity is absent. This is an early version of a criticism that continues throughout Hegel's work. In the "Preface" to the *Phenomenology,* for example, he provides a condensed sketch of the historical unfolding of Spirit:

> Culture and its laborious emergence from the immediacy of substantial life must always begin by getting acquainted with *general* principles and points of view, so as at first to work up to a *general conception* of the real issue, as well as learning to support and refute the general conception with reasons; then to apprehend the rich and concrete abundance [of life] by differential classification, and finally to give accurate instruction and pass serious judgment upon it. From its very beginning, culture must leave room for the earnestness of life in its concrete richness; this leads the way to an experience of the real issue. (PdG 5 / PS 4)

The culture that emerges with the help of a Platonic articulation and defense of general conceptions fails to leave room for life in its concrete richness. Hegel's point is to contrast this with the image of pure life as a childlike spirit. This spirit is represented by Jesus as a son; thus, it maintains its particular existence in its communion with the divine. Jesus separates the divine from what is restricted but then *reunites* them in a way that is absent, it would seem, in Plato. The fulfillment of faith, then, is the point where the opposition of the pure and the restricted falls away. *Contra* the personality and distinctiveness of Jesus alone, this beautiful relation is described in terms of the living union of lovers (Matthew 19:6: "So they are no longer two but one flesh"). The great achievement of love is finding oneself in another, and, for Hegel's Jesus, the very fact of the harmony *is* the divine. This relation of love is extended to the harmony characterizing friendship, so the harmonious gathering of friends itself constitutes the presence of Jesus and communion with him (Matthew 18:20; see W 1:387 / SC 271). Is this not Hegel's articulation of what the author(s) of "The Oldest Program" will describe as "the overthrow of all belief in a hinterhaven"? (OP 10). The idea of a *kingdom* of heaven, which completes the Christian religion as Jesus founded it, is a rather inappropriate way of designating what is nothing other than a living harmony of those free from domination.[28] This beautiful relation is a *return* to unity; as such, it is like a return to childhood: "the culmination of faith, the return to the Godhead whence man is born, closes the circle of man's development" (W 1:389 / SC 273). Hegel's description of the movement of this return carries in it the kernel of what is taken to be the essential movement of the Hegelian dialectic as such:

> the child carries the unity, the connection, the concord with the entire harmony, undisturbed though undeveloped, in itself. It begins with faith in gods outside itself, with fear, until through its actions it has [isolated and] separated itself more and more; but then it returns

> through associations to the original unity. The child now knows God, i.e., the spirit of God is present in the child, issues from its restrictions, annuls [*aufheben*] the modifications, and restores the whole. God, the Son, the Holy Spirit! (W 1:389–390/SC 273)

An original unity is divided and the increasing intensity of the alienation arising from this division culminates in the triumphant return of this prior union but in a developed form.

And yet the child does not return. The fleeting nature of the love between Jesus and Mary Magdalene and the vanishing union of the friends at the Last Supper repeats itself. Hegel describes a near presence of union that melts away and dissolves before its full realization. And he does so with the pathos of one who wishes it were otherwise. "Is there an idea," Hegel asks,

> more beautiful than that of a nation of men related to one another by love? Is there one more uplifting than that of belonging to a whole which as a whole, as one, is the spirit of God whose sons the individual members are? Was there still to be an incompleteness in this idea, an incompleteness which would give a fate power over it? Or would this fate be the nemesis raging against a too beautiful endeavor, against an overleaping of nature? (W 1:394/SC 278)

The Idea *will* provoke a *fate,* whether as a result of incompleteness or an excess of beauty. Hegel does circle back, but what he circles back to is the inherent contradiction within the Idea of love itself, and he will come to state directly what he had previously only intimated. Love carries within itself the contradiction that will produce the fate that attacks it. Jesus is not the victim of his times, as Hegel argued in the *Positivity.* The objective development of Christian history is the immanent development of Jesus's conception of withdrawal in the service of love.

Logic of Love

As the *unification* of life, love presupposes division, and the act of withdrawal is, initially, a form of division. As Hegel writes, "The more variegated the manifold in which life is alive, the more the places in which it can be reunified; the more the places in which it can sense itself, the deeper does love become" (W 1:395/SC 279). Life is seen to develop out of an immature unity into a more complex, differentiated world, structured by an increasing number of the oppositions that reflection produces. When compared to Hegel's own time, those living in Jesus's era "regarded fewer things as objects and so handed fewer things over to intellectual treatment" (W 1:414/SC 297). As the objective world becomes more variegated, love becomes ever richer since it is able to cancel and reunify the divisions that account for this increased complexity. As Hegel writes in the *Love* fragment, "In love the separate does still remain, but as something united and no longer as something separate; life senses life" (W 1:246 / L 305). As such, love then finds itself everywhere. The expansionist drive comes from within love itself, so that "it seeks out differences and devises unifications *ad infinitum*" (W 1:248 / L 307). Yet the movement of love is also that of a *concentration* and *intensification*. At its most intense, the lovers—both lover and beloved at once—are two struggling to be one. The struggle exists between, on the one hand, completely surrendering to unity, thereby destroying all opposition, and, on the other, maintaining a degree of individual independence. Through this struggle, a kind of self-sufficiency can arise. The lovers feed off one another so that, to cite once again the lines from Shakespeare that Hegel reproduces in the fragment, "the more I give to thee, / The more I have." But this is a potentially stifling, claustrophobic self-sufficiency. It becomes increasingly exclusive and more indifferent to the lives of others. Love *expands* to the extent that the joy of love is a recognition of the repetition of one's self in another, and it thus communes with all other life as other life reflects it. It *withdraws,* however, if it senses individuality in another. Difference is an affront to the joy of *melding,* of *intensification* (*Innigkeit,* W 1:395 / SC 279). Anything held back by one of the lovers as private is an affront to the union, yet love cannot shake the threat of *property,* of what is held back. This only accentuates the fragility of the union and the cancellation of the cancellation of opposition that it has achieved.

In the *Love* fragment, the mutual withdrawal of the lovers from others and from other things is plagued by shame (the language of spirit and fate is absent from the text): "This raging of love against individuality [any remnant of property held by one of the lovers exclusively] is *shame*" (W 1:247 / L 306). Shame, not resentment, is the negative power inherent to love that drives its expansion. It arises with the experience of the *incompleteness* of love, yet it also presupposes the experience of it, for someone who does not love cannot feel shame. Women who, as Hegel writes, "will not yield their charms except for money" or those who use their body to "fascinate" (ibid.) are distinctly shame*less* because they ascribe intrinsic wealth to their mortal bodies. Real value comes instead from the unity of love. Shame, as the awareness of an incomplete love, arises with the recollection of the materiality of the *body,* thus with the awareness of being individuated. Shame is not, in Hegel's words, the "fear *for* what is mortal" (ibid.); it is not the fear for the loss of what is merely one's own; it is, instead, the fear *of* it, a fear of what can stand as distinct and proper to oneself as an individual. But love overcomes fear, so that "it has no fear of its fear, but, led by its fear, it cancels separation, apprehensive as it is of finding opposition which may resist it or be a fixed barrier against it" (W 1:247–248 / L 307). Given this, shame would appear to be, as Hamacher writes, "the organ of the self-sublation of love."[29] Yet he also argues that the supplement, shame, as the means toward the fulfillment of love, "goes behind Hegel's back, and goes, in his own text, beyond this goal, which would at the same time be its origin; it splits the unity by itself and works towards a further unity. But there is no unity which would not necessarily be dissolved as a restriction by shame."[30] As an *expansionist* force, shame *exacerbates* desire. In the "Letter to D'Alembert," a text from which Hegel made an excerpt, Jean-Jacques Rousseau describes the phenomenon in this way: "The apparent obstacle which appears to make this object distant is, at bottom, that which brings it closer. Desires veiled by shame become only the more seductive; in obstructing them, modesty inflames them."[31] If love, as desire *fulfilled,* is the name for the logic wherein "the more I give to thee, / The more I have," then with desire, with what is by nature *unfilled,* (Rousseau continues) "the less he obtains, the more the value of what he obtains increases; and it is thus that he enjoys at once his privations and his pleasures."[32] Or, we could say, the less I have, the more it is.

In *The Spirit of Christianity,* Hegel acknowledges the failure of love to achieve *plērōma,* although he makes no reference to the experience of shame in this text. While the two unified lovers represent the concentration and intensification of love in its extreme, the same logic exists in larger communities based on love. Hegel writes that "the more isolated men stand in respect of their culture and interest, in their relation to the world, and the more idiosyncrasies they have, the more does their love become restricted to itself" (W 1:395/SC 279). Thus, the essence of Christianity, defined as it is by love and withdrawal, harbors within itself the isolationist tendencies that Hegel finds among early Christians, as well as the monastic ideal that will come to play such an influential role in subsequent Christian history. Hegel goes as far as to say that the isolation needed to secure their peculiar form of happiness "must even *create* enmities for itself" (ibid., emphasis added). The unifying force of love, when it encounters individuality, provokes division and produces disunity and hostility. Thus, a fate is born. Compare this with Freud's analysis, written in 1929, of the necessary supplement of the Idea of love:

> It is always possible to bind together a considerable number of people in love, so long as there are other people left over to receive the manifestations of their aggression. . . . When once the Apostle Paul had posited universal love between men as the foundation of his Christian community, extreme intolerance on the part of Christendom towards those who remained outside it became the inevitable consequence. To the Romans, who had not founded their communal life as a State upon love, religious intolerance was something foreign, although with them religion was a concern of the State and the State was permeated by religion. Neither was it an unaccountable chance

> that the dream of Germanic world-dominion called for anti-Semitism as its complement.[33]

For Freud, universal love is a flawed Idea because it ignores the aggression that is the manifestation of the drive toward death. Recalling his analysis in *Beyond the Pleasure Principle,* Freud contrasts this with the desire to "preserve living substance and to join it into ever larger units." Instead of this drive toward *extension,* a contrary instinct seeks "to dissolve those units and to bring them back to their primeval, inorganic state."[34] This latter drive, "the constitutional inclination of human beings to be aggressive towards one another,"[35] undermines the command of universal love because of its severity, which is, in effect, the pleasure we take in aggression toward others. If the imperative to love in this way is followed, it will give rise to unhappiness, revolt, or neuroses. Love thy neighbor as thyself? "The commandment is impossible to fulfill; such an enormous inflation of love can only lower its value, not get rid of the difficulty."[36] Instead of the shame intensifying desire, those who carry saintliness to an extreme will, as Freud writes, "reproach themselves with the worst sinfulness."[37]

Beyond the appeal to the human constitution, the hindrance to "civilization" posed by universal love, is contained within the concept of love itself. This is the case for both Freud and Hegel. Freud writes, "A love that does not discriminate seems to me to forfeit a part of its own value, by doing an injustice to its object,"[38] and Hegel states, "the love which a large group of people can feel for one another admits of only a certain degree of strength or depth [*Innigkeit*] and demands both a similarity in mind, in interest, in numerous relationships of life, and also a diminution of individualities" (W 1:395/SC 279). If the essence of Jesus's teaching is the unity grounded in a love born of withdrawal, the essence of the Christian community founded in his name is the forceful dissemination of the faith: "this is the sole activity of the Christian community, proselytizing is that community's essential property" (W 1:396/SC 280). This proselytizing mission, then, leads to a direct and *inevitable* collision with the character of love. Thus, we return to the guiding problem of the *Positivity.* In this earlier essay, however, Hegel did not interpret the source of this outward drive of Christianity to be of the essence of Jesus's teaching; the positive elements were mere concessions to the times. In *The Spirit of Christianity,* this source is inherent to his teaching. As the community that is united by love expands, love is sacrificed. On the one hand, the drive toward intensification inherent in the Idea of love leads to greater isolation, which, in turn, fosters a resistance to individualities and the production of enmities. On the other, the community can remain unified only through expansion, and the single-mindedness of this proselytizing mission has the effect of warding off the possibility of individuality arising *within* the community and clashing with it. But this only serves, again, to accentuate the fragility of this love. To engage in any activity other than love's task would initially sever the union by introducing difference and the concomitant individuation. This would then give rise to the possibility of a clash between these individualities. Thus, "for the sake of a petty interest, a difference of character in some detail, love would have been changed into hatred" (W 1:397/SC 281).

The legacy of the founding gesture of withdrawal as the flight from fate is that the Christian community can function only if it sets itself against the world. In severing themselves from the world in this way, Christians only court conflict with what they set against themselves. Love for one another in the community is necessarily bound together with a separation from others, and this coupling defines the essence of Christian love in its unfolding. This union by way of withdrawal ultimately reveals itself to be empty. It is an "undeveloped love" that avoids all forms of genuine individuation, and it manifests itself solely in expansionist zeal. The *fate* of Christianity is an expansion through withdrawal or the paradox of a universal withdrawal. This flight from all determinate modes of living, from all objectivity, gives rise to "the contranatural expansion of love's scope" that was "bound to become the father of the most appalling fanaticism" (W 1:397/SC 281). As Hegel presents it in the *Philosophy of Right,* fanaticism comes from a misunderstanding of the nature and relation of thinking and the will, a misunderstanding that is particularly endemic to "faculty" psychology:

> Those who regard thinking as a particular and distinct *faculty,* divorced from the will as an equally distinct *faculty,* and who in addition even consider that thinking is prejudicial to the will—especially the good will—show from the very outset that they are totally ignorant of the nature of the will. . . . Only *one aspect* of the will is defined here—namely this *absolute possibility* of *abstracting* from every determination in which I find myself or which I have posited in myself, the flight from every content as a limitation. If the will determines itself in this way, or if representational thought [*Vorstellung*] considers this aspect in itself as freedom and holds fast to it, this is *negative* freedom or the freedom of the understanding.—This is freedom of the void . . . [and] if it turns to actuality, it becomes in the realm of both politics and religion the fanaticism of destruction, demolishing the whole existing social order, eliminating all individuals regarded as suspect by a given order, and annihilating any organization which attempts to rise up anew. Only in destroying something does this negative will have a feeling of its own existence. (W 7:49/PR 37–38)

According to the *Zusatz* to this section, Hegel added that "this negative freedom or freedom of the understanding is one-sided, but this one-sidedness always contains within itself an *essential determination* and should therefore not be dismissed; but the defect of the understanding is that it treats a one-sided determination as unique and elevates it to supreme status" (W 7:51 / PR 38–39, emphasis added).[39]

The distinctive quality of Christian fanaticism is not the elevation of a particular, one-sided determination to supreme status but the attempt to withdraw from *all* determination. Despite this withdrawal, however, the flight from all fate as such gives rise to the greatest fate: "here is the point where Jesus is linked with fate, linked indeed in the most sublime way, but where he suffers under it" (W 1:397/ SC 281). Although he will proceed to describe the unfolding of the fate of Christianity, this is, once again, Hegel's final word in *The Spirit of Christianity* on the Idea embodied in the figure of Jesus: the attempt to withdraw from fate in the service of a union between subjective feeling and objective expression *produces* a fate that disrupts any fleeting experience of unification in something beautiful. The tragedy of Jesus's life would, thus, seem to be marked by sublimity and not beauty. Hegel has asked,

> Is there an idea more beautiful than that of a nation of men related to one another by love? Is there one more uplifting than that of belonging to a whole which as a whole, as one, is the spirit of God whose sons the individual members are? Was there still to be an incompleteness in this Idea, an incompleteness which would give a fate power over it? Or would this fate be the nemesis raging against a too beautiful endeavor, against an overleaping of nature? (W 1:394 / SC 278)

The Idea of love is incomplete because it is *too* beautiful, because it attempts to avoid objectivity and fate as such. The most colossal fate is born of the withdrawal into the wilderness, not by an individual but now by a whole community. For Hegel, this withdrawal has lasted for close to two millennia. The tragedy of the life of Jesus stems from his attempt to fulfill a merely subjective love through religion and, thus, to produce what Lukács calls an "objectivity without objects."[40] This repeats all of the contradictions of love, and it ultimately produces a form of subjectivity that is simply a hallowed-out, empty interiority.

The Crucifixion of Jesus, as an act of self-sacrifice, was deemed necessary by Hegel, and Hegel's Jesus, to the extent that it opened the way for the disciples to separate the essence of Jesus from his individual person. Without his sacrifice, the disciples would have continued to understand the divine as residing in the individual self of Jesus alone. They would have been unable to grasp the divine spirit as subsisting in *them;* thus, they would have fallen short of the fulfillment of faith. In this regard, Hegel refers to a passage in Matthew's gospel (12:30ff: Jesus is addressing the Pharisees) where Jesus contrasts blasphemy against an individual—blasphemy against the man, Jesus of Nazareth—with blasphemy against the spirit of the whole, that is, blasphemy against divine nature itself. The former act can be redeemed, but to blaspheme the spirit is to destroy the blasphemer's own holiness to such an extent that he becomes "incapable of annulling [*aufheben*] his separation and reuniting himself with love" (W 1:389/SC 273). This is a crime over which the power of forgiveness has no sway. In his *Lectures on the Philosophy of Religion,* Hegel paraphrases the same passage from Matthew in this way: "The injuring of absolute truth, of the idea of this unification of the infinite antithesis, is described, therefore, as the highest offense."[41] The union of the antithesis between "humanity, death, infinite limitation" and "the divine idea"[42] is, in Hegel's later philosophy, the condition of a free, communal subjectivity. The unforgivable offense, the offense that destroys the possibility of realizing this union, is the rejection of "spirit" itself, which is to say, the element of freedom as such. And at precisely this point in *The Spirit of Christianity,* where Hegel refers to Jesus's warning against this offense, the Furies reappear. He interprets the unforgivable with reference to tragedy:

> The Eumenides of your being could be terrified, but the void left in you by the Daemons thus chased away would not be filled by love. It will only draw your furies back again, and, now strengthened by your very consciousness that they are furies of hell, they complete your destruction. (W 1:389/SC 273)

The fate of absolute crime is the inability to tame the Erinyes and house them within the *polis.* Is this the void that is left as a result of Jesus's attempt to fulfill the law? Instead of fulfilling the law, has he, in truth, simply *abolished* it, leaving nothing in its place? In the *Lectures on the Philosophy of Religion,* in a section on "Rupture," Hegel remarks on the cleavage that knowledge or consciousness introduces: "It is what produces the disease and is at the same time the source of health."[43] Instead of assuming the role of *pharmakon,* has the movement of withdrawal that defines Christianity—the attempt to separate from separation, to "battle . . . the entire genius of his people" (W 1:387/SC 271)—served to produce only a more intense separation?

The Fate of Christianity as Tragedy

The destructive fate that Jesus's spirit unleashes is first revealed as an antagonism toward his age. He is presented as untimely, out of season. While he was first received with indifference, he was soon met by hatred: "the effect of this hatred on him was an ever increasing bitterness against his age and his people" (W 1:398/SC 283). But the conflict does not exist solely as a result of those who greet his call with hatred. It also results from a misunderstanding on the part of Jesus: "With great good nature, with the faith of a pure-hearted dreamer, he interpreted their [his disciples'] desire as a satisfied heart, their urge as a completion, their renunciation of some of their previous relationships, mostly trivial, as freedom and a healed or conquered fate" (W 1:398/SC 282). He misjudged both the character of his disciples and the readiness of his people to hear of the kingdom of God.

Faced with the animosity that his call elicited, Jesus resorts to silencing his religious opponents with *ad hominem* arguments, which reveals that he does not entertain the possibility of conversion and, thus, has abandoned any hope of reconciliation. There is no pretense to a universal reason that might reconcile opposition. Instead, we have the contradiction of Jesus proclaiming the gospel of pure life—of a living equality—at the same time that he stands in a relation of equality with no one.[44] Ultimately, he withdraws from the fate of his people and encourages his friends to do the same. While he actively severs himself from this fate, his flight from it means that he nevertheless assumes an utterly passive relation to it and, as a result, to the Roman state. Since an aspect of the fate that he renounces was paying taxes to Rome, this passivity is exemplified by his advice to his followers to render to Caesar the things that are Caesar's (Matthew 22:21; see W 1:398/SC 283). While the kingdom of God, as the substance of the transformation that Jesus heralds, is organized by the most "disinterested love" (W 1:400/SC 285), rather than the law, his relation to this law is willing subjection. As such, he renounces all active, living relations with his people, as well as the larger political order. Hegel's view is that, while Jesus saw it as contradictory that he and his friends were subject to the same taxation as the Jews, he acquiesced, and this exemplified his wholly passive relation toward the fate of his people. What is gained with this flight from fate is isolated individuality. This "beauty of soul" has as its *negative* attribute "the highest freedom, i.e., the potentiality of renouncing everything in order to maintain oneself" (W 1:350/SC 236). To maintain beauty and the ideal of love means a resignation from much, if not all, that is essential to life. What is gained as a result of this sacrifice is, thus, "freedom . . . in the void" (PR 38):

> Every modification of life was in bonds, and therefore Jesus isolated himself from his mother, his brothers, and his other relatives. He would love no wife, beget no children; he would neither become a father of a family nor a fellow-citizen and enjoy a common life with his fellows. The fate of Jesus was that he had to suffer from the fate of his nation; either he had to make that fate his own, to bear its necessity and share its joy, to unite his spirit with his nation's, but to sacrifice his own beauty, his connection with the divine, or else he had to repel his people's fate from himself, but submit to a life underdeveloped and

> without pleasure in itself. In neither event would his nature be fulfilled. (W 1:401 / SC 285–286, translation altered)

This is the double bind in which Jesus finds himself. It is the insoluble tragedy of love, as manifested in the son of man. By choosing to struggle against the fate of his people in the name of the beauty of his relation with the divine, he sacrifices the communal bonds of family and political life. It also means, as we have seen, that Jesus, as individual, as personality, must be sacrificed so that the disciples' dependence on him as an external point of authority ceases. Only his irrefutable mortality could reveal their shared essence. Jesus's individual self is sacrificed to revive concrete, but corrupted, life. Yet he and his disciples *flee* from life in all of its concrete forms. To remain within the spirit of his people would allow him to grasp only fragments of his nature and would lead it to become contaminated.

Jesus refuses to sacrifice his own beauty and instead withdraws. Thus, he is able to bring his nature to consciousness but only as a "splendid shadow" (W 1:401 / SC 286)—this is freedom in a void. While the essence of his nature is the highest truth of genuine reconciliation, it will never live in his action. Jesus *chooses* to withdraw, and Hegel makes a point of adding that he *chooses* the fate that it produces. If he was naïve in his judgment about the character of his disciples, he knows what his fate will be. If he rejects involvement in political life, he knows a hostile state nevertheless exists and will not be cancelled. As his fate plays itself out, he feels the separation more deeply, and he struggles against it. This struggle is "pure and sublime" (W 1:402 / SC 286), *precisely because* Jesus knows the entire scope of the fate that he is confronting. Through his opposition, the corrupt nature of what he sets himself against is raised to consciousness for *both* that which is corrupt *and* that which is fighting against it. The *sublimity* of the struggle rests in the severity of the division created by the withdrawal of Jesus and his followers.

Jesus knows of his fate but nevertheless struggles against it, despite its inevitability. Further, this very engagement marks a *break* from the purity of absolute withdrawal and leads to contamination. The "sublime sight" (W 1:402 / SC 286) of a righteous struggle against corruption and death turns into its opposite. At this point, Hegel slips from the fate of Jesus to that of his disciples, or, more accurately, he indicates the point at which the fate of the community established in Jesus's name becomes implicated in his fate.[45] The atrocity of holiness marred by unholiness is damaging because a purity that has been contaminated does not recognize the loss of purity. Thus, it continues to rage against fate without realizing its implication in it. Jesus foresees the full horror of the destruction that will arise from the campaign that he initiates, but he does not check himself or his followers in order to spare the world. Hegel quotes the lines from Matthew 10:34–36: "I came not to bring peace on earth, but a sword; I came to set the son against the father, the daughter against her mother, the bride against her husband's kin." What has been partially freed from fate and partially bound to it "must destroy both itself and nature all the more frightfully" (W 1:402/SC 286).

With the consequences before him, Jesus does not back down in order to lessen the "convulsions" (*Zuckungen,* W 1:403/SC 287) but spurs them on. Thus, Jesus's activity involves *separation* from the earthly world and a *restoration* of life, but this restoration takes place only in *Idealität.* He captures sight of his Ideal—the God of the *whole*—through the flight from the world and simultaneous collisions with it. His is an "enrapturing unification" (*verzückende Vereinigung,* W 1:418/SC 301). He joins with the divine, however, only by renouncing all multiplicity, including his own personality, and this is a feat that can only be achieved through death. Jesus is bound to succumb to the realities—the objectivities—that he battles against. The sacrifice of Jesus, then, is explained from within the logic of his own Idea. In an earlier draft of the essay, Hegel describes Jesus as the kind wishful dreamer (*Schwärmer;* W 1:405/SC 289n) who imagines the fulfillment of a great plan, rather than as someone who merely dreams for himself alone. The latter welcomes death, while the former (Jesus) feels nothing but grief as he leaves the stage on which his plan was to have been enacted.

The fate of the early Christian communities follows from the individual fate of Jesus, although it is not a simple repetition of it. While these communities also separated themselves from the world, they were able to do so in the company of like-minded people and, thus, were able to withdraw *further* from it. Because they had less contact with the world, they were less inclined to clash with it and, thus, were not so thoroughly defined by the activity of struggle. Hegel summarizes their position succinctly: "The essence of their group was love for one another and separation from others; and both are necessarily bound together" (W 1:403/SC 287, translation altered). The members of the Christian community, united in love and common faith, surrender their rights to one another—that is, they transcend the level of *Verstand* and abstract communal ties. They are, for Hegel, united by feeling alone. Love is a unique feeling in that it both encompasses everything as a single essence and is experienced as distinct in each individual consciousness. As Hegel has claimed, whatever the pleasures of the pure single-heartedness of love may be, it nevertheless falls short of religion because it lacks objectivity. As *feeling* alone, this unity cannot be *known,* for to know anything is to know it as severed. The love uniting the early Christian community was specifically a love understood as a union *in* God, not a "union of individualities" (W 1:403/SC 287). This is to say, again, that all relations to objectivity were shunned. When he was alive, Jesus acted as the living bond that united the disciples, and he united reality and spirit, the visible and invisible, for them. When he was gone, separation returned. Because of the degree to which their unity in pure life depended on the *individuality* of Jesus, in his absence, they were "like sheep without a shepherd" (W 1:407/SC 291). In this immediate sense, then, Jesus's sacrifice fails, in that it does not bring about an awareness beyond faith of the disciples' freedom from fate. As Derrida writes of this passage, "The *Christian* religion remains sublime."[46]

Far from being the reconciliation of fate as such, the unique fate of the early Christian communities was simply the reverse of that which they were fighting against. While the spirit of independence that Hegel attributes to Judaism reduced the relations of life to mundane realities, the Christian community comes to dread all contact with the world in general. If, for Hegel, Judaism marks the extreme of objectivity, Christianity marks the opposite danger of an excess of subjectivity. If the Jewish spirit renders all living relations into relations of *Objekte,* it is not ashamed of this but takes pride in it. The Christian spirit of love, in its opposition to the world, also makes all of life into the consciousness of *Objekte;* thus, it sees the same reality, but it takes this as an enemy. Hegel concludes, then, that Judaism and Christianity are equally impoverished (see W 1:404/SC 288). Both spirits fall short of the proper aim of religion, of fulfilling the fundamental need to "unite subject with object, to unite feeling, and feeling's demand for objects, with the intellect, to unite them in something beautiful" (W 1:406/SC 289).

True beauty is embodied in neither Judaism nor Christianity but in a middle position between these two extremes. Is it necessary to traverse both the extremes of objectivity and subjectivity to arrive at this point? Does Christianity bring us closer to it? The objective cannot be a world populated by *Objekte.* It must be, as Hegel has told us, animated by the imagination if it is to be beautiful. This is lacking in Christianity because, on Jesus's death, the disciples do not recognize their essential unity with him. This failure stems, in part, from the nature of the *image* left to the disciples of Jesus on the cross. While the disciples could remember the sacrificed Jesus and while, in their recollection of him, the image of a purer humanity could be enjoyed, nevertheless, this *sublime* spirit would always have as its opposite his vanished existence. Once again, for Hegel, the remembrance of Jesus always entails a longing, which denotes the lack of the fulfillment of religion. The sublimity of the image signals the distance of that which the image presumes to present.

The Hovering God

While Jesus on the cross does not prove to be an image of sufficient beauty to mend the divide between subject and object, can the image of the Resurrection succeed in doing so? Hegel writes:

> Two days after his death Jesus rose from the dead; faith returned into their [his disciples'] hearts; soon the Holy Ghost came to them; and the Resurrection became the basis of their faith and their salvation. Since the effect of this Resurrection was so great, since this event [*Begebenheit*] became the center of their faith, the need for it must have lain very deep in their hearts. (W 1:407n/SC291n)

Hegel includes this scene but then crosses it out. He rejects the inclusion of the Resurrection at this point, presumably because he is more concerned with the need that it fulfills in the disciples than he is with the Resurrection itself. This stricken passage could be read as sanctioning the view that the Resurrection was an "objective," historical occurrence. Hegel's position, however, is that to attempt to understand a properly religious phenomenon as an event of this kind entails the activity of division, and this signals its death. The risen Jesus must instead be considered as an *image,* a product of *Phantasie,* that attempts to give shape to love in its beauty. As the objective aspect of God, love given shape would be "simply the presentation of the love uniting the group, and it contains nothing not already in love itself . . . , contains nothing which is not at the same time feeling" (W 1:409/SC 293). As such, it would serve to heal the opposition of life and death and, so, in its beauty, satisfy what Hegel describes as our deepest need. The image of the risen Jesus *fails* to bring forth the fulfillment of religion, however, because it is not love given shape alone. As the "deification of a man present also as a reality" (W 1:409/SC 292), Jesus of Nazareth, who was crucified and buried, is appended to the pure image of love. The Resurrection, then, as love given shape, is the image of an actuality in the world of actualities; as such, the understanding cannot be kept at bay. As an individual, Jesus becomes the fixed, objective counterpart to the *Verstand.* As fixed and individualized by the understanding, his humanity, in turn, becomes a "mundane reality hanging on the deified one like lead on the feet and drawing him down to earth" (W 1:409/SC 293). Thus, the Christian is saddled with a dual nature in a way that mars the beauty of the image of the resurrected Jesus. The failure of the image is measured, not surprisingly, against the manifestations of the Greek imagination:

> Just as Hercules soared aloft to become a hero only through the funeral pyre, so too the deified one was glorified only through the grave. But with Hercules, altars were dedicated and prayers offered only to courage configured, only to the hero who had become god and who neither fought nor served anymore. It is different with Jesus, because it is not the risen one alone who is the cure to sinners and the ecstasy of their faith; prayers are also offered to the man who taught, who walked on earth and hung on the cross. It is over this monstrous combination [*ungeheure Verbindung*] that, for many centuries, millions of

> God-seeking souls have fought and tormented themselves. (W 1:409–410 / SC 293, translation altered)

As Derrida writes, "the altars and the prayers of the Greeks appeal to a god who no longer continues to fight on the earth, who no longer remains in his body."[47] With the Christian God, by contrast, the human form is not merely a veil covering the divine but belongs to its essence. The human form does not fall away but remains as a fixed and permanent aspect of God.

The "sad need" (*traurige Bedürfnis,* W 1:410 / SC 293) for the mundane reality—the body—of Jesus that Hegel finds in the disciples is not accidental but is the proper fate of Christianity and its Idea of love. It is the fate of a love that does not manifest itself as life; for this reason, the early Christian communities did not manifest in themselves something like the beautiful relations that characterized the citizens of a free republic. Because they lacked the experience of a union created through love itself—and, therefore, lacked a measure against which to recognize life—they needed an external criterion, something actual, to unite them. Faith in a common master and teacher, who, as such, ultimately remains divided from them, served this purpose. Thus, their God, as that which united them, assumed the form of something *given.* Yet, for Hegel, "to spirit, to life, nothing is given" (W 1:411 / SC 294). The proper movement of spirit as the conquering of a fate is only the appropriation of what was erroneously perceived to be alien to the self. Their faith, by contrast, required that they assume the role of a servant who attributes whatever it is that he might have to the generosity of his master. It is the absence of "life" that, in turn, allows love to overreach itself. By attempting to unite an assembly of people in a way that is beyond love's power, Christianity loses a necessary intimacy; thus, the Idea becomes alien. Love becomes a dogmatic principle, rather than a lived experience. As the Idea of love is rendered empty in this way, *positivity* emerges at the core of the Christian movement (although, again, in contrast to his position in *The Positivity of the Christian Religion,* this positivity is now presented as an internal consequence or *fate* of Jesus's life and teaching). It is not, however, their God who is foreign. He assumes the form of sublimity, since, instead of being their equal, he contains within himself "the whole spirit of those who are united" (W 1:411 / SC 295). What is specifically foreign to the early Christians is that which stands against the group and that against which it is deemed inferior, namely, a positive *Objekt.* Positivity arises, then, through the doctrine of the deification of Jesus, through the image of God marked by humanity. Jesus of Nazareth is a nondivine being who must also be worshipped, and at precisely this point, with the emergence of positivity and a foreign object on which the community is dependent, fate reemerges. The fate that plagues the attempt to avoid all fate, all objectivity, is manifested in the practice of worshiping a nondivine *Ob-*

jekt that, as such, cannot unite the finite and infinite. So far as this positive, external element exists, the Christian community will remain a "community of dependence" (ibid.).

The spirit of love that shuns ties to the existing social and political world becomes extended over a greater number of people, and, the more thinly this love is stretched, the more developed the fate becomes, to the point where it begins to correspond with the fate of the world. As I have stressed, Hegel's focus is ultimately trained on his own contemporary world insofar as the modern world is a product of this fate. This world was born of the "oriental" spirit, a spirit that regarded fewer things as objects and thus subjected fewer things to the faculty of division (*Verstand*) than is the case in modernity. Therefore, the "oriental" spirit, which still "breathed upon" earlier Christians, is characterized by a greater *embodiment* of spirit (W 1:414/SC 297). The *fate* of this spirit, however, as it becomes enveloped by the history of Christianity, is the excessive sundering of spirit and world. Hegel elaborates on this by comparing the Resurrection as it appeared to the early Christians with what we moderns understand as the immortality of the soul. Both positions represent extremes relative to the Greek spirit.

In modernity, from the perspective of European *Verstand,* "soul" is that which is severed from materiality and then set in opposition to it. Immortality, in turn, is the separation of "soul" from "body." As Hegel writes, "Our [modern] extreme is the outlook of reason [*Vernunft*] which sets a soul—something negative in the sight of every intellect [*Verstand*]—over against the intellect's object, the dead body" (W 1:414/SC 298). Modern *Vernunft* is characterized by this *negative* capacity. When it attempts to unify life and death—to recognize the continuity of life through death—it works only negatively, by positing an empty signifier—"the soul"—to bridge the abyss between the two. In other words, the activity of *Vernunft* in modernity is so dominated by the logic of *Verstand* that, when something beyond *Objekte* is thought, it is determined by this logic. It is understood as an *opposite,* as simply that which is not an *Objekt.* As such, the soul is entirely without substance; it is shapeless, *gestaltlos,* a mere placeholder. For the earlier Christian, "oriental" extreme, "immortality" is not the separation of "body" and "soul" but the resurrection of the body. The body dies, but, at the same time, the overcoming of death is figured as the return of this same body. According to Hegel, the body's persistence manifests "a *positive* capacity of *Vernunft* to posit the body as living although at the same time it has taken it for dead" (ibid., translation altered, emphasis added). This indicates, for Hegel, that the early Christian extreme still retained a more robust sense of spirit. An early Christian could still allow his or her spirit to meld with that of another.

For the early Christians, then, the body is distinct from the soul, yet it is a part of it as well. So long as the soul is immortal, the body accompanies it. This conceptual vagueness allows for a conjoining of the crucified and risen Jesus; thus, it illustrates, at the very least, the *attempt* to fulfill the deepest drive toward religion. Yet, at the same time, the body posited as both living and dead marks the beginning of the division that is so determinative of modernity. The "cognition" (*Erkenntnis*) that defines the "oriental" spirit, in comparison to European *Verstand,* "is more like a vague hovering [*Schweben*] between reality and spirit" (W 1:417/SC 300). This *hovering* signals an original separation of spirit and reality that will become entrenched through the Christian tradition, such that the hovering quality will itself eventually be lost as spirit and reality become fixed in their opposition. For the early Christians, "both of these [reality and spirit] were separated, but not so irrevocably, and yet they did not coalesce into a pure nature but already themselves afforded the clear opposition which, with further development, was bound to become a pairing of living and dead, divine and real" (ibid., translation altered). Yet the longing instituted by this vague, hovering union of the crucified and risen Jesus means that, while the opposition is set or fixed, there is movement between the extremes of God and world that takes the form of an interminable oscillation. The fate of Christianity dictates that the opposition of everything associated with body and soul—state and church, life and worship, virtue and piety, spiritual and worldly action—will not dissolve into one. The inability to effect this unification precludes the possibility of achieving any kind of living beauty. It is, Hegel concludes, contrary to the spirit and fate of Christianity "to find peace in a nonpersonal living beauty" (W 1:418/SC 301).

Thus, the "oriental" and the "modern" are presented as opposing extremes, yet the oriental spirit is also seen to be an integral, determinative part of the birth of the modern spirit itself. That is, the two extremes are present as both *logically* opposed and *historically* fluid and intertwined. Insofar as there is this determinative relation, they are united in their failure to experience the body and soul, world and spirit, as a living whole. In accordance with the logic of *opposition,* the living beauty of Greece remains, for Hegel, the middle point that unites spirit and world in a way that avoids the hovering and interminable oscillation that comes to characterize the history of Christianity. Between the early Christian extreme of the Resurrection of the crucified body and the modern extreme of the thorough separation of soul and body, Hegel finds "the Greek view that body and soul persist together in one living shape" (W 1:415/SC 298).[48] If the Greeks' ability to achieve this unity was grounded in their *Volksreligion* and the tragic narratives that were so central to it, why, then, does the hovering Jesus fail as a tragic hero? The indeterminacy and ambiguity of this state of *hovering* are certainly not absent from Greek tragedy. As Vernant argues, Attic tragedy arises only when every action has its source *both* in the *ethos,* or character, of the actor *and* in a *daimōn* operating *through* the self. The condition of tragedy is a self that is the source of its own actions and, at one and the same time, *possessed,* insofar as the medium for the will is a *daimōn*. The presentation of Greek tragedy, then, must imply two things simultaneously: "It is his character, in man, that one calls *daimōn* and, conversely, what one calls character, in man, is in reality a *daimōn*."[49] If these two disappear, or are seen as mutually exclusive, tragedy disappears. Vernant notes that they are deemed to be mutually exclusive for us today and were to a large extent already seen in this way by Aristotle.[50] The image of the coupling in Jesus of the mortal and immortal leaves him *merely* hovering, in part, because of the expectation of unity that the Idea of love introduces and the unwillingness that follows from it to reside within the tension and ambiguity of the tragic self. If there remains the possibility of moving beyond the Christian impasse as Hegel presents it in Frankfurt, what would the destination be? Is a "unification" beyond the interminable oscillation that Hegel describes possible, and would it be defined in terms of the tragic beauty of Greece or another kind of beauty all together?

Dissolution/*aufheben*

The Christian God ultimately "hovers midway between heaven's infinity, where there are no barriers, and earth, this collection of plain restrictions" (W 1:409/SC 293). A hovering ghost exists between the two objects of worship: the *Gegenstand,* the sublime God, the absolutely distant father, and the nondivine *Objekt,* Jesus of Nazareth, the crucified, who will never be divine. Miracles, as emblematic of everything that Hegel designates by the term "positivity," fail to bridge the gap between finite and infinite, despite the fact that Jesus's miraculous acts "do not simply hover about him" (W 1:412/SC 295) as an accidental characteristic, but instead *seem* to proceed from an inner, divine nature. However, when the *Verstand* attempts to apply its own concepts—in particular, cause and effect—to the miraculous act, the spectacle of an infinite power, or cause, having a finite, restricted effect presents itself. What is *unnatural, qua Verstand,* is "not the annulling [*Aufhebung*] of the intellect's sphere but its being posited and annulled simultaneously" (W 1:413/SC 296). The action that is understood as miraculous both *undermines* the domain of causality—an infinite force cannot have a finite effect—and *relies* on the logic of causality to be persuasive—miracles are only miraculous from the perspective of *Verstand,* for it expects causality to occur solely between *determinate* beings, one active, the other passive. For *Verstand,* the cause—the infinite—is simply assumed to be a means of explaining a finite effect where no finite cause can be found. God, as infinite cause, has the same status as the soul; it is shapeless, an empty signifier. As such, it will fail in uniting finite and infinite. But as Hegel recounts the historical fact of the merging of the world's fate with that of the "monstrous combination" found at the heart of the Christian spirit, he presents the method for realizing the passage between finite and infinite. This could be called "spiritual causality."

Spirit takes the infinite to be *being,* which is itself the whole. Its "effects" are specific determinations of this whole. Hegel now writes not of spirit *knowing* spirit but of spirit *working on* spirit (see W 1:413 / SC 296). The labor of spirit is not the cause of an effect on an external object; rather, this causality "assumes an object [*Gegenstand*] on which the effect is wrought, but the effect wrought by spirit is the sublation [*Aufhebung*] of it" (ibid.). Hegel continues, "the outgoing of the divine is only a development, so that, in sublating [*aufheben*] what stands over against it, it manifests itself in a union with that opposite" (ibid.). Spirit works only on itself or on a union (Hegel writes of *"eine Vermählung,"* a marrying [W 1:414 / SC 297]) with another who is, in truth, only an extension of the self. The manifestation of this unity is the "developing of a new being" (W 1:414 / SC 297). *The creation of new life stands in the place of miracles.* As Hegel presents the manifestation of love's labor in the fragment *Love,* it is, as a unifying power, as spirit, embodied; it is erotic. The mortal element of the lovers, the body, as what is most an individual's own, is unified into a whole through the lovers' touching, and it does this to the point of "unconsciousness" (*Bewußtlosigkeit,* W 1:248 / L 307), to the point of cancelling all differences. Yet, if consciousness is lost, the body does not disappear, for what comes into existence is *ein Keim der Unsterblichkeit* (ibid.), a germ of what is eternally self-developing and self-begetting. Hegel speaks initially of *ein Keim*[51] but later in the fragment of *das Kind.* Through the new life, as the new unity of the child, "God has worked and created" (W 1:248 / L 307). While the lovers separate, their union becomes inseparable in the child. The child is born as a *point,* but, in the way that all life—as *hen kai pan*—develops, she becomes a *manifold, ein Dasein,* and does so through the process of "drawing into itself," "setting over against itself," and "unifying with itself" (W 1:249 / L 307). The spirit has not left the body behind. This drawing-in entails both the material and the ideal, eating and education.

One cannot help but recognize in this kind of "spiritual causality" an inchoate form of the movement of the later dialectic. According to Hegel's analysis in Frankfurt, it is also something that Christianity does not achieve. This early articulation of the dialectic describes the movement through the spirit and fate of Christianity toward its fulfillment, but this fulfillment is not achieved within the sphere of Christianity itself. Jesus forgives Mary Magdalene, but that is all. There is no third. There is no objectivity that is simultaneously subjectivity. In the tragic register, Christianity fails to harbor the Erinyes within itself. Traversing the extremes of objectivity and then subjectivity does not effect a turn to the middle point of living unity. It does not fulfill our highest desire for a union of subject and object "in something beautiful, in a god, by means of the imagination" (W 1:406 / SC 289). Objectivity remains a fate. Indeed, the spirit of Christianity calls forth the most colossal fate, and modernity is shaped in an essential way by its inability to reconcile itself with it. As Hegel argues, we moderns, in contrast to the Greeks and early

Christians, are so thoroughly defined by the thought of the *Verstand* that, when we see another, we see only something actual—an objective being. For Hegel, this way of being follows from the rise of the Christian mode of subjectivity that is defined by the interiority secured through withdrawal. The loss of unity that comes with grasping all beings, including human beings, in terms of the categories of *Verstand* (which is to say, as *objects*) characterizes modernity, and, if there is a distinctly *modern* experience of tragedy, it is born of enduring this separation. Hegel was particularly attuned to the experience of this loss of a nonreflective relation to the world through his study of the Greeks and through the discussions he must have had with his friend Hölderlin. Even if there was not a total absence of this self-distancing, self-alienating kind of reflection in, for example, Greece, it was the exception; Socrates was the exception. In modernity, *not* distancing ourselves from the other is the exception.

Although Hegel's Idea of Greece is less than univocal, it remains, at the end of *The Spirit of Christianity,* the figure of a living union. This is not the Greece of moral harmony but of the beauty born of a tragic imagination. Despite Hegel's attempt to view the life of Jesus and his fate through the lens of Greek tragedy, the death of Jesus does not effect a union of pure life, where the extremes of subject and object, culture and nature, organic and "aorgic," come to be "harmonized" through the sacrifice of the individual. In his essay "The Basis of Empedocles," written in August or September of 1799, Hölderlin formulates the tragic solution that Hegel's Jesus fails to achieve:

> At the midpoint lies the death of the individual, namely, the moment where the organic dispenses with its ego, its particularized existence, which went to the extreme, where the aorgic dispenses with its universality, not in ideal mixture, as it was at the commencement, but in its real supreme struggle; . . . *so that in this moment, in this birth of supreme hostility, the supreme reconciliation appears to be actual.*[52]

In this passage, Hölderlin sketches a solution to the intense opposition between *nature,* as the unformed and unlimited (aorgic), and *culture,* as the formed and limited (organic). In Hegel's terms, this maps broadly onto the opposition between *life* and the petrified world of *positivity;* it is an opposition that is *experienced* as the "objectivization" of being—all beings, including human beings, are experienced as objects. Dastur summarizes the spirit of the passage well when she writes of the Hölderlinean idea of tragedy that "the highest joy, that is, the reunion of man and god, can be expressed, metaphorically, in sorrow and mourning, which is to say, in the death of the hero."[53] Thus, for Hölderlin, the reconciliation through tragic beauty takes the form of "harmonious opposition" between *art* and *nature* or, to apply this logic using Hegel's categories, a harmonious opposition of *law* and *love.*[54] As Hölderlin writes in "The Basis of Empedocles,"

> When life is pure, nature and art oppose one another merely harmoniously. Art is the blossom, the perfection of nature; nature first becomes divine when it is allied with art, which differs from it in kind but is in harmony with it, first when each is everything it can be and when each allies itself with the other, supplying what the other lacks, and lacks necessarily if it is to be everything it can be as a particular; at that point perfection is achieved and the divine stand at the midpoint of the two.[55]

Art is a rupture from nature, yet, in its highest, tragic form, it also allows nature itself to appear by staging "the dynamic conflict of nature and culture itself."[56]

The failure of the spirit of Christianity to reconcile itself with the fate that it brings into being through the tragic presentation of the self-sacrifice of Jesus is precisely what provokes the call found in the "The Oldest Program" to create a new mythology. Hölderlin's attempt to write a modern tragedy based on the life of the poet-philosopher Empedocles, rather than Jesus, can be conceived as a part this unprecedented project.[57] *The Death of Empedocles* is, for Hölderlin, the translation of the most profound intensity (*die tiefste Innigkeit;* FH 1:860) into "a foreign, *analogical* subject matter [*Grundstoff*]" (FH 1:866), for only through this translation can the poet's experience, as something more divine than the poet himself, achieve objective form. This most profound experience reflects, in turn, the contradictions of the poet's epoch, and these are to be reconciled "using the mediation of a story that is foreign to him."[58] (They are presented, in Hegel's terms, "in something beautiful, . . . by means of the imagination" [W 1:406/SC 289]). In this case, the foreign material is Agrigentum and Mount Etna in the fifth century BCE, for Hölderlin finds a hidden historical analogy between fifth-century Greek world and his own: "A different world, foreign surroundings and characters, are called for, and yet, as with every likeness of a bolder sort, all these things must be adapted to the underlying material all the more intensely; they are heterogeneous only in the extrinsic configuration" (FH 1:866).[59]

Hölderlin, however, abandoned the attempt to write a modern tragedy based on the death of Empedocles. One could argue that he abandoned the form of ancient tragedy and the conventions of the Greek tragic hero as the means of expressing modernity's most "profound intensity" because he came to acknowledge the necessity of enduring separation. He came to recognize that the failure of the speculative drive to unite with the infinite—the failure in Hegel's terms of *plērōma*—is the authentic experience of *modern* tragedy. As Hölderlin writes in a letter to his friend Böhlendorff (April 12, 1801), "This is the tragedy for us: that we quietly leave the world of the living packed in a box, and not consumed by flames. We atone for the flame that we did not know how to master" (FH 2:913).[60] The tragic sacrifice of Empedocles, consumed by the flames of Aetna, is not required of us.

Hegel will come to reject ancient Greek ethical life and its expression in Greek tragedy, as the ideal for a revitalized modernity. In doing so, he is, in turn, opening up the possibility of reconceiving and reevaluating Christianity and the fate of what he calls its "monstrous combination" of humanity and the divine. The Christian aspiration to an immanent transcendence ends, as Hegel understands it, in the state of an unending, itinerate "hovering" only insofar as it is judged according to an idealized notion of Greek unity and the idea of a pure love beyond the law. When this ideal is abandoned, it is not only Christianity and its fate that is open to being reevaluated but modernity and the modern subject as well.

CONCLUSION

Comedy, Subjectivity, and the Negative

Ohne ihn gelesen zu haben, läßt sich kaum wissen, wie dem Menschen sauwohl sein kann.

—Hegel on Aristophanes (W 15:553)

In the *Phenomenology*, "the revealed religion," Christianity, is not a failed tragedy as is the case in *The Spirit of Christianity and Its Fate*. By 1807, Christianity is presented as the fulfillment of the religious forms found in ancient Greece. What has happened in the interim? How do we explain this conversion, or inversion (*Umkehrung*)?[1] Whereas Hegel presents Christianity in Frankfurt as *die ungeheure Verbindung* (a monstrous combination) over which "millions of God-seeking souls have fought and tormented themselves" (W 1:409–410/SC 293), he now sees Jesus as "a tragic hero translated from the stage into real life."[2] As a clue to the reason this transformation takes place, we might consider the fact that the movement from "the spiritual work of art" of Greece to "the revealed religion" passes through comedy as the sublation of tragedy. If, as Hegel discovers in Frankfurt, beauty is tragic and tragic beauty is not only the presentation of life but its dissolution as well, "religion in the form of art" must also be the art of its own dissolution. This occurs in the laughter of comedy. Hegel writes in the *Lectures on Fine Art* that comedy—as opposed to the laughter of derision, scorn and despair—implies "an infinite lightheartedness and confidence felt by someone raised altogether above his own inner contradiction . . . : this is the bliss and ease of a man who, being sure of himself, can bear the frustration of his aims and achievements" (W 15:528/LFA 1200).

In the *Phenomenology*, Aristophanes and Socrates are united in destroying the divided substance that is presented in ancient Greek tragedy.[3] Comedy may not be the best or highest type of the art with respect to literary form, but, in terms of the movement of spirit, it is the most self-conscious moment of art and is, thus, both the culmination of "religion in the form of art" and the figure of its demise.[4] The gods of epic and tragic poetry, who took the form of individuality and were considered to be separate from human beings, are revealed to be the products of the Greek imagination. The truth, then, of the substantive world is the *self* as negative power, and it separates itself from the substance in which it had previously been absorbed.[5] From behind his mask, the actor proclaims "the irony of such a property [the abstract universal property assigned to the individual gods: beauty, justice, love, etc.] wanting to be something on its own account" (PdG 485 / PS 450). That is to say, from behind their masks, the actors unmask the gods. As subjects, the gods are comic because they are reduced to an abstract moment, that is, a single property. The comedy arises from the discrepancy that exists between the extravagant claims made by these divine beings and their weakness—a weakness also shared by those who do the unmasking.[6] As Hegel writes, the actor/self "plays with the mask" (PdG 485 / PS 450). While the self hides behind it in order to play a part, ultimately, it "breaks out again from this illusionary character and stands forth in its own nakedness and ordinariness, which it shows to be not distinct from the genuine self, the actor, or from the spectator" (ibid.). As Nietzsche says of the most comic of tragic poets, "Euripides brought the spectator onto the stage."[7] And this sounds the death knell of tragedy for both Nietzsche and Hegel. The actors play the spectators, and spectators assume the role of actors in all the scenes of their own lives. The resolute, polarizing, and even fanatical conviction found in a play like *Antigone* evaporates as the irony that was initially directed toward the gods is directed toward the (human) self as well.[8] To the extent that there is laughter, it is that of the "actors" laughing at themselves, for actor and spectator reflect each other to the point where the distinction between them collapses. The substantiality of Greek ethical life, the substance undergirding the prior moments of "religion in the form of art," is consumed not in fire but by this self-directed laughter. Subjectivity without substance: "What this self-consciousness [that of the actor who coincides with what he imitates] beholds is that whatever assumes the form of essentiality over against it, is instead dissolved in it—in its thinking, its existence, and its action—and is at its mercy" (PdG 487–488 / PS 452).[9]

The rehabilitation of Jesus arises, for Hegel, out of this comic conflagration of substance. It does so because this radical suspension of all substantiality marks the appearance of the power of the subject as *negativity*. Comedy's "triumph" over tragedy comes from standing above the substance in which the tragic heroes were firmly entrenched. This is a kind of withdrawal, something like the renunciation of all that is most beloved. Yet, at least initially, the distance produced is marked by light-heartedness. The subject is structurally "comic" in that it is able to detach itself from all substantiality at the same time that it recognizes itself in it. And comedy is truly comic only when it performs the comedy of tragedy, only when the substance that the tragic heroes adhere to with such fervor is exposed as self-created. What, then, is the fate of fate? It remains the recognition that what we took to be our nemesis is nothing but ourselves misperceived as another. Yet, if this is first experienced as an ungrounded, dizzying, ecstatic, and perhaps hysterical light-heartedness, we would be remiss not to mention its underside.

> We see that this Unhappy Consciousness constitutes the counterpart and the completion of the comic consciousness that is perfectly happy within itself. Into the latter, all divine being returns, or it is the complete *alienation* of *substance.* The Unhappy Consciousness, on the other hand, is, conversely, the tragic fate of the certainty of self that aims to be absolute. It is the consciousness of the loss of all *essential* being in this *certainty of itself,* and of the loss even of this knowledge about itself—the loss of substance as well as of the Self, it is the grief which expresses itself in the hard saying that "God is dead." (PdG 490/PS 454–455)

A *Volksreligion* that is to mend the *Entzweiung* (division) that Hegel had diagnosed as the essence of modernity will have to confront this hard saying. However, it does not merely announce the *division* of substance, but the *flight* of substance itself. To the extent that ancient Greek tragedy is grasped as the radical self-polarization of ethical life, it will not suffice. Hegel, like Hölderlin, is brought to abandon the attempt to compose a *modern* ancient Greek tragedy, albeit with very different consequences.

NOTES

Introduction

1. In *The Future of Hegel,* Catherine Malabou describes this openness concisely: "Hegel's idea of the arising, the event, belongs in this place of contrasts where form forms itself and at the same time deforms itself, where it acquires consistency and bursts out like a bomb" (187).

2. See Russon, *Reading Hegel's "Phenomenology,"* 164.

3. "In the advent of Christianity, which he saw as the 'axis on which the history of the world turns,' Hegel saw the emergence of the modern conception of subjectivity which dialectically sublates the earlier Greek conception [of subject as substance]." Malabou, *The Future of Hegel,* 16. Malabou's reference is to PH 319.

4. See Jamme and Schneider, *Mythologie der Vernunft,* 36–39. See also Krell, "The Oldest Program." H. S. Harris argues that "The Oldest Program" was likely the last theoretical essay that Hegel produced in Bern. He dates its composition, tentatively, as early as June or July 1796; Harris, *Hegel's Development,* 249, 520.

5. Although there is little in "The Oldest Program" that Hegel does not articulate in texts that are unambiguously his own, David Farrell Krell is surely right when he claims that "the oldest program toward a system in German Idealism develops out of an intense exchange of ideas and an interpenetration of styles"—an intense exchange, that is, between Hegel, Hölderlin, and Schelling. David Farrell Krell, *The Tragic Absolute,* 41–42.

6. Nietzsche, *The Birth of Tragedy,* 75.

7. See Nohl, *Hegels theologische Jugendschriften.*

8. See Hamacher, *Pleroma—Reading in Hegel,* 18.

9. I discuss the composition of Hegel's *The Spirit of Christianity and Its Fate* in greater detail below. See chapter 3, note 1.

10. Deleuze, *Spinoza,* 10.

11. The fragment titled "Religion ist eine . . . ," written in 1793, is also central to my understanding of the role that *Volksreligionen* play in the development of Hegel's early thinking. This fragment is often referred to in English as "The Tübingen Essay," although H. S. Harris argues that this title is misleading since the essay was likely written after Hegel had left the Tübingen *Stift.* See Harris, *Hegel's Development,* 1:119. It is the first of the "Fragmente über Volksreligion und Christentum," in *Frühe Schriften,* W 1:9–44. My thanks to Merold Westphal's comments regarding this point.

12. Terry Pinkard draws this connection between Hegel's "positivity" and Kant's "dogmatism" in *Hegel's "Phenomenology,"* 11.

13. "Schelling conducted his own education in public." Hegel, *Lectures on the History of Philosophy,* 3:515; cited by Harris in his introduction to Hegel, *The Difference between Fichte's and Schelling's System of Philosophy,* 6.

14. "In due course his [Hegel's] efforts to formulate the right interpretation of Kant brought him face to face with those aspects of Kant's doctrine that were irreconcilable with his Hellenic ideal." Harris, *Hegel's Development,* 1:xx.

15. Henrich, "Hölderlin on Judgment and Being: A Study in the History of the Origins of Idealism," in *The Course of Remembrance and Other Essays on Hölderlin,* 73; Krell, *The Tragic Absolute,* 41; Harris, *Hegel's Ladder,* 1:20n19.

16. This engagement with tragedy is evident in, for example, Schelling's *Philosophical Letters on Dogmatism and Criticism* (1795) and the drafts of Hölderlin's *The Death of Empedocles* (1797–1799), as well as the theoretical essays related to Hölderlin's attempts to write a modern tragedy based on the philosopher-poet's leap into Etna.

17. As Heidegger states in his 1924–1925 lecture course on Plato's *Sophist,* to interpret Plato properly, one must follow the hermeneutic principle of moving from the light into the dark. In this particular case, the "light" is Aristotle:

> We will presuppose that Aristotle understood Plato. Even those who have only a rough acquaintance with Aristotle will see from the level of his work that it is no bold assertion to maintain that Aristotle understood Plato. No more than it is to say in general on the question of understanding that the later ones always understand their predecessors better than the predecessors understood themselves.

Heidegger, *Plato's "Sophist,"* 8. Heidegger operates according to the principle that what is most essential in a body of thought is not always what the thinker necessarily presents as such: "Precisely here lies the element of creative research, that in what is most decisive this research does not understand itself" (ibid).

Yet are Hegel's earlier writings, in fact, clearer than the later systematic works? If so, it would be perfectly appropriate to proceed from the earlier to the later writings. Beyond the way in which the later writings reveal what is decisive in the research that Hegel undertakes in his Bern and Frankfurt studies, the fragmentary state of these earlier texts, as well as the fluid character of the ideas that they address, poses its own interpretative difficulties such that the mature works can sometimes be clear by comparison.

18. Harris, *Hegel's Development,* 1:xix. Whether the young Hegel harbored the aspiration to be a *Volkserzieher* himself remains a question. Regardless, he certainly aspired to understand both the role that *Volkserzieher* have played in past historical transformations and, in accordance with the final lines of "The Oldest Program," their role in inaugurating future revolutions in spirit: "A higher spirit, sent from heaven, will have to found this new religion among us; it will be the last and the grandest of the works of humanity" (OP 13).

19. Harris, *Hegel's Development,* 1:xxxii.

20. Ibid.

21. Harris, "L'etica del sapere," *Clio* 27, 4 (1998): 619.

22. Harris points in particular to the way in which his immanent approach was partially responsible for the fact that he overlooked the significance of the changes that Hegel made to the 1799–1800 draft of *The Spirit of Christianity and Its Fate* (see Harris, "L'etica del Sapere," 618). Harris's considered opinion is that the mature conception of *Aufhebung* emerges in the revised draft of the work. See also Harris, *Hegel's Development,* 1:330.

23. Harris, "L'etica del Sapere," 619.

24. Ibid.

25. Harris, *Hegel's Ladder,* 1:xiii.

26. Ibid., 2:783.

27. Russon, *Reading Hegel's "Phenomenology,"* 3. Consider, for example, Derrida's claim concerning the often "profound affinity" between his discourse and that of Hegel, albeit an affinity within which his attempts at achieving an "infinitesimal and radical displacement" of Hegel's discourse take place. Derrida, "Différance," 14. Kevin Thompson documents this in a very clear and concise way, concluding that "a deep affinity becomes manifest between the concept of *Aufhebung*—the 'speculative concept par excellence' as Derrida recalls—and *différance*"; Thompson, "Hegelian Dialectic and the Quasi-Transcendental in *Glas,*" 239.

28. Critchley, *Continental Philosophy,* 64.

29. Ibid., 66.

1. Positivity and Historical Reversal

1. See Kroner, introduction to Hegel, *Early Theological Writings,* 7.

2. Žižek, "Against Human Rights," 115.

3. See chapter 1, note 6 for a more detailed description concerning the composition of Hegel's essay *The Positivity of the Christian Religion.*

4. In this, it is distinguished from a "rationalistic liturgy," which reduces the religious text to what can be corroborated by the laws of the understanding. See Hamacher, *Pleroma—Reading in Hegel,* 14.

5. Hegel writes this in an early fragment cited by Karl Rosenkranz in *Georg Wilhelm Friedrich Hegels Leben,* 515. Cited in Hamacher, *Pleroma—Reading in Hegel,* 15, translation altered.

6. The fragmentary writings gathered in *Die Positivität der christlichen Religion* were first titled and published roughly seventy-five years after Hegel's death by Herman Nohl in his *Hegels theologische Jugendschriften.* Nohl divides *Die Positivität* into six distinct parts ordered in the following manner:

(1) "Die Überarbeitung von 1800," N 139.
(2) "Ursprüngliche Fassung," N 152.
(3) "Die religiöse Phantasie der Deutschen," N 214.
(4) "Unterschied zwischen griechischer Phantasie und christlicher positiver Religion," N 219.
(5) Über Wunder," N 230.
(6) "Über positive Religion und die kantischen Postulate," N 233.

With the exception of the first, all of these texts were written between 1795 and 1796.

These fragments are rearranged and renamed in later editions of Hegel's work. For the most part, I will use *Die Positivität der christlichen Religion* in *Frühe Schriften,* the first volume of Hegel, *Werke in zwanzig Bänden,* 104–229. Instead of following Nohl in dividing the text into six distinct sections, the Suhrkamp edition is organized in the following way:

(1) "Die Positivität der christlichen Religion," finished by 1795 (also known by its first words, "Man mag die widersprechendsten Betrachtungen"; Nohl's "Ursprüngliche Fassung"), W 1:104–190.

(2) "Zusätze"

   (a) *Ein positiver Glauben,* December 1795–March 1796 (Nohl's "Über positive Religion und die kantischen Postulate"), W 1:190–196.

   (b) *Jedes Volk hat ihm eigene Gegenstände,* May–June 1796? (Nohl's "Die religiöse Phantasie der Deutschen," "Unterschied zwischen griechischer Phantasie und christlicher positiver Religion" and "Über Wunder"), W 1:196–215.

(3) "Neufassung des Anfangs," begun September 24, 1800 (also known by its first words, "Der Begriff der Positivität"; Nohl's "Die Überarbeitung von 1800"), W 1:217–229.

Unless there is specific need to be more precise, I will simply refer to those texts written in Bern, that is (1) and (2) of the Suhrkamp edition, as the *Positivity.* A partial English translation of Nohl's text has been published in Hegel, *Early Theological Writings,* 6.

7. See Hamacher, *Pleroma—Reading in Hegel,* 24.

8. Gadamer, *Hegel's Dialectic,* 31.

9. Dostoevsky, *The Brothers Karamazov,* 240.

10. I refer to "The Oldest Program" and its contested authorship in my introduction.

11. The original source for Hegel's view of Greece and Greek religion comes from Plato, Herodotus, and Thucydides, as well as, of course, the tragedians. It was also gleaned from his reading of modern accounts, those of Friedrich Schiller and J. J. Winckelmann above all else. See Harris, *Hegel's Development,* 1:145, 152.

12. In *Faith and Knowledge,* Hegel raises the infinite finitude, or empirical infinite, in the context of a criticism of Jacobi's interpretation of Spinoza. Spinoza's "infinity of the intellect" corresponds with what Hegel calls "the absolute and true concept [*Begriff*]": it is "equal to itself and indivisible, which of its essence includes the particular or finite in itself at the same time, and is unique and indivisible" (W 2:345 / FK 107). The true infinite includes the particular finite within itself and is speculative, to the extent that it marks the identity of thought and being.

13. Hegel is paraphrasing Fichte's *Bestimmung des Menschen.* See Fichte, *Sämtliche Werke,* 2:189–190.

14. I examine this distinction between *Vernunft* and *Verstand* as Hegel employs it in his early, pre-Jena writings in the section titled "*Volksreligionen*" later in this chapter.

15. Hölderlin, *Hyperion,* in *Hyperion and Selected Poems,* 128–130.

16. See Henrich, "Hölderlin's Philosophical Beginnings," in *The Course of Remembrance and Other Essays on Hölderlin,* 66ff.

17. Harris, *Hegel's Development,* 1:97.

18. While in his third year at the Stift, Hegel spent a number of months at home recovering from an illness, during which time he immersed himself in botany and Greek tragedy. Ibid., 1:63n2.

19. Harris, "Introduction" to *Faith and Knowledge,* 40.

20. See ibid., 1:92–94; Crites, *Dialectic and Gospel in the Development of Hegel's Thinking,* 35–36.

21. See Krell, "The Oldest Program," 15.

22. For a sustained account of Hegel's engagement with questions of political economy, see Lukács, *The Young Hegel.*

23. The importance that Hegel places in philosophy is also evident in the manner in which he valorizes the philosophical community that grows up around Socrates over the religious sects that Jesus inspires. See W 1:120/P 82. This will be discussed in detail below.

24. Harris argues that Hegel first studied the *Critique of Pure Reason* in 1789, in his second year in the Stift, and the second *Critique* shortly afterward. See *Hegel's Development,* 1:83–84. We know from Rosenkranz's biography that Hegel made a detailed commentary on Kant's *Metaphysics of Morals* in 1798. See Rosenkranz, *Hegels Leben,* 86–88.

25. Malabou, *The Future of Hegel,* 13.

26. Ibid., 192.

27. Compare the following passage from the *Phenomenology* concerning the movement of Spirit itself: "Spirit is never at rest but always engaged in moving forward. But just as the first breath drawn by a child after a long, quiet nourishment breaks the gradualness of merely quantitative growth—there is a qualitative leap, and the child is born—so likewise the Spirit in its formation matures slowly and quietly into its new shape, dissolving bit by bit the structure of its previous world, whose tottering state is only hinted at by isolated symptoms" (PdG 10/PS 6).

28. This anticipates Hegel's analysis of the absolute monarch in the "Culture" section of the *Phenomenology of Spirit,* as much as his reconstruction of the dialectic of *Rechtszustand* in the Roman world. The monarch who claims to *be* the state is, in truth, entirely dependent on those who hear and acknowledge the claim. The role of luxury is present in the phenomenology of culture as well, in that those who affirm and underwrite the absolute monarch's position as absolute do so because of the material benefits of doing so (see PdG 338–339/PS 312). In this later dialectic of culture, however, Hegel emphasizes the role of speech in addition to luxury. Speech allows the cultured consciousness to transcend the natural negation—the simple, biological death—found in what Hegel calls the "silent" service of heroism. Through the act of talking itself to death, consciousness is able both to negate and preserve itself. This form of self-sacrifice—the oath, as well as the language of flattery—allows state power to exist as an exterior manifestation of the "I" (as the universal self in the form of an absolute monarch), while also preserving itself as an individual

standing opposed to state power. Like the Greeks who give the aristocratic class their privilege, the power of the monarch is dependent on those who recognize his authority.

The contradiction found in the context of an absolute monarch, wherein the individual is alienated from a substance that it has produced, is also at the core of the "silent revolution" that will lead to the demise of paganism. But whereas Hegel attributes to the Greek masses a perfect awareness of their position of power, this is lacking in the royal subject. See PdG 342/PS 310–311.

29. A tendency toward the concentration of wealth that disrupts the cohesion of the political whole is also present in Hegel's dialectic of ancient Greek *Sittlichkeit* in the "Spirit" section of the *Phenomenology of Spirit*. See PdG 298/PS 272.

30. Hegel names Montesquieu as the source of the view that sacrificing one's life is the principle of a republic. See W 1:206/P 156.

31. The Roman world that develops out of the "beautiful harmony and tranquil equilibrium" of the Greek ethical nation is described in the *Phenomenology of Spirit* as follows:

> The universal being thus split up into a mere multiplicity of individuals, this lifeless Spirit is an equality, in which all count the same, i.e. as *persons*. What in the ethical world was called the hidden divine law, has in fact emerged from its inward state into actuality; in the former state the individual was actual, and counted as such, merely as a blood-relation of the family. As *this* particular individual, he was the departed spirit, devoid of a self; now, however, he has emerged from his unreal existence. Because the ethical substance is only the true Spirit, the individual therefore withdraws into the *certainty* of his own self. He is that substance as *positive* law, but in his actuality, he is a *negative* universal self. . . . But it is an *abstract* universality because its content is this rigid unyielding self, not the self that is dissolved in the substance. (PdG 316/PS 290, translation altered)

32. "The free power of the content determines itself in such a way that the dispersion of the content into a sheer multiplicity of personal atoms is, by the nature of this determinateness, at the same time gathered into a single point, alien to them and soulless as well. . . . Cut off from this multiplicity, the solitary person [the caesar] is, in fact, an unreal, impotent self" (PdG 318/PS 292).

33. See Dilthey, "Die Jugendgeschichte Hegels"; Haering, *Hegel, sein Wollen und sein Werk;* and Lukács, *The Young Hegel.* See also Peperzak, *Le Jeune Hegel et La Vision Morale du Monde,* xii–xiii.

34. See Harris, *Hegel's Development,* 1:119. It is the first of the "Fragmente über Volksreligion und Christentum," in *Frühe Schriften,* W 1:9–44.

35. For the most part, I will leave *Vernunft* and *Verstand* in the German, but, when necessary, I will translate *Vernunft* by "reason" and *Verstand* by "understanding" or, occasionally, by "intellect."

Hegel continues to reinterpret the contrast between *Vernunft* and *Verstand* in his later work. A crucial moment in this process is found in the *Jenaer Realphilosophie* of 1805–1806, where he reinterprets the *Vernunft*/*Verstand* distinction in terms of that between *Begriff* and

Vorstellung. This innovation is correlative with the priority that Hegel comes to afford to philosophy over religion in the Jena period. By the time of the *Jenaer Realphilosophie,* Hegel clearly defines philosophy—the "absolute science"—by its "*Form des Begriffs,*" and he distinguishes this with equal clarity from religion, which he defines in terms of "*ein vorgestellte Geist.*" See Hegel, *Hegel and the Human Spirit,* 181. The *content* of a true, "absolute" religion—Christianity for Hegel in 1805–1806—is the same as the content of the absolute science of philosophy; but, in religious discourse, it is presented in the limited form of *Vorstellung,* that is, in a form that, like *Verstand,* is unable to unify opposites adequately—God and humanity, for example. According to Hegel, philosophy can, by contrast, unify this same content in conceptual form through the synthetic power of *Vernunft.* Thus, the limitations that Hegel had attributed to Christianity in his pre-Jena writings are, by 1805–1806, conceived as necessary structural limitations of religious discourse as such, so not something unique to Christianity. Within this context, then, Hegel comes to affirm Christianity. Further, he criticizes, in a way that anticipates the "Religion of Art" section of the *Phenomenology of Spirit,* what he calls in the 1805–1806 text the "beautiful"—that is, Greek—religion because its "depth" is nothing more than "unknown destiny." This lack of depth is contrasted to the "the depth brought to daylight" found in the "absolute" religion of Christianity. Hegel, *Hegel and the Human Spirit,* 176. Thus, we see the triumph of (Hegel's idea of) Christianity over the Greek *Volksreligion* that he had championed in his earlier writings.

Hegel's reinterpretion of the *Verstand/Vernunft* distinction in his 1805–1806 *Jenaer Realphilosophie* helps clarify the transition that takes place from his early theologico-political texts, marked as they are by his confrontation with the history of Christianity, to the affirmation of Christianity in the *Phenomenology.* I am grateful to Merold Westphal for his comments regarding this issue.

36. In a letter to Christian Ludwig Neuffer, dated February 17, 1797, Hölderlin describes his attachment to Hegel with reference to *Verstand:* "I love calm *Verstandesmenschen,* because one can orient oneself so well by them, when one does not rightly know in what case one is with oneself and the world" (FH 2:650).

37. Kant, *Critique of Practical Reason,* 77. See also Kant, Ak 4:400; Kant, *Groundwork,* 13–14.

38. "Consequently, we see a priori that the moral law as a ground of determination of the will, by thwarting our inclinations, must produce a feeling which can be called pain." Kant, *Critique of Practical Reason,* 76.

39. Ibid., 81, translation altered.

40. Hamacher, *Pleroma—Reading in Hegel,* 30.

41. This is a locution that I have borrowed from Lukács. See *The Young Hegel,* 7.

42. Aristotle, *Poetics* 1449b29.

43. Hegel was obviously aware of Athenian slavery, and he makes mention of it in the fragment *Jedes Volk hat ihm eigene Gegendstände,* from the Bern period (W 1:199/P 148). It does not, however, seem at this point to disturb his admiration for Greece. One way of understanding Hegel's later reconciliation with Christianity is that it comes at the expense of a demotion of ancient Greece due, in part, to a full acknowledgment of the absence of universality in this idea of freedom. He says as much in the "Introduction" to his *Lectures on*

World History: "The consciousness of freedom first awoke among the *Greeks,* and they were accordingly free; but like the Romans they only knew that *Some,* and not all men as such, are free. . . . The *Germanic* nations, with the rise of Christianity, were the first to realise that man is by nature free, and that freedom of the spirit is his very essence." LWH 54.

44. As Yirmiyahu Yovel argues in *Dark Riddle* (31), Hegel's view of Judaism reflects what he calls "a special anti-Semitic genre developed within the Enlightenment movement itself" that also includes the writings of Voltaire, H. S. Reimarus, and Baron d'Holbach, among others.

45. See Fackenheim, *The Religious Dimension in Hegel's Thought,* 158.

46. This is not the case with the German Hegelian *schools,* which are, as Fackenheim says, "infected" with anti-Semitism, rather than a pro-Greek bias. See ibid., 179n.

Fackenheim's position on the mature Hegel is that "the *religious* significance of Jews and Greeks for the absolute [Christian] *religion* is equal, if indeed Judaism does not have the edge" (ibid.) For the Christian faith, Jews and Greeks each have what the other lacks, and thus one must take Hegel to mean that they have equal value (ibid., 199). For Hegel's Christian, the Jewish God is one and infinite, but one and infinite alone. He is a transcendent Lord, rather than an infinite Creator, which has the effect of reducing the human to the merely finite. As for the Greeks, their gods are finite, although they are projections that reveal an awareness of a beauty that is both above and within the human (see ibid., 136). An argument can be made that Judaism is "*religiously* superior, and far closer to a truth acceptable to modern man" (ibid., 157), because it demythologizes nature. It is, however, because of Hegel's Aristotelianism that Greeks are deemed higher than Jews "in their *philosophical* significance . . . for they attain 'freedom' and hence philosophical thought on their own ancient soil whereas the Jews . . . must be transplanted on to modern Christian soil" (ibid., 179n.). Fackenheim's argument operates within Hegel's own position on the Christian character of the "absolute religion." We see here in the *Positivity,* and even more so in *The Spirit of Christianity and Its Fate,* that, although Hegel denies Christianity's absoluteness, the bias against the Jews and for the Greeks is far more severe. Fackenheim's position is, as he says, more persuasive when applied to the later Hegel.

47. For example, Hegel writes, "Greek and Roman religion was a religion for free peoples only" (W 1:204/P 154).

48. Harris argues that, even in Tübingen, Hegel had at least an "intuitive awareness" that the Athenian ideal ended with Socrates. See Harris, *Hegel's Development,* 1:152.

49. All biblical quotations are from *The New Oxford Annotated Bible.*

50. Consider in regard to this polarizing view of "law" contra "love" (or "law" contra "love conceived as the *plērōma* of the law") Jacob Taubes's *The Political Theology of Paul,* in which he argues that Paul's critique of the law is "assessed not as a Christian polemic against Judaism but as a Jewish potential for liberation, one in a series of Jewish forms of liberation from the law." Further, the "theme of *law* is not related to Jewish law as the paradigm fixation on the letter and self-righteousness, as Christian exegesis would have it. Rather, Taubes demonstrates in what sense Paul's critique of law is directed against the Hellenistic theology of the sovereign." Hartwich et al., "Afterword," 116–117. Although Hegel does not focus in an explicit fashion on the way in which Paul's writings have informed his understanding of

Jesus, or the way it has been informed by the reception history of these writings (indeed, Paul is not referred to by name at all in *The Positivity* or *The Spirit of Christianity*), Paul is present. In fact, there is evidence in a letter from Hölderlin (November 25, 1795) that Hegel entertained the idea of turning to the Epistles after completing, *The Positivity.* See Harris, *Hegel's Development,* 1:208.

51. The later Hegel reflects on the conflation of the teachings of Socrates and Jesus—along with those of Kant—that we find in his own early writings. When discussing Islam in the transcripts from his 1824 series of *Lectures on the Philosophy of Religion,* he notes that, from the perspective of the Enlightenment, that is, reflective, abstract thinking, Jesus is reduced to a mere teacher. For Enlightenment theology, "Christianity is valid only as a doctrine, and Christ counts as the emissary of God, as a divine teacher, in other words as a teacher like Socrates, only even more excellent than Socrates, since he was without sin." *Qua Verstand,* Socrates and Jesus would have been essentially indistinguishable, but for Socrates' sins. LPR 3:244n215.

52. Plato, *Symposium* 221c.

53. Lacoue-Labarthe, "History and Mimesis," 221.

54. Did the "thirteenth apostle," Paul, who did not know Jesus personally, produce an "artistic *mimēsis*" of this kind? Taubes goes so far as to claim in *The Political Theology of Paul* "that Christianity has its origin not properly in Jesus but in Paul" (40).

55. Hegel is making use of Kant's distinction between Idea (*Idee*) and Ideal (*Ideal*) in the *Critique of Pure Reason.* At the outset of the "Transcendental Dialectic," Kant explains that, "Ideas are even further removed from objective reality than are categories, for no appearance can be found in which they can be represented *in concreto.* . . . By the Ideal I understand the Idea, not merely *in concreto,* but *in individuo,* that is, as an individual thing, determinable or even determined by the Idea alone." Thus, "Virtue, and therewith human wisdom in its complete purity, are Ideas. The wise man (of the Stoics) is, however, an Ideal, that is, a man existing in thought only, but in complete conformity with the Idea of wisdom." Kant, *Critique of Pure Reason,* A568/B596. I will leave both *Idea* and *Ideal* capitalized in the text when employing them in this technical sense.

56. And it is "for the people that the single individual abandons himself to the danger of death [in war]." Hegel, *Schriften zur Politik und Rechtsphilosophie,* 465–466; *System of Ethical Life (1802/3),* 147–148.

57. Aristotle, *Nicomachean Ethics,* 1155a23–a29.

58. Allan Bloom interprets Book VIII of the *Republic* in this way. Bloom, "Interpretive Essay," 421–422.

59. Taubes cites the following passage from the beginning of the third chapter of Carl Schmitt's *Political Theology.* It draws a stark connection between miracles, as exceptions to an immanent, law-governed cosmos, and political practices:

> The state of exception in jurisprudence is analogous to the miracle in theology. Only by being aware of this analogy can we appreciate the manner in which the philosophical ideas of the state developed in the last centuries. For the idea of the modern state based on the rule of law triumphed together

with deism, a theology and metaphysics that banished the miracle from the world. This theology and metaphysics rejected not only the transgression of the laws of nature through an exception brought about by direct intervention, as is found in the idea of a miracle, but also the sovereign's direct intervention in the valid legal order.

Schmitt, *Political Theology,* 36–37. Cited in Taubes, *The Political Theology of Paul,* 66; see also 85.

60. Reference to *eine exzentrische Bahn* appears in two early drafts of *Hyperion,* the "Fragment von Hyperion" from 1796 (FH 1:489) and the preface to the "Vorletzte Fassung" (FH 1:558). Although Hölderlin does not use the phrase in the final version of *Hyperion,* he does have Hyperion describe his friend Alabanda in this way: "We had argued, too, gaily and ardently, over many things during the voyage; as so often before, I had taken the most heartfelt delight in watching that spirit on its bold, erratic course, following its path in such unconstrained gladness still for the most part so unfaltering." FH 1:635; Hölderlin, *Hyperion and Selected Poems,* 22.

61. See Brown, "The Eccentric Path," 112.

62. *Bildungstrieb,* formative force, is not Hegel's word; he writes of *"der Stempel eigener Originalität"* (W 1:120/P 82). Hölderlin uses *Bildungstrieb* in a short fragment, *Der Gesichtspunkt aus dem wir das Altertum anzusehen haben,* in which he laments the kind of slavish appropriation of antiquity that turns it into something "positive." He writes of "that which was the general reason for the decline of all peoples, namely, that their originality, their own living nature succumbed to the positive forms" FH 2:62; Hölderlin, "The Perspective from Which We Have to Look at Antiquity," in *Essays and Letters on Theory,* 40. Hölderlin also refers to this form-giving drive when working out the theoretical basis of his tragic play about Empedocles. See *Grund zum Empedokles,* FH 1:868; for an English translation, see Krell, "The Basis of Empedocles," in *The Death of Empedocles,* 144.

63. See Badiou, *Saint Paul,* 2.

2. On Expansion

1. I am grateful to Tina Chanter for reminding me of this passage from *Beloved.*

2. The original text of Mark's gospel, which follows Matthew in the New Testament but was chronologically the first of the four canonical gospels to be written, ends with a small group of women, including Mary Magdalene, fleeing the tomb of Jesus after discovering that his body had disappeared. The last words of this gospel of the empty tomb are "for they were afraid" (Mark 16:8). The account of the resurrected Jesus was later added to the text of Mark, thus bringing it in line with those written after it.

3. Plato, *The Republic of Plato.*

4. When Hegel turns from positive to natural law some six years later in his essay *The Scientific Way of Treating Natural Law* (published in the *Critical Journal* in two parts, December 1802 and May 1803), he divides his idea of absolute ethical life—a fulfilled, harmonious polity—into three separate classes. As is the case in the *Republic,* this division is tripartite. Hegel's class formation, however, acknowledges the importance of the modern bourgeoi-

sie and assigns to it the role of the second, "silver" class in his hierarchy. This middle class is consumed by the law of property, so, for Hegel, it does not willingly assume the threat of death and, therefore, lacks freedom. Hegel characterizes this second class with reference to the *Statesman:* they "have no capacity for courage or *sōphrosynē* and the other qualities which tend toward virtue, but by the force of an evil nature are carried away into godlessness, arrogance [*hubris*], and injustice" (308e–309a). In other words, this class, which is united into a cohesive system based on the kind of "formal legal relationship which fixes, and posits absolutely, individual separate existence" (W 2:492/NL 102), is a contemporary descendent of positivism. The free, "gold" class engages in a life that is "wholly devoted to the public interest" (W 2:489/NL 100). Its negative work is that of death in the service of the preservation of the whole. The third, elemental class works on the earth directly; it lacks the power of differentiation, that of *Verstand,* which characterizes the second class, but shares with the first the courage of sacrificing itself in war.

5. Hegel will later reject this approach to the life of Jesus that presents him as one moral teacher among others:

> If we consider Christ only in reference to his talents, his character and his morality, as a teacher, etc., we are putting him on the same plane as Socrates and others, even if we place him higher from the moral point of view. . . . If Christ is only taken as an exceptionally fine individual, even as one without sin, then we are ignoring the representation of the speculative idea, its absolute truth.

Hegel, *Philosophy of History,* 325, translation altered. Cited in Malabou, *The Future of Hegel,* 116. Insofar as Jesus is later conceived in the representational terms of religion as the union of divine and human nature occurring at a particular point in time, he is, as Malabou puts it, the "figure of a pure event," and thus singular (116). That is, with Jesus, the "the very relationship between the substantial divine content and its representation changes." Slavoj Žižek, *The Monstrosity of Christ,* 81. While Socrates may *resemble* God, Christ directly *is* God, "*which is why he no longer has to resemble God,* to strive to be perfect and 'like God'" (ibid). As such, "the Incarnation is not a move by means of which God makes himself accessible/visible to humans, but a move by means of which *God looks at himself from the (distorting) human perspective*" (ibid., 82).

6. W 5:114; Hegel, *Science of Logic,* 107.

7. Hegel, *Encyclopaedia of Philosophy,* §473.

8. "*To sublate,* and the *sublated* (that which exists ideally as a moment), constitutes one of the most important notions in philosophy. It is a fundamental determination which repeatedly occurs throughout the whole of philosophy." Hegel, *Science of Logic,* 106–107.

9. In his later writing, Hegel thinks of life as "reflection into self" and, thus, in a manner informed by the modern orientation around the subject. The Greeks, by contrast, "think of that which moves itself or that which has the origin of motion in itself, as primary." Gadamer, *Hegel's Dialectic,* 29.

10. "The *pharmakon* is neither remedy nor poison. . . . Neither/nor, that is, *simultaneously* either *or.*" Derrida, *Positions,* 43.

11. Commenting on the Sermon on the Mount in *The Spirit of Christianity and Its Fate,* Hegel acknowledges Jesus's concerns regarding material wealth and cites Matthew 20:24 ("it is easier for a camel to go through the eye of a needle than for a rich man to enter the kingdom of God"). While positivity *qua* property is acknowledged in this later text, he claims that it must simply be endured: "The fate of property has become too powerful for us to tolerate reflections on it, to find its abolition thinkable" (W 1:333/SC 221).

12. The material condition for the rite was walking in open sandals on dusty roads. A host would present water to a guest to wash his feet; according to Mark 1:7, washing the feet of a guest was considered to be the most menial task that a servant could be asked to perform. According to John, and John's gospel alone, Jesus performed this service for his friends and disciples at the Last Supper. The early church developed the rite of *pedilavium* as both a symbol portending Jesus's death as the cleansing from sin and as an example of humility. See Bromily, *International Standard Bible Encyclopedia,* 2:333.

13. Bergson, *Laughter,* 25.

14. Ibid., 18.

15. In relation to this concern with living, localized references, Hegel claimed that in his work he intended to make philosophy speak German. To the German translator of Homer, J. H. Voss, he writes, "Luther has made the Bible speak German; you, Homer—the greatest gift that can be presented to a people; for a people is barbarous and does not consider the excellent things it knows as its own until it gets to know them in its own language;—if you would forget these two examples, I should like to say of my aspirations that I shall try to teach philosophy to speak German." *Briefe von und an Hegel,* 1:99; cited in Harris, *Hegel's Development: Night Thoughts,* 409, translation altered. His aim is to overcome the estranged language of *die Schulmetaphysik,* with its foreign phrases and artificial expressions. According to Gadamer, Hegel infused this dead language with "the concepts of ordinary thought, succeeded in recovering the speculative spirit of his native tongue for the speculative movement of his philosophizing, and thereby restored a way of doing philosophy which is the natural inheritance of the Greek thinkers" (*Hegel's Dialectic,* 31).

16. We know from Aristophanes' plays that Athenian Old Comedy would ridicule the Olympian gods, as well as men of prominence in the contemporary society. Hegel will come to interpret the Greeks' ability to laugh at their gods as a sign of their freedom. The distance afforded by comedy will be explicitly associated with the levity experienced with overcoming domination, rather than with the preservation of it. See Hammond and Scullard, *Oxford Classical Dictionary,* 269.

17. Kant, Ak 8:20–21; "Idea for a Universal History with a Cosmopolitan Intent," 31–32. I will look briefly at Kant's writings on universal history, but, in addition to his essay, see also Schiller's 1789 essay, "Was heißt und zu welchem Ende studiert man Universalgeschichte? Eine akademische Antrittsrede," in *Schillers Werke in zehn Bänden,* 8:435–458); and Fichte, "Die Grundzüge des gegenwärtigen Zeitalters," in *Johann Gottlieb Fichtes Sämtliche Werke,* 7:3–15.

18. Kant, Ak 8:21; "Universal History," 32.

19. Ibid.

20. Ibid., 8:27; 36.

21. Ibid., 8:21; 32.

22. One could also think of any number of secular challenges rising against the church. If we look forward to Hegel's analysis of the Enlightenment in the *Phenomenology of Spirit,* secular dissent from a positive religious order can be deemed "internal" as well, to the extent that he presents the dialectical union of belief and reason. The rise of Pietism and a rationally grounded secularism in the eighteenth century stems from the same source. Hegel writes, for example, "Just as faith and pure insight belong in common to the element of pure consciousness, so too do they belong to the return out of the actual world of culture. . . . [E]ach is related within pure consciousness to the other" (PdG 352/PS 324, translation altered). Both oppose, as Terry Pinkard puts it, the "stultifying effects of inherited religious orthodoxy." Pinkard, *Hegel's "Phenomenology,"* 167.

23. Bataille, *The Accursed Share,* 1:109. Bataille's remark concerning monasticism refers to Buddhist and not Christian monks, although it is applicable to Christianity: "And it is strange to bring forward Lamaism, instead of the Christian Church, to describe an unarmed society. But the contrast is clearer, the play of elements is more intelligent when one gives extreme examples" (ibid., 1:93).

24. "Hence, the Absolute itself is the identity of identity and non-identity; being opposed and being one are both together in it" (W 2:96/D 156).

25. See, for example, Lukács, *The Young Hegel,* 105, 119, 186, 198.

26. In *The Spirit of Christianity,* Hegel claims that the distinction between "religious, moral, and civil laws" was first introduced by Jesus. W 1:318/SC 206.

27. Kant, Ak 8:38–39; "What Is Enlightenment?" 43.

28. This is Foucault's translation. See Michel Foucault, "What Is Enlightenment?" in *The Foucault Reader,* 35.

29. Kant, Ak 8:37, 8:41; "What Is Enlightenment?" 42, 45, emphasis added.

30. Ibid., 8:37; 8:42.

31. Cited in Lukács, *The Young Hegel,* 51.

32. In Knox's English translation, the fragment is titled "Is Judea, then, the Teutons' Fatherland?" Harris holds that it was likely written in May and April of 1796. See Harris, *Hegel's Development,* 1:232, 520.

33. For Hegel, in this instance, the Ideal appears to be the Idea both *in individuo* and *in concreto.* See Kant, *Critique of Pure Reason,* A568/B596.

34. Harris argues that Hegel found this image of the "sacred groves" in Friedrich Gottlieb Klopstock's "Der Hügel und der Hain." Harris, *Hegel's Development,* 1:286n2.

35. "The external existence of this picture-thinking, *language,* is the earliest language, the Epic as such, which contains the universal content of the world, universal at least in the sense of *completeness,* though not indeed as the universality of *thought.* The Minstrel is the individual and actual Spirit from whom, as a subject of this world, it [the world] is produced and by whom it is borne. His 'pathos' is not the stupefying power of Nature but Mnemosyne, recollection and a gradually developed inwardness, the remembrance of essence that formerly was directly present" (PdG 475 /PS 440–441).

36. Since both Harmodius and Aristogiton were killed as a result of their assassination attempt, their descendents received the "punishment" that, according to the *Apology,*

Socrates claimed for himself: free meals in the Prytaneum. See Hammond and Scullard, *The Oxford Classical Dictionary,* 112.

37. Hegel's mature system can be seen, in part, as fulfilling what is only hinted at here, in that it defends a dialectical logic that unites Greece and modernity. And it does so in such a way as to incorporate within itself mytho-poetic narrative. It is, in part, a presentation of this unfolding, but one that is philosophically defensible. As Hegel shows in the "Art of Religion" section of the *Phenomenology,* the epic and tragic narratives of Greece are, in effect, the precondition of this rise of Socratic philosophy. See PdG 474–488 / PS 439–453, especially PdG 486–488 / PS 451–453. The scope in the mature system is, of course, much broader than the German nation. If Hegel's philosophy presents the dialectical unity of the global "community," the question to pose, then, is: what narrative can feed the imagination of *this* community?

38. That is to say, very broadly, that the resources that fueled Luther's writings came from within Christianity, and, when he condemned the decadence of Rome, it was on the basis of his own understanding of the significance of the life and teaching of Jesus.

39. Is Hegel simply endorsing nationalist self-aggrandizement? Or is he making the point that nationhood is always based on self-mythologizing? Perhaps the myths proper to a *free* society ultimately work to *undercut* the self-aggrandizing or chauvinist tendencies in any national mythology. One could argue that tragic myths work in exactly this way. If so, a mythology of this kind ought to present a tragic figure like King Agamemnon instead of Harmodius and Aristogiton in their role as heroic tyrannicides.

40. Who, then, would be the modern Paul? Taubes argues in *The Political Theology of Paul* that the "thirteenth apostle" aimed to repeat the achievement of *Moses* and found a people: "For Paul, the task at hand is the *establishment and legitimation of a new people.*" Taubes, *The Political Theology of Paul,* 28. As an apostle from the Jews to the Gentiles, Paul's task was, however, "unprecedented and unique" (ibid., 41).

41. The first detailed sketch of the play, the "Frankfurter Plan," dates from the summer of 1797, and the first and second drafts of *Der Tod des Empedokles* were produced over the next two years. The theoretical essay *Die Tragische Ode . . .* is said to have been written in August or September of 1799, and the third and final draft was abandoned by 1800. These writings can be said to have occupied roughly a quarter of Hölderlin's most fertile writing life if we date this liberally from the time he leaves the Tübingen Stift late in 1793 to his forced return to Tübingen in September 1806. See Constantine, *Hölderlin,* 397–399.

42. Krell, "The General Basis [of Tragic Drama]," in *The Death of Empedocles,* 142. Both Françoise Dastur and Krell follow Heidegger's 1934–1935 lecture course on Hölderlin's two hymns *Germanien* and *Der Rhein* when they resist translating *Innigkeit* as "inwardness" or "intimacy." They both suggest translating this highest experience of the poet as "intensity," but, from this point on, I will leave it untranslated to underscore that the translation of this term is really the labor of tragedy itself. Dastur also notes that it does not signify the closed interiority of the "subject," and she goes on to say that it indicates instead *"the non-exteriority of all things in relation to all others."* The thought is the thoroughly Greek one of the Heraclitean "one divided in itself," and it points toward the ideal of harmonic opposi-

tion that we will encounter below. See Heidegger, *Hölderlins Hymnen 'Germanien' und 'Der Rhein,'* 117; Dastur, *Hölderlin, Le retournement natale,* 46; Krell, *Lunar Voices,* 25, 40.

43. Krell, "The General Basis [of Tragic Drama]," 143.

44. See the "*Volksreligionen*" section in chapter 1.

45. Harris proposes that Herder was the source of the appeal to this truth of the imagination and, thus, the second canon of the *Volksreligion.* Hegel refers to Herder's *Über Mythen* in a letter to Schelling. Hegel, *Briefe von und an Hegel,* 1:11. Harris, *Hegel's Development,* 1:237n1.

46. Nietzsche, *On the Genealogy of Morals,* 93–94.

47. See Szondi, *Versuch über das Tragische.*

48. This is Philippe Lacoue-Labarthe's formulation. See "Caesura of the Speculative," 215.

49. Ibid.

50. Dastur, *Hölderlin, Le retournement natale,* 37–38.

51. Lacoue-Labarthe, "Caesura of the Speculative," 216–217, emphasis added.

52. Vernant, "The Historical Moment of Tragedy in Greece: Some of the Social and Psychological Conditions," in Vernant and Vidal-Naquet, *Myth and Tragedy in Ancient Greece,* 27.

53. By extension, the subservience of a society would be revealed by the perceived need to censor a poet's stories because they portray gods who transform themselves and mislead in speech and deed. See *Republic* 383a.

54. Terence, *The Eunuch,* 2:278, l.589.

55. Hegel does not, however, interpret this slave revolt as the condition for a higher form of universality—namely, the Pauline claim that "There is neither Jew nor Greek, there is neither slave nor free, there is neither male nor female" (Galatians 3:28). Badiou interprets this sentiment in the following way: "To declare the nondifference between Jew and Greek establishes Christianity's potential universality; to found the subject as division, rather than as perpetuation of a tradition, renders the subjective element adequate to this universality by terminating the predicative particularity of cultural subjects." Badiou, *Saint Paul,* 57. Hegel does not argue that the collapse of pagan freedom clears the way for a universal that is indifferent to a specific religious, ethnic, gender, or class qualities. This is compatible with his account of Christian expansionism as grounded in resentment.

56. See Kant, *Critique of Pure Reason,* A529/B557.

57. Hegel quotes these lines from an early version of Schiller's *Resignation.* See W 1:184.

3. The Idea of Freedom as Independence

1. The texts gathered under the title *Der Geist des Christentums und sein Schicksal* were written between 1798 and 1800, while Hegel was a Hofmeister in Frankfurt (W 1:274–418/SC 182–302). These are an even more complicated array of fragmentary works than those collected in *The Positivity of the Christian Religion.* The one long essay reconstructed as *The Spirit of Christianity and Its Fate* is really a series of shorter texts, and, while Nohl's ordering was guided by preparatory sketches made by Hegel, there is no way of knowing with certainty how Hegel wished them to be arranged. It is clear, however, that the ordering of topics and arguments underwent substantial changes. Hegel initially composed a number of

longer texts on Christianity in the winter of 1798/1799, and he then began revising them, making substantial additions, during the following year. Thus, commentators speak of two distinct drafts of the various essays. See Harris, *Hegel's Development,* 1:330–331. When I refer to *The Spirit of Christianity* as a whole, it is to the final version.

2. See Jamme, "Hegel and Hölderlin," 364.

3. See, for example, W 1:349/SC 235. Hegel does not use *zurückziehen* in a rigorous way throughout the text. He also describes this general movement of withdrawal as *entnehmen* (W 1:392/SC 276), *entwinden* (W 1:391/SC 275), *heraustreten* (W 1:319/SC 207).

4. See Wood, *Hegel's Ethical Thought,* 45.

5. Henrich, "Hegel and Hölderlin," in *The Course of Remembrance,* 139.

6. Lukács, *The Young Hegel,* 99.

7. Harris, *Hegel's Development,* 1:294.

8. Hamacher, *Pleroma—Reading in Hegel,* 44.

9. Ibid., 46.

10. This is also the case in Luke, although Hegel claims that Matthew's account is the most spiritual (W 1:390/SC 274). In Luke's gospel, the call to baptism is merely an expression of the repentance of sins rather than a rebirth into the spirit. Hegel also notes that the scribes who brought the ending of Mark in line with the other gospels by adding the injunction to baptize the world did so in a dead, customary way.

11. This descent from the stage is preceded by the unmasking of the actor in Greek comedy: "The self, appearing here in its significance as something actual, plays with the mask which it once put on in order to act its part; but it as quickly breaks out again from this illusory character and stands forth in its own nakedness and ordinariness, which it shows to be not distinct from the genuine self, the actor, or from the spectator" (PdG 485/PS 450).

12. See Hegel, *Wissenschaft der Logik,* W 5:387; *Science of Logic,* 327.

13. The citation is found in the "Zusatz" to §107. Hegel, *The Encyclopaedia Logic,* 170.

14. Hegel, *Wissenschaft der Logik,* W 5:390; *Science of Logic,* 329.

15. Compare the following passage from the "Preface" to the *Phenomenology* concerning truth and its apparent opposite: "The evanescent itself must, on the contrary, be regarded as essential, not as something fixed, cut off from the True, and left lying who knows where outside it, any more than the True is to be regarded as something on the other side, positive and dead. Appearance is the arising and passing away of that which does not itself arise and pass away, but is 'in itself', and constitutes the actuality and the movement of the life of truth. The True is thus the Bacchanalian revel in which no member is not drunk; yet because each member collapses as soon as he drops out, the revel is just as much transparent and simple repose" (PdG 35/PS 27).

16. Hegel's conclusions are not, perhaps, quite this unambiguous. It can be argued that there is a discrete moment of fulfillment in the Last Supper. I will return to whether fulfillment takes place at this very intimate level in chapter 4.

17. *The Spirit of Christianity and Its Fate,* as it stands, begins with an account of the spirit and fate of the Jews. The Greeks are not afforded nearly the same kind of detailed analysis, but they are located within the same universal history. Nohl begins his construction of the essay with the fragment *Mit Abraham, dem wahren Stammvater* (summer/fall 1798;

W 1:274–277 / SC 182–185), but Harris argues that this would be more accurately categorized as a sketch and that the proper *incipit* for the *The Spirit of Christianity* is the more substantial essay *Abraham in Chaldäa geboren hatte schon* (Fall 1798; W 1:277–297 / SC 185–204). Harris, *Hegel's Development,* 1:330n2.

18. Dastur, *Hölderlin, le retournement natale,* 72.

19. "Love is born into every human being; it calls back the halves of our original nature together; it tries to make one out of two and heal the wound of human nature." Plato, *Symposium* 191d.

20. Sallis, *Crossings,* 17. He is referring to Nietzsche's use of the phrase *ein ungeheurer Gegensatz* in the opening paragraph of the first section of *The Birth of Tragedy.*

21. Nietzsche describes the critical, rather than creative, instincts of Socrates as "a monstrosity *per defectum!*" *The Birth of Tragedy,* 66. Sallis (*Crossings,* 124) explains the "defect" in this way, "What is monstrous is the lack of the natural relation between instinct and conscious knowledge, that is, the divergence from nature lies in the inversion."

22. Friedrich Hölderlin, "Seyn, Urtheil, Modalität," FH 2:50. For Hölderlin, the judgment "I am I" is a relation of *Identität* alone, which is to say that separation remains between the "I" as subject and object. *Seyn* is the unity of subject and object where "no separation [*Trennung*] can be undertaken without violating the essence of what is separated" (FH 2:49).

23. In his *Praeparatio Evangelica,* Eusebius (260–340 CE) cites Alexander Polyhistor (circa 105–135 BCE) quoting Eupolemus's popular history *Concerning the Jews* (circa 150 BCE): "The Assyrian city Babylon was first founded by those who escaped from the flood, and they were giants and built the historically famous tower." Reference found in N 245; SC 184n6.

24. As we noted above, this is the aim, according to Gadamer, of the dialectic. Gadamer, *Hegel's Dialectic,* 31.

25. This story is recounted by both Apollodorus and Ovid. I will focus on the richer account provided by Ovid.

26. Ovid, *Metamorphoses,* l. 355–356.

27. Ibid., l. 383–385.

28. Ibid., l. 388–389.

29. Ibid., l. 406.

30. Hegel addresses the question of a nostalgic relation to the past as it arises within the history of Judaism. He criticizes the attempt to resort to "languishing *daimōnes*" (*erschlafften Dämons,* W 1:295 / SC 203) as a means of rekindling their former *Genius* after it had been thoroughly defeated. He claims that, when the genius of a nation (*der Genius einer Nation*) has fled, inspiration (*Begeisterung*) cannot call it back (W 1:295 / SC 203). Inspiration can, however, call forth a new spirit from the depth of life, *if*—Hegel makes the qualification—this nation is constituted by a pure and living people. As Hegel interprets it, the Jewish prophets, who were determined to revive the former spirit, are unable to call forth a new, living one. Instead, they turn away from all the complexities of the present and become mired in reminiscences of bygone times. This approach fails both to address the present and resurrect the past. The question to pose to Hegel's investigation is whether the danger of becoming mired in mere reminiscences exists in his own appropriation of Greek culture.

31. Ovid, *Metamorphoses*, 1.385.

32. Hegel's account of the spirit of Judaism is found in the fragment *Abraham in Chaldäa geboren hatte schon*. The fragment I examined in the previous section addressing the different ways of reacting to the revolt of nature, *Mit Abraham, dem wahren Stammvater*, also begins with the claim that Abraham, rather than Noah and Nimrod, is the progenitor of the Jews.

33. This stands in stark contrast to Johannes de Silentio's interpretation of Abraham as a man of faith, beyond ethics, tragedy, and philosophical concepts. For Søren Kierkegaard's de Silentio, Abraham does not defeat love but exhibits it in its greatest form. His is the love that expects the impossible, that is, the return of Isaac after his sacrifice:

> [Abraham] acts by virtue of the absurd, for it is precisely the absurd that he as the single individual is higher than the universal. This paradox cannot be mediated, for as soon as Abraham begins to do so, he has to confess that he was in a spiritual trial, and if that is the case, he will never sacrifice Isaac, or if he did, then in repentance he must come back to the universal. He gets Isaac back again by virtue of the absurd. Therefore, Abraham is at no time a tragic hero but something entirely different, either a murderer or a man of faith.

Kierkegaard, *Fear and Trembling*, 56–57.

34. See Psalm 119:19. Parts of the earlier draft can be found in Nohl, "Entwürfe zum Geist des Judentums," in N 368. The fragment is also known as "Joseph. jüd. Alterth." See Harris, *Hegel's Development*, 1:521.

35. See Psalm 111:10, cited in Hodgson, *Hegel and Christian Theology*, 232. In the master/slave dialectic in the *Phenomenology*, Hegel claims that "although the fear of the lord is indeed the beginning of wisdom, consciousness is not therein aware that it is a being-for-self. Through work, however, the bondsman becomes conscious of what he truly it" (PdG 135/PS 117–118).

36. Lukács, *The Young Hegel*, 74.

37. Hamacher, *Pleroma—Reading in Hegel*, 52.

38. Although the context is labor rather than political liberation, compare Hegel's description of the "unhappy consciousness" in the "Freedom of Self-Consciousness" section of the *Phenomenology*:

> The active force appears as the *power* in which actuality is dissolved; for this very reason, however, the consciousness to which the *intrinsic* or essential Being is an 'other', regards this power which it displays in its activity to be the beyond of itself. Instead, therefore, of returning from its activity back into itself, and having obtained confirmation of its self-certainty, consciousness really reflects this activity back into the other extreme, which is thus exhibited as a pure universal, as the absolute power from which the activity started in all directions, and which is the essence both of the self-dividing extremes as they at first appeared, and of their interchanging relationship itself. (PdG 151/PS 133–134).

39. Discussed in the previous section, "The Abrahamic Tear."

40. Aristotle, *Poetics* 1453a1–10.

41. Although Hegel notes that the early Jewish laws prohibited idolatry, he does grant that a kind of beauty arises in this context, but it is an "oriental beauty" (W 1:287/SC 195). As such, it takes the form of a threat. This is the image that Moses gives to accompany God's law, which, according to Hegel, is nothing other than its own image, that is, the terror of physical force.

42. This is Dastur's translation, *Hölderlin, le retournement natale,* 74.

43. Deleuze, *Difference and Repetition,* 58.

44. In reference to Adolf von Harnack's *Marcion: The Gospel of the Alien God,* Jacob Taubes draws attention to the "history of the secret Marcionism" that shapes German Protestantism from Luther on. Taubes, *The Political Theology of Paul,* 61. This Marconite "thought-structure" is characterized by the severing of the Old from the New Testament, justice from love, law from redemption, and is evident in eighteenth- and nineteenth-century attempts to isolate the "essence of Christianity." See Hartwich et al., afterword to *The Political Theology of Paul,* 132–133.

45. Please see the section titled "Resentment and the Imperial Will" in chapter 2.

46. To the extent that Hegel can be seen as engaged in this kind of philosophical debate, his most consistent interlocutor is Moses Mendelssohn, whom he cites directly in his early writings (W 1:134ff/P 95ff; W 1:287/SC 195). In *Jerusalem,* Mendelssohn draws the distinction between the state, as the domain of legality, and religion, as that of morality, and he argues for their rigorous separation. Hegel's position on the relation of church and state in the *Positivity* is situated by that of Mendelssohn, but, while Hegel clearly employs this distinction, he does not endorse their separation in the same way. He argues for a kind of state beyond the state (as the sphere of legal coercion), where the spheres of legality and morality operate in a quasi-organic manner—one that is guided, again, by his image of ancient Athens. See Harris, *Hegel's Development,* 1:221.

47. Nancy, *Hegel,* 5.

48. These *Lectures* were given at two-year intervals beginning in the *Wintersemester* of 1822–1823 until the *Wintersemester* of 1830–1831. Both of these quotations are from Hegel's original 1822–1823 manuscripts.

49. Needless to say, the history of the Jewish covenant can be interpreted as revealing a very different logic. Richard Bautch shows the way in which the intermingling of a *conditional* covenant that calls for the free participation of the Jewish people and an *unconditional* promise made by God to his people underlies the evolution of the covenant from the Noahic and Abrahamic periods through to the monarchic, exilic, and postexilic periods. There is an attempt to reconcile "divine commitment and human obligation" (as Bautch notes, this is the title of an article by David Noel Freedman). Far from the absolute transcendence of the Jewish God that Hegel describes, the evolution of the covenant is the narrative of the communion between God and man. Bautch, *Glory and Power, Ritual and Relationship,* 26–32. For his reference to Freedman, see 29.

50. Compare Taubes's observation that "nothing is more engrained in the Jewish soul and in the Jewish body than to die for the sanctification of the name of God. For that you don't need to be a Messiah, you don't need to be a Rabbi, for this the communities in Worms

slaughtered their children, so they wouldn't fall into the hands of the Crusaders." Taubes, *Political Theology of Paul*, 9.

51. In the *Poetics*, Aristotle claims, famously, that tragedy "through pity and fear accomplishes the catharsis of such emotions" (1449b26) and that it is distinguished from comedy insofar as "the latter [comedy] tends to represent people inferior, the former [tragedy] superior, to existing humans" (1448a16).

In his *Lectures on Fine Art*, Hegel writes of the tragic heroes of Sophocles in particular: "It is the honor of these great characters to be culpable. They do not want to arouse sympathy or pity, for what arouses pity is not anything substantive, but subjective grief, the subjective depth of personality. But their firm and strong character is one with its essential 'pathos', and what excites our admiration is this indestructible harmony and not the pity and emotion that Euripides alone has slipped into expressing" (W 15:546/LFA 1215).

52. In the *Lectures on Fine Art*, Hegel contrasts Macbeth and Hamlet. He presents Hamlet as a figure of beauty, but of a distinctly modern shade. Hamlet has a "beautiful, inner soul" (W 14:208/LFA 584), a "beautiful heart [that] is indrawn" (W 13:300/LFA 231), and, although he is defined by inner strength and is inwardly quick for revenge, he is not, as Hegel writes, "carried away like Macbeth" (W 13:208/LFA 583). Hegel singles out the one-sided, self-dependent individuality of Macbeth. He is untouched by any religious feeling and is driven by an immediate, unreflected passion of ambition that exemplifies the Romantic nature of Shakespeare's characters. Although Macbeth is driven by this "dreadful passion" (W 13:271/LFA 208) and is, thus, criminal, through Shakespeare's pen, he rises above this evil passion and is endowed with a "greatness of spirit" and "force of imagination" (W 13:538/LFA 420). Yet he is never described as *beautiful*.

In the *Lectures*, Hegel distinguishes modern (Romantic) tragedy from Greek tragedy as such. Hamlet's collision is *not*—as would be the case in Greek tragedy—the result of his pursuing an ethically justified revenge for his father's murder that simultaneously results in a violation of the ethical order. In *Hamlet*, there is no justification for Claudius's act of regicide; thus, Hamlet must wreak "revenge only on the fratricide king in whom he sees nothing really worthy of respect" (W 15:559/LFA 1225). Thus, there is no conflict between one ethical pathos and another; rather, the collision turns solely on Hamlet's personal character.

53. "Natural consciousness will show itself to be only the Notion of knowledge, or in other words, not to be real knowledge. But since it directly takes itself to be real knowledge, this path has a negative significance for it, and what is in fact the realization of the Notion, counts for it rather as the loss of its own self, for it does lose its truth on this path. The road can therefore be regarded as the pathway of *doubt*, or more precisely as the way of despair" (PdG 61/PS 49).

54. This connection is prevalent, at least at the level of metaphoricity, throughout Hegel's subsequent writings. In the *Phenomenology of Spirit*, for example, a new historical era "comes on the scene for the first time in its immediacy or its Notion" (PdG 11/PS 7). In the later *Philosophy of World History*, to cite just one of many examples, Hegel writes that "in the theatre in which we are about to witness its operations—i.e., the theatre of world history—the spirit attains its most concrete reality" (W 12:29/LWH 46).

55. William McNeill argues that interpreting catharsis in either one of these one-sided ways misunderstands what can be called, anachronistically, Aristotle's phenomenological approach. See McNeill, *The Time of Life,* 185–186.

56. Aristotle, *Poetics* 1451b5–10.

57. Dastur, *Hölderlin, le retournement natale,* 37.

58. Schmidt, *On Germans and Other Greeks,* 89, emphasis added. This theory is distinctly *speculative* in that the idea of the tragic, which presents life as "torn, conflicted, and agonized," is wedded to "the idea of speculation, which seeks to grasp all things, in their mutuality and belonging together, that is, as a unity." This may seem like the marriage of opposites, but "speculative philosophy does not want to be another metaphysics or philosophy of identity: the unity that is the sign of the speculative is not above or outside or other to the phenomenal world, it is rather the very system of this world itself" (ibid.).

59. Aristotle, *Poetics* 1451a11–15.

60. Ibid., 1450b25.

61. The Knox translation renders this as "distinct ethical substances," but there is only one substance (PS 266).

62. Hegel writes of pathos in the *Lectures on Fine Arts:*

> Now, lastly, the universal powers which not only come on the scene explicitly in their independence but are equally alive in the human breast and move the human heart in its inmost being, can be described in Greek by the word *pathos.* To translate this word is difficult, because "passion" always carries with it the concomitant concept of something trifling and low, for we demand that a man should not fall into a passion. "Pathos" therefore we take here in a higher and more general sense without this overtone of something blameworthy, froward, etc. So, e.g., the holy sisterly love of Antigone is a "pathos" in the Greek meaning of the word. "Pathos" in this sense is an inherently justified power over the heart, an essential content of rationality and freedom of will. Now "pathos" forms the proper center, the true domain, of art; the representation of it is what is chiefly effective in the work of art as well as in the spectator. (W 13:287/LFA 232).

63. Vernant, "The Historical Moment of Tragedy in Greece," in Vernant and Vidal-Naquet, *Myth and Tragedy in Ancient Greece,* 27.

64. Ibid.

65. Aristotle, *Nicomachean Ethics,* 1155b5.

66. Christophe Jamme argues that Hegel and Hölderlin came to this idea of "beauty" during the years 1797–1800: "the friends became increasingly aware of the concept of fate in Sophoclean tragedy, the idea that beauty does not belong merely to nature and life but also to their demise." Jamme, "Hegel and Hölderlin," 364.

67. Hölderlin, *Grund zum Empedokles,* FH 1:872. Hölderlin elaborates on this in the following way, drawing a direct connection to tragedy in the process: "Thus Empedocles was to become a sacrifice of his time, *the problems of destiny in which he grew up were to be apparently solved, and this solution was to show itself to be an apparent solution a temporary solution, as*

is the case more or less with all tragic personages, all of which, in their characters and in their utterances, are more or less attempts to solve the problems of destiny" (FH 1:872–873; Krell, "The Basis of Empedocles," 148).

68. The philosophical history of the world "adopts a general perspective, but without focusing on a single aspect abstracted from national life to the exclusion of the rest. The general perspective of philosophical world history is not abstractly general, but concrete and absolutely present; for it is the spirit which is eternally present to itself and for which there is no past" (LWH 23–24).

69. In the *Phenomenology,* Hegel contrasts the hero with his valet in the dialectic of "Conscience," situated at the culmination of the "Spirit" chapter and, thus, immediately before the transition to "Religion": "No man is a hero to his valet; not, however, because the man is not a hero, but because the valet—is a valet, whose dealings are with the man, not as a hero, but as one who eats, drinks, and wears clothes, in general, with his individual wants and fancies" (PdG 437/PS 404).

70. As an admirer of the French Revolution, the young Hegel was very much concerned with the manner in which state and religious power collude to impose autocratic force. However, Hegel's account of Jesus is, for the most part, framed in terms of his religious and moral challenges to the Temple. Any opposition that Jesus had toward Roman political rule and its false universality is largely absent from Hegel's account of him.

4. Withdrawal and Exile

1. In *The Spirit of Christianity,* Hegel does not use *aufheben* in its later technical sense. It does not consistently denote the three moments of preservation, cancellation, and uplifting—a preservation that, in its preserving, cancels the immediacy of what is preserved without annihilating it or reducing it to nothing. He is, instead, in the very process of uncovering the complexity of this movement of reconciling apparently irreconcilable opposites. *Aufheben* is the crucial term that he uses in his conceptualization of what he names in Greek *plērōma* and in German, more often than not, *erfüllen* and *versöhnen.* Whether all three moments of *aufheben* are implied can be determined by how fulfillment itself is described. Although Hegel does not yet exploit the speculative wealth of the word, the different moments are evident. The labor of this text is, in part, that of bringing the three moments together.

The difficulty of translating *aufheben* stems from precisely the speculative richness that Hegel will later appreciate. I will render it in different ways according to the context in which it is used. I will reserve the term "sublation" for those instances when Hegel unites in one verb preservation, cancellation, and the lifting up of the two opposites into a unity.

2. Žižek, *The Ticklish Subject,* 84.

3. Hölderlin recognizes the one-sidedness of the emphasis on the universality of cognitive interest and the autonomy of human nature, but it is, he concedes, the only possible philosophy for the epoch. See FH 2:726.

4. Kant, Ak 4:423; *Groundwork,* 32.

5. Ibid., 4:409; 21.

6. Hegel is referring to Kant's *Die Religion innerhalb der Grenzen der bloßen Vernunft* in *Immanuel Kants Werke,* 6:326; *Religion within the Limits of Reason Alone,* 164.

7. Kant, *Werke,* 6:175; *Religion . . . ,* 31.

8. Ibid., 6:171; 27.

9. Ibid., 6:158; 16. In a letter to Herder (June 7, 1793), Goethe describes this as a moment of what Hegel would call "positivity": "Kant required a long lifetime to purify his philosophical mantle of many impurities and prejudices. And now he has wantonly tainted it with the shameful stain of radical evil, in order that Christians too might be attracted to kiss its hem." Cited in Allison, *Kant's Theory of Freedom,* 270n1.

A defense of Kant against this charge of rigorism would locate the source of evil in *Willkür,* rather than sensibility (*Sinnlichkeit*) or *Wille.* This is a line of argumentation that Allison develops. To *forget* the moral law is to act according to natural inclination alone; it is to be driven by "*mechanical* self-love": the impulse to self-preservation, sexual self-propagation, and social interaction. Kant, *Werke,* 6:165; *Religion . . . ,* 22. If our sensuous nature provides the ground for our actions, we renounce the incentives which spring from freedom and are banished from the realm of morality entirely and relegated to that of animality. Thus, Kant is not advocating the view that evil originates in our sensuous nature. See Allison, *Kant's Theory,* 150. At the other extreme, morally legislative reason cannot be corrupted. A consistently evil will (*Wille*), "diabolical" evil, one that *knows* the moral law and chooses as its maxim the *principled* and *systematic* opposition to it, is an impossibility:

> Man (even the most wicked) does not, under any maxim whatsoever, repudiate the moral law in the manner of a rebel (renouncing obedience to it). The law, rather forces itself upon him irresistibly by virtue of his moral predisposition; and were no other incentive working in opposition, he would adopt the law into his maxim as the sufficient determining ground of his will [*Willkür*]. (Kant, *Werke,* 6:175; *Religion . . . ,* 31; cited in Allison, *Kant's Theory,* 150)

In other words, a condition of being moral at all depends on recognizing the possibility that the categorical imperative *can* be valid and that it *does* evoke the feeling of respect.

An in-between position is dependent on the view that the source of evil is, again, neither sensibility nor *Wille* but *Willkür* (as the executive faculty of *choice*). It would involve following a principle that is a kind of deliberative tendency—a "propensity to evil," as Kant writes. See Allison, *Kant's Theory,* 153. Such a propensity is not an unreflective, "natural" impulse; rather, it determines the orientation of a person's *Willkür.* It defines one's *Gesinnung,* or moral disposition. As such, it is, as Allison concedes, "a very peculiar sort of principle or maxim, since it is not to be thought of as explicitly and self-consciously adopted by an agent" (ibid.,153). The adoption of this *Gesinnung* is timeless in the sense that it does not occur at one specific moment in time; it is not timeless in the sense of *atemporal.*

Perhaps the most important consequence of this reading of Kant for our purposes is that his claim that "man is evil by nature" is not a judgment about the human race per se. It only points to the impossibility of finite, sensuous beings like human beings achieving a perfect will. Our inclinations will never correspond perfectly with the moral law. This, however, does not exclude the possibility of acting in accordance with the moral law but indicates a tendency in the other direction. This should be kept in mind when Hegel presents *love* as the fulfillment of the moral law. The perfect correspondence of inclination and the law is precisely the point that, according to this reading, Kant is challenging.

10. On grace, see Schiller, "Über Anmuth und Würde," in volume 2 of *Schillers Werke in drei Bänden.*

11. Kant, *Werke,* 6:161, n.; *Religion . . . ,* 19n.

12. Ibid., 6:189; 44.

13. Ibid.

14. Kant, *Werke,* 6:197; *Religion . . . ,* 26.

15. Aristotle, *Nicomachean Ethics,* 1099a.

16. Aristotle, *Nicomachean Ethics,* 1105a29–34. In its fulfillment, one does not, for example, *have* courage; rather, one *is* courageous.

17. "Genius is a *talent* for producing something for which no determinate rule can be given, not a predisposition consisting of a skill for something that can be learned by following some rule or other; hence the foremost property of genius must be originality." Kant, *Critique of Judgment,* 175.

Terry Eagleton argues that, at the end of the eighteenth century, the aesthetic comes to be understood as the site of the extension of reason (the universal) to the life of pleasure, feeling, sensibility, the body, and so forth (the particular). Aestheticized reason does not dictate or command from on high, as the Kantian categorical imperative does, but it works instead, as Eagleton says, to dissolve the law to custom. The human subject is to be molded and cultivated like a work of art. See Eagleton, *The Ideology of the Aesthetic,* 20.

18. Compare Hegel's later discussion of the relation between the disciples in the 1821 manuscript to his *Lectures on the Philosophy of Religion,* 3:139:

> The relationship of the disciples is not one of friendship, for friendship is a relationship burdened by subjective particularity. . . . In brief the bond [uniting the disciples] is an objective content; it is not attraction as such, like that felt by a man for a woman (as this particular personality or beauty), but [lies] in the intuition of this speculative [element], the infinite love that comes from infinite anguish, i.e., from the worthlessness of the particularity and mediation of love through it.

The communal subjectivity that arises through the infinite suffering of the crucifixion, through the "monstrous unification" (W 3:125) of the extremes of divinity and death, is precisely what Hegel will not find in Christianity in these earlier writings. The speculative intuition that "the monstrous unification of these extremes is love itself" is missing, as is the love that is founded on it.

19. Was Plato only proving that he was a better comedian than Aristophanes when he argues in the fifth book of *Republic* that "[a]ll these women [those who are to be educated in the same manner as men] are to belong to all these men in common . . . and the children, in their turn, will be in common"? (357c–d). Allan Bloom, following Leo Strauss, draws attention to the parallels between Book V and Aristophanes' *Ecclesiazusae* (performed in 392 BCE).

Bloom, "Interpretive Essay," 380–381. In Plato's presentation of Aristophanic union in the *Symposium,* the reproductive function is diminished as the love between men takes center stage: "People who are split from a male are male-oriented. While they are boys, because they are chips off the male block, they love men and enjoy lying with men and being embraced by men; those are the best boys and lads, because they are the most manly in their nature. . . . [T]hese are the only kind of boys who grow up to be real men in politics. When they're grown men, they are lovers of young men, and they naturally pay no attention to marriage or to making babies, except insofar as they are required by local customs" (*Symposium* 191e–192b). Perhaps Aristophanes is just playing to the crowd that has gathered at Agathon's symposium, but, at least on the surface, erotic union is not subordinated to sexual reproduction: "Love is born into every human being; it calls back the halves of our original nature together; it tries to make one out of two and heal the wound of human nature" (*Symposium* 191d).

20. Hegel, *Wissenschaft der Logik,* W 5:78; *Science of Logic,* 74.

21. "Again you have heard that it was said to the men of old, 'You shall not swear falsely, but shall perform to the Lord what you have sworn.' But I say to you, Do not swear at all, either by heaven, for it is the throne of God, or by the earth, for it is his footstool, or by Jerusalem, for it is the city of the great King. And do not swear by your head, for you cannot make one hair white and black. Let what you say be simply 'Yes' or 'No'" (Matthew 5:33–37).

22. When Nietzsche states in the second essay of *On the Genealogy of Morals* (47), "To breed an animal *with the right to make promises*—is this not the paradoxical task that nature has set in the case of man?" he also understands the value of keeping promises in an immanent manner. Fulfilling promises was originally considered noble because of the mastery over the world and oneself that is required to makes claims about the future, as every promise does. The foundation for the trust that the promise will be kept is nothing more or less than the one who makes it. There is no external obligation that one follows when keeping a promise, and there is no appeal to an external author. Instead, keeping a promise fulfills what Nietzsche calls the "pathos of distance." *Genealogy of Morals,* 26.

23. "My bounty is as boundless as the sea, / My love as deep; the more I give to thee, / The more I have, for both are infinite." Shakespeare, *Romeo and Juliet,* in *Shakespeare,* 2.2.133–136. All subsequent citations from Shakespeare will be from this volume.

Hegel wrote a first draft of the "Love" fragment in November 1797 and then thoroughly revised it a year or so later, at the time of the first draft of *The Spirit of Christianity.* See Harris, *Hegel's Development,* 1:298n2.

24. Žižek, *The Fragile Absolute,* 23.

25. Ibid., 23–24.

26. Hölderlin, "On the Law of Freedom," in *Friedrich Hölderlin,* 33.

27. Ibid.

28. See "Seyn, Urtheil, Modalität," FH 2:50.

29. "Über die verschiednen Arten, zu dichten," FH 2:67; Hölderlin, "On the Difference of Poetic Modes," in *Friedrich Hölderlin,* 83.

30. Aeschylus, *The Eumenides,* in *Aeschylus I,* l.175.

31. Ibid., l.245–247.

32. Aeschylus, *The Libation Bearers*, in *Aeschylus I*, l.896–897.

33. Ibid., l.899.

34. Aeschylus, *Eumenides*, l.892. Michael Naas notes the growing humility of the *Eumenides* in *Turning*, 2.

35. Nietzsche, *On the Genealogy of Morals*, 81.

36. In the "Natural Law" essay, published in the *Critical Journal* in 1802/1803, Hegel refers to the *Oresteia* as an illustration of how the reconciliation of the Olympian gods and the Furies—the reconciliation of freedom and necessity in absolute ethical life—is achieved through "nothing else but the performance, on the ethical plane, of the tragedy which the Absolute eternally enacts with itself, by eternally giving birth to itself into objectivity, submitting in this objective form to suffering and death, and rising from its ashes into glory" (NL 104). At this point in the *The Spirit of Christianity*, we are still waiting for the rise to glory.

37. Aeschylus, *The Liberation Bearers*, l.1047–1050.

38. Marx and Engels, *The Communist Manifesto*, 94.

39. Blanchot, "On One Approach to Communism," 93–94.

40. Marx and Engels, *The Communist Manifesto*, 94.

41. Nietzsche is writing of Aeschylus's Prometheus specifically, but the sentiment applies to the plays in the *Oresteia*. Nietzsche, *The Birth of Tragedy*, 51.

42. Aristotle, *Poetics*, 1453a19. See Krell, "A Small Number of Houses in a Universe of Tragedy."

43. Levinas, *Existence and Existents*, 57.

44. Ibid. To paraphrase Levinas, the element of horror is the haunting specter, the phantom, that is, the *return* that the corpse always portends.

45. Nostalgia can be understood as a desire to return to an idealized past; as such, it is the impossible desire to return to a past that never existed, a past that "could only be the future of our inchoate desires." Krell, *The Tragic Absolute*, 113.

46. F. W. J. Schelling, *Philosophische Briefe über Dogmatismus und Kriticismus*, 107; idem, *Letters on Dogmatism and Criticism*, 193.

47. Aeschylus, *Agamemnon*, l.1335–1341.

48. Vernant, "Tensions and Ambiguities in Greek Tragedy," in Vernant and Vidal-Naquet, *Myth and Tragedy in Ancient Greece*, 45–46.

49. Sophocles, *Oedipus the King*, l.884–895.

50. Ibid., l.897.

51. Ibid., l.898.

5. Dialectic of Love

1. Terry Pinkard puts this in the following way:

> Hegel broke from almost all of his contemporaries in seeing modern life as arising in principle at the end of antiquity with Christianity. Unlike those who saw history falling into three periods—antiquity, the Middle Ages, and the modern world—Hegel saw the so-called "Middle Ages" as continuous with modern life in its insistence on the newly discovered role of human subjec-

tivity and self-reflection that emerges with ancient antiquity. Like Nietzsche after him, he saw Christianity as the point at which history took its turn toward modern life. Hegel of course gave this a positive interpretation, in contrast to Nietzsche's rather negative view of the matter. (Pinkard, *Hegel's "Phenomenology,"* 388n36)

2. Hegel later writes of the possibility of a wound that heals without leaving a scar—"The wounds of spirit heal and leave no scars behind" (PdG 440/PS 407)—a wound that heals without a trace of the original tear. Cited in Schmidt, *On Germans and Other Greeks,* 120.

3. This sentiment is repeated in various formulations in *The Spirit of Christianity:* "Faith is a knowledge [*Erkenntnis*] of spirit through spirit" (W 1:355/SC 239); "Only spirit grasps and comprehends [*einschließen*] spirit" (W 1:372/SC 255); "Spirit recognizes [*erkennen*] spirit" (W 1:280/SC 265); and "Hence faith in the divine grows out of the divinity of the believer's own nature; only a modification of the Godhead can know the Godhead" (W 1:382/SC 266).

4. Hamacher, *Pleroma—Reading in Hegel,* 160.

5. In *Glas,* Derrida writes of this interruption in the logic of exchange: "to this pleroma, to this revolution in the circle of the restricted economy, to this humiliation without counterpart, a dissymmetry on the other side is going to answer. Forgiveness of sins is also raised above the law, that is, above the principle of reciprocity." *Glas,* 61, left column.

6. Krell writes, "Jesus can forgive Mary Magdalene because she knows the depths of human nature without having become a wife." *The Purest of Bastards,* 163.

7. *Kalon ergon:* Hegel tells us that Mary's act of anointing Jesus is the "only thing in the whole story of Jesus which goes by the name of 'beautiful'" (W 1:359/SC 243). See Matthew 26:10 and Mark 14:6.

8. Or, as John explains in his account of the meal and its interruption, "But Judas Iscariot, one of his disciples (he who was to betray him) said, 'Why was this ointment not sold for three hundred denarii and given to the poor?' This he said, not that he cared for the poor but because he was a thief, and as he had the money box he used to take what was put into it" (John 12:4–6). Judas's judgment, of course, was no less utilitarian, but, according to John, it lacks even the pretense to moral worth. Derrida cites this passage, *Glas,* 197, left column.

9. *Astragalos:* neck vertebrae; ankle bone; die, dice. This was the raw material of the *sumbolon,* the halves of a broken die or bone given by two friends to each other as a token of their friendship and as a means by which to identify each other in the future. In addition to a tally, token, and omen, *sumbolon* also denotes a passport, visa, treaty, and in the economic register, a contract between two states to protect commerce. Henry George Liddell and Robert Scott, *A Greek-English Lexicon* (Oxford: Clarendon Press, 1940). Although the 'living' symbol of the shared meal most readily evokes a relation of friendship, the erotic connotations of *sumbolon* are exploited by Plato in the speech he gives to Aristophanes in *Symposium,* "Each of us, then, is a 'matching half' [*sumbolon*] of a human whole, because each was sliced like a flatfish, two out of one, and each of us is always seeking the half that matches him" (191d). But as motivation for revering the gods, Aristophanes also wields the

threat of our becoming human *sumbolon* again—of being quartered and thus existing as a permanent relief: "So there's a danger that if we don't keep order before the gods, we'll be split in two again, and then we'll be walking around in the condition of people carved on gravestones in bas-relief, sawn apart between the nostrils, like half dice [*lispai,* a die cut in two by friends, each of whom kept half as a tally]" (193a).

10. Hamacher, *Pleroma—Reading in Hegel,* 101.

11. See the section entitled "A Different Genius" in chapter 4.

12. See Hamacher, *Pleroma—Reading in Hegel,* 106.

13. This is certainly not the only possible reaction to a dead body. Rather than the experience of sadness or melancholia at the thought of vanished life, for Levinas, the corpse provokes horror, and it does so precisely because it portends the *return* of life:

> A corpse is horrible; it already bears in itself its own phantom, it presages its return. The haunting spectre, the phantom, constitutes the very element of horror. . . . Specters, ghosts, sorceresses are not only a tribute Shakespeare pays to his time, or vestiges of the original material he composed with; they allow him to move constantly toward this limit between being and nothingness. . . . Hamlet recoils before the "not to be" because he has a foreboding of the return of being ("to dye, to sleepe, perchance to Dreame"). (Levinas, *Existence and Existents,* 56–57)

14. See Gadamer, *Hegel's Dialectic,* 31.

15. Hegel writes, "This is why beautiful souls who are unhappy, either because they are conscious of their fate or because they are not satisfied in the fullness of their love, are so full of charity—they have beautiful moments of enjoyment, but only moments" (N 389). Cited in Lukács, *The Young Hegel,* 187.

16. Hegel writes, "pure life is *being*" (W 1:371 / SC 254), and "the divine is pure life" (W 1:372 / SC 255). He also produced this inclusive disjunction "pure life or *Selbstbewußtsein . . . ,*" but then crossed out "self-consciousness" (W 1:370n / SC 254). "Self-consciousness" is most likely left under erasure in this way because it is so clearly associated with the reflective terminology of Kant and the opposition between subject and object, that both "pure life" and "love" attempt to supersede. See Harris, *Hegel's Development,* 1:352.

17. When focusing on the problem of "spirit grasping spirit" in and through *language,* one might consider Hegel's insistence in his later writings on the need to write philosophy in one's own ordinary, "natural" language, and the corresponding limitations that he finds in technical philosophical language. In Malabou's words, "Philosophy's role is to show how, in each language, the essential is said and exhibited through the idiom's accidents." *The Future of Hegel,* 171. The essential must be expressed in the language in which we live.

18. When he confronts the dead, atomized, bourgeois society of his own day, Hegel does so with reference to what he considers to be a "primitive" or "natural" people like the Arabs, not, it should be noted, those of the Christian Middle Ages to whom the German Romantics often appealed. As exemplary of the "primitive," the Arabs are presented as embodying a properly organic relation between part and whole. Hegel appeals to these "natural" peoples to defend his view that religion has the capacity to establish this kind of

social relation, but, to do so, he must posit an isolated and idealized past. See Lukács, *The Young Hegel,* 182. It is as if, within the logic of Hegel's text, the Arabs assume the place of an immediate unity that the Greeks once held before they were defined in terms of a tragic self-division. Thus, at the same time that Hegel is developing a logic—almost behind his own back—that undermines the possibility of an original and immediate life, the specific reference to Arabs exists as a kind of ghost of this natural life haunting Hegel's text.

19. Kant, *Werke,* 6:292n; *Religion . . . ,* 135n.

20. Harris, *Hegel's Development,* 1:362.

21. Hegel, "Systemfragment von 1800," W 1:422; "Fragment of a System," in *Early Theological Writings,* 312.

22. What Hegel is here presenting as the *failure* of faith to achieve an immediate union is, from the perspective of dialectical thought, the avoidance of any false pretense to immediacy. Lukács argues that the mysticism of an immediate identity of subject and object in the form of spirit destroys the dialectical advances Hegel had made in his Frankfurt writings. This mysticism is what underlies a claim like "spirit knows spirit" when the basis of this knowing is a "feeling of harmony" (W 1:382/SC 266). In the pretense to an immediate harmony, Hegel "abandons the very motif that was supposed to enable religion to overcome the limitations of love, viz. the notion that religion is the dialectical unification of love and reflection." Lukács, *The Young Hegel,* 191.

23. John Dominic Crossan describes Jesus's confrontation in the Temple in the following way:

> Cleansing or purification are, therefore, very misleading terms for what Jesus was doing, namely, an attack on the Temple's very existence, a destruction—symbolic, to be sure, but none the less dangerous for that. His action, in John and Mark, is quite clear. It is like going into a draft office during the Vietnam War and overturning drawers of file cards. It is a symbolic negation of all that office or Temple stands for. . . . My best historical reconstruction concludes that what led immediately to Jesus's arrest and execution in Jerusalem at Passover was that act of symbolic destruction, in deed and word, against the Temple. That sacred edifice represented in one central place all that his vision and program had fought against among the peasantry of Lower Galilee. In Jerusalem, quite possibility for the first and only time, he acted according to that program. (Crossan, *Who Killed Jesus?* 64)

24. See Steinberg, *The Sexuality of Christ in Renaissance Art and Modern Oblivion,* 11.

25. Ibid., 12–13.

26. Plato, *Phaedrus* 251a–b.

27. This and subsequent translations of the *Phaedrus* are from volume 1 of the Loeb Classical Library edition of Plato, 250d.

28. Hegel does not stress the point that to proclaim the coming of the kingdom of God within this context was an overt challenge to the Roman Empire and its local collaborators. By contrast, this political dimension permeates the language of the letter of Paul to the Romans. According to Taubes, from its opening, where Jesus is described with "those

attributes that are imperatorial, kingly, imperial," the letter is as "political theology, a *political* declaration of war on the Caesar." Taubes, *Political Theology of Paul,* 14, 16.

29. Hamacher, *Pleroma—Reading in Hegel,* 88.

30. Ibid., 89.

31. See Hegel, *Frühe Exzerpte,* in *Gesammelte Werke,* 3:237–238. The quotation from Rousseau is cited in Hamacher, *Pleroma—Readings in Hegel,* 87.

32. Hamacher, *Pleroma—Readings in Hegel,* 87.

33. Freud, *Civilization and Its Discontents,* 72–73.

34. Ibid., 77.

35. Ibid., 108.

36. Ibid.

37. Ibid., 87.

38. Ibid., 57.

39. Hegel explains the French Revolution in terms of this abstract, negative freedom: "The Reign of Terror . . . was a time of trembling and quaking and of intolerance towards everything particular. For fanaticism wills only what is abstract, not what is articulated, so that whenever differences emerge, it finds them incompatible with its own indeterminacy and cancels them [*hebt sie auf*]" (W 7:52/PR 39). In a letter from 1807, he evokes the element of baptism to describe the concrete effects of the "essential determination" of this manifestation of fanaticism: "Thanks to the bath of her revolution, the French nation has freed herself of many institutions which the human spirit had outgrown like the shoes of a child." Cited in PR 397n3.

40. Lukács, *The Young Hegel,* 202.

41. Hegel, *Lectures on the Philosophy of Religion,* 3:141n208.

42. Ibid., 3:140.

43. Ibid., 3:206. This passage is from 1924 lecture notes. In Hegel's 1921 manuscript, he writes, "Knowledge heals the wound that it itself is" (ibid., 3:106).

44. Harris, *Hegel's Development,* 1:371–372.

45. In the first draft of this text, Hegel concentrates on the fate of Jesus alone. In the second draft, he tries to unite the two fates, but Harris argues that he abandoned this attempt "in despair." Harris, *Hegel's Development,* 1:370. Insofar as there is a spirit and an historical fate, there must be such a—dialectical—relation, however, even if it seems to lead to despair.

46. Derrida, *Glas,* 91, left column, emphasis added.

47. Ibid., 92, left column.

48. With body and soul persisting in one living shape, it would seem as if Hegel's "Greek spirit" remains, in part, the fusion of Aristotelian *life* and the Platonic theory of *love.* See Harris, *Hegel's Development,* 1:377–378.

49. Vernant, "Tensions and Ambiguities in Greek Tragedy," in Vernant and Vidal-Naquet, *Myth and Tragedy in Ancient Greece,* 37.

50. Ibid.

51. *Keim:* fig. *seed;* but also *bud, spore, sprout, nucleus; embryo; origin;* and *germ,* with all that that entails, i.e., a rudimentary form of life *and* death.

52. Hölderlin, *Grund zum Empedokles,* FH 1:869; Krell, "The Basis of Empedocles," 145, translation altered.

53. Dastur, *Hölderlin, le retournement natale,* 49.

54. The logic of tragedy as harmonious opposition also captures Vernant's account of tragic action as having its source both in the *ethos,* or character, of the actor and in a *daimōn* operating through the self. As noted above (see the previous section, "The Hovering God"), if these two disappear or are seen as mutually exclusive, tragedy disappears. This is the case today, mired as we are in the logic of *Verstand.* Vernant, "Tensions and Ambiguities in Greek Tragedy," in Vernant and Vidal-Naquet, *Myth and Tragedy in Ancient Greece,* 37.

55. FH 1:868; Krell, "The Basis of Empedocles," 144.

56. Dastur, *Hölderlin, le retournement natale,* 35. Nature is unable to appear by itself. Dastur cites fragment 123 of Heraclitus in this regard, φύσις κρύπτεσθαι φιλεῖ, "nature loves to hide itself." For Hölderlin, this reconciliation "only *appears* to be actual" in that the hero's sacrifice is always temporary, for modern tragedy, as Hölderlin conceives it, is the tragedy of time itself, and time "never allows for a final repos, but continues its infinite processes tirelessly into ever new dissolutions and structurations" (ibid., 57).

57. I discuss Hölderlin's play and the theoretical writings associated with it in greater detail in chapter 2, "Excursus on Hölderlin's *The Death of Empedocles.*"

58. Ibid., 52.

59. Krell, "The General Basis [of Tragic Drama]," 143.

60. Cf. Dastur, *Hölderlin, le retournement natale,* 65.

Conclusion

1. Hegel claims that "the religion of art" of which tragedy is a part culminates in the worldly proposition "The Self is Absolute Essence," but this contains within itself the movement, or conversion, *Umkehrung,* that will establish substance as subject and degrade the self in such a way that we nevertheless avoid falling back into "natural religion" (PdG 487/PS 452). The *Umkehrung* is brought about, as Hegel says, "*for* and *by self-consciousness* itself" (PdG 488/PS 453). This "conversion" to the proposition that the "Absolute Essence is the Self," which is to say, the unhappy consciousness born of the knowledge that God is the only Absolute Essence or Self, is then united with its inverse in Christianity. This marks the unity of substance and subject. (This conversion moves through that of Roman legalism: "The Self as such, the abstract person, is Absolute Essence" (PdG 489/PS 454).) See Harris, *Hegel's Ladder II,* 651.

2. Harris, *Hegel,* 87.

3. Both comedy and philosophy attack the substantiality of God, nature, and the *polis,* but the pure ideas of philosophy are also subject to this treatment. See PdG 487/PS 452.

4. Harris, *Hegel's Ladder II,* 647n77.

5. Hyppolite, *Genesis and Structure of Hegel's "Phenomenology of Spirit,"* 556.

6. Ibid.

7. Nietzsche, *The Birth of Tragedy,* §11.

8. Hamacher describes this well when he writes of comedy that "it is the coincidence of an actor with a role that he knows can be set aside. The role is insubstantial and as such,

precisely because it is insubstantial and detachable, the actor always plays *himself* with this role and only ever *plays* himself as another. . . . It is a subject only insofar as it plays with itself, with itself as a mask, loosens itself from the mask, detaches itself through it, donning and discarding the mask and itself at will." Hamacher, "(The End of Art with the Mask)," 115.

9. Hamacher cites this passage in "(The End of Art with the Mask)," 106.

BIBLIOGRAPHY

Adorno, Theodor. *Minima moralia: Reflections from Damaged Life.* Translated by E. Jephcott. London: Verso, 2005.

Aeschylus. *Aeschylus I.* Translated by R. Lattimore. Chicago: The University of Chicago Press, 1953.

Allison, Henry. *Kant's Theory of Freedom.* Cambridge: Cambridge University Press, 1990.

Apollodorus. *The Library.* Loeb Classical Library. Translated by Sir James George Frazer. New York: G. P. Putnam's Sons, 1961.

Aristotle. *Nicomachean Ethics.* Translated by Christopher Rowe. Oxford: Oxford University Press, 2002.

———. *Poetics.* Loeb Classical Library Edition. Vol. 22. Translated by S. Halliwell. Cambridge, MA: Harvard University Press, 1995. 27–141.

Avineri, Shlomo. *Hegel's Theory of the Modern State.* Cambridge University Press, 1974.

Badiou, Alain. *Saint Paul: The Foundation of Universalism.* Translated by R. Brassier. Stanford, CA: Stanford University Press, 2003.

Bataille, George. *The Accursed Share.* Translated by R. Hurley. 2 vols. New York: Zone Books, 1991.

Bautch, Richard J. *Glory and Power, Ritual and Relationship: The Sinai Covenant in the Postexilic Period.* New York: T & T Clark, 2009.

Beaufret, Jean. "Hölderlin et Sophocles." In Friedrich Hölderlin, *Remarques sur Oedipe, Remarques sur Antigone.* Translated by Jean Breaufret and François Fédier. Paris: Union générale d'éditions, 1965.

Beistegui, Miguel de. "Hegel: or the tragedy of thinking." In *Philosophy and Tragedy,* edited by Miguel de Beistegui and Simon Sparks, 11–37. London: Routledge, 2000.

Bergson, Henri. *Laughter: An Essay on the Meaning of Comic.* Translated by Cloudesley Brereton and Fred Rothwell. Mineola, NY: Dover Publications, 2005.

Bertaux, Pierre. *Hölderlin und die Französische Revolution.* Frankfurt am Main: Suhrkamp, 1969.

Bertrand, P. "Le sens du tragique et du destin dans la dialectique hégélienne." *Revue de Métaphysique et de morale* 47 (1940): 164–186.

Blanchot, Maurice. "Hölderlin's Itinerary." In *The Space of Literature.* Translated by Ann Smock. Lincoln: University of Nebraska, 1982.

———. "On One Approach to Communism." In *Friendship.* Translated by E. Rottenberg. Stanford, CA: Stanford University Press, 1997.

———. "The 'Sacred' Speech of Hölderlin." In *The Work of Fire.* Translated by Charlotte Mandell. Stanford, CA: Stanford University Press, 1995.

Bloom, Allan. "Interpretive Essay." In *The Republic of Plato*, 307–436. New York: Basic Books, 1968.

Bromily, G. W., ed. *The International Standard Bible Encyclopedia*. Grand Rapids, MI: Eerdmans Publishing, 1982.

Brown, Marshall. "The Eccentric Path." *Journal of English and Germanic Philology* 77 (1978): 104–112.

Constantine, David. *Hölderlin*. Oxford: Clarendon Press, 1988.

Courtine, Jean-François. "Of Tragic Metaphor." In *Philosophy and Tragedy*, edited by Miguel de Beistegui and Simon Sparks, 59–77. London: Routledge, 2000.

Critchley, Simon. *Continental Philosophy: A Very Short Introduction*. New York: Oxford University Press, 2001.

Crites, Stephen. *Dialectic and Gospel in the Development of Hegel's Thinking*. University Park: Pennsylvania State University Press, 1998.

Crossan, John Dominic. *Who Killed Jesus? Exposing the Roots of Anti-Semitism in the Gospel Story of the Death of Jesus*. San Francisco: HarperSanFrancisco, 1996.

Dastur, Françoise. *Hölderlin, Le retournement natale: Tragédie et modernité & Nature et poesie*. La Versanne: Encre Marine, 1997.

———. "Tragedy and Speculation." In *Philosophy and Tragedy*, edited by Miguel de Beistegui and Simon Sparks, 78–87. London: Routledge, 2000.

Deleuze, Gilles. *Difference and Repetition*. Translated by Paul Patton. New York: Columbia University Press, 1994.

———. *Spinoza: Practical Philosophy*. Translated by R. Hurley. San Francisco: City Lights Books, 1988.

Derrida, Jacques. "Différance." In *Margins of Philosophy*, 3–27. Translated by A. Bass. Chicago: University of Chicago, 1982.

———. "From Restricted to General Economy: A Hegelianism without Reserve." In *Writing and Difference*, 251–277. Translated by A. Bass. Chicago: University of Chicago Press, 1978.

———. *Glas*. Translated by J. Leavey Jr. and R. Rand. Lincoln: University of Nebraska Press, 1986.

———. *Positions*. Translated by A. Bass. Chicago: University of Chicago Press, 1981.

Diels, Hermann, and Walther Kranz, eds. *Die Fragmente der Vorsokratiker*. 6th ed. Berlin: Weidmann, 1951.

Dilthey, Wilhelm. "Die Jugendgeschichte Hegels." In *Gesammelte Schriften*. Vol. 4. Stuttgart: B. G. Teubner, 1962–1965.

Dostoevsky, Fyodor. *Crime and Punishment*. Translated by C. Garnett. New York: W.W. Norton & Company, 1964.

———. *The Brothers Karamazov*. Translated by C. Garnett. New York: W.W. Norton & Company, 1976.

Eagleton, Terry. *The Ideology of the Aesthetic*. Oxford: Wiley-Blackwell, 1991.

Fackenheim, Emil. *The Religious Dimension in Hegel's Thought*. Bloomington: Indiana University Press, 1967.

Fichte, J. G. *Johann Gottlieb Fichtes Sämtliche Werke.* 8 vols. Edited by I. H. Fichte. Berlin: Veit, 1845–1846.

Foucault, Michel. *The Foucault Reader.* Edited by P. Rabinow. New York: Pantheon Books, 1984.

Freud, Sigmund. *Civilization and Its Discontents.* Translated by J. Strachey. New York: W.W. Norton & Company, 1989.

Gadamer, Hans-George. *Hegel's Dialectic: Five Hermeneutical Studies.* Translated by P. Christopher Smith. New Haven, CT: Yale University Press, 1976.

Gasché, Rodolphe. "Self-dissolving Seriousness: On the Comic in the Hegelian Conception of Tragedy." In *Philosophy and Tragedy,* edited by Miguel de Beistegui and Simon Sparks, 38–56. London: Routledge, 2000.

Haering, Theodor. *Hegel, sein Wollen und sein Werk.* Aalen: Scientia Verlag, 1963.

Hamacher, Werner. "(The End of Art with the Mask)." In *Hegel after Derrida,* edited by S. Barnett, 105–130. New York: Routledge, 1998.

———. *Pleroma—Reading in Hegel: The Genesis and Structure of a Dialectical Hermeneutics in Hegel.* Translated by N. Walker and S. Jarvis. Stanford, CA: Stanford University Press, 1998.

Hammond, N. G. L., and H. H. Scullard, eds. *The Oxford Classical Dictionary.* Oxford: Oxford University Press, 1970.

Harris, H. S. *Hegel's Development: Night Thoughts (Jena 1801–1806).* Oxford: Clarendon Press, 1983.

———. *Hegel's Development: Towards the Sunlight (1770–1801).* Oxford: Clarendon Press, 1972.

———. *Hegel's Ladder.* 2 vols. Indianapolis, IN: Hackett Publishing Co., 1997.

———. *Hegel: Phenomenology and System.* Indianapolis, IN: Hackett Publishing Company, Inc., 1995.

———. "Introduction to *Faith and Knowledge.*" In G.W.F. Hegel, *Faith and Knowledge,* 1–50. Albany: State University of New York Press, 1977.

———. "L'etica del sapere." *Clio* 27, 4 (1998): 615–632.

Hartwich, Wolf-Daniel, Aleida Assmann, and Jan Assmann. "Afterword." In Jacob Taubes, *The Political Theology of Paul,* 115–142. Stanford, CA: Stanford University Press, 2004.

Hegel, G. W. F. *Briefe von und an Hegel.* Edited by J. Hoffmeister and R. Flechsig. 4 vols. Hamburg: Felix Meiner, 1961.

———. *The Difference between Fichte's and Schelling's System of Philosophy.* Translated by W. Cerf and H. S. Harris. Albany: State University of New York Press, 1977.

———. *Early Theological Writings.* Translated by T. M. Knox. Philadelphia: University of Pennsylvania Press, 1971. Seventh paperback printing 1992.

———. *Elements of the Philosophy of Right.* Translated by A. Wood. Cambridge: Cambridge University Press, 1991.

———. *The Encyclopaedia Logic, with the Zusätze: Part I of the Encyclopaedia of Philosophical Sciences with the Zusätze.* Translated by T. F. Geraets, W. A. Suchting, and H. S. Harris. Indianapolis, IN: Hackett Publishing Company, Inc., 1991.

———. *Encyclopaedia of Philosophy.* Translated by G. E. Mueller. New York: Philosophical Library, Inc., 1959.

———. *Faith and Knowledge.* Translated by W. Cerf and H. S. Harris. Albany: State University of New York Press, 1977.

———. *Gesammelte Werke.* Edited by Rheinisch-Westfaelischen Akademie der Wissenschafen. Hamburg: Felix Meiner, 1968ff.

———. *Hegel and the Human Spirit: A Translation of the Jena Lectures on the Philosophy of Spirit (1805–6).* Translated by Leo Rauch. Detroit: Wayne State University, 1983.

———. *Hegel's Aesthetics: Lectures on Fine Art.* Translated by T. M. Knox. 2 vols. Oxford: Oxford University Press, 1998.

———. *Lectures on the History of Philosophy.* Translated by E. S. Haldane and F. H. Simson. London: Routledge and Kegan Paul, 1955.

———. *Lectures on the Philosophy of Religion.* Edited by P. C. Hodgson. Translated by R. F. Brown et al. Berkeley: University of California Press, 1995.

———. *Lectures on the Philosophy of World History, Introduction: Reason in History.* Translated by H. B. Nisbet. 3 vols. Cambridge: University of Cambridge Press, 1992.

———. *Natural Law: The Scientific Ways of Treating Natural Law, Its Place in Moral Philosophy, and Its Relation to the Positive Sciences of Law.* Translated by T. M. Knox. Philadelphia: University of Pennsylvania Press, 1975.

———. *Phänomenologie des Geistes.* Hamburg: Felix Meiner Verlag, 1988.

———. *Phenomenology of Spirit.* Translated by A. V. Miller. Oxford: Oxford University Press, 1977.

———. *The Philosophy of History.* Translated by J. Sibree. New York: Dover Publications, Inc., 1956.

———. *Schriften zur Politik und Rechtsphilosophie.* Edited by G. Lasson. Leibzig: Felix Meiner Verlag, 1923.

———. *Science of Logic.* Translated by A. V. Miller. Atlantic Heights, NJ: Humanities Press, 1969.

———. *System of Ethical Life (1802/3).* Edited by H. S. Harris and T. M. Knox. Albany: State University of New York Press, 1979.

———. *Three Essays, 1793–1795.* Translated by P. Fuss and J. Dobbins. Notre Dame, IN: University of Notre Dame Press, 1984.

———. *Vorlesungen über die Philosophie der Religion, Einleitung, Der Begriff der Religion.* Edited by W. Jaescke. Hamburg: Felix Meiner Verlag, 1983.

———. *Werke in zwanzig Bänden.* Edited by E. Moldenhauer and K. M. Michel. Frankfurt am Main: Suhrkamp Verlag, 1969–1971.

Heidegger, Martin. *The Basic Questions of Philosophy: Selected "Problems" of "Logic."* Translated by R. Rojcewicz and A. Schuwer. Bloomington: Indiana University Press, 1994.

———. "Hegel und die Griechen." In *Wegmarken.* Frankfurt am Main: V. Klostermann, 1967.

———. *Hegel's Concept of Experience.* Translated by K. Royce Dove. New York: Harper & Row, 1970.

———. *Hölderlins Hymnen 'Germanien' und 'Der Rhein.'* Gesamtausgabe. Vol. 39. Frankfurt am Main: V. Klostermann, 1980.

———. *Plato's "Sophist."* Translated by R. Rojcewicz and A. Schuwer. Bloomington: Indiana University Press, 1997.

Henrich, Dieter. *The Course of Remembrance and Other Essays on Hölderlin.* Stanford, CA: Stanford University Press, 1997.

———. *Hegel im Kontext.* Frankfurt am Main: Suhrkamp, 1971.

Hodgson, Peter. *Hegel and Christian Theology.* Oxford: Oxford University Press, 2005.

Hölderlin, Friedrich. *Friedrich Hölderlin: Essays and Letters on Theory.* Edited and translated by Thomas Pfau. Albany: State University Press of New York, 1988.

———. *Hyperion and Selected Poems.* Translated by Willard Trask. New York: Continuum Publishing Company, 1990.

———. *Poems and Fragments.* 3rd ed. Translated by Michael Hamburger. London: Anvil Press Poetry Ltd., 1994.

———. *Sämtliche Werke* (Grosse Stuttgarter Ausgabe). 8 vols. Edited by Friedrich Beissner. Stuttgart: Kohlhammer, 1943–1985.

———. *Sämtliche Werke und Briefe.* Edited by Michael Knaupp. 3 vols. Munich: Carl Hanser Verlag, 1992.

Hyppolite, Jean. *Genesis and Structure of Hegel's "Phenomenology of Spirit."* Translated by Samuel Cherniak and John Heckman. Evanston, IL: Northwestern University Press, 1974.

———. *Introduction to Hegel's Philosophy of History.* Translated by Bond Harris and Jacqueline Spurlock. Gainesville: University Press of Florida, 1996.

———. "Le tragique et le rationnel dans la philosophie de Hegel. In *Figures de la pensée philosophique,* 254–261. Paris: PUF, 1971.

Jamme, Christoph. "Hegel and Hölderlin." *Clio* 15, 4 (1986): 359–377.

———. *Ein ungelehrtes Buch: Die philosophische Gemeinschaft zwischen Hölderlin und Hegel in Frankfurt 1797–1800.* Bonn: Bouvier Verlag, 1983.

Jamme, Christoph, and Helmut Schneider, eds. *Mythologie der Vernunft: Hegels "Ältestes Systemprogramme des deutschen Idealismus."* Frankfurt am Main: Suhrkamp, 1984.

Kant, Immanuel. *Critique of Judgment.* Translated by W. S. Pluhar. Indianapolis, IN: Hackett Publishing Company, Inc., 1987.

———. *Critique of Practical Reason.* Translated by Lewis White Beck. New York: MacMillan Publishing Co., 1993.

———. *Critique of Pure Reason.* Translated by N. Kemp Smith. London: Macmillan, 1929.

———. *Kants gesammelte Schriften.* Edited by the Royal Prussian Academy of Sciences and Its Successors. Berlin: Reimer; later Berlin and New York: Walter de Gruyter, 1902–1938, 1968.

———. *Groundwork of the Metaphysics of Morals.* Translated by M. Gregor. Cambridge: Cambridge University Press, 2002.

———. *Religion within the Limits of Reason Alone.* Translated by T. M. Greene and H. H. Hudson. New York: Harper & Row, 1960.

———. "Idea for a Universal History with a Cosmopolitan Intent." In *Perpetual Peace and Other Essays on Politics, History, and Morals,* 29–40. Indianapolis, IN: Hackett Publishing, 1983.

———. "What Is Enlightenment." In *Perpetual Peace and Other Essays on Politics, History, and Morals,* 41–48. Indianapolis, IN: Hackett Publishing, 1983.

Kierkegaard, Søren. *Fear and Trembling.* Translated by H. Hong and E. Hong. Princeton, NJ: Princeton University Press, 1983.

Kirk, G. S., J. E. Raven, and M. Schofield, eds. *The Presocratic Philosophers.* 2nd ed. Cambridge: Cambridge University Press, 1995.

Krell, David Farrell. *The Death of Empodocles: A Mourning-Play.* Albany: State University of New York Press, 2008.

———. *Lunar Voices: Of Tragedy, Poetry, Fiction, and Thought.* Chicago: University of Chicago Press, 1995.

———. "The Oldest Program towards a System in German Idealism." *The Owl of Minerva* 17, 1 (1985): 5–19.

———. *The Purest of Bastards.* University Park: Pennsylvania State University Press, 2000.

———. *The Recalcitrant Art: Diotima's Letters to Hölderlin and Related Missives.* Albany: State University of New York Press, 2000.

———. "A Small Number of Houses in a Universe of Tragedy: Notes on Aristotle's περὶ ποιητικῆς and Hölderlin's 'Anmerkungen.'" In *Philosophy and Tragedy,* edited by Miguel de Beistegui and Simon Sparks, 88–116. London: Routledge, 2000.

———. *The Tragic Absolute.* Bloomington: Indiana University Press, 2005.

Kroner, Richard. "Introduction." In G. W. F. Hegel, *Early Theological Writings,* 1–66. Philadelphia: University of Pennsylvania Press, 1971. Seventh paperback printing 1992.

Lacoue-Labarthe, Philippe. "The Caesura of the Speculative." In *Typography: Mimesis, Philosophy, Politics,* 208–235. Translated by C. Fynsk. Stanford, CA: Stanford University Press, 1998.

———. "History and Mimesis." In *Looking After Nietzsche.* Edited by L. Rickels. Albany: State University of New York Press, 1989.

Levinas, Emmanuel. *Existence and Existents.* Translated by Alphonso Lingis. Pittsburgh, PA: Duquesne University Press, 2001.

———. *Time and the Other.* Translated by Richard A. Cohen. Pittsburgh, PA: Duquesne University Press, 2001.

———. *Totality and Infinity: An Essay on Exteriority.* Translated by Alphonso Lingis. Pittsburgh, PA: Duquesne University Press, 1992.

Liddell, Henry George, and Robert Scott. *A Greek-English Lexicon.* Oxford: Clarendon Press, 1940.

Lukács, Georg. *The Young Hegel: Studies in the Relations between Dialectics and Economics.* Translated by Rodney Livingstone. London: Merlin Press, 1975.

Malabou, Catherine. *The Future of Hegel: Plasticity, Temporality and Dialectic.* Translated by L. During. New York: Routledge, 2005.

Marx, Karl, and Friedrich Engels. *The Communist Manifesto.* Translated by S. Moore. New York: Penguin Books, 1967.

McNeill, William. *The Glance of the Eye: Heidegger, Aristotle, and the Ends of Theory.* Albany: State University of New York Press, 1999.

———. *The Time of Life: Heidegger and Ethos.* Albany: State University of New York, 2006.

Mendelssohn, Moses. *Jerusalem.* Translated by A. Jospe. New York: Schocken Books, 1969.

Morrison, Toni. *Beloved.* New York: New American Library, 1987.

Naas, Michael. *Turning: From Persuasion to Philosophy.* Atlantic Highlands, NJ: Humanities Press International, 1995.

Nancy, Jean-Luc. *Hegel: The Restlessness of the Negative.* Translated by J. Smith and S. Miller. Minneapolis: University of Minnesota Press, 2002.

Nietzsche, Friedrich. *The Birth of Tragedy.* Translated by S. Whiteside. New York: Penguin Putnam, 1993.

———. *On the Genealogy of Morals.* Translated by W. Kaufmann. New York: Vintage Books, 1989.

———. *Philosophy in the Tragic Age of the Greeks.* Translated by M. Cowan. Washington, D.C.: Regnery Publishing, Inc., 1962.

———. *Twilight of the Idols.* Translated by R. J. Hollingdale. New York: Penguin Putnam Inc., 1990.

———. *Werke: Kritische Studienausgabe.* Edited by Giorgio Colli and Mazzino Montinari. 30 vols. Berlin: Walter de Gruyter and Deutscher Taschenbuch Verlag, 1967–1978.

Nohl, Herman, ed. *Hegels theologische Jugendschriften.* Tübingen: J.C.B. Mohr, 1907.

Olson, Alan M. *Hegel and the Spirit: Philosophy as Pneumatology.* Princeton, NJ: Princeton University Press, 1992.

Ovid. *Metamorphoses.* Translated by A. D. Melville. Oxford: Oxford University Press, 1990.

Parry, David. *Hegel's Phenomenology of the "We."* New York: Peter Lang, 1988.

Peperzak, Adriaan. *La jeune Hegel et la Vision Morale du Monde.* La Haye: Martinus Nijhoff, 1960.

Pinkard, Terry. *Hegel's "Phenomenology": The Sociality of Reason.* Cambridge: Cambridge University Press, 1996.

Pippin, Robert B. *Hegel's Idealism: The Satisfactions of Self-Consciousness.* Cambridge: Cambridge University Press, 1995.

Plato. *Phaedrus.* Loeb Classical Library Edition. Vol. 1. Translated by H. N. Fowler. Cambridge, MA: Harvard University Press, 1956. 405–578.

———. *Phaedrus.* Translated by A. Nehamas and P. Woodruff. Indianapolis, IN: Hackett Publishing Company, 1995.

———. *The Republic of Plato.* Translated by Allan Bloom. New York: Basic Books, 1968.

———. *Symposium.* Translated by A. Nehamas and P. Woodruff. Indianapolis, Hackett Publishing, 1989.

Pöggeler, Otto. "Hegel und die griechische Tragödie." In *Hegels Idee einer Phänomenologie des Geistes,* 90–95. Freiburg: Karl Alber, 1973.

Ritter, Joachim. *Hegel and the French Revolution: Essays on the Philosophy of Right.* Boston: MIT Press, 1984.

Rosenkranz, Karl. *Georg Wilhelm Friedrich Hegels Leben.* Darmstadt: Wissenschaftliche Buchgesellschaft, 1963.

Russon, John. *Reading Hegel's "Phenomenology."* Bloomington: Indiana University Press, 2004.

Sallis, John. *Crossings: Nietzsche and the Space of Tragedy.* Chicago: University of Chicago Press, 1991.

Schelling, F. W. J. *Letters on Dogmatism and Criticism.* In *The Unconditional in Human Knowledge: Four Early Essays (1794–1796),* 156–196. Translated by F. Marti. Cranbury, NJ: Associated University Press, 1980.

Schiller, Friedrich. *Schillers Werke in zehn Bänden.* Basel: Birkhäuser Verlag, 1967.

———. *Werke in drei Bänden.* München: C. Hanser, 1966.

Schmidt, Dennis. *On Germans and Other Greeks: Tragedy and Ethical Life.* Bloomington: Indiana University Press, 2001.

Schmitt, Carl. *Political Theology: Four Chapters on the Concept of Sovereignty.* Translated by G. Schwab. Cambridge, MA: MIT Press, 1985.

Shakespeare, William. *Shakespeare: A Historical and Critical Study with Annotated Texts of Twenty-one Plays.* Edited by Hardin Craig. Chicago: Scott, Foresman and Co., 1958.

Sophocles. *Antigone.* In *Sophocles I.* Translated by David Grene, 159–212. Chicago: University of Chicago Press, 1991.

———. *Oedipus the King.* In *The Three Theban Plays,* 11–76. Translated by Robert Fagles. New York: Viking Penguin, Inc., 1984.

Steinberg, Leo. *The Sexuality of Christ in Renaissance Art and Modern Oblivion.* Chicago: University of Chicago Press, 1996.

Szondi, Peter. *On Textual Understanding and Other Essays.* Translated by H. Mendelsohn. Minneapolis: University of Minnesota Press, 1986.

———. *Poetik und Geschichtsphilosophie.* Frankfurt am Main: Suhrkamp, 1974.

———. *Versuch über das Tragische.* In *Peter Szondi: Schriften I,* edited by J. Bollack, 151–260. Frankfurt am Main: Suhrkamp, 1978.

Tacitus, Cornelius. *The Life of Cnæus Julius Agricola.* In *The Complete Works of Tacitus,* edited by Moses Hadas, 677–706. New York: The Modern Library, 1942.

Taubes, Jacob. *The Political Theology of Paul.* Translated by D. Hollander. Stanford, CA: Stanford University Press, 2004.

Terence. *The Eunuch.* In *The Complete Roman Drama,* edited by G. E. Duckworth, 254–311. New York: Random House, 1942.

Thompson, Kevin. "Hegelian Dialectic and the Quasi-Transcendental in *Glas.*" In *Hegel after Derrida,* edited by S. Barnett, 239–259. New York: Routledge, 1998.

Vernant, Jean-Pierre, and Pierre Vidal-Naquet. *Myth and Tragedy in Ancient Greece.* Translated by J. Lloyd. New York: Zone Books, 1990.

Westphal, Merold. *History and Truth in Hegel's "Phenomenology."* Bloomington: Indiana University Press, 1998.

Wood, Allen. *Hegel's Ethical Thought.* Cambridge: Cambridge University Press, 1990.

Young, William. *Hegel's Dialectical Method.* Nutley, NJ: Craig Press, 1972.

Yovel. Yirmiyahu. *Dark Riddle: Hegel, Nietzsche, and the Jews.* University Park: Pennsylvania State University Press, 1998.

Žižek, Slavoj. "Against Human Rights." *New Left Review* 34 (2005): 115–131.

———. *The Fragile Absolute—or, Why Is the Christian Legacy Worth Fighting For?* New York: Verso, 2000.

———. *The Monstrosity of Christ*. Cambridge, MA: The MIT Press, 2009.

———. *Tarrying with the Negative: Kant, Hegel, and the Critique of Ideology*. Durham, NC: Duke University Press, 1993.

———. *The Ticklish Subject: The Absent Centre of Political Ontology*. New York: Verso, 1999.

INDEX

PETER WAKE holds a PhD in philosophy from DePaul University. He is an associate professor of philosophy at St. Edward's University in Austin, Texas.